CANADA'S COMMUNITY COLLEGES

CANADA'S COMMUNITY COLLEGES

A Critical Analysis

John D. Dennison and Paul Gallagher

UNIVERSITY OF BRITISH COLUMBIA PRESS
VANCOUVER
1986

This book has been published with the assistance of a grant from the Social Science Federation of Canada, using funds provided by the Social Sciences and Humanities Research Council of Canada.

Canadian Cataloguing in Publication Data

Dennison, John D., 1929-
    Canada's community colleges

    Includes index.
    Bibliography: p.
    ISBN 0-7748-0249-9
    1. Community colleges—Canada. 2.
Technical education—Canada. I. Gallagher,
Paul, 1929- II. Title.
LB2328.D45 1986   378'.1543'0971   C86-091173-X

International Standard Book Number 0-7748-0249-9

Printed in Canada

CONTENTS

ACKNOWLEDGEMENTS

Colleagues throughout Canada assisted in the preparation of this book; they consented to interviews, provided materials, and reviewed drafts of the text. Among them, the following deserve special recognition for their patience, cooperation, and willingness to share their perspectives. The affiliations reported were those at the time of writing.

BRITISH COLUMBIA: Andy Soles, Ministry of Universities, Science and Communications; Grant Fisher, Ron Faris, Diane Morrison, all of the Ministry of Education; Hilda Rizun, Patricia Groves, Greg Lee, Jim Bizzocchi, all of Capilano College; Grant Kelly and Tony Manera, Vancouver Community College; Bill Day, Douglas College; Ann Kitching and Tony Wilkinson, Kwantlen College; Kathleen Bigsby, B.C. Council of College and Institute Principals; Valerie Giles; Jack Finnbogason.

ALBERTA: Fred Speckeen, Fairview College; Gerald O. Kelly, Grant MacEwan College; Bill Workman, Bastiaan Heemsbergen, Des Berghofer, Henry Kolesar, all of the Department of Advanced Education; Reno Bosetti, Department of Education; Abe Konrad, University of Alberta.

SASKATCHEWAN: John Biss, Ed Evancio, Jake Kutarna, Lorne Sparling, all of the Department of Advanced Education and Manpower; Michael P.J. Kennedy, L. Robertson, Allan McKenzie, all of Kelsey Institute; Terry Anne Brydges, Saskatoon Community College; Julius Friesen, Community College Trustees Association; Lenore Rogers and Greg Robart, Regina Plains Community College; Lew Riederer; Ken Gunn; Fred Davies.

MANITOBA: Terry Morrison, Neil Russell, Jack Heuvel, Brian Angood, Terry Lumb, all of the Department of Education; Lyman Ross, Ray Newman, Donna

Finkleman, and Don Unruh, all of Red River Community College; Alexander Gregor, University of Manitoba.

ONTARIO: Norman Sisco; Robert "Squee" Gordon, Humber College; Alan Thomas and Michael Skolnik, OISE; Ted Sheffield; Ken Hunter, Ministry of Colleges and Universities; Glen Crombie, Cambrian College; Doug Light, George Brown College; Bert Curtis, Confederation College; Fred Hamblin, Association of Colleges of Applied Arts and Technology of Ontario; Bruce McAusland, St. Clair College; William Cruden, St. Lawrence College; Harold Braun, Lakehead University; Bob La Rose, Association of Canadian Community Colleges.

QUEBEC: Joe Rabinovitch and Jean-Louis Hérivault, Vanier College; Pierre Imbeau, Federation des CEGEP; Yves Sanssouci, Collège Edouard-Montpetit; Sarah Paltiel, Dawson College.

NOVA SCOTIA: Gerald McCarthy, Blenis Nicholson, and Michael Kent, all of the Department of Education; Olga McKenna, Mount St. Vincent University; Rod MacLennan, Chairman, Royal Commission on Postsecondary Education; George Williams, Nova Scotia Technical Institute; George MacDonald; Darrell Mills; Ralph MacLean.

NEW BRUNSWICK: Jean-Guy Finn, Department of Community Colleges; Josephine Lynam, Gerald Raymond, and David Russell, all of New Brunswick Community College; W.B. Thompson

PRINCE EDWARD ISLAND: Hon. L. Bagnall, Charles Campbell, Lorne Morse, S. Stratton, and R. Rice, all of the Department of Education; Howard Jamieson, Hesta MacDonald, Dave Morgan, Ian Low, Frank Zakem, Pat Faulkner, Fred Hodge, Allan MacRae, Don Livingstone, and Simon Compton, all of Holland College; Ron Baker, President emeritus, University of Prince Edward Island.

NEWFOUNDLAND: Douglas Fowlow, Bay St. George Community College; Les O'Reilly, College of Fisheries; Malcolm MacLeod, Elayne Harris, and Phillip Warren, all of Memorial University; Cyril McCormick, Department of Career Development; Ken Duggan, College of Trades and Technology.

YUKON TERRITORY: D.P. Odin, Department of Education; John Casey, Yukon College; Dave Sloan.

NORTHWEST TERRITORIES: Ron Klassen, Department of Education; W.H. Stapleton and Ron Holtorf, Thebacha College.

Andre Le Blanc of Champlain Regional College in Quebec was a special collaborator. He provided the leadership for the development of the Bibliography in French, but he also served as critic-at-large for many parts of the book. And we are particularly proud to be associated with the cartography of Karen Ewing of Capilano College. The technical assistance of Jean Elliott of Vancouver Community College was most appreciated, and the book would not be as it is without the special wisdom and balance of Barbara Boyce of Capilano College.

INTRODUCTION

Educational institutions reflect as well as shape their societies. The history of education in Canada provides striking evidence in support of this view.[1] Until the end of the Second World War, English-Canadian colleges and universities east of the Manitoba border were selective and conservative, reflecting their church-related origins in an era in which the vast majority of Canadians could not aspire to the intellectual and social benefits of a university education.[2] In Atlantic Canada, church-affiliated colleges and universities provided quite satisfactory religious, educational, and business leadership. To Ontarians, the University of Toronto stood as the symbol of educational prestige within Canada, with its colleges modelled on English traditions and with Hart House designed specifically as the gathering place for the future business and cultural leaders of Canada.[3] In Quebec, though the language was different, the pattern was identical and even more obvious. The Archbishop of Montreal served as the Chancellor of l'Université de Montréal, and the position was far from symbolic. The rigid class structure of Quebec society, as late as the 1950's, was mirrored in the exclusivity of Quebec education, even in the powerful English community of that province.[4]

The evolution of the university system has been summarized by Ross as follows:

> It can be said in general that the universities in Canada, England and the United States responded to new opportunities and new resources between 1850 and 1950 and that they enlarged their horizons, their curricula, and their constituency. They became all-powerful in the educational system, exercising almost monopolistic control over that system in each country. Withal they remained conservative ideologically, bound to established goals, class-structured, and peculiarly unprepared to face new demands for reform after World War II.[5]

By 1956, the post-secondary sector in Canada also included a number of colleges. The majority were *collèges classiques* and other specialized schools in Quebec, where the adaptation of the European model created a category of institutions between the schools and the universities. These colleges were church-affiliated and offered a traditional classical curriculum designed to prepare students to enter the equally traditional university stream. The remainder of the colleges, scattered throughout the country, were either under university or church authority or were specialized institutions, such as military colleges or provincial normal schools for the training of teachers. In effect, the entire sector of higher education in Canada was synonymous with academic and professional preparation.

While it is true that technical, vocational, and agricultural institutes had been established in various provinces, their status was modest at best. These institutions, although post-secondary in their voluntary character and in the age of students, were operated directly by provincial governments and displayed few of the qualities generally associated with institutions of higher education. They had neither financial independence from government nor any measure of self-government.

What was evident in higher education in central and eastern Canada applied equally to the public schools.[6] Universal education was not seen as a requirement for an informed citizenry in a democratic nation. That all children should attend school for at least a few years came to be seen as socially desirable only in the most generalized sense. The public school—apart from initiating a useful verbal and arithmetical literacy—was a fine screen through which children could be shaken, with only the most capable and the most persistent coming through.[7] Children of more advantaged parents had access to the benefits of quality private schooling as early in life as possible.[8]

Central and eastern Canadian education—as well as education in the Canadian North—stood out in stark contrast to a far more democratic educational tradition in the American States to the south. There, public education was viewed as the avenue to material success and equality of opportunity and as an essential social responsiblity in a society requiring an educated electorate.[9]

In the region to the west of Ontario, practices differed. The enterprising and challenging atmosphere of a more venturesome and more individualistic environment, the view that the school and the university should be in part instruments of cultural assimilation of people from many lands, and the influences of a bustling American Midwest and Pacific all contributed to a more egalitarian educational system.[10] With Canadian education under provincial jurisdictions, Western Canada steered its own educational and cultural courses. Besides, as neutral observers have noted, education had never been a hot political issue anywhere in Canada; the professional educational community and the committed amateur had the field to themselves.[11]

MOVEMENT AND DEVELOPMENT

Significant changes followed the Second World War. The increased rate of industrialization and urbanization in most parts of Canada, the far easier access to news of the world and a broader range of social and educational philosophies through improved and expanded modes of communication, and the politicians' conviction that development of educational facilities and expansion of educational opportunity were investments in the future contributed to a much more sophisticated and complex view of the social potential of education everywhere in Canada.[12]

New universities were built from coast to coast as a response to the changing aspirations and needs of a growing Canadian population; access to higher education was clearly to be made available to a larger percentage of students.[13] Elementary and secondary schools experienced a similar expansion throughout Canada and were generally equipped well, if not lavishly, to meet a broader commitment to more students. And except in Quebec, where unique forces first weakened the private sector of education and then caused its regeneration, the public educational institution—or the university with relatively modest fees—came very visibly to centre stage.[14] More adult and continuing education—under private, public, and voluntary auspices—added a further dimension to educational opportunity everywhere in Canada. The most striking development of the last quarter century, however, has been the rise of new post-secondary educational institutions in all provinces—and new opportunities in some older post-secondary institutions—through the growth of provincial networks of a new Canadian phenomenon, the publicly funded college.[15]

In most parts of Canada, the apparatus to provide Canadians with a remarkably open, multi-faceted educational system which could become the envy of better-endowed nations has been put in place.[16] Educational energy, in most parts of Canada, has been consumed in building the structures for expanded educational opportunity; it is not a criticism to suggest that the structures have not yet been put to the best use.[17] Yet, just when the structures had been put in place, new and far more difficult economic conditions have confronted Canadians in the 1980's. The task now is to reassess what was built over generations and to make the adjustments or changes necessary to prepare Canadians for the 21st century. Within that broad task, reappraisal of the role and mission of Canada's new colleges is particularly crucial, because it is these institutions which reach the greatest number of adults in Canada. Additionally, these colleges have little tradition to live up to or down from. Their personnel were largely selected for their recognition of new needs, for their energy and enthusiasm, and for their willingness to be adaptive; their decision to stand pat or start in new directions without major institutional or societal disruption has yet to be made.[18]

THE SOCIETAL CONTEXT

The future of Canada's new kind of college should be situated in the context of several Canadian realities.

First and most obvious is the general state of the nation. Few observers of the Canadian scene would understate the range of political, social, and economic issues to be addressed. Although the Quebec Question, so dominant in the 1970's, now seems much more muted, the fact remains that many French-speaking Canadians in Quebec and beyond continue to feel a deep sense of estrangement—or at best misunderstanding—within the Canadian political community;[19] the 1984 language issue in Manitoba is seen by many as just one more in a long series of incidents that do not accord the French language and culture in Canada the dignity and opportunities to flourish that it deserves. Quebec's concerns will not go away, whatever constitutional alignments may develop.[20]

As well, Canada may be officially multicultural, but there remains a wide gap between legislation and practice in the view of many citizens who are members of ethno-cultural groups.[21] The 1984 national election results dampened expressions of Western alienation, but its residue is not far below the surface. Grievances of native people remain unresolved. Atlantic Canada seeks more opportunity to decide for itself what its future will be.[22] People of the North hold a close watching brief on conservation and resource utilization questions and will not be shut out from participation in Canadian public policy development.[23]

But, in the mid-1980's, all of the political and social issues are overshadowed by economic uncertainty. Coping with the size of the national debt, on the one hand, and stimulating employment, on the other, are personal as well as governmental problems. The interdependence of Western economies and the ability of Canada to influence external decisions in the economic domain are complex matters without simple solutions. Canada's economic relationship with the United States has again emerged as an important public issue, and no uniform Canadian economic strategy seems capable of satisfying all regions of the country.[24] All these issues are further compounded as Canada tries to break into the new world economy based on information and rapid technological change at a time when this nation's traditional place among trading nations is seriously challenged. How wealthy Canada will be and how that wealth should be distributed are unanswered questions of the highest order.[25]

One result of the political and economic turmoil of recent years is that strong public support for education in Canada can no longer be taken for granted. Politicians, businessmen, the increased number of people on fixed incomes, and taxpayers generally have lamented consistently rising costs of education. Public education is still popularly viewed as an investment in job training, and the taxpayer still insists that there is not sufficient visible return on this investment.

Disaffection with public education will likely increase as high levels of unemployment become the rule rather than the exception.

The concern that education is "not what it used to be" is expressed over and over again. Young people are seen as unruly and not properly appreciative of the opportunities afforded them. The work load, salary, and general working conditions of teachers are increasingly regulated by formal contracts rather than by "gentlemen's" agreements. Divisions between administrator and teacher are becoming sharper and more inflexible. There is a genuine anxiety that institutions supported by public revenues are simply not doing the job, however ill-defined, expected of them.

Most Canadians still want access to university and the social as well as academic and professional advantages of a university background for their children. However, with the pressure to be more economical, Canadian schools are likely to continue to offer a broad range of programmes for children of all aptitudes and interests, but graduate fewer students for university admission. Access to university is already becoming increasingly limited on financial rather than academic grounds.[26] Poorer levels of literacy of graduates of Canadian schools are already prompting higher standards for admission to university.

The Canadian university is likely to become more exclusive in the years ahead. Costs are on the rise, and public subsidy will become even more necessary for their operation. Ironically, young people already advantaged by scholastic achievements that warrant admission to university will receive an additional advantage at public expense by having most of the costs of their education defrayed through tax support to universities; the gap between the educationally advantaged and disadvantaged may well broaden. The illusion of universal accessiblity to higher education as an essential component of a free Canadian society will remain—and examples of those who "made it," despite being disadvantaged, will be identifiable—but the reality is that access to university is becoming more limited.

The young adult has already replaced the adolescent as Canada's major societal concern. More and more high school graduates are disenchanted with both their society and the post-secondary education it has provided. Many are "unqualified" for university; they are virtually unemployable because there are more limited employment opportunities, and many of these opportunities are being preserved for older and more experienced Canadians.

How should Canadian education respond to these forces? The truth is that there is not a Canadian educational system, even in the limited sense of differing institutions pursuing common goals.[27] In social as well as constitutional senses, Canadian education is still provincial, with some notable exceptions in the university sector. Outside the university and voluntary sectors, the only existing instrument to identify and advance common goals is the Council of Ministers of Education, Canada, whose members have an essential interest in preserving provincial prerogatives in education; to expect the Council to promote supraprovincial interests is to ask its members to violate their own individual mandates. Successive efforts to establish a national office of education have been unsuccessful,[28] and there is little reason to believe that similar efforts in the immediate future, however desirable in the common Canadian interest, would be any more successful. A national system of education for Canada, or even the articulation of common educational objectives for the variety of jurisdictions through a National Office of Education, has simply not been the Canadian way. Nevertheless, without at least a national consciousness and concern, if not explicit national goals, Canada will not become more equitable, and Canadian educational institutions will not put their educational apparatus to the best use of individual Canadians or of Canadian society as a whole.

Yet, it would be easy to exaggerate the seriousness of the issues currently confronting Canadian education. After all, few of the world's 900 million illiterates reside in Canada; even fewer of the 250 million children in the world who have no access at all to schooling are members of this favoured society.[29] However minor Canada's educational challenges may be on the world stage, they should still be addressed. One of these challenges—the place of the colleges and college systems that have emerged in the last twenty five years—is the subject of this book. It is certain that the longer established educational institutions—the schools and universities—will play important roles in the future of Canadian society. It is equally certain that new educational structures, organizations, and institutions will emerge in the years ahead to respond to new educational needs.

What is less certain is the place that the public colleges will take in the immediate future of Canadian education. Recent consultation with college people from coast to coast, many of whom have lived but not recorded their experiences, has led to this story of how and why these institutions were established, what they have become, and what tests they must face to the end of this century. The fundamental question of this book is: How might Canada's new colleges best serve Canadians and help shape the Canadian future?

The story of the origins and developments of the colleges and college systems relies heavily on broad but largely unassembled documentation; readers should have no difficulty, however, in distinguishing between the evidence and the authors' opinions and judgments which appear primarily at the ends of chapters and sections.

The issues presented in the second section of the book have been identified through a cross-Canada survey of college leadership concerns. While documented, they are intentionally judgmental and, it is hoped, controversial. Indeed, one of the primary objectives of this section of the book is to provoke discussion and debate about the future. The arguments presented are neither exhaustive nor totally dispassionate. In fact, they reveal the authors' biases that the diversity of college models within Canada is one of their strengths and that all college systems within the country have great potential for influencing the national future—but that this potential will not be realized without vision and deliberate action.

PART I

Origins and History

1

INFLUENCES ON COMMUNITY COLLEGE DEVELOPMENT

The decade of the 1960's was truly a "golden age" for public education in Canada. It was a period when public demand for more advanced education and the financial capability of governments in Canada to respond to these demands coincided in dramatic fashion. The result was educational activity at all government levels, and the legacy was an educational structure which introduced new concepts of accessibility to higher or post-secondary education, new curriculum designs, and new kinds of educational institutions. It was a decade of unprecedented growth at all levels and in all forms of education in Canada, but particularly within the post-secondary sector.

In fact, the term "post-secondary" emerged in this period. Previously, Canadian education was thought of as having four components: elementary and secondary schooling; higher education, which really was restricted to the work of universities and degree-granting colleges; trade, technical, and vocational training, some of which was provided in schools and others in specialized institutions which accepted both school age students and those who had completed their compulsory schooling; and adult education, which was often provided informally by volunteers without public subsidy.

With the establishment of new institutions in and after the 1960's, the term "post-secondary education"—and sometimes "tertiary education"—became increasingly popularized as a collective label which would incorporate all education after secondary school: universities, degree-granting colleges, specialized institutions which admitted students beyond school age, and the new institutions which most commonly referred to themselves as community colleges. The place of adult education in this new alignment of institutions remained ambiguous because at this stage in the development of Canadian education, it really did not fit. It had its individual advocates and practitioners across the land, but it remained at best on the fringe of the established educational structure in Canada.

The distinction between schooling and post-secondary education was a useful one because it reinforced another distinction: that between schooling, which by this time was to be universally available to children in Canada and compulsory by law, and voluntary education at the post-school level for adults who had completed their formal compulsory schooling. The new colleges in Canada were clearly "post" secondary and part of the voluntary sector, even though it was not long before they included instruction for people beyond school age who had not successfully completed their schooling. Why this surge in post-secondary education in Canada at this time? More particularly, why did new colleges and new college systems come into existence at this point in Canada's history? Although different factors influenced the substance and timing of post-secondary developments in different parts of Canada, there were some common contributing factors.

First and most urgent was the projection of demand for post-secondary education by a rapidly increasing segment of the eighteen to twenty-four age cohort. Enrolment in university and college programmes had reached 120,000 in 1960, but 250,000 were projected for 1967 and over 350,000 by 1970.[1] Clearly, there was widespread concern about the capacity of the higher education institutions, particularly the existing universities, to absorb such an increase. The primary issues were questions of access, of size and structure of institutions, and of effects of growth upon quality and academic standards. As Leslie noted, "It was not a period of thinking much about where the money was coming from or the conditions which in later years might be imposed upon the universities in return for continued public support."[2] In fact, the political consequences of inaction seemed to dominate and the imprecise phrase "democratization of higher education" entered the rhetoric of the period.

A second factor prompting growth in the post-secondary sector was the impact of scientific and technological change which accompanied the end of the Second World War. Constant reference was made to the economic consequences of sustaining a Canadian workforce without the skills necessary for the demands of that age. The role Canada would play in the new scientific era would depend heavily upon the quality of its workforce. In 1961, in proportion to the size of its population, Canada employed approximately one-half as many scientists and engineers as were employed in the United States.[3] Furthermore, the traditional practice of importing rather than training skilled workers as a solution to new manpower needs was becoming no longer politically or economically acceptable. If new cadres of skilled and semi-skilled manpower were to be produced quickly, the solution was perceived to lie in the development of technical and vocational programming in post-secondary institutions.

Yet another strong influence on Canadian political and public opinion was a series of well-publicized studies,[4] produced in the United States and Canada, extolling the human capital theory and the return which society could expect from investment in higher education. In particular, Canada's Economic Council Report of 1964 implicitly urged the expansion of post-secondary education as an important factor in economic growth and as an investment in the future.

THE AMERICAN EXPERIENCE

As with so many other public affairs in Canada, developments had taken place in the United States which became profoundly influential. Higher education in that country was rooted in traditions imported from Europe and reform and change had begun much earlier than in Canada and with a good deal of public support. By 1860 there were 246 universities and colleges in the United States but only seventeen of these were state universities. The Morrill (Land Grant) Act,[5] about the time of the Civil War, gave rise to a number of agricultural and mechanical arts colleges in almost every state. In fact, the early participation of the federal government in higher education in the U.S. was stimulated by "the belief on the part of the American people that all men and women must be given equal educational opportunity."[6] This goal could be achieved only by equalization of opportunity among the states, and only the federal government, through its taxing power, could accomplish the task.

The practical expressions of the idea of equal opportunity through education—the provision of free, comprehensive public schools, the avoidance of early selection or "streaming" of students as practised in Europe, and the multi-purpose curriculum in the secondary schools—all had consequences for the American post-secondary sector. The universities, state and private, were required to accommodate a heterogeneous student population, many of whom were academically and emotionally unprepared for the rigours of higher education. The growing concern with this impact upon university values was articulated by a number of university presidents—Tappan of Michigan, Folwell of Minnesota, Harper of Chicago, Jesse of Missouri, and Jordan of Stanford—all of whom advocated an "intermediary" level between the high school and college where academic maturity could occur.[7] The model suggested followed the American custom of adapting German institutions to American conditions. Just as the Americans had borrowed from the German kindergarten, they now borrowed from the "gymnasium," a thirteenth and fourteenth year for those planning to enter university.

A number of American school boards took the initiative suggested by the university presidents. Beginning with Joliet, Illinois, in 1901, "post graduate" grades were established in high schools; the term "junior" college was not used until some years later. Fresno in California established a college in 1910, and a system of colleges developed rapidly in that state. By 1922 a total of 207 junior colleges operated in the United States, of which 137 were under private control.[8]

Between 1901 and 1960, the colleges in that country underwent a considerable evolution. While there were variations among the states in finance, governance, and control, there were certain common characteristics. Curricula rapidly diversified to include technical and vocational training, community education, and pre-college remedial programmes. The colleges became gradually integrated into their communities, and, as the name change to "community" college implied, they became more and more responsive to the wide-ranging educational needs of citizens of all ages and backgrounds. Of more importance, perhaps, was the public acceptance of the college as a full partner in the spectrum of American post-secondary education and as a practical expression of the idea of equal opportunity for all citizens to pursue further education despite academic, socioeconomic, or geographic barriers. By 1960, there were public community colleges in virtually every one of the United States; the total number of two-year colleges grew from 678 in 1961 to 1,100 by the end of that decade.[9] The enrolment increase during the same period was from 750,000 to 2,500,000. There had been massive injections of public money into the new colleges with an abundance of political rhetoric accompanying the process.

Originally, these American developments had virtually no impact on education in Canada. Soles attributes the phenomenon to historical and philosophical differences:

> for reasons which are essentially historical, Canadian education has remained predominantly under the influence of the British school system with its sharp cleavage first between the elementary and secondary schools, and even more sharply between the secondary schools and the universities. Over the years Canadian educators have tended to reject the German concept of the gymnasium, as an intermediate step between the high school and the university, and for the most part they have been downright contemptuous of any ideas of "open door colleges". Implicit in the pedagogical thinking of Canadians has been an almost total acceptance of the assumption that subject matter content is distributed along an hierarchical scale of values. Thus certain studies, English Literature or mathematics, for example, are acceptable and appropriate to college curricula; others, such as cosmetology or gunsmithing, are not. The fact that it is extremely difficult on a rational basis to distinguish between two areas of study in terms of the intrinsic worth of either has never troubled the thinking of Canadian academicians. By tradition, certain subjects belong in the university; others do not. Therefore entry to higher education can be open only to those students who have demonstrated at least basic competence in acceptable subject matter fields. The notion of permitting automatic entry (after

high school graduation in any programme) to institutions of higher learning, where students may study either the so-called academic or the non-academic subjects, has largely been foreign to Canadian thinking at least up to the last decade.[10]

The reluctance to expand post-secondary education in Canada came to an abrupt end at the end of the 1950's, and the American experience of the previous fifty years was to become a major influence on the ways in which Canadian education was to respond to newly felt needs.

THE FEDERAL ROLE

Without doubt, Canada's national governments had a singularly practical effect on the growth of post-secondary education throughout Canada. Although the British North America Act had placed education under the jurisdiction of the provinces, a number of historic conventions have called for a large measure of federal intrusion into forms of education in Canada. The management of the national economy and its relationship to the growth and disposition of the workforce rests with the federal government. Beginning with the Royal Commission on Industrial Training and Technical Education in 1910, a series of federal acts provided direct assistance to agricultural, technical, and vocational education through capital grants and student financial support.[11] Further federal funding was provided under legislation applied to veterans and to various programmes of research.

More directly related to developments in the 1960's, high unemployment in the 1950's prompted the Diefenbaker government to introduce the Technical and Vocational Training Assistance Act (1960). This legislation placed major emphasis on the vocational and technical training required for workers to adapt to changes in technology and to meet the demands of industry. Eight hundred million dollars was provided for such training by the Canadian government over a ten-year period, under a cost sharing arrangement with the provinces. A 75% federal-25% provincial formula was developed which applied to capital costs but, under certain conditions, to operating costs as well. Another series of legislative changes increased the amount of federal financial support, which culminated in 1967 with the introduction of the Adult Occupational Training Act and The Canada Manpower Training Program.

A second dimension to federal involvement in post-secondary education followed the publication of the report of the Royal Commission on National Development in the Arts, Letters, and Sciences (The Massey Commission). The commission recommended direct federal grants to universities and the St. Laurent government responded in 1951 with a grant of fifty cents per capita to each province, distributed among their universities based upon enrolment. By 1966 the grants had grown to five dollars per capita, and the federal government strengthened and solidified its support by the passage of the Federal-Provincial Fiscal Arrangements Act (1967). Under this act 50 per cent of the operating costs of higher education was returned to the provinces, and federal financial support was extended to include "academic/technical" programmes in both the university and non-university sectors.

These two areas of federal initiatives to support post-secondary education proved a real incentive for provincial governments to expand educational opportunity in their provinces through a heavy injection of federal funds—and it offered them an equally attractive opportunity to gain political credits within their own constituencies for expanding post-secondary education.

THE TOTAL IMPACT

While all of these factors were influential in all parts of Canada within a common time frame, each province responded in its own way, at its own rate, as a result of considerations peculiar to particular provinces. The diversity of Canada, the regional and cultural differences rooted in history, geography, and sociocultural imperatives, and the variety of educational philosophies make the study of the conception and birth of the new colleges an adventure into the Canadian conscience. The origins of the new colleges, by province, demonstrate intriguing similarities and differences despite the common thread of heavy federal impact on post-secondary education throughout the country.

2

NEW COLLEGES ACROSS CANADA

New colleges—and whole systems of colleges—appeared in Canada in the 1960's and early 1970's, ushering in a completely new era in post-secondary education. When, why, and how they were established produce ten different accounts. These accounts follow, province by province, in the order in which new colleges came on the scene.

ALBERTA

The industrial growth which accompanied the opening of the Alaska Highway, together with the oil boom of 1947 which followed the discovery of the Leduc fields, led to a demand for technical skills for what had been primarily a rural society.[1] By 1951, Alberta supported a variety of institutions which could be described as post-secondary. The University of Alberta in Edmonton, facing a rapidly increasing demand by students and yielding to political realities, had established a branch campus in Calgary. The provincial normal schools operating in Edmonton and Calgary were incorporated into the respective university campuses in 1945. The Technical Institute in Calgary was under considerable pressure to expand its programmes because of increasing industrialization. Vocational training centres, largely for the use of veterans, had been established with federally funded programmes in five regions of the province. As well, agricultural colleges, which suffered from uneven demand, were located in three rural communities, while eight private church-related, degree-granting colleges were in operation in various localities. Three were affiliated with the University of Alberta with formal transfer credit arrangements in place.[2]

Despite all these institutions, social changes were occurring in the province which provided the impetus for yet another type of post-secondary institution.

A substantial improvement in secondary school retention rates in the 1950's had created a much larger pool of students seeking some form of post-secondary education. In the new affluence which accompanied the resource boom, many of these students were anxious to pursue professional careers which required academic preparation beyond that available in secondary school.

Of even greater practical influence, however, was promotion of the theme of democratization of social and economic opportunity through expanded post-secondary education. In Campbell's view, "from the beginning of the first public junior college in Alberta . . . the democratization of opportunity became a theme of educators, planners, and politicians alike."[3] To such persons, new colleges were to be a specific instrument to achieve a more democratic society. As a result, credit for formulating the contemporary concept of a public, comprehensive, community college, not just for Alberta, but indeed for Canada as well, should be given to a group in the city of Lethbridge under the leadership of Gilbert C. Paterson, a teacher turned lawyer, who chaired a Lethbridge Chamber of Commerce Committee on education.[4]

On Paterson's urging, S.V. Martorana of Washington State College was commissioned in 1951 to conduct a community and regional survey and to recommend a plan for a college in Lethbridge.[5] Martorana noted the narrow scope of curricular offerings available in Alberta's institutions of agriculture, technology, and art, but particularly the limited opportunities for post-secondary education in the Lethbridge region. Not surprisingly, Martorana drew heavily and enthusiastically upon the community college model in his own state as an educational design to meet the needs of a community and region similar in size and complexity to many in Washington.

The college proposed for Lethbridge advocated a comprehensive curriculum, including university equivalency programmes and occupational, remedial, and community education courses. Particular reference was made to the needs of mature students and the advantage of part-time study opportunities. Martorana's implementation recommendation was that the college begin through the addition of a thirteenth year to the secondary school.

School boards, education committees, and community groups kept up pressure locally for the establishment of a real community college, and this pressure led to discussions in 1955 with the two most influential voices in higher education in Alberta: the University of Alberta and the Minister of Education. The university, largely through its prime advocate for the college idea, W.H. Johns, advanced the view that several options in structure were possible: "(a) A branch of the university, as in Calgary; (b) a college affiliated to the university, such as the private institution, Mount Royal College; (c) a college under a local authority which may or may not be recognized by the university."[6] Johns made clear that he felt the best course of action would be to establish a two-year junior college, primarily academic, under the aegis of the university. The Minister of Education thought otherwise, noting that public financial support would become available for a college only if it would offer vocational training as well as university transfer courses.

The eventual decision to establish a college in Lethbridge was precipitated by an application from Lethbridge District School Board to the Minister of Education under Section 178 of the School Act.[7] The application provided for the establishment of a school district college, affiliated with the University of Alberta, with credit courses equivalent to the first two years of an arts degree. Financial grants would be available under the School Grants Act for this purpose. The University of Alberta set conditions for affiliation on the advice of its General Faculty Council. The restrictive terms were expressed in the following manner:

> [1] A minimum staff of six teachers giving the major part of their time to junior college work must be maintained. The members of the staff must be university graduates with special training in their particular fields and have at least one year of post-graduate study. [2] Junior college work may be associated with the work of the high school, but must be dissociated both in organization and in buildings from the work of the primary grades. [3] Library and laboratory equipment must be reasonably adequate in the subjects taught in the junior college. [4] The examinations of the junior college will be the regular university examinations of the first year. The conditions of entrance and of advancement to junior college will be those which obtain in the university. [5] Except in the case of high schools which may obtain junior college affiliation and receive the regular department grant, junior colleges will be affiliated on the basis of private financial support only.[8]

After the approval of affiliation, in April 1957, Lethbridge Junior College, the first public two-year community college in Canada, was established by Cabinet order in the following fall (See Appendix D).

The presence of the Lethbridge College stimulated legislation in the form of a Public Junior Colleges Act (1958).[9] The provincial government correctly anticipated that demands would follow from other parts of the province for similar institutions once the precedent had been set. The act expressed a clear statement of the main role of a college but also reiterated the influential presence of the University of Alberta in college development. While the colleges were to be given the authority to offer both university equivalent courses and vocational programs, no college would be established unless " . . . (a) the Minister gives his consent thereto, and (b) the board of Governors of the University of Alberta has approved, in writing, the affiliation of the junior college with the University."[10] In fact, college instructors for university equivalent courses were to be approved by the university, and students would have to face the same admission requirements as the university demanded of its applicants. The colleges were to be governed by a board consisting of members appointed by participating school boards. Funding of colleges was to be from local taxation, student tuition fees, and revenue from both provincial and federal sources.

Despite the new legislation, it was clear that a conflict was developing between two views of an appropriate community college concept for the province of Alberta. The university feared the dilution of university-level studies in these new institutions and was therefore determined to control their development, even though the university community saw colleges as essentially "junior" institutions. They paid little attention to other elements of the proposed college curriculum. Conflicting with this perception of colleges was the provincial government's desire to see the decentralization of vocational training; it viewed the colleges as job preparation and community education centres.

In 1959, a Royal Commission on Education in Alberta chaired by Senator Donald Cameron[11] restated the need to decentralize non-university education throughout the province. The commission's report made a clear distinction between junior colleges and public community colleges and argued that non-university education should be the prime role of Alberta public community colleges.

Several Alberta communities, attracted by the prestige associated with universities, took the initiative to establish colleges which would be predominantly university-transfer institutions. Their preference was reinforced by the availability of federal financial support for academic programmes and by interest expressed by students in university level studies. Following the "Lethbridge pattern," public colleges were established in Red Deer in 1964, Medicine Hat 1965, and Grande Prairie 1966. In each case the enrolment was small, the students were primarily of college age, and the curriculum was university oriented. Camrose Lutheran College had also gained affiliation as a private college in 1959 as a consequence of approval of the Lethbridge transfer policy.

In a policy departure from earlier positions,the Ministry of Education established a college financing system in 1964[12] which appeared to favour and encourage university equivalent programming for colleges. Indeed, the legislation even allowed the offering of second year university courses. Ambivalence by the government towards the essential role of the public colleges persisted. By 1965 the government's approach to college developed further in response to local school board initiatives. School boards in both Edmonton and Calgary requested colleges. The government rejected the Edmonton bid but agreed to award public status to Mount Royal College in Calgary, which had enjoyed an affiliated status as a private institution since 1931. In 1966, when the conversion of Mount Royal College was approved, a coincidental decision was made to grant autonomy to the Calgary campus of the University of Alberta, creating the University of Calgary. From that point, Mount Royal's affiliation was with the University of Calgary, and, for the first time, the University of Alberta no longer had sole authority in the politics of university transfer studies.

One other event significant in the historical development of Alberta colleges was the establishment, in 1965, of a Special Study on Junior Colleges under the chairmanship of Dr. Andrew Stewart.[13] Stewart was asked to advise government on the role, governance, and financing of the emerging colleges. The prime recommendation in his report was that colleges should be a valid alternative to university education for those unable or unwilling to attend university, but that they should also provide a variety of non-university programmes. The report additionally recommended that the province should be divided into college districts, under a provincial board, to advise the government on college development. This system approach would clearly diminish the role of universities in shaping the college movement in Alberta. While recognizing that the pressure of numbers on the university was a reality, Stewart did not see colleges as mere service stations for universities. In his view, colleges should become comprehensive regional post-secondary education centres, separate and distinct from the secondary schools and from the universities. He also rejected the Ontario model of colleges of applied arts and technology which was being put in place at this time, noting that such an approach would only encourage the construction of expensive satellite university campuses throughout the province without reducing to any significant extent the need for college facilities for other kinds of programmes.

Public reaction to the Stewart Report was generally positive, but the University of Alberta expressed reservations. A series of meetings followed publication of the report to allow for public discussion of its recommendations. The newly appointed Deputy Minister, T.C. Byrne, organized a conference on post-secondary and continuing education and, to aid discussion, prepared draft legislation calling for regional and provincial boards of post-secondary education. Although the draft legislation did not become law, the government did establish a Provincial Board of Post-Secondary Education in 1967. The creation of this new body, by amendment to the Public Junior Colleges Act, further eroded the influence of the University of Alberta over college development. The transfer of credit issue and such matters as the qualification for admission of students to the college academic programmes were no longer under full control of the university.

The major influence of the provincial board was the proposal to establish an intermediary body called a Colleges Commission, which would have responsibility for planning the future of a college system. There was also some pressure to create a commission which would oversee both colleges and university development, but this was rejected by cabinet. The provincial board, in response, drafted a set of proposals for the non-university sector which would form the basis of new legislation. With one exception, these proposals were accepted by cabinet and provided the nucleus for the 1969 Colleges Act[14], which was to provide the structure for colleges in the future. The one exception was the inclusion of institutions of technological, agricultural, and vocational education under the act. The cabinet decided that they should not be included under the new legislation, and these institutions were left under the direct jurisdiction of the appropriate ministries of government.

In summary, Alberta set its own path for college development. The University of Alberta was prestigious, influential, and determined to see the post-secondary universe unfold as it felt it should. Local communities, largely through pressures from boards of school trustees, counterbalanced the university influence and were eventually given the right to develop their own post-secondary alternatives in their own regions. The passage of the Colleges Act brought legitimacy and security to colleges after a stormy period of parochialism and university domination over the new intruders into Alberta's post-secondary educational system. The government opted for local initiative until financial and administrative considerations called for a brake on the speed with which new colleges should be established. The public preference was primarily for academic, university-like junior colleges, which would, in the anticipation of many, eventually become degree granting institutions in their own right. The government wanted the new colleges to be primarily educational centres which would concentrate on occupational preparation, while also providing access to wider educational opportunity to a broader segment of society—in fact, to democratize post-secondary education. In the process of their initial development, the colleges were buffeted by conflicting opinion, confusing directions, and unclear agendas. Finally, firm and deliberate leadership was provided by government. The result was the creation of a college system with a plan, a legislated structure, and a rule of procedure ensured through the Colleges Act and with a provincial commission to oversee evolution. From the modest but tenacious "Lethbridge movement," Alberta witnessed the growth of an educational vision which was to capture the imagination and obtain the support of both rural and urban communities.

BRITISH COLUMBIA

British Columbia is often regarded by other Canadians as different, both geographically and spiritually, from the rest of Canada. Regardless of the accuracy of this perception, British Columbia, since the Second World War, has been the beneficiary of continuing in-migration from the other provinces. With population increases consistently well in excess of the national rate, and a "boom or bust" economy based largely upon natural resource exploitation, this province would seem to be an ideal location for the development of diversified institutions of post-secondary education. However, prior to 1964, there had been little development or diversification. The University of British Columbia, established in 1915, had maintained a fundamentally conservative course of development. Enrolment reached 3,000 by the end of the Second World War, and, following a brief period of growth when war veterans flocked to the campus during 1947-48, it continued to expand slowly.

The university had established one satellite college in Victoria,[15] the capital city. The two university campuses, in addition to one small private college[16] and the tiny Notre Dame University in Nelson, represented the entire spectrum of post-secondary education in British Columbia until 1965. A number of vocational schools had been constructed throughout the province by the Ministry of Education, but these schools were narrow in scope and not generally regarded as post-secondary institutions even though their students were beyond school age. As well, a number of high schools throughout the province offered a grade thirteen, one year beyond the standard high school diploma. By staying in high school this extra year, some students could accumulate a limited number of academic credits for transfer towards a degree at the University of British Columbia.

While the 1965-1975 period was the era of growth in number and kinds of post-secondary educational institutions in British Columbia, a master plan for a comprehensive college system for the province had been developed in a thesis written by Knott as early as 1932.[17] This manuscript, entitled "The Junior College in British Columbia," prepared a systematic rationale for a number of "junior" colleges in various locations in the province. Though modelling his proposal on the California college system, Knott saw the advantage of a Canadian version which reflected the educational philosophy of the time.

Knott emphasized the need for a level of education beyond grade twelve which would offer both academic and "vocationally oriented" programmes. The prime reason for the establishment of the junior college, in Knott's view, was to correct the unacceptably high level of student drop-out in British Columbia's high schools at that time. Knott's figures revealed that of the students in British Columbia who entered the first year of high school (grade nine) in 1926, only 44 per cent graduated in 1930. Further, of 3,008 seniors in high school in 1929, only 1,848 continued their education in the following year, a loss of almost 40 per cent. By comparison, the rate of drop out at the end of high school in California during the same years was 6 per cent.[18] Knott's conclusion was that the junior colleges in that state provided both an opportunity and an incentive for students to continue their education. Knott notes that "[the college] is an institution with a guidance function designed to give terminal course training to students who do not wish, or should not go to college, and prepare them for occupations in life."[19] However, perhaps the most prophetic of Knott's recommendations were the proposed locations for his junior colleges. In virtually every case, the centres he proposed in 1932 became realities some thiry-five years later.

While the Knott thesis remained simply an idea, unappreciated and forgotten, many of his concerns continued into a period of adjustment and social change which accompanied the end of the Second World War. In his perceptive study of the forces which led to the establishment of British Columbia's colleges, Beinder notes:

> Social change is a slow and generally erratic process. Crystalization of changing public perceptions is not an overnight phenomenon. It seemed as though the war had changed the world. There was no returning to the old ways. We had entered the era of the global village. The new and disturbing imperative of growing international interdependence was upon us.
>
> With it came speculation on the future of us all, and the place of the individual in the emerging panorama. Perhaps the drive to provide veterans of the conflict with university opportunities was a signal of the change. Some of the remarkable success stories emanating from that experience may have been the forerunner of the drive to continue to find motivation for people to whom opportunity has traditionally been denied.[20]

Practical consequences in education of social change in the post-war years were improved high school retention rates, rapid increases in enrolment in grade thirteen classes, and pressures from school boards and other local community agencies for expanded educational opportunities for citizens of all ages. The government responded positively if not immediately to these forces. In 1958, the Public Schools Act was amended to allow for the establishment of two types of institutions of higher learning—those organized by the government and those which would be the responsibility of school boards. The act gave permission to the Council of Public Instruction to:

> Authorize the establishment, maintenance, and operation, in affiliation with the University of British Columbia, of school district colleges by a board in which may be offered such courses as may be deemed desirable, and authorize the prescription of rules covering the operation of such colleges.[21]

The critical line in the legislation was the "affiliation" clause—the expression of a concern about academic standards in any "new" non-university institutions.

Presumably, the university would ensure the academic quality of the new school district colleges.

Following the legislative amendment, the Kelowna school district initiated a series of studies on the feasibility of establishing a college.[22] On many counts—potential enrolment, public interest, operating and capital costs, and local demand for various kinds of post-secondary education—the case for the college was well-supported. But a college was not established.

In 1960 the Report of a Royal Commission on Education (The Chant Commission) was tabled.[23] The report included among its proposals a recommendation for the extension of the grade thirteen programme throughout the province by the creation of "collegiate academies" which would include grades eleven, twelve, and thirteen. The academies would offer a two-stream curriculum: one leading to the university and the other to employment or advanced technical training. The major reason for the proposal to expand grade thirteen, rather than establish new institutions, seemed to be the cost of post-secondary education, to both the province and the individual. The report noted that:

> Fees charged for Grade XIII are considerably lower than those for first year university and particularly for pupils who reside in parts of the province other than Vancouver or Victoria. The cost of living at home is much less than that incurred by either living in university residences or boarding when attending university.[24]

While many of the recommendations in the report directed at the school system were implemented, no immediate action was taken to establish the collegiate academies. Part of the reason for the government's hands-off approach to post-secondary education must be attributed to the stance of the administration of the University of British Columbia. The university had devoted considerable energy in a continuing struggle with the provincial government for increased financial support and now saw the growth of alternative post-secondary institutions as a further dilution of funds that should be made available to the university. There was little support from the university, even for expansion of the grade thirteen classes, primarily on academic grounds; university administrators viewed high schools as inferior substitutes for the intellectual climate required for university studies.

However, some demographic and economic facts could not be ignored. The size of the college-age population was growing rapidly and the percentage of this group seeking higher education was also increasing—to 18 per cent by 1961, as compared to 12 per cent in Canada as a whole and 40 per cent in the United States[25], with projections to 25 per cent by 1971.[26] The University of British Columbia was projecting an enrolment of 30,000 by 1970—an unacceptable figure in the view of most academics of that day. Even to the most conservative of university administrators, it was evident that some action had to be taken.

Several options were open. The University of British Columbia could allow itself to expand dramatically; a number of affiliated "branch colleges" could be established throughout the province; or a set of new and different post-secondary educational institutions could be developed. The first option was unacceptable to the university. The second seemed at least to allow the university to maintain suitable standards and had broad support. It was the third choice, however, which was implemented, in large part as a result of an important decision—the appointment in 1962 of John B. Macdonald as President of the University of British Columbia.

Macdonald was a man of remarkable energy, foresight, and determination. Coming from a research position at Harvard University, he immediately announced his intention to make a study of the long-term needs in post-secondary education for the province. He brought together a group of faculty colleagues and began a tour of the interior of the province to hear first-hand the educational aspirations of the people.

The Macdonald study was unusual in one important respect—the initiative was essentially his own. His report was not commissioned, or even requested, by government or by any other agency, private or public. Macdonald had a strong personal sense of the future and foresaw the need for a detailed plan of action if British Columbia were to keep pace educationally and economically with the rest of Canada.

As the Macdonald team listened to the numerous presentations from individuals and groups in each community throughout the province, it became evident that limited access to post-secondary education was a major public concern. The barriers to accessibility were many and varied: geographic, sociocultural, economic, academic, and psychological. But, essentially the problem was that university studies, available only in Vancouver and Victoria, were remote if not unrealistic goals for many people of college age in most parts of a province with poor transportation and communication systems among its numerous small communities.

Among the most active of groups articulating views to the Macdonald Committee were the boards of school trustees throughout the province. Both individual boards and the parent body, The B.C. School Trustees Association, had long held strong positions on the structure of new institutions of further education. They were to be community based, community oriented, and community controlled. The association's position was clear and unequivocal.

Boards of School Trustees should be responsible for meeting all educational needs in a community which may reflect the needs of the community for adults as well as children, in academic and vocational fields alike, including the development and operation of community colleges, which properly are extensions of the public school programme of a community.[27]

Further, the School Trustees Association brief to Macdonald drew attention to the government adult vocational schools in operation in some parts of the province, and viewed the existing and pending ones "with alarm," as "entities separate from the school system, and which look upon various technical, commercial, etc., activities and programmes as being quite apart from general schooling."[28] The influence of school trustees on the shaping of post-secondary education in British Columbia cannot be overestimated. The post-secondary model Macdonald proposed was quickly adopted by government, and was one in which local communities were to play the central role, rather than the provincial government. British Columbia was to have colleges that would be the products of grassroot activity, even to the extent of requiring local referenda to provide for their establishment. Clearly, the school trustees had made a major impact on the Macdonald Committee.

The Senate of the University of British Columbia was the other major influence upon the Macdonald Committee.[29] It presented its own brief to Macdonald in which it reviewed several arguments regarding diversification of higher education. The Senate acknowledged that those seeking higher education would increase but it rejected outright any plan either to enlarge the University of British Columbia or to create more universities. It recommended the development of a differentiated system of post-secondary education throughout the province, to include new institutions which would be independent from the university and multi-purpose in curriculum. In doing so, the brief stated that:

> Many people feel that a system of differing institutions is basically undemocratic, will give rise to feelings of discrimination, will deepen feelings of class consciousness and resentment, because such a system necessarily makes distinctions between student interests and abilities, and tailors education accordingly.
>
> English experience is often cited in this regard; however, we do not find it relevant. If there are problems of this sort in England they seem traceable largely to education at the lower level, not under discussion here, and in any case Western Canada does not begin with a class heritage even remotely analogous to England's.[30]

The publication of the Macdonald Report aroused considerable public and educational reaction, mostly positive. In a rare display of personal initiative, a university president had dealt critically and comprehensively with the future of higher education in the province. Furthermore, he proposed a detailed plan of action to introduce a new structure for higher education. Macdonald's stature as the university president was undoubtedly an important factor in the immediate and widespread support for his plan.

The tone of the Macdonald argument was set in the opening chapter:

> The persons who will make the greatest contribution to society will be those educated to the limits of their capacities and talents, by the best kinds of educational institutions we can finance and staff. Human resources are our most important asset for tomorrow. The nation making inadequate use of its citizens through failure to educate them will be a nation doomed to economic distress at best, and economic disaster at worst.[31]

The introductory chapter concluded with an impressive analysis of statistical data which revealed that British Columbia had invested little in its young people's future relative to the investment in other provinces and other nations. The report continued with a powerful plea for "excellence in education" as the prime criterion for the form post-secondary education should take in British Columbia. In Macdonald's words:

> Two requirements are fundamental to the promotion of excellence in British Columbia's higher education. These are first, diversification of opportunity, both in respect to the kinds of educational experience available and the places where it can be obtained. The second requirement is self-government of individual institutions in respect to setting objectives, standards, admissions, selection of staff, curricula, personnel policies, administrative structure, and all the other things that go to make up the operation of a college. These two elements—diversification and self-government— together will not insure excellence, but in their absence an excellent system of higher education in British Columbia would be unattainable.[32]

The practical application of Macdonald's plea for diversification of opportunity was that development of four-year liberal arts universities was necessary— but that a number of two-year colleges, which would offer both academic courses of university equivalent value and technical programs designed to prepare students for employment, primarily in their own communities, was equally necessary. The second condition, self-government of institutions, led to the recommendation that colleges be established with their own boards which would generate their own policies, without the paternal hand of the university. Macdonald's position certainly undermined the concern that only universities could ensure the academic standards of post-secondary institutions.

The report supported the views on governance so aggressively argued by the school trustee groups. Macdonald recommended that:

Within the province those agencies which have the evident knowledge and experience in financing and developing educational facilities are the boards of school trustees . . . . In my opinion they are well suited to appraise the educational needs and goals of the areas within the province, and for that reason, they should have a large measure of responsibility of higher education in two-year regional colleges.[33]

That responsibility, in Macdonald's view, would include a substantial financial contribution to the operating costs of the colleges from local taxation. The report made specific recommendations for the locations of the new institutions and projected cost estimates for both operating and capital needs.

The more detailed proposals included a description of what two-year colleges ought to become, with emphasis upon the plan to develop characters consistent with the needs and the nature of the different communities to be served by the colleges. Even in the case of the "university-transfer" courses, Macdonald's emphasis was upon courses parallel to those of universities, rather than courses identical to those of universities. The colleges were to be teaching institutions with demands upon faculty quite different from those on professors in the university. The major responsibilities of college faculty would be instruction and community service. Unlike university professors, college teachers would not be required to conduct research.

The government responded to an enthusiastic reception throughout the province for the Macdonald Report with uncharacteristic haste. In 1963 the first of a series of amendments to the Public Schools Act provided legislation which authorized school boards to "establish, maintain, and operate" colleges and to prescribe the rules governing the operation of such colleges.[34] There was no reference to the role of the university in the process of establishing, maintaining, or operating the new colleges.

The legislated procedure for establishing a new college in British Columbia is worthy of note. A single school district, or several districts in co-operation, could establish a college by following a series of steps calculated to ensure that community initiative and support were evident before the provincial government would co-operate in the venture of establishing a college. On application to the Ministry of Education, a school district could establish a college "steering" committee, generally composed of interested school trustees, business and community leaders, and educators. Their first task was to conduct a publicity campaign leading to a plebiscite in all co-operating districts. The plebiscite, requiring a 50 per cent majority for success, was to determine the extent of district and regional support for the new institution. Successful passage of the plebiscite would lead to the formal establishment of a regional or district College Council.[35]

The second step proved to be more difficult to complete successfully. It involved the presentation of a funding by-law, requiring a 60 per cent majority for success, to provide for the capital financing of the college. With one exception (West Kootenay Region), the first referenda failed to receive the majorities required. Nevertheless, operating funds were made available through the co-operating school districts and leasing arrangements were made for the facilities for the new institutions, many of which began with evening classes in high schools and similar locations. In the initial period, college operations were funded through a formula by which 50 per cent of operating costs were funded from local tax sources and student fees with the remainder from the provincial budget.

The establishment of colleges, following the procedure outlined, was a gradual process. In 1965, Vancouver opened a district college, Vancouver City College, created through the amalgamation of its adult continuing education centre, a vocational institute, and an art school. Selkirk College, a regional institution with several participating school districts, opened in 1966. Capilano and Okanagan Colleges followed in 1968, Malaspina and New Caledonia Colleges in 1969, and Douglas and Cariboo Colleges in 1970. In each case the community steering groups overcame local skepticism and negative criticism, presented defensible feasibility studies, and developed wide support for a kind of educational institution with a new and exciting orientation and appeal.

In every college plan, the ideas of increased accessibility to further education for college-age and mature students; of opportunity to live at home while pursuing higher education; of a multi-purpose curriculum including university-equivalent courses, advance technical and career programmes and general studies; and of the general concept of democratization of education were incorporated. All proved to be decisive factors in gaining increasingly broader support for the college concept advocated by Macdonald.

The wide range of interest in the new institutions was reflected in the rapid expansion of programmes to include a variety of continuing education courses and vocational and remedial programmes. The colleges quickly became factors in changing the quality of community life in many parts of British Columbia. Their special contribution to British Columbia life was expressed in the distinctive character of their programmes.

The governing bodies, composed of community representatives—chosen in part locally and in part by the provincial government, proved to be effective voices in enlisting government support at the provincial level. An academic board, established by the Minister of Education as a province-wide body charged with the supervision of academic standards in the new colleges, was instrumental in converting some initial skepticism from the universities into mutually satisfactory arrangements for the transfer of credits from colleges to university. The practical extension of the college idea in British Columbia was underway.

Summarizing the development of non-university post-secondary education in British Columbia, the major factor was the role by the wider community in the process of establishing colleges. Neither the products of provincial government initiatives nor of massive injection of government funding, British Columbia's colleges were conceived, born, and nurtured through the expression of local and regional support for an idea which represented a new concept of educational opportunity. The Macdonald Report and the legislation which followed, while important in themselves, were in reality only the instruments for the marshalling of wider public attitudes, expressed by community groups and agencies with a distinctive vision of the future and a deep commitment to the democratization of education beyond high school.

> The community college in British Columbia represents the crystallization of a dream of service to people. It is something more than and different from the old community of scholars concept of higher education. It represents an idea of dynamic involvement of the total community. It was seen as an entity subservient to no other institution. It was not to be an extension of the public school, nor a mini-university. It was a social invention, whole and legitimate in its own right, designed to solve a particular kind of problem created by a highly complex society.[36]

ONTARIO

The conceptual roots of the Ontario public college system were beginning to form as early as 1950, with the release of the report of the Royal Commission on Education in Ontario. Reacting to the perceived needs for more employment training and expanded opportunity for technical education, the report recommended the establishment of "Junior Colleges" to be operated by local education authorities. The proposed colleges appeared to be more akin to senior secondary schools, however, as graduates would be expected to enter either "the first year honours course in university" or "a specialized Provincial Technical Institute".[37] No specific actions on the recommendations of the commission were taken at that time, but at least a problem had been publicly identified.

In 1955, E.F. Sheffield, at the then Dominion Bureau of Statistics, reported to the annual meeting of the National Conference of Canadian Universities a projection on university enrolment in Canada indicating a 100 per cent increase in demand by 1965.[38] Anticipating this pressure, Ontario responded with two parallel but quite independent moves: a steady and unprecedented expansion of the university sector and the development of a large non-university post-secondary sector. Expansion came about both through the conversion of denominational colleges into public universities and through the establishment of new public universities.[39] In 1954-55, seven universities—three of them denominational—were receiving provincial financial support. In rapid succession several previously church-related colleges obtained public university status: McMaster (1957), Waterloo (1960), Laurentian (1960), Windsor (1962), Ottawa (1965) and Wilfrid Laurier (1973). York (1960), Lakehead (1962), Trent (1964), Brock (1964) and Guelph (1964) were all established as public universities.

The roots of the development of a non-university post-secondary sector in Ontario can be traced to the publication of a report entitled Post-Secondary Education in Ontario 1962-1970, issued by the Committee of Presidents of provincially assisted universities.[40] Apparently after a prepublication revision, the January 1963 version of the report examined and rejected two options for relieving the pressure of numbers upon their institutions. The first involved the conversion of Ontario technological institutes and teachers' colleges into "composite junior colleges," from which students would transfer with advanced credit to universities, as was the case with the Ryerson Polytechnical Institute. This option was rejected on the grounds that composite junior colleges would be regarded by the public as inferior substitutes for universities—or they would soon want to add a third year and a baccalaureate degree and create, in effect, a second class university system. It is interesting to note the irony in this admonition in the light of a recommendation of the Wright Commission ten years later, which recommended degree-granting status for the colleges.

The second option in the 1963 report described, and also rejected for Ontario, the United States junior college model on the grounds that one of its prime functions was to accommodate the wide variations in standards in the United States secondary schools, a condition which, the university presidents argued, did not apply to Ontario because of its standardized examination system through grade thirteen. The positive recommendation from the university presidents was to create 18,000 additional student places in existing technological institutes to meet the increased demand for an alternate form of post-secondary education.

At this time, there were many provincially operated institutions providing technical and vocational training: institutes of technology in Ottawa, Hamilton, Kirkland Lake, Windsor, and Toronto; Vocational Centres in Sault Ste. Marie, London, Ottawa, and Toronto; Trades Institutes with particular specialties in other centres of population. All of these were to be influenced dramatically by developments which followed.

Evidently public opinion did not coincide with the views of the university presidents, for in June 1963, the supplementary report from the same committee noted, "the extraordinary interest of the people of Ontario in the development and expansion of the educational system at the post-secondary level."[41] The supplementary report, which again rejected the American model for essentially the same reasons as before, produced an "Ontario" alternative which provided the conceptual framework for the college model which was eventually to be created.

The Committee of University Presidents proposed to correct a number of perceived deficiencies in the Ontario educational system. The first deficiency was a striking lack of opportunity for adult education in the province. Although 4,200 such students were then enrolled in Ryerson's evening programmes, only some 800 were enrolled in other institutes. The committee also recognized the need to expand the non-university sector, particularly in vocational and technical areas, for students graduating from the secondary system without aptitudes required for university study.[42] Adult education and vocational and technical training needs prompted the proposal of a "Colleges of Technology and Applied Arts" model which would "resemble the American community college in its emphasis on terminal vocational courses and adult education, but would be compatible with the Ontario system." Anticipating that some students might wish to go on to university after college studies, the committee noted that "Arrangements for transfers of very good students from these colleges either to the Provincial Institutes of Technology or the universities might be worked out as experience develops."[43] It was proposed that the colleges be under local control but that the Department of Education be charged with the supervision of standards and the control over unnecessary duplication of programmes.

The thrust of the report reflected the university bias of its authors. The need to preserve and protect the university system underlay most of their recommendations. The university presidents viewed with justifiable alarm the pressure on their institutions to admit more students who might lack the intellectual competencies to benefit from the university experience. They emphasized the diversity of educational needs in a complex industrialized society and the need for highly trained personnel in various technological fields, given the particular character of the Ontario economy. They underscored the social and economic value of wider choice for youth through the operation of a diverse set of educational institutions.

Another factor which contributed to the character of Ontario's colleges was a reassessment of the nature and function of grade thirteen of the secondary school, conducted by a Ministry of Education Grade Thirteen Study Committee in 1954.[44] While not specifically addressing the college idea, this committee noted that there was no opportunity for grade twelve graduates to continue their education other than the university-oriented grade thirteen. The solution proposed by the Grade Thirteen Study Committee was the establishment of "community colleges" which would "logically extend" the variety of alternatives offered in secondary schools under the Robarts Plan.[45]

The final document which led to the shaping of the character the new Ontario colleges would take came in the form of the second Supplementary Report of the Committee of University Presidents entitled *The City College*.[46]

While again strongly opposing the notion of university equivalent programmes in new institutions, the committee now argued its case on both ideological and empirical grounds. A further expansion of university facilities could bring 90 per cent of Ontario's population within twenty-five miles of a university, and so university-transfer courses in colleges were unnecessary and indefensible. The Ryerson model was promoted for the new colleges arguing that,"The Ontario Institute of Technology at its best is neither a glorified high school or an ersatz university."[47] The university presidents were still anxious to maintain the status quo, particularly with respect to the sole right of the universities to offer university level courses.

But public debate began to generate around the proposed "city college" model, and the issue of university-transfer courses in particular. Murray Ross, then President of York University, strongly supported the view that there should be transfer opportunity for college graduates as a matter of provincial policy, not merely at the discretion of the universities in individual cases. Ross feared that, without such a policy, the colleges could become "a dead end for students able to profit from university."[48]

The stage was now set for the introduction of legislation to establish new colleges in Ontario. While their possible structure had been debated in the public press, little comment came from professional educators, other than the university presidents. Bartram summarized the situation as follows:

> Above all, it was the presidents of Ontario's universities who seem to have most influenced the shape of the colleges. The recurrent themes in their reports were: that the colleges should not interfere with the unique position of the universities in that only they should do degree-level work; and, that any colleges should be created in such a way as to preserve the perceived superiority of Ontario's educational system as compared with the United States and, by implication, other Canadian provinces.[49]

Furthermore, the university presidents were determined, despite advice to the contrary, that grade thirteen should be retained.

The other dominant influence on the model of post-secondary education to be adopted in Ontario was R.W.B. Jackson, Director of the Department of Educational Research at the University of Toronto and later the founding Director of the Ontario Institute for Studies in Education. Apart from his influence as an advisor to the Committee on University Affairs and as secretary to the 1950 Royal Commission on Education, Dr. Jackson was a close associate of the Minister of Education and accompanied him on fact-finding excursions prior to the introduction of legislation to establish new colleges in Ontario. Jackson's influence on the government's policy concerning colleges was particularly significant.

On May 21, 1965, Ontario's Minister of Education, William Davis, introduced an amendment to the Department of Education Act which established Colleges of Applied Arts and Technology. In January 1966, a rationale and accompanying legislation for the colleges was published in a document entitled Colleges of Applied Arts and Technology: Basic Documents. In this statement the minister noted that the colleges were designed to serve a new student population:

> directly related to the Applied Arts and Technology, for full-time and for part-time students, in day and in evening courses, and planned to meet the relevant needs of adults within a community, at all socioeconomic levels, of all kinds of interests and aptitudes, and at all stages of educational achievement.[50]

It was confirmed that the university transfer concept was not to be part of these institutions. The curriculum of the colleges was to be occupationally oriented, with an additional emphasis upon general adult education and upgrading for those adults wishing to return to further study. Admission would be based upon either grade twelve or grade thirteen completion with an "open admission" to applicants nineteen years of age and older. Coordinated development of the college system would be the responsibility of a Council of Regents for the province, and financing for the new colleges would be provided largely by the provincial government. As well, the colleges would be under the jurisdiction of the Department of Education through its Committee on College Affairs.

Reaction to the legislation was extensive and mixed. Claude Bissell of the University of Toronto appeared to offer university support for the idea, although the more liberal position articulated by Murray Ross was that, without formal transfer policy from college to university, the colleges would become second-rate institutions. The *Globe and Mail* noted the ambiguous position of the minister when he authorized transfer only in individual cases, at the discretion of the universities. Further editorial comment drew attention to the easy availability of federal funds for both the capital and operating costs of the new colleges.[51]

In fact, access to federal funds through the Technical and Vocational Training Assistance Act (TVTA) of 1960 was especially influential on the course that Ontario colleges would take.[52] This legislation was one of a series of federal measures to support training programmes designed to prepare individuals to enter the workforce with appropriate levels of skill in needed occupations. The 1960 act allowed the federal government to enter into an agreement with any province for a period not exceeding six years to provide funding for programmes in technical and vocational training. The federal government agreed to reimburse the provinces 75 per cent of the cost of new buildings and equipment to a limit based on the provincial population, and thereafter at 50 per cent of cost. The total appropriation for the programme was $920 million. The TVTA became the catalyst for a massive programme of construction in most provinces, but particularly in Ontario with its heavy concentration of population.

Ontario, recognizing the importance of increasing the number of skilled workers if its industrially based economy were to continue to expand, took full advantage of the new federal funds to achieve this objective. Ontario even managed to obtain more than its expected share of federal funds for buildings and equipment when several other provinces did not capitalize on the allocation of funds which their populations warranted. The "instant" system of Colleges of Applied Arts and Technology in Ontario, with heavy and sustained emphasis upon technical and vocational education, might never have materialized in the absence of the federal financial support.[53] While the universities, through their prestigious spokesmen, supplied ideological justification for the particular orientation of Ontario colleges, the practical fuel for their development came via initiatives of the national government.

The special role played by the Canadian Association for Adult Education (CAAE) in the developmental period of Ontario's colleges should not pass unrecognized. As expected, the CAAE emphasized the mandate of the colleges to expand opportunities for adult learners. In the association's view, the transfer-to-university issue simply clouded more profound questions. At the 1965 Annual Meeting of CAAE the banquet speaker was Murray Ross, who argued eloquently for the colleges as centres for broad general and liberal education, noting that: "The community college should be an intellectual and cultural centre in many of these communities in Canada which are now cultural wastelands."[54]

The CAAE also took the initiative by sponsoring a National Seminar on the Community College in Canada in 1966. (See Chapter 9). At this meeting, an interesting debate centred on the use of the term "community" as it might apply to Ontario colleges. Alan Thomas, a prominent adult educator, had promoted the formal use of the title, but Education Minister Davis rejected the term in his keynote address to the seminar, again emphasizing the unique nature of the Ontario model as his justification for not using an American college label. At a later session of the seminar, insights into government plans for the new institutions were provided by Norman Sisco, Director of the Applied Arts and Technology Branch of the Ministry of Education. Sisco underscored the vocational bias of the curriculum, the relationship to be developed by the colleges with business and industry, and the status of the colleges as unique educational institutions.

In fact, it was the determination and aggressive leadership of Norman Sisco which kept the Ontario colleges on the firm path which had been set for them in their legislated mandate. Many of the new colleges had previously been provincial institutes of trades and technology; imposition of the "college" model on them in no sense compromised their functions, but expanded their curricula and increased their responsiveness to the manpower needs of business and industry through the influence of their quasi-autonomous boards of governors. Ontario's new colleges were conceived and born at a time when several complementary factors converged. The acceleration of student demand for post-high school education and the crystallization of public policy to expand manpower development coincided conveniently with the adoption of the federal Technical and Vocational Training Assistance Act. As Sisco recounted,

> Emboldened by our success in developing previous programmes, and realizing as a result of the experience in other countries and as a result of the numerous commissions and studies that had been made on the educational needs of our population in Ontario and in other provinces, we embarked on the development of a new and greatly expanded level of education . . . .
>
> I think the ten provincial Departments of Education realize that if they are going to participate in the development and operation of a national manpower policy, they are going to have to take a new look at some old traditions and a few sacred cows, and develop programmes and policies which have a direct relationship to the economic needs of the nation. I believe that, in a spirit of goodwill and mutual understanding, a new basis of federal-provincial cooperation can be developed which will be in tune with the philosophy of the present Federal Government.[55]

In summary, Ontario faced an explosive demand for participation in post-secondary education, as did other provinces, but Ontario also had a number of prestigious universities with a highly articulate lobby to protect their interests. The universities promoted growth in the university sector rather than the development of alternative institutions for post-secondary education. Graduates of secondary schools were hampered by the lack of further educational opportunities for the non-university bound students. The period was one of economic buoyancy, with general public support for educational expansion, and for a future with the expectation of both growth in the business and industrial sector and an accompanying need for trained manpower to sustain it. The opportunities available for adults to continue their education were limited, disorganized, and haphazard. Federal initiatives made financial support available for capital development in vocational-technical curriculum areas. The Ryerson Institute model was highly regarded by a broad segment of society, particularly in the occupational sector. Finally, provincial legislation creating new colleges was adopted in a political climate supportive of the creation of a complete educational system from kindergarten to graduate school, which would be unique and, because it would be Ontario-made, intrinsically superior to its counterparts across the nation.

QUEBEC

From the establishment of the first college in Quebec in 1635, provision of post-secondary education in this predominantly French and Roman Catholic province, and indeed education at all levels, was the prerogative of the Roman Catholic hierarchy.[56] The provincial government played no active role on the grounds that education was a family and church matter to be protected from political vagaries and pressures. The result was the gradual growth of an extraordinary variety of institutions all largely autonomous and independent one from another and from government intrusion.

A Council of Public Instruction was established in 1856 to monitor and direct the modest public school sector, but in 1875 it effectively subdivided into a Catholic Committee and a Protestant Committee, each with separate and unlimited responsibilities for the different public schools for which the languages of instruction were for the most part French and English respectively. In the French and Catholic sector, secondary level education was private and provided by the clergy. The English and Protestant sector, however, established "public" secondary schools as well as private ones, and they in time provided instruction up to the eleventh grade. Graduates could progress from these schools through a public grade twelve, into one of the three anglophone universities or into universities outside Quebec for their higher education.[57]

By the 1950's, French-language classical colleges had been founded in every part of the province by the Roman Catholic clergy. Most were affiliated with the universities of Montreal and Laval, and students could be admitted to these institutions after fifteen years of elementary, secondary, and post-secondary education to pursue studies primarily in theology, law, and medicine.

The "Quiet Revolution" in Quebec, which touched directly every important aspect of life in that province, was triggered by the defeat of the Union Nationale government in 1961 and the victory of the Lesage Liberals. For the next five years, change of all kinds was the order of the day. The changes brought to the education system were but an important part of a much grander social and economic reorganization, but they had a profound effect upon every aspect of education. The new government came to recognize that if its vision of a new Quebec—powerful, proud, and a full participant in the business and industrial life of Canada—the emphasis of education must be changed. The changes would have to include a universal and compulsory secondary school system, followed by widely expanded and structured access to technical and vocational training. The government's concern for the future of the predominantly francophone province was expressed in documentation which ushered in many of the changes:

> The generations of young people now beginning or pursuing their studies will live in a society that will present a set of characteristics a complete list of which would not be easy to draw, both because not all the required data are available and because unanimity of opinion could not be confirmed: the society of tomorrow will be more numerous, more educated, more mobile, and it will change more rapidly than that in which we now live.
>
> The pursuit of economic, social and cultural development will be more active and will proceed at a faster pace than at present. In order to be able to survive and grow in such a context, this society must find it possible to rely upon a mass of conscious and educated citizens.
>
> On our continent, the rapid development that will characterize the society of tomorrow will bring along particularly rigid requirements. There is no need to dwell upon the enormous difference between human resources available to us and those available to the remainder of the North American continent: this difference is even more marked because of the considerable advance enjoyed by the whole of the continent in relation to Quebec, as regards the qualitative development of human resources. In Quebec only 8 per cent of the people of working age have had more than twelve years of schooling; only about 50 per cent have studied beyond the elementary level.[58]

Quebec was by no means the first "nation" state to stimulate social, economic, or political reform through the manipulation of its sociocultural and economic institutions. However, in the context of a comparative analysis of the forces which led to the creation of new colleges in Canada, the Quebec episode is demonstrably unique. While in no other provinces were political motivations unknown, Quebec elevated such motives to the degree that a college system was itself an instrument of political and social change in a direction clearly determined by government. The details have a particular fascination and deserve further elaboration.

The educational reforms did not begin with legislative action but with a government-initiated study. On April 21, 1961, the government established a Royal Commission of Inquiry on Education.[59] The mandate for the commission noted, inter alia, "Whereas education at all levels is beset by many problems and it is therefore expedient to have a thorough and impartial study of the state of education in the Province made by a Royal Commission of Inquiry."[60] The appointed chairman was the Alphonse-Marie Parent, a Vice-Rector of Laval University. The eight other members included five francophones and three anglophones. Two members, Gerald Filion and Paul Larocque, were not educators, the first being a Director of "Le Devoir" but a former school trustee, the second in private industry. It is interesting to note that the government, perhaps in reasonable anticipation of recommendations which would radically alter the status quo and even the role of the church in education, chose a widely respected man of religion to fill the chair. The Royal Commission's original mandate was only for a few months, but its studies of all aspects of Quebec education lasted several years.

The central recommendation of its five-volume report was that there should be a Minister of Education appointed by government. Of almost equal importance was the recommendation that a lay Superior Council of Education be appointed by government to advise the minister and government on all aspects of education in the province. With the implementation of these recommendations, the process of wresting control of education from the Roman Catholic Church was begun.

An understanding of the Royal Commission's recommendations on post-secondary education requires an appreciation of the structure of the non-university sector as it had evolved to 1960.[61] Initially, note should be made of the differences between English-language (and Protestant) education and the French-language (and Catholic) systems. Francophone students spent seven years in elementary school; some then took four years of public "superior" schooling, but others followed the eight-year private "cours secondaire" at a classical college to obtain the baccalaureate. This qualified for admission to university for the more specialized upper level undergraduate studies common to English-language universities.

In all, the francophone spent as much as eighteen years of study before obtaining a university degree. By contrast, the student from the anglophone sector entered university directly from the public secondary school after completing the eleventh grade, and a four-year programme at university led to an undergraduate degree after a total of fifteen years of study. One of the realities was that although there were three French and three English-language universities in Quebec at the time, the number of university students in each segment was approximately the same—despite the fact that 80 per cent of the population of the province used French as its first language.

In 1963, prior to the implementation of reforms recommended by the Parent Commission, the French language non-university institutions were many in number, scattered throughout the province, varying considerably in quality and type, without co-ordination, mostly private, and operated by religious communities. They included about one hundred colleges classiques which offered eight-year programmes after elementary school, sixty to seventy government subsidized one and two-year normal schools and between fifteen and twenty technical institutions.[62] Other specialized institutions included thirty-two "institut familial," most of which received students after grade eleven. And, while English-language students could proceed to university, often at the age of sixteen, they had virtually no post-secondary alternative to university. Opportunities in technical-commercial training beyond school for English-speaking students were limited to small English sections of French institutions such as l'Institut de Technologie de Montréal. Clearly the need for educational reform was not limited to either of the two language groups in Quebec.

The report of the Parent Commission made comprehensive recommenda-tions which included a fully co-ordinated and unified educational system for both French and English education from kindergarden to university and adult education. After an elementary level of six years and a public secondary of five years, students should enter a composite "Institute," which would include pre-university and vocational studies for two years. After the institute, some students would proceed to university where a baccalaureate degree would require three years of study, while others would immediately enter the workforce.[63]

For the French language student the "Institute" would be a tuition-free unified multi-programme educational institution, replacing the variety and range of other post-school institutions that had operated throughout the province. For the English-language student, the proposal represented a totally new arrangement which would require the creation of new post-secondary institutes, cause the universities to relinquish their lower division courses and reorganize their undergraduate programmes, and add a year of study for an undergraduate university degree. The old and new structures are illustrated in Table 1.

TABLE 1
QUEBEC EDUCATIONAL STRUCTURE (PRE AND POST 1967)

PRE 1967

	Elementary	Secondary		Higher	Total
French	0 0 0 0 0 0 0 (7)	0 0 0 0 cours secondaire	0 0 0 (8) cours collegial	0 0 (3)	18 yr.
English	0 0 0 0 0 0 0 (7)	0 0 0 0 (4)		0 0 0 0 (4)	15 yr.

POST 1967

	Elementary	Secondary	CEGEP	Higher	Total
French or English	0 0 0 0 0 0 0 (6)	0 0 0 0 0 (5)	0 0 (2) 0 0 0 (3)	0 0 0 (3) → *work*	16 yr.

The rationale for these dramatic proposals was provided in considerable detail. Among other observations, it noted that, "It must be boldly asserted that every person has a right to access to all the various fields of knowledge, a right to the full development of his capacities and to the exercise of all his intellectual aptitudes. Only thus can he develop fully in what may properly be called a well-rounded humanism."[64] The report also emphasized the increasing number of students remaining in school and the lack of a well articulated post-school system to accommodate their need for further study. The existing system was unable to meet the challenge:

> The same motive which led to the proliferation of institutions—the motive of helping the greatest possible number of students—today requires a carefully considered re-organization of this phase of education in more orderly and better integrated terms; otherwise only a minority will continue to have the advantage of an education of high quality, whereas the majority will receive instruction of no great value.[65]

The report also addressed in some detail the questions of the relative importance of general education and specialized studies and the need to integrate academic studies with technical and vocational studies. "Integration into a composite institute will bring these schools the resources and the climate necessary to raise the level of their general studies and the quality of their specialized instruction."[66]

The commission was well aware of the implications of its proposals. Many traditions, many assumptions, and many established procedures would have to be abandoned. But the firmly established conservatism of the Quebec educational establishment would not be coerced easily. Nor would the institutions which had sustained the structure of English-language Quebec. However, the report was aggressive: "Hence it may be said that a preoccupation with an educational system at once richer and broader, more flexible and direct, and more generous and democratic had led us to propose this composite stage between the secondary course and higher education."[67]

The curriculum for the proposed institutes was also discussed in considerable detail. Two stages, a time for orientation and a time for specialization, were described. At the first stage a limited group of basic courses was suggested—the mother tongue, a second language, physical education, and philosophy. This would be supplemented, at the second stage, by various specialized and complementary courses depending upon the education or career goal of the student. In this manner, it would be possible to ensure that each student would have a balanced programme of courses of a general education nature as well as a specialized education in a particular field of interest.

The role of institutes in adult education was not neglected in the report. The needs of adults to return to formal education, to study part-time, and to take courses at unusual hours were recognized. The possibility of using radio and television to provide educational services was identified. Indeed, the institute was expected to become an educational resource in the widest sense of the term: "It will therefore have an obligation to serve as a guiding light for its neighbourhood, to offer its collaboration with other bodies in educational ventures and to lend its assistance to every form of popular culture."[68]

The Royal Commission Report emphasized the differences between the institute and the American "junior college," the English "A Levels," "gymnasia" in Germany, and the Grandes Ecoles of France. The institutes were in part to be preparatory to university, and they were to be totally disassociated from the secondary schools. Although the institutes were to be co-ordinated by the newly constituted Ministry of Education, they were to be governed by their own boards from their own regions. In a very real sense, they were to be community institutions. In the words of the report, "[the institute] must be the cherished possession of the local population, which must have a feeling of commitment to, and interest in it, and which must assume some share of responsibility for it, be active in it and be represented in it."[69]

Following publication of the popularly supported Parent Report, the government initiated a planning process designed to prepare for implementation of its recommendations. A consultative committee, known as the "Comité de Planification de l'Enseignement pré-universitaire et professionnel," met from January 1965 to June 1966. It was responsible for the preparation of legislation and supporting material necessary to establish a system of institutes. One of the first recommendations of the committee was to reject the term "institute" and replace it by "Collège d'Enseignement Général et Professionnel" (CEGEP). The pre-university stream was designed as a two-year post-secondary programme, and the occupational training or vocational programmes were to be of two or three years duration.

Following the system planning stage, provincial legislation was introduced to permit establishment of the new CEGEP. Some features of that legislation are particularly noteworthy. As a public corporation, the CEGEP was to belong to its immediate community, but it was also be a partner of the state. To reinforce its community orientation, a widely representative board of governors was to include regional appointees of government, elected members of the faculty, students and administrators, members from interest groups in the region, and parents of students. In all, the board was to consist of nineteen members.[70] The governance of CEGEP required a balance between local autonomy for each institution and some degree of centralized co-ordination by the Ministry of Education. The government role was expected to be prominent in the initial stages of development, but government was also expected to relinquish major authority for policy and governance to the local board after the first phase of college development.

The reorganization of existing institutions required to establish CEGEP in the French sector involved an integration or "melding" of a number of different institutions in some regions (classical colleges, technical institutes, normal schools), and, in others, the conversion of a single institution to a new status. In September 1967, the first twelve French language CEGEP opened. One, CEGEP de Trois Rivières, involved the fusion of nine institutions. On the other extreme, CEGEP de Maisonneuve involved only an extension of the role and function of a former classical college. By early 1969, twenty-three CEGEP, all French language, were in operation. The first of their English counterparts, Dawson College in Montreal, did not admit students until September 1969.[71] As a conscious effort to advance the principle of equality of opportunity to post-secondary education for all citizens, all CEGEP were to be tuition free for full-time students.

The reason for the delay in establishing CEGEP in the English sector was primarily of a practical nature. There were no English language post-secondary institutions that could conveniently be converted. In addition, within the English language universities, there was considerable skepticism about the need for English language CEGEP and certainly no enthusiasm for losing their first year of undergraduate studies to the CEGEP.[72] However, in response to government insistence that there be equity in both language sectors as quickly as possible, Dawson College opened in 1969, with 1900 students at its first downtown campus, and soon became a larger multi-campus urban college. For the first time, English-speaking students were able to undertake training in a variety of post-secondary technical-vocational programmes. Until three additional English language CEGEP were established, the English language universities were permitted to offer "pre-university" courses as a pragmatic way of finding space for English language post-secondary students and of easing the adjustment for the English language universities.

The CEGEP curriculum, authorized by the Ministry of Education, required a common core of general education. Admission requirements were generous and flexible. Students paid no tuition fees. A great experiment in Quebec education was underway.

One early CEGEP development is worth particular note. The general planning assumption was that two-thirds of CEGEP students would choose to pursue vocational or technical studies, with one-third preferring a pre-university orientation. In the first years, the actual enrolment completely reversed this plan. This had serious implications for the number of places planned for enrolment in the universities and student unrest soon emerged as far more CEGEP students than originally anticipated demanded the opportunity to proceed to university. In short order, to meet the increased demand, the government developed a major new multi-campus university, the Université du Québec.

The educational changes were dramatic, not only in structure, but more in the upheaval of the traditional magisterial relationship between professor and student, and for the erosion of the role of the church. Change often came with resentment and fear. In fact, several classical colleges elected to remain outside the new system, and hence accepted the prospect of the elimination of public funding, which did not in fact materialize for most of them, because government was able to rationalize continued public support for private institutions deemed to be "in the public interest."

Within CEGEP, the requirement of democratic governance and administrative practices and structures challenged the imagination and ingenuity of educational leaders. The change did not come about without turmoil and dissent, as the early years of several CEGEP document.[73] However, in the process, Quebec, in education as in so many other areas, more than entered the twentieth century. Rarely had social change been so rapid, so profound, and so irreversible. The new colleges of Quebec were educational institutions but even more instruments in a sociopolitical plan to restructure an entire society.

PRINCE EDWARD ISLAND

> It was not until the late 1960's that Prince Edward Island experienced the explosive growth in post-secondary education that had begun in other parts of Canada a generation earlier. When it did come, however, the Island's break with its past was singularly abrupt.[74]

Prior to an unprecedented initiative by the Prince Edward Island government in 1968-69, secondary school graduates had few choices within their own province: they could begin their working lives, they could receive some vocational training, or they could continue on to university studies at one of two long-established academic institutions: St. Dunstan's University, a Roman Catholic institution, or Prince of Wales College, originally a denominational college which later became a public institution. These two academic institutions constituted the post-secondary sector in Canada's smallest province. They were constant rivals in a province in which the issue of religion in education was a recurring and sensitive bone of contention frequently flaring as a political issue.

As in other provinces, public acceptance of vocational training as a legitimate part of the post-secondary sector came only with the end of the Second World War, when the training needs of returning veterans prompted the addition of a special vocational wing to Prince of Wales College. This wing was for the exclusive use of veterans until 1948 when it was opened to more general use.

Vocational education for Islanders received its next boost in 1962 with the opening of Prince County Vocational High School, but it was not until 1964 that post-secondary vocational and adult education began to come into its own. In that year, with federal assistance, the Prince Edward Island government was able to establish the Provincial Vocational Institute in Charlottetown, which served not only as a vocational high school but also as an apprenticeship training centre and an adult trade school.

The dramatic developments of 1968-69, however, can be traced to events in the university sector, rather than in vocational training or adult education. In 1951, the Massey Report[75] had recommended that federal financial assistance be extended to all universities and colleges affiliated with the National Conference of Canadian Universities to allow them to develop new courses and to expand their facilities. Although both St. Dunstan's and Prince of Wales became eligible for—and received—this new federal money, the provincial government saw fit to supplement this support only for Prince of Wales College on the grounds that its public resources should be used to subsidize only public institutions. As a result, St. Dunstan's survived with federal support, but Prince of Wales was able to thrive and expand with both federal and provincial funds. The traditional rivalry between these institutions was hardly ameliorated by these decisions.

The appointment of a Royal Commission on Higher Education in 1964, chaired by M.E. LaZerte, was the stimulus for the 1968-69 developments. The report, released in January 1965, recommended that the two post-secondary rivals should "study the feasibility of federation" with the co-operation and assistance of the provincial government: one University of Prince Edward Island should be crafted from St. Dunstan's University and Prince of Wales College.[76] Before this recommendation was acted upon, the provincial government undertook some ambitious economic planning. Through the Economic Improvement Corporation, established under the aegis of the Federal Department of Regional Economic Expansion, an economic development plan was underway. The result was an ambitious fifteen-year projection of social and economic programmes for the province.[77] And it became apparent that this plan could not be realized unless it included training opportunities in skilled occupations at a level well beyond that which was available on the island at that time.

Faced with both the recommendation for university federation and the need to provide more advanced training to support economic expansion, Premier Alex B. Campbell expressed his government's intention to play a strong leadership role in higher education. In a major address to the Legislature in April 1968, he concluded that "the present institutions of higher education are not necessarily the most efficient or best suited to the financial capabilities of the Province."[78] The climax of the premier's lengthy statement of his government's philosophy and view of higher education in the province was the announcement of a three-pronged action programme: extension of student aid in the form of bursaries and scholarships; the creation of a single, non-denominational university; and the creation of a College or Institute of Applied Arts and Technology. The purpose of this action programme was:

> To remedy a long-standing deficiency in our post-secondary educational system. It is fully expected that such facilities will be developed to meet both provincial and regional needs. This programme will significantly increase the opportunities available to our students. The technical and applied arts aspect of the programme is estimated to cost approximately $30 million over the next ten years.[79]

Legislation to enact the programme was prepared. The first draft—The Universities Grants Commission Bill—envisioned the maintenance of both St. Dunstan's University and Prince of Wales College as a federated institution. Faced with strenuous opposition from Prince of Wales College on the grounds of political interference and the potential erosion of academic freedom, the government chose to withdraw the bill and replace it with another one establishing two committees, one charged with establishing a new college.

Implementing the new legislation was no simple task, particularly with the resignation of Frank MacKinnon as Principal of Prince of Wales College on the grounds of "extra-ordinary intervention" by government. The government responded by inviting Edward F. Sheffield of the University of Toronto to provide advice on implementing the legislation. His solution was the formation of a University Planning Committee and a College Planning Committee, with himself serving as pro-tem chairman of both. By December 1968, presidents-designate had been chosen for the two new institutions: Ronald Baker for the university and Donald Glendenning for the college.

Charters for both institutions were proclaimed on April 23, 1969, and both new institutions began operations that year. The University of Prince Edward Island was centred at the former St. Dunstan's University site, and the new Holland College gradually relocated to the former campus of Prince of Wales College. A new structure for post-secondary education on the island was in place, and new opportunities for the people of Prince Edward Island were on the horizon.

The new Holland College quickly became new in far more than name.[80] From the outset, at a time when preparatory or remedial education was still in its pioneering stage in other parts of Canada, it welcomed adults who had not completed secondary school. As a result, it quickly established a broad base of citizen support. Its emphasis in the curriculum on education for employment provided it with additional popular support. It encouraged community advice on college policy and programme development and became a "community" college from the start.

But Holland College's reputation in the rest of Canada, as well as at home, rested primarily on its instructional methods. From the beginning, its programmes were organized for individualized, self-paced learning which subdivided course materials into modules or building blocks so that all students could progress through these programmes at their own paces, with instructors serving as tutors of individuals rather than as teachers of classes.

The events of 1968-69 reshaped post-secondary education on Prince Edward Island. In so doing, they caused the establishment of a new community college which not only broadened access to post-secondary education on the island and provided new kinds of post-secondary education, but also stood out among the new Canadian colleges as a centre for innovation in curriculum development and instructional technology. At the same time, Holland College became a key element in the economic planning for the province; its performance was perceived as critical to the economic and social future of Canada's smallest province.

MANITOBA

The year 1942 marked the beginning of a new era for post-secondary education in Manitoba. University education had long been available in the province; some vocational instruction had also been provided, but only in conjunction with the existing high school curriculum. Impetus for expansion of vocational training came from the federal government's Vocational Training Co-ordination Act in 1942, which established cost-sharing arrangements with the provinces for building vocational training facilities. This act was also the vehicle used to transfer funds to the provinces specifically for training for returning war veterans and the unemployed, all the while recognizing education as a provincial responsibility. The Manitoba government displayed particular enthusiasm for taking full benefit of the act and its first students were registered in war emergency training classes. A further surge in enrolment was experienced with the war's end as thousands of returning veterans looked to vocational training as preparation for jobs in civilian life.

By 1967, a more direct involvement in vocational training was sought by the federal government which adopted the Adult Occupational Training Act. This legislation permitted, with the consent of a provincial government, the federal government to purchase training provided by provincial public educational institutions, private trade schools, and industry. Within but a few years, the Manitoba institutions offering vocational training came to rely heavily on federal sources of revenue; effectively, the federal government—not the institutions themselves and not the Manitoba government—determined the number and type of courses offered in the province, since it not only subsidized the training institutions themselves through the vocational training purchase plan but also subsidized as many as 80 per cent of the students who took vocational training.[81] Manitoba felt it necessary to co-operate with the federal government because withdrawal of the latter's support for vocational training would have been catastrophic for Manitoba training institutions and students.

Manitoba established its first permanent post-secondary vocational institution, the Manitoba Technical Institute (MTI) at Winnipeg in 1948. The growth of population and industry in the province warranted establishment of a second vocational institution: The Brandon Vocational Training Centre was started in 1961 in rented facilities, offering classes in automotive repair, construction, the electrical trades, and business education. Years later additional courses were added to the curriculum to upgrade the basic education of adults who had not been able to complete secondary school.

The Manitoba Technical Institute acquired its own large campus by 1963 and immediately offered two-year technology programmes at the post-secondary level. Concurrently, the Brandon Vocational Training Centre was expanding and its permanent facility was constructed in 1966. It was renamed the Manitoba Vocational Centre that year, offering twenty-four training programmes.

The Northern Manitoba Vocational Centre was opened in 1966 at The Pas to serve students in the northern areas of the province. It began with an ambitious list of twenty trade and vocational programmes, an upgrading programme, and a two-year technology programme.

Throughout the late 1960's post-secondary enrolment continued to expand. An Applied Arts Division was added to MTI, which in 1966 became known as MIT (Manitoba Institute of Technology). The new division, the Manitoba Institute of Applied Arts, offered twenty-three courses in business, commercial studies, and teacher education.

Throughout this period of expansion, all vocational training and all training centres were under the direct jurisdiction of the provincial government. But the expansion also brought growing public acceptance for non-traditional non-academic education. The sense of involvement and public commitment to education on a community level was manifested by the December 1969 switch in nomenclature from "vocational centre" to "community college" for Manitoba's career-oriented educational institutions. The Manitoba Vocational Centre at Brandon became Assiniboine Community College; the Northern Manitoba Vocational Centre at The Pas was renamed Keewatin Community College; and the Manitoba Institute of Technology/Manitoba Institute of Applied Arts in Winnipeg became Red River Community College. The names chosen reflected the perceived wish of the citizens in each area that the location and sense of community be incorporated in the new names of institutions. In practical terms, the change of name and focus also encouraged increased use of public school facilities and resources for post-secondary education, as well as a new emphasis in these institutions on extension courses in vocational training for adults.

Well into the 1960's, the kinds of post-secondary education made available in Manitoba were determined by Manitoba industry, which specified to the government what its labour requirements were. However, a shift in societal values which occurred in much of North America in the late 1960's affected attitudes towards educational opportunity. By the early 1970's in Manitoba as elsewhere, individual aspirations rather than industrial needs began to shape post-secondary education. The prime purpose of education was being redefined as a vehicle for individual enrichment, with occupational development relegated to a motivating factor instead of a purpose of education.

In a September 18, 1970 speech, the Minister of Education, Saul Miller, reflected the prevailing sentiments in Manitoba about education: "We are not just feeding an economic machine. We are attempting to offer educational opportunities which will be rewarding to the individual in personal and social as well as economic terms."[82]

With the conversion to community colleges in 1969, the forty-five-member Technical and Vocational Advisory Board, which had for years influenced the character of post-secondary education in the province, underwent a major reorganization. It was pared to twenty people: four faculty members, four students, six community representatives, three government appointees, two regional school board chairmen, and the chairman of the previous advisory board. Directly responsible to the Minister of Education, this body was to advise on recommended additions to and deletions from training programmes throughout the province and to make general recommendations for improvements to the entire post-secondary educational system. In addition, it had responsibility for Red River Community College, the largest of Manitoba's new colleges. Although Red River, like the other colleges, was a government institution, it had an advisory board in place of a board of governors, and the provincial advisory board doubled as the Red River Community College Advisory Board. An organized approach to province-wide post-secondary planning had begun. The regional boards were also reorganized into advisory boards for the other two community colleges (Assiniboine and Keewatin).

In December 1970 a Community Colleges Division within the provincial Department of Education was formed. Its purpose was to facilitate planning, utilization of facilities, programme development, and budgeting for the college system. The council also endorsed a statement about what they considered a community college to be:

> an organization of learning environments responsive to the needs of the community, offering flexible technical and liberal educational programmes for a type and variety which will inspire and enable individuals to develop

themselves to the fullest and thereby contribute to the enrichment of their community.

The programmes, on full or part-time basis, provide continuing education, re-training, and upgrading for individuals seeking personal and occupational development.

Instruction may be carried out with accreditation in any effective location, on the campus or in other locations such as industrial or commercial sites, urban or rural centres, remote communities, or through correspondence, the communications media, or any combination of these.[83]

In the fall of 1971 the provincial Youth and Education portfolio was divided into the Department of Colleges and Universities Affairs and the Department of Education. This split, which acknowledged the growing complexity of post-secondary education in the province, testified to the provincial government's support for further development. A preliminary study on community colleges had pointed out the need for an in-depth analysis of how government developments relating to education should be organized, managed, and staffed. The report of a management consulting firm resulted in streamlining the post-secondary system for students, employers, and the general public by the establishment of a separate Department of Colleges and Universities Affairs.

In 1972 attention was turned to the internal operation and governance of Manitoba's community colleges. To encourage greater participation in the internal matters of the community colleges, internal general boards were established with representation from students, faculty, and administrators. They reported directly to the Chief Executive Officer of the institution. A pattern for consultative committee decision-making style was established.

In the same year, a task force under the chairmanship of Michael Oliver of Carleton University was charged with studying and recommending on a variety of aspects of post-secondary education. The report, released on July 30, 1973, addressed the planning, organization, delivery, governance, and financing of education of the province's colleges and universities. Twenty-two recommendations resulted, some specific to certain colleges, but most related to the overall post-secondary system. Significantly, the task force went beyond its mandate with the recommendation that a commission on post-secondary education be established and "undertake immediately a detailed study of the colleges' future in line with the principles enunciated by the Task Force."

Recommendations of the Oliver Report on governance supported the view that students and faculty should be represented on governing and advisory boards. Faculty leaves for the purpose of professional renewal were encouraged for vocational and technical teachers, in addition to academic instructors. Promotion of education for minorities was supported by those recommendations that urged colleges to recruit women and Indian teachers. Greater co-operation was encouraged between universities and other post-secondary institutions in articulating courses and allowing students to register at both types of institutions simultaneously.

By 1973, Manitoba had a provincial college system in place. Its major emphasis was occupational training. Its development was clearly controlled by the provincial government, with the explicit objective of serving the economic and labour force needs of that province. Unlike the colleges which preceded them in other parts of Canada, Manitoba's colleges had little sense of community and even less of local autonomy. It was not certain, however, that this system would remain unchanged in the years immediately ahead.

SASKATCHEWAN

The roots of the community college idea in Saskatchewan grew in the same soil which nurtured the strong tradition of self help and community problem-solving which has been so characteristic of Canadian prairie life and survival. Saskatchewan has long nurtured voluntary organizations which included adult education in their services as a means of social, economic, and intellectual betterment. The University of Saskatchewan, from its inception, developed extension services to farmers, homemakers, and 4H clubs in urban and rural communities.[84] In 1944, the first Adult Education Branch of government was established. While funding and leadership came from Regina, the branch encouraged local committee initiatives in planning for regional communities. The aims of the branch were both intellectual and social—to sustain and improve the quality of life in small communities as well as in larger centres throughout the province.

A gradual deterioration of the quality of life in rural Saskatchewan prompted the Saskatchewan provincial government to establish a royal commission[85] in 1956 to examine and recommend means to stimulate the quality of life in rural communities. This commission, under the chairmanship of W.B. Baker of the University of Saskatchewan, produced sixteen separate reports on aspects of rural living in the province. Particular reference was made to the role of continuing education and the report noted that "opportunity should be provided for the stimulation of self-study and personal growth, for man is almost inherently a curious creature."[86] While the commission recognized supportive roles for government and university, it expressed the view that the real forces for education were the voluntary citizen organizations which were the catalysts for self help within a community. It also noted that greater use should be made of school facilities for adult education, and professional leadership in adult education should be accepted as a responsibility of the university.

The commission also affirmed that rural adult education should be conducted in an "atmosphere of free enquiry," not to advance government policy. The role of government should be to provide funding for education, but that education itself should be then placed under the control of community voluntary organizations. However, the commission also recognized that a political dimension to community education was inevitable "to the extent that continuing education is concerned about increasing citizen knowledge of social and economic affairs, then it must in fact reflect some political or philosophical view of life." The commission was to have a profound influence upon the design of community college education in the province some fifteen years later.

The report of the Royal Commission of 1956 led to a number of practical adult education initiatives. Professional programmes for the preparation of adult educators began at the universities and the newly formed Continuing Education Branch of the Department of Education engaged regional field staff to provide leadership for adult education in rural communities. Dr. Baker, through the Institute for Community Studies at the University of Saskatchewan, focused attention on the problems and issues of rural life, on the impact of changing economic and social environment, on education, and on ways of preserving values of community-based society. Although vocational training had been available in Saskatchewan during the depression years under the Dominion-Provincial Youth Training Programme, the real impetus for growth of vocational training was the Second World War. During the 1939-45 period, centres for the training of military maintenance personnel (The War Emergency Training Programmes) were established in a number of temporary locations in Saskatchewan. By 1945, since the rehabilitation and training of war veterans became a major federal initiative, centres for both vocational and academic study were established in Moose Jaw, Prince Albert, Saskatoon, and Regina.[87]

The demand for such training eventually diminished and vocational training did not again become a priority until the late 1950's when the resource-related economic future of the province gave rise to concern over a lack of skilled manpower for such an economy. As one result, in 1958 the Normal School at Moose Jaw was converted into the first of Saskatchewan's Technical Institutes, where a variety of trades and technology programmes were made available.

With enactment of the federal Technical and Vocational Training Assistance Act, the Saskatchewan government took full advantage of federal financial support available for capital construction by constructing the Saskatchewan Central Technical Institute in Saskatoon in 1963. The curriculum was directed to job training in a wide range of occupations including trade apprenticeships, nursing assistants, cooks, draftsmen, and farm mechanics. In keeping with its curriculum orientation, the institute was renamed the Saskatchewan Institute of

Applied Arts and Sciences. Demand for pre-employment and occupational training at all levels created a rapid increase both in enrolment and in the number of programmes offered. But, vocational training available only at central locations within the province caused considerable movement of people from rural areas into urban centres seeking new job skills.

The government elected in 1964 showed an evident preference for a more centralized, conventional approach to post-secondary education by phasing out the Continuing Education Branch of the Department of Education in 1966, and by placing increased emphasis upon the creation of technical training institutions in larger centres of population. Although vocational training was already provided in a number of composite high schools throughout the province, a third technical institute was planned for Regina, and vocational centres were established in Weyburn and Prince Albert.

Prince Albert was the locale for another innovative development in post-secondary education in the late 1960's. Following the provision of adult training courses as a night school activity at the technical high school, the local school board pressed the Minister of Education to establish in Prince Albert a college which would provide a comprehensive set of programmes for adults. The plan finally materialized in 1969, when the Prince Albert Vocational Centre became the Prince Albert Regional Community College, the first community college in the province. Created under the Societies Act, but funded through the Department of Education, the college was governed by an elected community board, which included a faculty representative and a student as members.

In 1967, a joint committee from the University of Saskatchewan and the government, under the chairmanship of J.W. Spinks, presented a report on the future needs of tertiary education.[88] Although it gave particular emphasis to the potential of extension activities of the university, the report recommended the formation of a coherent, co-ordinated tertiary education system for the province. After a supplementary study, an internal committee of the ministry under L.A. Riederer[89] recommended the gradual phasing in of a number of "junior" colleges, modelled on the Alberta colleges, to provide comprehensive programmes for adults in both urban and rural centres. This proposal appealed to the government of the day and was consistent with its more centralized view of a co-ordinated provincial system of junior colleges, to be operated by a province-wide commission.

Public reaction to the recommendation was mixed. Despite some obvious strengths and support, the plan was viewed as inconsistent with the Saskatchewan tradition of rural community-based, self-help approaches to life-long learning. Further, given the lack of job opportunities requiring technical expertise in Saskatchewan, it was feared that technical training would only contribute to an exodus of skilled individuals from the province. The proposal to establish Alberta-style colleges in Saskatchewan was not implemented immediately.

A new thrust in political philosophy emerged with a change of government. The new N.D.P. administration reaffirmed the concern for quality of rural life, the impact of technology on small communities, the erosion of the rural culture, and the disturbing emigration of population from farms to cities and often out of the province. The proposal for a college system was officially placed on hold while two conferences, featuring wide representation from all areas of the province, were convened in 1971 to study the college plan and to investigate alternatives. The result of the conferences was the establishment of yet another advisory committee by the new Minister of Continuing Education, Gordon MacMurchy. The committee was charged with proposing a more appropriate community college model.[90] It initially devoted its attention to hearing first hand the views of individuals and groups throughout the wider community, and then it developed a set of assumptions and principles for college development which provided the basis for recommendations which followed. The assumptions included the following:

> The sense of community in rural Saskatchewan, built on traditions of community participation and cooperation blended with self-help, is among the province's most valuable attributes. Learning continues throughout life and access to learning opportunities should be continuous.[91]

The principles also stressed the community role in the planning of adult education, and included the thesis that college programmes should reflect the expressed and identified needs of the people in each college region. In rural areas, the colleges should serve as mechanisms for the maintenance and development of a viable way of life, should co-ordinate but not duplicate educational services, and should be governed at the regional level rather than the provincial. Consistent with this view, the colleges should be under the purview of the Minister of Continuing Education. The specific recommendations presented by the minister's advisory committee included a college model quite unlike those which had developed in other provinces. The term "community" was to be used to describe each institution; degrees or diplomas would not be granted; rented facilities would be used wherever possible; programmes needed by a community would be acquired by contract with established educational institutions; college services would be distributed throughout each region; and the number of permanent college staff would be restricted because most educational services would be provided by contract with other institutions rather than by the college itself. The college would primarily be a broker for educational services.

The brokerage model was, at the time, unique and ambitious. Even though the universities and technical institutes, all located in urban centres, were geographically inaccessible to a large percentage of the rural population, their programmes were to be "leased" through the colleges and made available throughout the province in response to expressed community needs. Programmes and services were not to carry on year after year as in most colleges elsewhere; once needs were met, educational programmes and services would no longer be offered. With this model, commitments to the maintenance of expensive facilities or to the retention of permanent teaching personnel would be unnecessary. While the community colleges were to be managed by boards appointed from their regions, even further public participation was to be ensured by the creation of "contact" committees of volunteers from each small centre of population. Although funding was to come primarily from provincial government grants, the colleges were to belong to the people of the different college regions.

The final report of the advisory committee was submitted to the Minister of Continuing Education in August, 1972. Implementation began immediately. Four pilot areas for colleges were designated and community college developers were appointed to assess the educational needs in each of these regions. The legislation necessary to establish the colleges was passed in April 1973.[92] In tabling the act, the minister again reiterated the philosophical framework for Saskatchewan community colleges. He stated, that "the end of formal schooling is not the end of learning," that "learning opportunities need to be made available to adults where they are," and that "college programmes would help people keep pace with knowledge relating to social and economic change and also with opportunities for recreational, cultural, and educational activities. "These ideas were to be translated into practice through a field representative, employed by the Department of Continuing Education, in each region to act as a consultant to the college board and to provide a liaison between the department and local committees. Colleges in the four pilot regions—Parkland, Carlton Trail, Cypress Hills, and La Ronge—had, by the end of the 1973-74 year, involved participation of 14 per cent of the adult population in 750 educational activities throughout 150 community locations. The Saskatchewan community college concept had become reality.

College development in Saskatchewan was unlike that in other provinces of Canada. The social history of the people, the rural geography, the powerful political philosophies which had been so influential in this province, the continuing anxiety about movement of population from rural to urban communities and then an exodus of many from the province itself, limited opportunities for post-secondary education, the individuality of the prairie people, their strength and their independence—all of these factors collectively contributed to a college concept which was different, viable, and vital.

Faris has commented that:

    The colleges without walls in Saskatchewan were founded on a firm historical base, cemented by a tradition of community cooperation and a special breed of dedicated educators in Saskatchewan. Educational traditionalists have predicted that Saskatchewan colleges will devolve into conventional colleges. The Advisory Committee and the Department have attempted to prevent this seemingly inexorable process by structural, legislative and other means. In the end, however, the response of Saskatchewan people will determine the efficacy of their college system.[93]

Non-university, post-secondary education in Saskatchewan in the period between 1943 and 1973 again demonstrated how much educational policy can become an expression of political philosophy as interpreted by the government of the day. In Saskatchewan, governments have fluctuated between a social democratic orientation and a conservative, more conventional approach. Official views on appropriate forms for community college education have changed accordingly; governance, curriculum, staff policies, and facilities issues were all influenced by the way in which governments viewed colleges. Notwithstanding the realities of government's authority to manage public education at any level, Saskatchewan's model for post-secondary education is testimony to the effectiveness of a people-based movement despite shifts of government policy. The early success of the Saskatchewan colleges was, in large part, a credit to the perseverance of ordinary citizens.

NEW BRUNSWICK

New Brunswick shares many of the characteristics associated with the development of post-secondary education in its sister provinces of Atlantic Canada: a variety of educational institutions rooted in denominational differences, strong regional identification, and a long established commitment to liberal and traditional forms of higher education. A distinctive characteristic, however, is the linguistic and cultural composition of New Brunswick, which had made bilingualism within social organizations—including post-secondary education—an added dimension to the complexity of providing access to educational opportunity in this province.[94]

By 1960, with a population of 600,000, New Brunswick supported six degree-granting institutions, two French and four English. The oldest and largest of these institutions, the University of New Brunswick, traced its history from 1785, while the other five had all been established during the nineteenth century. However, while three-quarters of the university students in the French-speaking sector were from New Brunswick, less than half of the English-speaking students resided in the province.[95] Despite the relatively large number of institutions and despite the fact that the enrolment of New Brunswick residents in universities and colleges increased by 40 per cent during the previous five years, the proportion of the province's youth receiving higher education had not kept pace with the rest of Canada.[96] In 1961-62 the percentage of the eighteen to twenty-one age group enrolled as full time university and college students in Canada was 12.2 per cent, while in New Brunswick the figure was 8.6 per cent.[97] Of additional concern was the fact that the participation of the French-speaking population in the province was considerably lower than for their English-speaking counterparts.

In 1961, aware of developments in post-secondary education in other provinces, and concerned with the capacity of the existing higher education institutions to accommodate the expected demand for post-secondary education in the years ahead, the government of the province established a royal commission on higher education, under the chairmanship of John Deutsch. This was the second such commission on this subject in New Brunswick history, the first having reported in 1854. The Deutsch Commission released its findings in 1962 and recommended several significant changes to the structure and financing of higher education in New Brunswick. The rationale which preceded the recommendations contained a succinct statement of difficulties which faced the New Brunswick higher education system at the time:

> In the past decade higher education in New Brunswick has encountered problems of an unprecedented kind and magnitude. Both the number of New Brunswick high school graduates and the number continuing to universities and colleges are increasing at a remarkable rate. The growth is particularly significant among the Province's French-speaking students, who are coming forward for higher education in significant numbers for the first time. Nevertheless, the proportion of the Province's young people receiving higher education is falling well below the national average. At the same time, the number of students from other Provinces seeking entry to New Brunswick institutions is increasing very rapidly. The total impact of growing student numbers has serious implications for university and college finance in the Province. At present the costs of higher education in New Brunswick, as elsewhere in Canada, are increasing more rapidly than student numbers and the existing sources of university and college support. The Province's universities and colleges have consequently experienced rising deficits, and are unable to make reasonable provision for the increased enrolments which must be accommodated in the years ahead. In fact, these institutions are now finding it exceedingly difficult even to maintain existing academic standards for their present student numbers.[98]

The recommendations which accompanied the report presented an organizational and financial blueprint for the future of post-secondary education in

New Brunswick. However, it focused entirely upon the university sector; no discussion or recommendation made reference to the needs of students for technical or vocational training, nor were any new institutional models proposed to respond to such needs.nor was there reference to the non-university sector in post-secondary education in the report of another investigative body which presented its recommendations in 1967.[99] Its major recommendation, pertaining to the financing of higher education in New Brunswick, was the establishment of an intermediary body, the New Brunswick Post-Secondary (later Higher) Education Commission, to be responsible for the orderly planning and financing of higher education. This commission was given broad terms of reference to make recommendations about institutions other than universities. The commission was to advise "with respect to the needs and the appropriate pattern of future development of all forms of post-secondary education in New Brunswick, including, without restricting the generality of the foregoing, universities, colleges, teachers' colleges, and technical schools."[100] Despite this mandate, no reference to new institutions was made.

Yet another study of New Brunswick post-secondary education was made in 1969.[101] John Crean reported on behalf of the Association of Atlantic Universities to the Maritime Union Study. His committee studied the range and scope of post-secondary education in the Maritimes with a view to co-ordination and planning of all the institutions in the four provinces. This report led to the creation of the Maritime Provinces Higher Education Commission in 1974.

One section of the Crean study involved a discussion of alternative models for post-secondary education, including "junior" colleges. While noting the development of similar institutions in other provinces, the committee expressed concern that this kind of college, in attempting to meet widely diversified needs, was susceptible to the compromising of academic standards. The committee's advice was essentially conservative, noting that

> A slow and steady growth is preferable to the attempt to offer too much with the danger of inferior quality. To ensure academic standards and a highly qualified staff, close integration with an existing university seems essential, for the new college must be protected from the possibility of undue local pressures now experienced by similar institutions elsewhere.[102]

The impetus for new colleges in New Brunswick eventually came from the grass roots, not from provincially commissioned studies or other government initiatives, through an opportunity provided by a provincial higher education advisory body.

In 1972 the New Brunswick Higher Education Commission held public hearings throughout the province which acknowledged the high quality of New Brunswick's traditional higher education institutions, but it also heard that these institutions did not respond well to educational needs perceived by the ordinary people in communities throughout the province. Responding to this concern in 1973, the provincial government passed the New Brunswick Community College Act for the "purpose of providing a means of improving communications links between the citizens and the government with respect to understanding the needs for specific training within the community."[103]

The new community college model for New Brunswick was consistent with the community college vision in other provinces and in the USA, but adapted to the specific needs, history, and educational tradition of that province. Because of the size of New Brunswick and the dispersal of population in several small communities, to establish either one college for the whole province or one college in each community was simply unrealistic. Moreover, the province already operated two institutes of technology with trade school components, three other trade schools, and a county vocational school—all administered by the Vocational Branch of the Department of Education[104]—which had not been considered a part of the higher education system of the province.

The act produced a community college model like no other in Canada. New Brunswick was organized into five regions, each of which would sustain a campus of a single provincial institution, the New Brunswick Community College, utilizing the facilities of the institutes of technology and trade schools. The change, however, was to be far more than just of name. "The College is neither a school nor a training programme but is a comprehensive educational institution designed to provide a wide range of educational opportunities throughout the Province."[105] All post-secondary, non-university educational needs were to be identified and responded to on a regional basis. To ensure effective responsiveness, regional advisory boards were created to include representation from citizens, staff, and students, and were to report to the Board of Governors for the province-wide college. The single but multi-campus college retained the principal features of community colleges elsewhere—open admissions, flexible programming, a heterogeneous student body, and an ongoing close working relationship with federal and provincial manpower training agencies.

Despite the number of degree-granting institutions in the province, the New Brunswick government had become convinced that it had to add the new community college if it was to meet changing manpower needs of the province and the demand by many citizens of New Brunswick for educational opportunities quite different from those which had been available through the degree-granting institutions. At the same time, the act addressed the traditional concern about the potential quality of education in new institutions by making the distinction between "quality" and "level" of education in the rationale provided for the new legislation. This rationale noted that high quality was the goal of all programmes and, as such, is unrelated to level, which is determined solely by the objectives.

By 1973, New Brunswick had its distinctive community college model. That institution and all its regional campuses were determined to become an equal partner with the degree-granting institutions for the development of a more complete and more responsive provincial system of post-secondary education.

NOVA SCOTIA

"The history of university education in Nova Scotia has been marked by sectarian squabbles and religious dissent, resulting in a proliferation of institutions backed by nearly every religious denomination active in the province."[106] Most of the universities were established by churches, and most of the churches established universities.[107]

By 1974, in a province with 800,000 people, Nova Scotia could boast of twelve degree-granting institutions, of which five were comprehensive universities and the remainder a group of academic colleges, public and private, and technical institutes which offered a variety of programmes and courses at various levels. However, it did not then have, and does not now have, any institution which Nova Scotia would classify as, or that would fit, the general description of a college such as those developed in the decade of the 1960's in other parts of Canada.

Every discussion of higher education in the Atlantic provinces makes reference to the number and variety of post-secondary institutions and their easy accessibility to people anywhere in this region. The hallmarks of Nova Scotia are diversity and specialization of institutions; the case can be made that all of the curriculum elements of a new college in other parts of Canada are available in Nova Scotia, but not within any single institution. The state of the post-secondary education system in the province, its history and the special group interests involved, and the financial consequences of continuing with the same approach to post-secondary education contributed to the establishment in 1971 of a Royal Commission on Education, Public Services, and Provincial-Municipal Relations, under the chairmanship of John Graham.[108] A major part of the report was devoted to university issues, but other post-secondary institutions were also reviewed. While many of the recommendations stressed the need to increase co-ordination and reduce unnecessary duplication at the post-secondary level, there was an evident reluctance to recommend an adaptation of the community college concept. There are several explanations for this reluctance. The Graham commission took a very broad interpretation of the term "community college" and noted that:

The community college is usually advocated as a means of bringing post-secondary education to all at a reasonable cost. What a community college offers varies markedly from one such college to another. Some community colleges offer advanced technological training such as is provided by the Nova Scotia Institute of Technology and the Nova Scotia Eastern Institute of Technology. Others offer the first two years of university work, allegedly at a lower cost than in the universities. An example of such a college is Xavier College in Sydney, lately known as the Sydney Campus of St. Francis Xavier University and now to be part of a new institution in Cape Breton. Many courses at Collège Sainte-Anne also fit this pattern. A few courses offered by some institutions elsewhere might be said to fit into a third type—a two-year programme in arts and science complete in itself—but little attention has been paid to this concept in Nova Scotia.[109]

The commission was not convinced that the amalgamation of several of these institutions into one multi-purpose or comprehensive college would produce significant educational or economic benefits in Nova Scotia. On the other hand, the report noted:

On the basis of the Ontario or Quebec ratio of community colleges to population, Nova Scotia would have between two and five community colleges. Though it is seldom recognized, we have at least that many, though all tend to be more specialized than the CAATs or CEGEPs. There are two institutes of technology, a land survey institute, an agricultural college offering university-level and vocational courses, Xavier Junior College, and Collège Sainte-Anne, excluding the marine navigation and engineering schools. What comes closest to the wide range of functions most often attributed to the community college is the new institution in Cape Breton County. This institution has been formed by wedding the Nova Scotia Eastern Institute of Technology and Xavier Junior College. The latter has placed a good deal of stress on community involvement through an active extension department. The degrees of the new institution are to be conferred subject to the approval of St. Francis Xavier University. It has the makings of a very good community college.[110]

While it might appear that no community colleges—in the conventional sense of the term—operate in Nova Scotia, that conclusion would have to be based on a definition of term rather than an interpretation of function. Most functions performed by the new colleges in other parts of Canada have indeed been found in Nova Scotia by institutions with other names.

But what about Nova Scotian adult education and technical-vocational education? In each case the record is impressive. In 1945, Nova Scotia became one of the first provinces in Canada to establish a government agency for adult education. Of even more significance, movements such as that established at

Antigonish by Moses Coady in 1922 and the Home and School in 1934 had raised public consciousness to the educational needs of adults far earlier than in most other parts of Canada.[111] Nova Scotia's tradition in adult education had included services in a wide variety of settings and structures such as agricultural field work, leadership training, folk schools, community arts, and minority group programmes.

Vocational and technical education in Nova Scotia can be traced back to 1872 with the establishment of the Halifax Marine School, later the Nova Scotia Nautical Institute.[112] In the next hundred years a variety of specialized institutions for agriculture, land survey, engineering, and navigation were established. As was the case in other provinces, the federal Technical and Vocational Training Assistance Act brought major injections of capital funding (fifty million dollars) to the province for vocational education.[113] Between 1961 and 1967 Nova Scotia established four technical institutes and fifteen adult training centres.

One other consideration is central in any assessment of the development of post-secondary education in Nova Scotia. The three Maritime provinces have taken a number of steps, albeit some tentative, to establish an interprovincial post-secondary system. Two organizations, the Association of Atlantic Universities (AAU), a voluntary body, and the Maritime Provinces Higher Education Commission (MPHEC) are designed to ensure that the needs of students in these provinces are met in a cost effective and co-ordindated fashion. However, Holmes has commented:

It is worth noting that, in the same session that the MPHEC Act was passed, the New Brunswick government passed an act establishing the New Brunswick Community College—an umbrella institution which does not appear on the schedule of institutions for which the commission has responsibility. At the same time, the Nova Scotia government was passing an act to establish the College of Cape Breton, by merging the Sydney campus of St. Francis Xavier University (Xavier College) with the Nova Scotia Eastern Institute of Technology. A charitable interpretation would be that the governments of the two provinces did not wish to over-burden the commission with responsibilities in its formative months.[114]

In summary, Nova Scotia is a province in which 70 per cent of the population resides within thirty miles of a university. In Halifax alone there are seven degree-granting institutions. In addition to the universities, Nova Scotia has numerous other specialized post-secondary institutions. The need for and appropriateness of even more post-secondary institutions is not at all obvious.

NEWFOUNDLAND

> Since education must reflect the living and cultural standards over any given period, considerable attention must be given to the effects of scattered population and the blighting factors of isolation and scaring poverty, which until comparatively recent times were the perennial lot of the Newfoundland people.[115]

Newfoundland had indeed been a colony of scattered population, isolation, and poverty. The limited educational opportunities it provided, particularly at the post-secondary level, were a product of these circumstances. University College had offered university level courses from 1925 and had supplemented these courses with vocational training through evening programmes for as many as 450 students at one time. A few years later, a number of "opportunity" schools were established in various parts of the island. Peripatetic teachers presented eight-week courses for adults in one community and then, at the end of each session, would move on to the next community. A unique format for adult education developed with group night classes followed by visits from instructors to the students' homes.

In 1936, under the direction of Dr. Vincent Burke, the first Adult Education Branch was formed within the Department of Education. It became the stimulus for rapid expansion of both instructors and the number of centres where adult classes were conducted.[116] A permanent centre for adult education was established in St. John's; this, in addition to expansion of the evening and extension courses by University College, provided a range of learning opportunities for adults from boiler making, labour studies, and navigation to pharmacy, commercial law, and music appreciation.

The climax of this evolution of adult, vocational, and academic education was the granting of a charter to award university degrees to Memorial University of Newfoundland—one of the earliest actions of the first provincial government.

Entry into the Canadian Confederation in 1949 was accompanied by a community development model emphasizing cultural and intellectual enrichment within isolated communities of the province. Although the St. John's Centre continued to provide formal academic programmes for an increasing number of adults, greater demand in small communities for similar opportunities brought the establishment of similar centres in nine additional communities of the province. Rowe summarized the rationale for the increase of adult education centres:

> Newfoundland's functional illiteracy has always been high, the result of numerous interrelating factors, the most potent of which were scattered population and the economic conditions of the people prior to 1949. The

need is still great for increased emphasis upon adult education, but with centralization, vocational development, and the equalization of educational opportunity, it is reasonable to assume that Newfoundland's adult education problem will decrease steadily as such new measures take effect.[117]

Formal vocational and technical education grew very slowly in Newfoundland because of the resource-based economy and the absence of large centres of population. Some initiatives had been taken by the denominational colleges, which had played key educational roles in the early years of the territory, but Newfoundlanders favoured academic studies, and so little was offered in the way of alternate programmes. The predictable result was a large drop-out rate by those with limited aptitude for, or interest in, traditional academic courses.

The first real impetus for the expansion of vocational education occurred following the Second World War. The General Rehabilitation Committee of the Newfoundland government recommended the establishment of a vocational institute to provide ex-servicemen with job skills. As a result of this recommendation, the Vocational Institute for Ex-Servicemen was opened in St. John's in 1946, offering trades training in nine occupations. The institute was scheduled to close in 1948, but after some public pressure, it continued to operate for another year.[118]

Newfoundland's decision to join the Canadian Confederation in 1949 opened the avenue to support from the Canadian government for vocational training. With the signing of Vocational Training Agreements in 1950 and 1951, federal funds became available for secondary schools to provide vocational training. In 1961, a familiar impetus, the federal Technical and Vocational Training Assistance Act, provided funds for the construction of eleven vocational schools (for students who had completed high school) located in different centres of the province, as well as a College of Trades of Technology in St. John's. This massive injection of federal dollars provided unprecedented opportunities for trades, apprenticeship, and technical training for thousands of Newfoundlanders. Although The College of Trades and Technology was originally a provincial government institution, it acquired its own board of governors by legislation in 1969.

A second non-university institution in Newfoundland, the College of Fisheries, Navigation, Marine Engineering, and Electronics (commonly called the College of Fisheries) was established in 1963, largely on the initiative of Premier J.R. Smallwood. The province, though dependent upon the fishing industry, had previously provided no opportunity for formal study or research into this activity. Indeed, no such facility existed in Canada, and the founding of the college attracted federal financial support much in the fashion of agricultural colleges in other provinces. The College of Fisheries began with a general education upgrading programme for a student clientele with little formal preparation for the sophisticated study of the science of fishing. With federal funding, the college then concentrated on vocational training for an industry vital to the economy of the province and previously ignored everywhere in Canada as a formal area of study. Two observations by Rowe reflect the contribution made by the college to the development of the province:

> In retrospect, it is clear that the creation of the College of Fisheries was a vital part of the educational revolution of the post-Confederation period, affecting as it has the lives of thousands of Newfoundlanders whom that revolution would otherwise have missed. Indeed, without the College it is difficult to see how the tremendous fishery development of recent years could have taken place in the Province.
> The College of Fisheries is not merely a Newfoundland institution. It is a national asset held in high regard by all connected with fishing and the sea. This explains why deep-sea fishermen from Nova Scotia and merchant marines from British Columbia are to be found registered there. And this approbation is not confined to Canada. Competent observers from other great fishing countries have described it as the best and most comprehensive college of its kind in the world.[119]

During 1966-67, the province of Newfoundland founded two more specialized post-secondary institutions in Stephenville for the training of people to work on the massive Churchill Falls Hydro Project. These were an Adult Training Centre and a Heavy Equipment School, both at the abandoned U.S. Air Force Base.

Despite all these initiatives and despite the Newfoundland commitment to community development, the province did not establish community colleges as had been done in other provinces in this period, nor had communities in Newfoundland pressed the provincial government to establish new colleges as communities in other provinces had done. The community college idea was, however, explored, debated, and recommended as desirable for the province. The source of this recommendation was a Royal Commission on Education and Youth, under the chairmanship of P.J. Warren, which reported in 1968.[120] The general mandate of the commission was to recommend policies for improving the entire educational system of the province, and its report did contain a chapter entitled "Further Education." In this chapter the commissioners noted the lack of attention to the needs of youth who had left secondary school, and reviewed the opportunities provided by Memorial University, the College of Trades and Technology, and the College of Fisheries. The report also reviewed developments in the non-university sector in Alberta, British Columbia, Quebec, and Ontario. It noted with alarm the high failure rate of grade eleven graduates at university, attributing the problem to their lack of preparation, immaturity, and lack of an adequate range of educational programmes at the post-secondary level. The report continued by stating:

> The problem, then, is that of providing quality educational programmes for the many individuals seeking post-secondary education—students going to university, students who wish more general education but do not have the ability or the desire to do a university degree, students who wish to do vocational training, and adults who wish to continue their education in their leisure time.[121]

The solution, the commissioners concluded, lay with the establishment of "regional" colleges in six regions of the province. These colleges should provide combinations of four curriculum areas: university transfer, terminal general education, vocational training for local employment, and continuing education for adults. The specific curriculum for each regional college should complement that of Memorial university and the College of Trades and Technology. Direct reference was made to need for affiliation with Memorial University in cases when courses for university transfer were to be offered by the regional colleges.

The royal commission recommendations for the colleges were creative attempts to acknowledge the educational history of the province, but also to recognize the needs of a generally under-educated populace, a less than robust economic climate, a limited range of vocational opportunity, and a desire to redress the deficiencies of the past within a spirit of hope for the future. Regional colleges as one component of post-secondary education were viewed as an important contributor to the process of sociocultural change which was underway.

Economic difficulties, which had been so much a part of the history of Newfoundland, and which had in part stimulated the need for development through education, became the determining factor in the ultimate rejection of the recommendations of the commission. Newfoundland decided that six additional regional colleges simply could not be afforded. Despite the comprehensive and co-ordinated approach to post-secondary education featured in the Warren Report, the provincial government decided only to expand vocational education by the construction of six more district vocational schools between 1970 and 1973, which by that time numbered seventeen in total. Newfoundland's government opted for many small and dispersed institutions rather than a system of larger regional colleges. The province, by the mid 1970's, contained a large number of single purpose post-secondary facilities; only two were quasi-autonomous from government in their governing structure. The District Vocational Schools were operated directly by one division of the Ministry of Education while adult education was administered by another division.

Newfoundland, as in so many other respects, went its own way in the development of post-secondary education in the post Second World War years. What was happening in most of the rest of Canada during the 1960's bore little relationship to the particular circumstances of a province that had never considered itself, or had been considered by others, to be advantaged.

3

CHARACTERISTICS OF CANADA'S
COMMUNITY COLLEGES

The origins of new colleges in Canada have been reviewed in the preceding chapter. What characteristics these new institutions had in common, in spirit if not always in practical application from their first days, are the focus of this chapter.

In some respects, it is easier to describe what these colleges were not rather than to identify them by what they were or what they aspired to become. The new colleges were quite different from universities or university-affiliated institutions which provided degree programmes. In fact, several universities were also established during the period in which the new colleges were created, and several university colleges, usually denominational in character, acquired a new legal status during this same period. The distinctiveness of university institutions was their research orientation, their degree preparation work, and, to some extent, the public services they provided.

The new colleges were also quite unlike the institutes of technology which had pre-dated them and the new ones which came into existence in the 1960-75 period. The institutes of technology were like the new colleges only in that, with the exception of Ryerson Polytechnical Institute in Toronto, they did no degree preparatory work. They were specialized institutions limited to technical programmes, each with a combination of academic and applied studies; the explicit objective of all programmes was to prepare graduates for employment in applied fields of endeavour well beyond the job-entry level. Some level of controversy still exists within Canadian post-secondary educational institutions about the performance level of graduates of institutes of technology; whether these institutes train technicians or educate technologists, or both, is a topic of continuing debate, particularly as the need for more advanced, applied education (as distinct from the more theoretical studies at university) becomes more evident in Canada. The institutes of technology were also distinguishable from most of the new colleges by the fact that they were uniformly provincially mandated to serve province-wide needs; they did not, at least officially, have local constituencies.

In addition, there were several single-purpose, specialized institutions across Canada, and, by that characteristic, they distinguished themselves from the new colleges. The specialized institutions—called institutes or schools or colleges— focused their work on one or few related programme areas and, like the institutes of technology, commonly had a provincial rather than regional or local mandate. Some of these institutions had long and illustrious histories while others were even newer than some of the new colleges of Canada. Most were publicly supported, but there was also a network of private single-purpose institutions, such as trade schools licenced by provincial governments to offer their services.

Private colleges also continued to operate in Canada. Most offered only post-secondary academically oriented instruction (and many at the secondary school level as well) in a religious denomination context and provided a rich extra-curricular as well as curricular experience to students. In some instances, they received public subsidy, but most were primarily supported by tuition fees and voluntary contributions.

All of these institutions were, and remain, quite different from the new colleges which began to appear across Canada in the early 1960's. What, then, were the distinguishing characteristics of the new colleges?

CURRICULUM COMPREHENSIVENESS

The new colleges were first characterized by the comprehensiveness or multi-purpose dimensions of their curricula. The principle of comprehensiveness required that they offer a mix of different programmes, for a mix of students with different abilities and past achievements, with a mix of educational goals, within a single institution, usually on a single campus. The mixes differed from province to province and from institution to institution, but the mixes were designed and deliberate, not the result of programme evaluation or historical accident.

The common—but not universal throughout Canada—curriculum components of the new colleges could be categorized as follows:

1. *Vocational and trades training programmes of different but usually short durations, intended to lead directly to employment by graduates who would be job-ready.* The general practice was for most students to be selected from the rolls of the unemployed, by government, to undertake this job-specific training so that they could enter or return to the workforce with marketable skills as economically

and as effectively as possible. Both federal and provincial governmental officials saw the adult orientation of the new colleges as appropriate to people who commonly had previously experienced both educational and employment frustration, and directed students to these new colleges for a fresh start. Indeed, the success of the new colleges with this form of training frequently resulted in long waiting lists of candidates for these programmes. Such programmes were provided for both full-time and part-time students.

2. *Apprenticeship training programmes for those trades requiring this form of work preparation.* The new colleges not only offered the pre-apprentice training but also provided the institution-based annual period of training of tradespersons at the apprentice level in co-operation with employers and unions. Although this form of training was hardly the exclusive domain of the new colleges, it was a major and unpredictable share of many of them, as the number of apprentices to be trained fluctuated with the state of the economy. In the bustling 1960's and 1970's, this problem was not nearly as acute as it became later with the deterioration of the economy virtually throughout Canada.

3. *Career, technical, and para-professional programmes of bewildering variety, of two or three years duration, intended to prepare graduates for employment at technical, mid-managerial, or professional assistant levels.* The new colleges were genuine innovators in the design of such programmes in fields as varied as engineering, business, health sciences, social service, cultural arts, public safety and criminology, medical technologies, recreation—and many more. These programmes were not directly job preparatory but analogous to the applied programmes of institutes of technology, with special emphasis on new areas of employment. Graduates did not normally receive advanced standing at universities for the studies they had undertaken at the new colleges, but more and more of them decided to continue their education at university, frequently on a part-time basis, upon completion of their college programmes and upon obtaining employment— usually immediately upon graduation.

4. *University transfer programmes made up of courses parallel or equivalent to those offered by universities themselves.* In some cases, arrangements for transfer of credit from college to university were established on a bilateral basis between individual colleges and universities, but in other cases transfer arrangements were established on a provincial basis. The two largest provinces varied from this pattern in two different ways: in Ontario, university transfer was not an integral part of the C.A.A.T system; in Quebec, the university-type courses and programmes were preparatory to the newly structured undergraduate university programmes but at least equivalent in standard and rigour to courses offered in universities at the undergraduate level prior to the educational reforms in that province. Perhaps the purest form of university transfer programming was in British Columbia where each college and each university agreed upon transfer arrangements for a great variety of courses at the first and second year level.

5. *General academic programmes, with courses not intended for transfer to university but responding to locally recognized need for post-secondary instruction of an academic, rather than job training, nature.* Labour studies, women's studies, and interdisciplinary programmes of many kinds began early to fall into this category; graduates of such programmes were commonly recognized as worthy of college certification as much as those who completed successfully any other programme at a new college.

6. *Personal interest and community development programmes—of cultural, recreational, or community-based character—which did not carry credit toward any college diploma or certificate but which satisfied the intellectual or technical interests of individuals or groups of citizens within a community.* Such programmes were normally offered on demand at any time of the day of week or year and were not repeated year after year unless demand was sustained. Courses as varied as foreign language conversation to Playing Bridge to Building Your Log Cabin and to Beginners' Typing were early offerings of some new colleges, and the list became longer and more varied as the new colleges came to know their communities better.

7. *Pre-college level or upgrading programmes, or basic skill training.* When the new colleges began, there were many adults throughout Canada who had interest in, and aptitude for, the various programmes offered by these colleges, but who did not have the academic background to pursue them effectively or confidently. As a result, new colleges in Canada quickly entered the field of make-up or remedial education in addition to their other instructional activities and by that measure opened the door to many people who would otherwise have been unable to continue their education or acquire new employment skills. While the original focus of these programmes was on basic literacy and mathematics as a preparation for vocational training, several of the new colleges also quickly developed second language programmes as the immigration policies of Canada brought people of a great variety of languages and cultures to this country.

8. *Contract programmes.* Initially in Ontario and later in other provinces, the need for the new colleges to develop close ties with the businesses and industries in their communities or regions was emphasized particularly by governmental officials. The leap from that principle to the step of colleges entering into contract with corporations and community agencies and government departments or services to supply the training they needed was a short one, and this form of training quickly became a significant part of the total package of offerings of many new colleges.

The mix of programming—and each college had its own particular mix—was a revolutionary approach to post-secondary education in most provinces of Canada in that it crossed the traditional curriculum boundaries of earlier institutions, many of which considered themselves to be already multi-purpose and mult-dimensional. However, the new colleges quickly became more comprehensive in curriculum than any previous post-secondary institutions, and even more multi-purpose than the secondary schools, which were intended to be responsive to the educational needs of all youth within the compulsory sector of public education.

The advantages of comprehensive curricula for the new colleges were obvious. The same facilities and equipment could be used by students in different programmes; central services such as purchasing could take advantage of economies of scale; savings and expertise should have resulted from a single administrative structure for one institution rather than separate if smaller administrations for several institutions. But the real gains originally anticipated were educational. The new colleges were to allow for considerable mobility by students between programmes and to bridge the traditional gap between academic studies and vocational forms of training. Contrary to practices in single-purpose institutions, the new colleges would give students an opportunity to change programmes as their educational objectives changed (a common reality with young and older adults, particularly those returning to formal education after a long lapse of time), without having to withdraw from one institution and enrol at another—usually without receiving any credit or recognition for work successfully completed at the first institution. Expected to be at least as common at colleges would be the student without specific career or further education goals; in these cases, the new colleges were to organize themselves to encourage students to shop around before making a commitment to a specific programme, all the while defining more sharply their educational and employment objectives. Programme mobility, together with improved counselling services, it was claimed, would be of great advantage to uncertain students and more economical for institutions and for the public purse.

STUDENT HETEROGENEITY

With a variety of programmes, the new colleges immediately attracted students of great variety of interests, aptitudes, abilities, and goals—of far greater heterogeneity than single purpose or more specialized institutions. In fact, many colleges soon became in student make-up a reflection of the communities they served. The new colleges attracted younger and older adults, men and women, full-time and part-time students, wealthy and impoverished, and all stages in between—people of all races, creeds, and colours that were represented in their communities.

This student body complexion was seen as advantageous since, outside the context of the classroom or laboratory or shop or studio, students of quite different backgrounds could rub shoulders one with another and in that process learn from one another. The new colleges could become democracy in action, rather than retain the segregated character of single purpose or more specialized institutions. Some of the more adventuresome colleges even made it policy, and practice, to have students from different programmes taking courses together. The vision was that a great deal of valuable informal learning, as well as the more formal studies, would result from having people who wished to be welders, police officers, and chemical technologists sitting in class with university-bound students, senior citizens, and nurses in training. The social mix in new colleges was something quite new to Canadian post-secondary education.

OPEN ADMISSIONS

The social mix and the comprehensiveness of programming could not have been achieved without admission standards quite unlike those of more established post-secondary institutions. The new colleges uniformly adopted more "open admissions" policies than Canadian education had ever seen before. Essentially open admissions meant in principle that, other things being equal, applicants could "try" programmes of their choice regardless of previous scholastic performance and regardless of the length of time they had been out of formal education. In effect, it would be relatively easy for a student to be allowed into a programme, but the student would have to perform to institutional standards in order to graduate, in contrast to some of the other post-secondary institutions, which made it very difficult for applicants to gain admission but not very difficult for the successful enrollees to graduate.

Of course, all other things were never equal, and applicants were rarely admitted by lottery. In some cases, it was obvious that applicants had no reasonable chance of succeeding in the programmes of their choice, and they were denied admission until they had successfully completed "make-up" work that would indicate a reasonable chance of success. In other cases, the demands for some programmes far exceeded the ability of the college to respond properly, and so admission quotas were used, with those applicants with the greatest chance of success commonly being given preference over more high-risk applicants. In fact, not all programmes were open to all applicants simply at their request, but the spirit of "taking a chance" on applicants who did not always have the traditional paper credentials was characteristic of the new colleges.

STUDENT SERVICES

In other post-secondary institutions, professional counsellors were viewed as necessary for dealing with problem students, if necessary at all; in the new colleges, counselling—and then a whole range of other student services—was not seen as peripheral but as integral to the character of this kind of institution. All applicants—indeed, in some cases, all people in the college region—were to be able to receive professional advice and assistance in career and educational planning, and this service was held to be just as important to the success of students and the institution as the teaching services provided. In short order this service was expanded to include financial management advice, special services for minority group students, and a whole range of non-instructional services calculated to support students or to provide them with the confidence they needed to become successful. Because the new colleges were to admit a much broader segment of the population than other institutions, it was incumbent upon these institutions, it was claimed, to provide those services necessary to ensure that students would not merely flounder once they were admitted. The student service function became an early, important, and integral function of Canada's new colleges.

OPERATIONAL FLEXIBILITY

Just as admission standards were malleable, the new colleges in Canada pioneered flexibility in several aspects of their day-to-day operations; the principle was that the college should adapt to the student rather than the student accommodate to the inflexibility of the institution.

The most obvious example of flexibility was in the scheduling of activities. In some instances, classes literally operated around the clock, but the more common practice was to run educational activities—courses, laboratories, libraries, individualized learning centres, shops—in mornings, afternoons, and evenings, and on weekends to meet the requirements of full-time students, part-time students with domestic obligations, shift workers, and people who could be students only in the evening or on weekends. Of course, the new colleges could achieve the ultimate in flexibility of scheduling only at prohibitive cost, and so in practice they were not as flexible as they would have liked to be—but the intent of flexibility was there, and many new colleges experimented freely with way of accommodating to student constraints to the extent that their resources would allow.

A second example of flexibility was the organization of the college year. Some colleges operated on a semester basis, others on a trimester, still others on a quarter basis, and even some on a twelve-month year; it was not uncommon even from the start for the new colleges to offer different programmes on different cycles. The objective was to make the college accessible to as many potential students as possible, and the timing of instruction was seen as one of the real barriers to accessibility that had to be overcome. The new colleges were far more responsive in this connection than the more established post-secondary institutions. From the start, Canada's new colleges were to be year-round institutions and they responded immediately to this challenge.

Yet another form of flexibility was the individualization of college instruction for some students. It was not uncommon for new colleges to allow if not encourage some students to design their own learning programmes under the supervision of an instructor, to grant credit for work done by students at other institutions or for skills they had acquired without any formal training, or to design special programmes for groups of students who found conventional instruction intimidating, boring, or unchallenging. At several of the new colleges, students were able to contract with the college to achieve the institution's requirements in their own ways and, upon meeting their contractual obligations, to become graduates.

In all, most new colleges looked for new ways to respond to their student's time and place constraints rather than insist that students follow, in lock-step fashion, the predetermined institutional rhythm. In fact, most colleges did not have a single rhythm and were proud of it.

DECENTRALIZATION

Consistent with other features of student responsiveness, the new colleges quickly recognized that they had to reach out to potential students rather than expect that all potential students could reasonably attend a single campus within a college region of substantial size. Geography and distance were obvious barriers to universal access, despite the numbers and locations of the new colleges.

Accordingly, it was not long before many of the new colleges established satellite campuses, store front centres, or other college locations in centres distant from their main campuses. Most often, colleges rented community halls, libraries, and schools in more remote locations and provided a presence and basic information services, if not instruction, in these centres. More daring colleges did not have main campuses at all, but operated mobile classrooms and other means of bringing educational service to their constituents. Even in the earliest years, the potential of radio and television as means of bringing educational opportunity to people was recognized if not fully translated into reality.

RESPONSIVENESS TO GOVERNMENT

All of the new colleges had as at least one primary function: the preparation of adults for the workforce of Canada, of their province, of their region, or of their community. To fulfil this function, the colleges across the country established ties quickly not only with potential employers, but also with the federal and provincial government agencies which attempted to project manpower needs and to place unskilled workers in training programmes. The new colleges built close relationships not only with their own provincial government department dealing with these issues, but as well with Canada Manpower (later to be known as Canada Employment and Immigration Commission).

Indeed, Canadian government agencies viewed these new colleges as important agencies for meeting many of their own objectives. They selected candidates for training, retraining, or skill upgrading; they, directly or through the appropriate provincial agency, placed students in college training programmes; they provided financial support to students during their training sessions; they placed graduates in jobs. In fact, some of the new colleges came rather quickly to resent the dependence they had on both federal and provincial employment-related agencies, which could significantly influence the planning of the institutions themselves by a quick change of policy or practice which could virtually overnight increase or decrease their planned intake of students.

Nevertheless, the new colleges and government agencies established working relationships—sometimes to their mutual satisfaction, other times stressful—which had been unknown in Canadian post-secondary education. Previously, government institutions had provided training for employment directly, but government relationships with more autonomous post-secondary institutions had been of an arms-length nature. With the appearance of the new colleges, many with their own governing bodies and a large measure of institutional autonomy, new government-institution relationships had to be built—and they were.

TEACHING AND LEARNING

Being a college teacher, instructor, or master was quite unlike being a university professor, much to the surprise and chagrin of many college instructors who had themselves been nurtured through the university system. University professors were expected to be researchers who also taught, and they spent more that a little time participating in the governance and administration of their department, their faculty, or their university. College instructors were expected to teach—or, more precisely, to do whatever was necessary to help students learn. Unlike university professors, college instructors came from many directions: business, the universities, social service and professional agencies, schools. Most had considerable competence in their subject areas and disciplines, but few were experienced teachers and even fewer were familiar with the most current methods of helping students learn. A very high proportion, in the first years, were employed only on a part-time basis by the colleges and so could not devote their full attention to college priorities.

That some of the first college teachers simple floundered did not deter the new colleges from placing major emphasis on teaching potential in the selection of the many teachers who had to be found to staff the new colleges. Rather, it prompted some of them to insist upon the regular evaluation of the teaching performance of their staff members and for the more perceptive and insistent colleges to provide programmes to help instructors improve their skills as teachers.

This emphasis on the teaching function meant that college instructors had teaching loads well in excess of those carried by their university counterparts. It also meant that they were expected to be available to students outside the classroom to a far greater extent than was the case in universities, or indeed in many secondary schools. The general expectation for teachers in the new colleges was that they would spend the vast majority of their time, in and out of the classroom or its equivalent, helping students, but not doing research, not running the institutions, not staying ahead of the new developments in their areas of teaching. In fact, one of the first concerns of college instructors was that they were being treated as technical workers rather than as autonomous professionals, and that concern did not evaporate in the early years of the new colleges.

But there were other expectations related to teaching that were placed on the shoulders of the new instructors. They were clearly expected to become personally involved, informally and formally, with community life and activity, so that they could never be charged with working in an ivory tower; rather, they were to be seen as contributors to the general quality of life in the communities which supported their institutions. The emphasis on new colleges as teaching-learning institutions with deep roots in the community was very much a characteristic which set these institutions apart from others in the post-secondary sector.

COMMUNITY ORIENTATION

In a real sense, all of the distinctive characteristics already associated with the new colleges grew out of yet another of their characteristics, namely, their community orientation.

As the previous descriptions of the origins of new colleges in different provinces have illustrated, only a most general and generous definition would permit the designation of all the new colleges as "community" colleges. In fact, some of them were to respond more to provincial requirements than to the local needs; some were, in fact as well as in name, regional colleges with several distinct communities within the region. Nevertheless, almost all of the new colleges had from the beginning far more of a community orientation, however narrowly or broadly community may be defined, than other post-secondary institutions. Their community or localized orientation was reflected in their programme mix, in their student mix, in the employment placement of their graduates, and in their specialized services and activities. Special programmes for native students, for senior citizens, for penitentiary inmates, as examples, gave each new college the opportunity to individualize itself and to respond in its own way to its constituents, rather than merely to duplicate the offerings of neighbouring institutions.

In some cases, the community orientation of the new colleges was emphasized by the requirement that they be supported at least in part by local taxation; in other cases, that orientation was expressed through municipal appointments to college boards; and in yet others, it was explicitly expected that the new colleges would develop close ties with local business and industry.

The community orientation of the new colleges was also equally associated with their governance. Most of them had governing boards separate from the provincial governments, and board members—whether elected or appointed, —were clearly expected to bring a local or regional perspective to board deliberations. And the board members in the early years of the colleges developed strong identification with their new colleges, even if they had been appointed at a provincial level.

The community focus of the new colleges was further reinforced by the fact that they were, almost universally, expected to be "commuter colleges"; that is, colleges which could be reached by public transportation at least in urban areas and which would not need residences. Students would be able to live at home and avoid the high costs of relocation associated with other forms of post-secondary education.

Many of the new colleges, regardless of the label used, also became community colleges to the extent that they became a new community resource in the locales in which they were established. Especially in non-metropolitan centres, the new colleges were viewed not only as educational and training centres to which people had convenient access but also as cultural, artistic, and recreational centres available to enrich the lives of all citizens. Indeed, in many cases, the new colleges were major community employers themselves, and not a few acrimonious inter-municipal debates surrounded the choice of location for the new colleges precisely for this reason.

In no sense could most of Canada's new colleges be considered community colleges as the term was used in the U.S. Nevertheless, they had a community flavour to a far greater extent than other Canadian post-secondary institutions, and the general attempt was more to enhance than suppress community or regional identification.

THE ESSENCE—THEIR PUBLIC CHARACTER

There were two universal characteristics of the new colleges in every province in which they were established: first, their financial support came substantially if not totally from provincial and federal sources; secondly, provincial legislation either brought them into being or enabled their establishment. In this sense, the common characteristic was that they were public colleges—publicly established, publicly supported, publicly maintained—to achieve public purposes, to serve all citizens without discrimination, as public agencies.

It is for this reason that, in the following chapters, these new Canadian colleges are referred to at different times as public colleges, or community colleges, or public community colleges.

4

TRANSITION TO TODAY:
THE EMERGENCE OF COLLEGE SYSTEMS

The decade of the 1960's saw the establishment of new public colleges in many parts of Canada and, by the mid-1970's, the framework for a nation-wide network of public colleges was becoming evident. This had been a period of growth and reorganization in the entire post-secondary sector: new colleges had come into being, new universities had been established, institutional mergers had taken place, older institutions had begun to take on new mandates. For people within the field of post-secondary education, it was a period of excitement and expansion; there seemed to be no limit to what might be accomplished. For the people of Canada, it was a time of optimism, confidence in what could be achieved through education, and trust in educators and politicians to do what was right and necessary in all sectors of education, but particularly in the post-secondary arena.

Commitments to universal accessibility to all the education and training Canadians might need or want, to equality of educational opportunity for all citizens, to higher education as a means of more satisfying employment and an enriched quality of life, and to the pursuit of knowledge as a value in itself were driving forces for educators and public alike. Altruism converged with economics and there seemed little limit to government support of post-secondary education.

Propelled by buoyant economic conditions, favoured by free-spending politicians, and buttressed by widespread public support, higher education during the 1960's became one of Canada's major growth industries. Between 1960 and 1970 full time enrolment across the country almost tripled to 316,000. In the same period expenditure by Canadian universities increased 600 per cent to $1.6 billion. And between 1945 and 1970 the number of institutions offering university-level training doubled to sixty. All of this was to say nothing of the massive expansion of community college education for the training of students in technical and vocational areas. The spin-off effects of educational investment into other areas of regional economic life, if uncalculated, was unmistakably evident. Popular faith in the economic value of post-secondary education reached unprecedented heights.[1]

In fact, the prospect of further economic development for Canada drove educational expansion. A belief in the return on investment in post-secondary education, for both individual Canadians and Canadian society as a whole, really motivated government action in education with full concurrence of the electorate.[2] Fuel for this support came from prestigious sources as varied as the Economic Council of Canada, the Industrial Foundation on Education, and several sectors of the Canadian business community.[3] Canadian educators were only too happy to accept this support and to promise, at least implicitly, that dreams of a new and more dynamic Canada would be the result of still heavier investment in education.

A CHANGE OF MOOD

This generous support, both financial and moral, to publicly subsidized post-secondary education was not, however, to be sustained. By the mid-1970's, the impact of the oil crises of 1972 and 1974, high levels of inflation combined with even higher levels of unemployment, and stiffening international competition conveyed the message to politician and public alike that anything approaching universal prosperity was some years away. Combined with these economic realities was growing political tension quite the opposite of the common pride expressed throughout Canada during Montreal's Expo '67. The prospect of an "independantiste" government in Quebec and then its reality in 1976, the mounting expressions of regional disaffection in the West, the inability of federal and provincial governments to deal with constitutional issues and other common concerns in a mutually acceptable manner added a political dimension to the economic difficulties being experienced across the country.

Despite these difficulties, governments within Canada did not abandon support for public post-secondary education or for other social programmes, but the government plea for the lowering of expectations became louder and louder. No longer was expansion going to be uncritically financed. At one extreme, post-secondary institutions were urged or required to do more careful planning; rationalization of the plans of separate institutions was called for;

governments took initiatives to set up co-ordinating mechanisms for system planning; labour relations in post-secondary education produced high profile contentious issues as governments saw it necessary to have more checks on the costs of providing post-secondary services; government grants to colleges and other institutions were now based less on trying to satisfy the institutional quest to serve more people and more on government ability to finance these institutions in addition to so many other public services; the words "retrenchment" and "priorities" entered the vocabulary of Canadian education, beginning in a whispered way in most parts of the country.

At the other extreme, colleges and other post-secondary institutions began to plead with different levels of government to communicate better with one another as they came to sense, if not fully appreciate, that a new era in the financing of post-secondary education was about to dawn and as they came to recognize that the attainment of their objectives was intimately related to the degree of co-operation that existed between their chief sources of funding. By the early 1980's, deterioration of the economy in most parts of Canada, the lack of political concensus and a common sense of direction, and the revenue pressures on governments had become more severe. By the mid-1980's, the previously high level of moral and material support for colleges, universities, and other post-secondary institutions had been replaced by public skepticism about theories of return on investment in education, public and private criticism of the work of educators at all levels, caution on the part of politicians in sustaining existing levels of educational support, and a dramatic lowering of the public priority that had been assigned to education. This disillusionment was further aggravated by the seemingly insatiable financial appetites of post-secondary institutions at the very time governments were hard-pressed to maintain their own revenues and avoid further public debt. And as new institutions tried to establish their mark within Canada, the public colleges were affected by these new circumstances as much as other components of Canadian education. Just as Canada's new colleges were getting their head of steam, they were confronted by new imperatives:

> Recession, rationalization, and restraint—these were the watchwords which shaped higher education in the 1970's and early 80's. Against such obvious debilitating pressures, the goals of widening accessibility, fostering social criticism, enhancing cultural development, and preserving institutional autonomy struggled to assert their priority in the framing of post-secondary educational policy.[4]

This comment was a description intended to apply particularly to Canada's universities. It applied to an even greater extent to the public colleges, which were perceived by the Canadian public and politicians in quite a different light from the universities. The colleges did not enjoy the mystique of the university tradition. They were commonly regarded as means rather than institutions of inherent value in their own right, and they were closely tied to government, not only for their funds but also for their rationale as producers of graduates who ought to be able to satisfy immediate manpower needs of the country, the province, or the community.

THE FEDERAL ROLE

Although public education remained constitutionally the prerogative and responsibility of provincial authorities, as in the earlier era, actions by the federal government had substantial impact on the course of Canadian post-secondary education. Through the greater part of the 1970's, the federal presence in post-secondary education was muted though important. Through the Department of the Secretary of State, the government of Canada continued to share the cost of funding the various kinds of post-secondary education via fiscal arrangements with the provinces. Similarly, Canada Manpower (and later Canada Employment and Immigration Commission) continued to purchase seats in colleges and to subsidize students to obtain training that would allow them to enter or return to the work force. Canadian research councils expanded their support of scholarly research. The Canadian government continued to share in the funding of student aid programmes for needy post-secondary students.

In 1977, a new five-year agreement between federal and provincial governments was reached for the joint funding of both health care and post-secondary education through Established Programmes Financing (EPF) under the Fiscal Arrangements Act.[5] Before the term of that agreement had expired, however, the federal government was to adopt a new position in its relationships with its provincial counterparts in all matters pertaining to post-secondary education. In fact, the federal government took several separate but related steps in the early 1980's as expressions of disaffection with the status quo.

The start of the process was an attempt by the federal Secretary of State to articulate a set of national goals for education with the objective of reaching national support for these goals. Buttressed by an earlier report by the Organisation for Economic Cooperation and Development (OECD) on Canadian education[6] which praised the level of support provided in Canada to public education but also commented on the lack of direction in Canadian education, officials of the Department of the Secretary of State developed and sought consultation throughout the country on national goals for education. The process did not excite Canadian educators nor did it produce anything close to national consensus, but it did raise the public profile of the government of Canada in matters of education.

A much stormier part of the process was the 1982 effort on the part of the federal government to establish new terms for its fiscal arrangements with the provinces for its continued support of post-secondary education. From a federal perspective, the provinces had been distorting the intent of the 1977 agreement by failing to continue to pay their share of the costs of post-secondary education, when the clear intent was that the support be 50 per cent federal and 50 per cent provincial. Adding coals to the fire that at times was close to being out of control, federal officials charged that the federal government was not receiving public credit for the support it was providing, and that provincial governments were attempting to back out of their financial commitments to an effective joint post-secondary student aid programme. The issue became more heated when the Secretary of State announced to his provincial counterparts that he would expect accountability from the provinces so that the Canadian government could confirm that federal funds were being spent as intended.[7] From a provincial perspective, apart from being high-handed in its dealings with another level of government with constitutional authority, the federal government had made faulty financial calculations, was in no position to tell another government how it should spend its funds, and should not only maintain but increase its support to post-secondary education. An acrimonious public debate ensued, and one result was that a new federal-provincial fiscal agreement was not reached by the time of expiry of the 1977 agreement. In a fashion not atypical in Canada, an interim agreement to extend the basic terms of the 1977 scheme for 1982-83 was reached while discussions of a new agreement were to continue. Throughout the saga, post-secondary institutions did some lobbying but largely sat on the sidelines and faced uncertainty as they felt like pawns in a game that they could not play, even though their futures were very much at stake.

On quite a different front, the federal government was also making its presence felt in other ways in the early 1980's. As the Canadian unemployment situation worsened, and as talk about high technology, without definition, as the way of the future increased, a Parliamentary Committee on Employment Opportunities for the 80's was established.[8] Almost simultaneously, Canada Employment and Immigration established a Task Force on Labour Market Development in the 1980's.[9] Both of these bodies expressed some level of alarm about the lack of match between actual and projected labour market needs, on the one hand, and the training capacity of industry and institutions, on the other. With constitutional responsibilities for economic and industrial development and with a long history of support for various forms of training, the Canadian government was clearly preparing to launch a major new training initiative.

In fact, the reports of the parliamentary committee and the task force came to be recognized as the prelude to new training legislation. The National Training

Act of 1982, drafted after intensive consultation across the country, received quick passage.[10] Unlike the debates about Established Programmes Financing, the consultations with provinces and territories, the business and labour communities, institutions and community groups revealed substantial agreement that a major new training initiative by the federal government was desirable. While there was disagreement on details of implementation, there was broad support for new training objectives and programmes.

The National Training Act was a comprehensive piece of legislation with many provisions which would have a direct and pronounced effect on colleges throughout the country. The most dramatic notion within the act was that the federal government would identify national occupations for special support. It would, in co-operation with the provinces, identify those occupations where there were nation-wide shortages of skilled workers and direct its funding primarily to training in those occupations. The act also set up a Skills Growth Fund, a capital pool to allow training institutions and industry to update their equipment and modernize their facilities for new types of training to meet the labour requirements of the 1980's. To monitor and keep current the concept of national occupations, the new act also provided for the establishment of a Canadian Occupational Projection System which was to integrate labour market information from the private sector and from both federal and provincial levels of government. The legislation complemented its priority for national occupations with a priority for those who should have the opportunity to receive the new training: women, native peoples, and the physically disabled. Finally, to ensure that no single set of agencies in the public or private sector could monopolize training, the legislation and its supporting regulations were to guarantee that both non-profit training organizations and public institutions would be able to bid on the funds made available to implement the act. All of these features of the new legislation were to have direct influence on the colleges, on the capacity of provinces to provide the kinds of training they saw as priorities to meet local or regional labour market needs, and on the visibility of the federal government in the task of training. That the legislation specifically excluded universities from access to the new funding—they were to have their day in court later with exclusive access to funds for the development of Centres of Excellence—was at least in part a signal that the federal government acknowledged the importance and the potential of the new colleges in a national affort to improve human resource planning and training for employment.

PROVINCIAL VARIATIONS

Just as the new colleges came into being in different ways and at different times in different parts of the country, the impact of the new imperatives was not identical for all colleges; nor indeed were the new conditions uniformly evident in all parts of Canada. The following pages present major college developments in each province and in the territories during the second phase of development of Canada's no-longer-new public colleges and indicate issues with which those institutions were grappling as this second phase became the present.

THE EMERGENCE OF COLLEGE SYSTEMS

By the mid-1970's, most of Canada's colleges could no longer be described as new. They had passed the years of establishment and early frantic activity. Conditions in Canada were also changing, with important economic shifts and equally significant differences in public attitudes towards the support of post-secondary education. As in the first era of college development, the institutions themselves, the provincial systems, and the provincial governments were to take measures that altered dramatically the face of Canadian post-secondary education. How each province and territory responded to the new circumstances—or anticipated them—is described below.

Alberta

In the twenty-five year period which followed the establishment of its first public community college at Lethbridge in 1958, Alberta experienced an unprecedented surge in economic growth, matched by a similar expansion of post-secondary education. In particular, the application of generally stable and consistent government policy for post-secondary education after 1970 resulted in a new level of accessibility within a widely diversified galaxy of institutions. Unlike several other provinces, Alberta moved towards decentralization of social services, and the same trend was evident for the geographically dispersed public colleges, which expanded their comprehensive curricula to accommodate the various ranges of needs in different communities. Although many of Alberta's colleges had originally been "junior" universities in the sense that their major preoccupation was with academic "transfer" courses,[11] in more recent years a deliberate process of evolution has been apparent. Six of the ten colleges still offered university transfer programmes in 1985,[12] but the proportion of students in such programmes has diminished while growth in the technical, trade, vocational upgrading, and community education components of the curriculum has reshaped the provincial pattern of college education. Similarly, the character of the student population has changed from a predominantly full-time, college-age cohort to a more representative group of more mature, part-time learners engaged in a much broader range of studies.

Since the dissolution of the Colleges Commission in 1972, the Alberta colleges have been under the aegis of the Ministry of Advanced Education. This ministry now has responsibility for the entire provincial post-secondary enterprise, which includes four universities, the Banff Centre, ten public colleges, three institutes of technology, the Alberta Petroleum Industry Training Centre, twenty-one vocational centres, and a variety of post-secondary educational "consortia"—a true "system" of post-secondary educational institutions to serve a population of two million.

Efforts to coordinate this system have been continuous since the mid-1970's. While the ministry has assigned a high priority to rational development, the inevitable consequences of historic roles of institutions (with the accompanying territorial prerogatives) have produced some anomalies. The colleges, universities, and, as of 1981, the technical institutes operate with autonomous governing boards, while the vocational centres are under direct ministry control. In large regions such as Edmonton, further rationalization may be indicated. In several respects, rationalization of the system through the Ministry of Advanced Education has proved to be advantageous. The provincial programme approval system, while sometimes lengthy, produces a measure of province-wide co-ordination, yet provides to individual colleges the scope necessary to ensure responsiveness to perceived needs in different parts of the province. Issues of articulation and transfer of credit, a longstanding problem in the structure, have largely been overcome through ministry initiative. In recent years the Ministry of Advanced Education subsumed the Department of Manpower, and this arrangement provided for a co-ordinated approach to the allocation of federal funds and to the planning of federally subsidized programmes. This element of co-ordination ceased, however, in 1983 when manpower functions were withdrawn from the Ministry of Advanced Education. Since the Colleges Act in 1969, legislative changes have been relatively few. The most significant have been with respect to labour relations, an area in which Alberta has introduced several unique approaches which are described in Chapter 7.[13]

In 1981, Alberta's technical institutes were constituted under their own act,[14] which provided for the creation of institute boards. As in the case of colleges and universities, institute boards include the institutional president, lay appointees of the Lieutenant Governor-in-Council, and members nominated by and from the academic staff association, the students' council, and the non-academic staff. Potential "conflict of interest," so often an issue of debate in other provinces with respect to student and faculty participation on policy-making bodies, is not an issue unknown in Alberta, but there is general acceptance that such conflict can be addressed satisfactorily. In fact, the notion that employee board members are nominated by, but do not sit as representatives of, their peers is an important distinction made in this province.[15]

Professional staff in Alberta colleges have an additional legislated role in institutional governance. The legislation provides for the creation of an "Academic Council" in each institution, to include administrators, academic staff, and students; these councils may make recommendations to their boards on any matters they deem desirable.[16] While the powers of councils are clearly advisory, their presence reinforces in law the legitimacy of the role of employees and students in institutional governance.

Side by side with system rationalization and ministry-influenced co-ordinated planning of post-secondary education is a clear policy to decentralize the delivery of post-secondary education service. In 1978 the decision was made to extend apprenticeship trades training beyond the institutes of technology in Calgary and Edmonton. The policy objectives were to accommodate the increasing demand for such training as a consequence of economic growth, to overcome the concentration of these opportunities in the two major cities, and to provide training seats closer to the new industrial centres of the province. Coincidental with this government initiative, the colleges had been planning to broaden their programme offerings to accommodate a wider cross-section of community needs. The end result was the provision of apprenticeship, trades, and occupational training in colleges, which had thus become more comprehensive in their programming while maintaining the strong community identification they had struggled to establish in their early years.

Further evidence of dispersal rather than consolidation or centralization of educational opportunity is found in the trend towards the establishment of college satellite campuses. In addition, some colleges have been selected as sites for the construction of cultural centres. Adult and continuing education in both urban and rural areas has been enhanced through the creation of eighty-eight adult education co-ordinating agencies throughout the province to rationalize but disperse the offerings of public schools, private agencies, and post-secondary institutions in this field.

Another structural innovation developed in Alberta has been the higher education "consortium." In four rural regions of the province, consortia of outside institutions have been established to deliver local programming. These consortia, as an alternative to the establishment of still more post-secondary institutions, provide courses by contract with the university, college, and technical institute members of the consortia. Instruction in these regions is offered in leased facilities, an arrangement which offers maximum flexibility at minimal cost.

Despite these positive developments, those concerned with the development of Alberta colleges identify problems not yet resolved. Participation rates in post-secondary education appear not to have grown during the past decade.[17] Although measurement presents some difficulty, there is concern that all qualified students are not obtaining access to post-secondary education. Alberta, as much as any Canadian province, is perplexed that in the light of a massive increase in the number and diversity of institutions since 1970, participation rates in post-secondary education in Canada do not yet approach those in the United States.[18]

The character of and methods of providing general education for students in technical and occupational programmes is a concern to many Alberta educators. Although isolated attempts have been made in some colleges to develop a general education core, the practice is not common. There is broad support for reform in this area from both the ministry and the colleges, but only modest initiatives have been apparent to date.

The lack of systematic programmes for professional development of instructors, particularly in the area of instructional competence, is also a concern in Alberta because it represents a lack of determination to bring credence to the notion of colleges as teaching institutions. While there is widespread recognition of dramatic advances in instructional technology, there appear to be few efforts to develop related skills at the classroom level.

Programme evaluation—more properly, the absence of a systematic approach to evaluation—is yet another Alberta concern. This concern is prompted by the suspicion that there are too many graduates being produced by programmes which are not appropriate in a rapidly changing technological society and that, as a result, continuation of the current output of these programmes will merely lead to higher levels of unemployment of graduates; the speculation is that a number of these programmes may need major restructuring if they are to remain current. Programme evaluation, in a systematic way, is seen as the best way to address the issue of programme relevance.

In summary, during the last decade Alberta colleges, individually and collectively, have made important adjustments which have increased their ability to meet the needs of a widening clientele of students. The province has, until recently, enjoyed a relatively buoyant economy coupled with a high level of public commitment to post-secondary education; the general approach from the ministry has been to encourage growth in the college sector but in a planned, rationalized, and co-operative manner; college education has been brought to a larger spectrum of Alberta society as the individual colleges have expanded their curricula; working relationships between governments and institutions have been more than cordial with a higher level of mutual trust than in some other provinces; the Ministry of Advanced Education is, and is perceived as, an advocate for colleges before government. In Alberta, the colleges have developed into an effective and functional system or sub-system of post-secondary education. Anticipating a future with much greater fiscal restraint, Alberta's college educators look to further adjustments to their practices. As an example of forward planning, these colleges have already initiated study of the relative roles of institutions and industry in training, partly as a realistic assessment of their own limitations. Indeed, Alberta seems well placed to lead Canada in the provision of more sophisticated training through industrial-institutional co-operation.

From their original mandate as institutions to "fill the gap" between secondary school and university for a select segment of the population, Alberta's colleges have evolved into community educational resources of broad scope and vision, moving systematically to a role as centres for lifelong learning for a continually expanding portion of the Alberta population.

British Columbia

British Columbia's colleges were one of the first Canadian adaptations of the American community college concept. They grew from grassroots initiative at the community level and reinforced their community focus through measures such as local taxation and school board representation on college governing boards.[19] The number of colleges increased slowly, in part owing to the time-consuming processes required at the community level prerequisite to their establishment. However, by 1975, fourteen colleges had been established. They enjoyed considerable autonomy: they built their own buildings, they designed their own courses and programmes, and they hired their own personnel according to their own personnel practices. The colleges were loosely associated one with another, but they were characterized more by their differences than by their similarities, reflecting the diverse economies and social circumstances of the difference regions of the province.

The strengths of these colleges, their independence and their regional identification, became their weaknesses. By 1975, the provincial government was contributing heavily to the operating costs of colleges and was defraying new capital costs as colleges expanded to meet heavy demands in every region of the province. Not unexpectedly, provincial governments wished to protect their investment; first, they appointed members to the governing councils, then they imposed restrictions on college expenses, and finally they established a post-secondary division of the Ministry of Education to control institutional development.

During the same period there were shifts in the expectations which government had for the colleges. The New Democratic Party, elected in 1972, saw colleges primarily as educational resources to serve the wider community, particularly the disadvantaged and under-educated. The colleges' commitment to community education, to remedial programmes, and to social service programmes became much more visible. Vocational and trades training had already been melded into the curricula of most colleges after a government-directed amalgamation of colleges with regional post-secondary vocational schools in 1971.[20] The N.D.P. government also recognized a need to accelerate the construction of college facilities and to provide access to college in all parts of the province. This priority required more direct government intervention on both a financial and policy level than had previously been the case. In 1974, a government-appointed task force presented a report which laid the ground for a more systematic, ministry-directed group of institutions in the province. While much attention in the report was given to democratic governance procedures and community involvement in curriculum and admissions policies, the government's stake in the direction that colleges should take was made very evident.[21].

Another initiative taken by the N.D.P. government was to award a new status to the British Columbia Institute of Technology.[22] An act specifically concerned with that institution provided for its corporate status through a widely representative Board of Governors. This status allowed B.C.I.T. to explore new curriculum initiatives and also served to set that institution apart from the colleges.

In 1976, a new government with different priorities added considerably to the pressures on colleges to conform to government direction. Several communications from the ministry, both formal and informal, indicated that job training was to be the first priority for colleges, while the university-transfer and community education components were to be of lower priority. Operating budgets and programme approval processes were also more carefully monitored from Victoria as the staff in the post-secondary branch of the ministry expanded in both number and influence. The Minister of Education also established two new bodies of inquiry, one addressed to vocational and technical education and the other to adult education in the province. The former proposed a formalized structure to co-ordinate the procedures of the widely diverse agencies, provincial and federal, which were involved in funding and initiating occupational training. The second commission presented a comprehensive blueprint for adult education, addressed contentious funding questions, and attempted to resolve jurisdictional disputes between school boards and colleges in this area. Little action resulted from this report, a reflection of the priority that government accorded the education of adults in programmes that did not lead to some form of college certification.

Until 1976, the colleges had operated under legislation buried in the Public Schools Act. While college councils were responsible for governing and managing these institutions, they held no corporate power and, for example, were not able to borrow money or sign contracts. A further, less direct consequence of the legislative arrangement was that colleges were still often perceived as mere extensions of the secondary schools. But public and college pressure upon government to place colleges under their own legislation was building. The prime catalyst for a new era in college education was the tabling of the Colleges and Provincial Institutes Act[25] in September 1977. The structural changes which were ushered in were many, but a major one was the distinction made between colleges—which were to retain a local or regional orientation, and the institutes—which were to serve province-wide needs in more narrowly defined programme areas. The latter were the Pacific Vocational Institute, Marine Training Institute, Emily Carr College of Art and Design, Justice Institute, B.C.

Institute of Technology, and Open Learning Institute. Both colleges and institutes were given corporate status under the legislation, which effectively removed any direct legal relationship with school boards. Even more significant was the removal of local taxation as a source of college funding. A trend from colleges with a local or regional orientation to a system of provincial colleges was underway.

The act also provided for the creation of three intermediary councils between the minister and the colleges and institutes to co-ordinate programme development and the distribution of funds to these institutions. Further systematizing was the objective, and the result was to reduce the autonomy of the governing bodies of the institutions, now called boards, as well as to relieve the minister and his officials of some difficult political decision-making. Other controversial sections of the act, notably those pertaining to labour relations, were left unproclaimed from the start.

The period from 1977 to 1983 witnessed a consistent pattern of increasing provincial responsibility for the colleges. Both the spirit and the reality of community involvement which had characterized the early years of the colleges slowly faded; and provincial government priorities for the colleges took precedence over the local and regional interests.

By the 1980's, as the operating and capital demands of the college and institute system continued to increase while the province's financial condition deteriorated, British Columbia colleges experienced the introduction of formal system strategic planning. In 1982, a document was circulated by the Ministry of Education which prescribed a well-defined future for a "a system."[26] The blueprint identified eight goal areas as bases for the planning process (governance; comprehensiveness; quality, relevance and cost effectiveness; manpower development; lifelong education; accessibility; social development; and accountability), supplemented by over thirty specific objectives. While this planning document reiterated a commitment to many of the qualities which had characterized the institutions to that point, it also was explicit that the interests and priorities of government—such as financial restraint, avoidance of programme duplication, and high levels of accountability—were to be basic assumptions upon which the colleges would develop their five-year plans.

The prime thrust of the new initiative was further centralization. Occupational training was again elevated to a primary goal for the system. Anxiety within the colleges and institutes grew as the Ministry of Education took a much more active role in college development, despite ministry assurances that system planning was to be a joint enterprise with these institutions. The planning document included a mission statement which expressed in succinct fashion a future direction for colleges and institutes as a system:

The Mission of the College and Institute System of the Province of British

Columbia is to provide educational opportunities to assist adults to meet continuing and changing individual, economic, and societal needs. These opportunities will be provided recognizing the aspirations of individuals, the present and future requirements of Provincial and Canadian society for economic development, priorities of government, and the structure of the educational system of the Province as defined through legislation.[27]

The next step in the development of an integrated college and institute system occurred in the summer of 1983. Following its re-election, the government introduced amendments to college and institute legislation. School board representation on the college boards was eliminated, leaving only provincial government appointees. The three provincial councils were discontinued with co-ordination of programming and funding reverting to the Ministry of Education. Coupled with the restraint programme of government which affected all publicly supported institutions and agencies, the overall impact of the new legislation was dramatic.

The 1983 governmental legislative program is seen by some as the last nail in the coffin. All governors are to be appointed by Order in Council; tight restrictions are to be placed on collective bargaining which is still done at an institutional level in B.C. colleges; the government has empowered itself to regulate the working conditions and compensation of management personnel; the educational and financial planning of all colleges must by approved by the Ministry of Education; formula funding is to be introduced by 1984-85, threatening in particular the viability of the colleges in the outlying regions of the province—the very institutions for which the original legislation had been adopted.[28]

The record of non-university, post-secondary education in British Columbia has been impressive. The number of institutions and the diversity reflected in their programmes are testimony to a commitment to broad educational opportunity for adults. In fact, British Columbia has been in the forefront of innovative Canadian post-secondary education. For example, the Open Learning Institute, whose creation was accompanied by some skepticism, has incorporated a unique distance education model offering programmes ranging from adult basic education to university degrees. The Justice Institute has been an exciting concept in the field of public safety and security. Several research projects strongly support the claim that colleges indeed serve diverse needs in their regions and attract students of great number and variety.[29] Nevertheless, many people concerned about college education in British Columbia see restraint, centralization, system planning, and ministry influence as the death knell of their institutions. Less pessimistic observers see reorganization of the post-secondary system as both necessary and urgent, with a new interplay of forces in the immediate future.

There are many college people in British Columbia who are willing to struggle for retention of local or regional control. That control is likely to produce, in the years ahead, a new relationship between the colleges and the provincial government which will see the colleges become a co-operative network of post-secondary institutions balancing the legitimate needs for some rationalization on a provincial basis and the equally legitimate need for regional and local responsiveness on the part of individual colleges.

Ontario

In little more than fifteen years, Ontario has been able to develop a coherent system of twenty-two colleges of applied arts and technology which operate from ninety campuses and offer programmes to more than 100,000 full-time and over half a million part-time students.[30] Indeed, it has become a system with stability and a widely recognized sense of purpose which contributes to its positive profile in the educational and economic structures of the province.

Stability is not a quality shared by many college systems in Canada but there are several reasons why Ontario is an exception. The extended term of office of the Progressive Conservative government, with its tempering of economic planning with political pragmatism, provided a consistency in leadership of and in support for the colleges; essentially the same political ideology prevailed throughout the periods of conception and early development of the college system: the colleges were established as essential ingredients in the economic plan of the province and this priority of role has never wavered. While the more imprecise notions of broader accessibility and democratization of educational opportunity, characteristic of some other provinces, have always been recognized in Ontario, they have been subsidiary to a more pragmatic economic objective. Furthermore, it should not go unobserved that the recently retired premier has been an important factor in the success of the colleges: as Minister of Education, William Davis provided leadership for the development of the Ontario college concept and articulated the interpretation of that concept which was translated into reality. The idea of the college of applied arts and technology, while unique to Canada at the time, was consistent with the Davis view of the purpose of the non-university, post-secondary sector. His subsequent role as premier must be associated with the accomplishments of these institutions since their early days.

From the beginning, the general mandate of the colleges was clear: the preparation of individuals to enter the workforce, with training of both quality and relevance, to contribute to the economic progress of the province. In the highly task-oriented Ontario society, the original mandate has been re-emphasized and strengthened. During the process, a distinctive identity for colleges, so difficult to establish in many other provinces, has been established with clarity and accepted by government, the educational community, and society at large. It is, for example, important to note the relationship which exists between the colleges and the university sector. The latter represents a powerful force in Ontario, but universities assume a role which is neither confused with nor superior to the colleges. The exclusion of a formal "transfer" arrangement between the two sectors has contributed to a certain "parity of esteem"[31] in which the college sector is not placed in a subservient role to the university interests. While it would be an overstatement to imply that questions of institutional status are absent from Ontario post-secondary education, the focus is more upon differentiation rather than confusion of roles of different institutions.

The question of status with respect to the colleges arose in the report of the Commission on Post-Secondary Education in Ontario which was published in 1972. Although there were few recommendations which were specifically addressed to the college system, one was universally rejected. The commission suggested that individual colleges should have the authority to issue "distinctive" bachelors degrees in technologies. Apparently the commissioners were of the opinion that, in a credential conscious society, the colleges would ensure equality with the universities by participating in the awarding of degrees. The issue was addressed in an article by Campbell in which "parity of esteem" played a major role.[32] Since that period, however, the issue of status seems to have been set aside.

Further evidence of the continuing role of the colleges in the province's economic plan is to be found by noting the initiatives which the provincial government has taken in recent years to stimulate occupational preparation. Programmes such as BILD (Board of Industrial Leadership and Development), G.I.T. (General Industrial Training), TIBI (Training in Business and Industry) and the activities of local Community Industrial Training Committees have been funded provincially. Concurrently, the federal government's involvement through the National Training Act, the Skills Growth Fund, and similar initiatives has added a further financial stimulus. The end result has been a massive injection of additional, albeit designated, funding into the college system. Action of this kind, apart from the economic implication, reflects a strong expression of confidence in the CAATs.

The criterion of graduate job placement, as a yardstick for the success of the colleges, is applied with vigour in the Ontario college system and is accorded consistent prominence. While it is debatable whether job placement is better or worse than in the university sector,[33] the colleges have clarified their major function and can document its attainment. In an environment where jobs are of critical value, the public image of the college has remained very positive.

The evolution of the CAAT, however, has not been entirely without disruption or dissent. In the early years, the impact of innovation coupled with a climate of economic buoyancy was evident. Between 1967 and 1972, a combination of administrative freedom and easy access to funding allowed relatively ad hoc management at both the provincial and institutional level. Growth was the order of that time—in student enrolments, programmes, personnel, and acquisition of massive capital assets. Federal financial support supplemented by provincial initiatives produced an instant "system." By 1972, however, a trend towards less spontaneous development was underway and this pattern has continued. Several factors have contributed to the perceived need for more formalized structure. In 1972, the Colleges Collective Bargaining Act came into force and had immediate implications for management practices at the institutional level.[34] One result of that act is that labour relations had been relatively free of acrimony until 1984, but it did limit the independence of institutions.

As well, consequences of unchecked growth became more evident and more numerous over time. The tendency for students to transfer between institutions, with the inevitable problem of portability of credit, prompted concern that programme requirements in different institutions be more standardized so that employers could be assured of the equivalence of credentials of graduates of the same programmes in different colleges. More recently, an increasing employer demand for more sophisticated training in technology-related occupations and the financial consequences of providing such training have created pressure for rationalization of programme distribution among institutions. As a result, colleges have now developed specialized programme areas as an antidote to expensive duplication. In continuing education, Ontario has not escaped the jurisdictional disputes among school boards, universities, and community agencies over responsibility for programmes which colleges have initiated and the search for coherence in the organization of continuing education has prompted a more deliberate, system-wide approach for post-secondary problem resolution.[35] All these factors have contributed to an increased need for more systematic planning and centralized decision-making, which in turn have limited the independence of the the individual institutions within the system. Recently, further rationalization has been sought by government by placing adult basic education within the scope and responsibility of the school boards rather than the colleges, a clear break from the original span of responsibility of the college.

Three other developments have also contributed to system rationalization. After considerable study and refinement, the college system has developed a method of funding colleges which is calculated to ensure equity among these institutions but also produce adequate planning at various levels in the system. The mechanism, in reality an allocation formula applied to the total provincial grant for colleges, takes into consideration several institutional factors but puts a particular premium on programme and enrolment growth. The formula, as a result, places the individual institutions in the position of promoting their own growth in relation to the system if they are to retain their share of provincial grants. Formula funding in Ontario has been an important development in the more systematic planning of college education in Ontario. The second development has been the changing role of the federal government in influencing programme development. In most Ontario colleges the federal contribution to college funding has been so substantial as to shape, indirectly, the programme offerings of these institutions. To reduce this influence and to make Ontario colleges less susceptible to changes in federal government policy and practice, greater provincial intervention in dealings with federal government authorities has been seen as necessary.The third factor has been the development of a centralized data bank (Ontario College Information System). This step has meant that planning and decision-making have been based upon a provincially developed body of information rather than upon individual institutional data. The general expectation in Ontario colleges is that, with increased financial restraint throughout the 1980's and no abating of the public demand for greater accountability for the expenditure of public funds, further rationalization and centralized decision-making is likely.

Centralization of decision-making for Ontario colleges has not, however, been ham-handed; it has involved an imaginative process for the delegation and dispersal of power at a central level which still leaves substantial autonomy for individual institutions. The pre-decisional consultative process involves a delicate relationship among three central bodies—the Ministry of Colleges and Universities, the Council of Regents of the Ontario Colleges, and a voluntary organization, formed collectively by the colleges themselves, known as the Association of Colleges of Applied Arts and Technology of Ontario. The interaction of these influences merits examination.

For their first decade, the colleges were grouped with the universities as the responsibility of a Minister of Education and then a Minister of Colleges and Universities. Despite some early concern that the college sector would be dominated by the interests of the higher profile universities, the fears proved generally groundless because colleges quickly established their own identity and power and were treated by government with equity. In 1979, however, the Ministry of Colleges and Universities was combined administratively with the Ministry of Education with one minister for both ministries, and one deputy minister with an assistant for the college sector. The minister, the assistant deputy minister, and his ministry colleagues are an obvious influence on college developments.

The Council of Regents, however, as an intermediary advisory body composed of fifteen lay appointees of the government, complements or counterbalances the potential influence of the ministry on the colleges. The council retains responsibility for making recommendations on such matters as new programme approvals, establishment of new campuses, and labour relations and has the unique task of recommending new appointees for institutional boards. The role of the council as a quasi-independent agency has become generally regarded as effective, even though the final, formal authority on all policy matters rests with the minister.

The third system-wide influence is a provincial organization made up of representatives of the Boards of Governors and the Committee of Presidents of the institutions themselves called the Association of Colleges of Applied Arts and Technology of Ontario (ACAATO). ACAATO addresses a wide range of matters of concern to the college sector and maintains broad participation with a comprehensive committee structure. The association combines a low-key lobby function with a professional approach to college issues and has acquired by its style of operation an important role in the planning process at a provincial level. It also chooses to make policy recommendations to the minister on matters which it considers appropriate.

These three forces collectively create a climate of dynamic tension in the resolution of college-related issues and provide for diffusion of power within the system, an arrangement seen to be beneficial to the success of the system, the institutions, and their public image.

It is of more than passing importance to note that boards of governors of Ontario colleges tend to consist of individuals with a regional identification and a high level of responsibility for the progress of their own institutions. There are no faculty, staff, or student representatives on the college boards as a consequence of the view that direct involvement of faculty and students on a policy-making body leads to problems of conflict of interest. Students and faculty are both involved, however, in internal advisory committees.

Despite the indisputable success story of Ontario's colleges, there is no lack of further issues to address. While the employment-oriented curriculum has documented its value, the place of general education as a curriculum component remains under debate. Although the original statement of college mission included specific reference to general education and while the Council of Regents decreed that one-third of the curriculum in any programme should be allocated to this aspect of learning, the reality has not conformed to the ideal. In 1980 a report on general education noted that: "There is no common working definition of general education throughout the college system and there is confusion and disparity within individual colleges about the definition and administration of general education."[36]

The report concluded that fourteen of nineteen responding colleges were offering less than the one-third of the curriculum which had been specified for general education. Indeed, studies such as those by Klemp[37] and reports from employers have made reference to the need for graduates to have cognitive and interpersonal skills as essential attributes for success in the rapidly changing workplace of the 1980's.[38] A resurgence of support for more careful consideration of the importance of general education within employment-related programming has become evident in Ontario colleges.

In summary, the Ontario college system has enjoyed considerable success: growth; documented record of job preparation and placement; and credibility with government, the business community, and society at large. The colleges have remained true to their original mission and continue to represent a viable alternative to the universities. The quality of their programming has remained high, and internal problems have been manageable. A sensitive provincial governance and consultative structure have been developed to avert concentration of power within an increasing government bureaucracy. The colleges of Ontario display justifiable confidence in their future.[39]

Quebec

The years which have elapsed since the creation of the college system in Quebec have been characterized by political turmoil, economic uncertainty, and a high degree of volatility among that province's social institutions. All of these conditions have had a marked impact upon the colleges. Conceived in a period of political ferment and planned as instruments of social reform, the CEGEP were to play a highly visible role in the turbulence experienced in that province in the 1970's and early 1980's. "The conception was a global one—at once philosophical and political—of life within society."[40] It is now possible to assess the impact of the colleges and, in the process, to weigh the success to date of a unique educational experiment in post-secondary education and social reform.

In 1967, there were three major goals established for the new colleges.[41] It seems appropriate to take each of these goals in turn and comment upon the extent to which they have been realized. The first, democratization and accessibility to post-secondary education, may be partly measured in statistical terms. Within the francophone sector the enrolment has increased from 58,000 in 1966, all in private colleges, to over 115,000 in thirty-eight colleges in the public CEGEP sector alone. The comparable figures from the anglophone colleges are 8,800 and 23,000. Enrolment in private colleges is now approximately 15,000. Furthermore, the demographic picture shows major increases in the percentage of females (22 per cent in 1967 to 53 per cent in 1982) and in the participation rates of the seventeen to twenty-one age group.[42] In a province where participation in post-secondary education was not long ago a privilege for the few, Quebec now reports one of the highest rates of all Canadian provinces. This increase is particularly significant in the francophone sector and reflects one of the major goals of the Quiet Revolution, to correct the wide divergence in educational opportunity which had existed between the two linguistic groups.

For the second goal, reorganization and standardization of the post-secondary sector, the record is equally impressive. The widely diverse collection of over 250 post-secondary institutions has been replaced by forty-six public colleges which form a coherent system with a recognized level of commonality in admissions, curriculum, requirements for certification, and governance. A number of private colleges which, for a number of reasons, elected to remain in the private sector have also developed a degree of standardization.

The CEGEP slowly established an identity of their own. They are recognized as a separate level of education between the secondary schools and the universities, clearly distinct from both. Articulation among the three levels of education, in a structure unique to Quebec, has been encouraged through both government regulation and institutional initiative. For the anglophone population, the CEGEP as a pre-university institution had been initially received with little enthusiasm; but over time, partly as a consequence of maturity and partly on the record of achievement, the English-speaking population has more than accepted the CEGEP as an integral and effective part of the Quebec educational apparatus.

The high level of standardization so quickly established in the Quebec colleges was a consequence of centralized ministerial initiative of far greater magnitude than that usually found in other provinces. Many matters, including the academic structure (régime pédagogique) of the CEGEP, have been decided by government regulation, which has been accommodated somewhat differently in the francophone and anglophone colleges. On the other hand, a balance between the two principles of "provincial system" and "institutional autonomy" has been sought through several devices, including the democratization of college boards, with their wide representation of faculty, staff, students, parents, administration, and the external community.

The third goal established in 1967 was the diversification of programmes and comprehensive schooling. In the pursuit of this goal, the record has also been noteworthy. The great gulf which so often exists elsewhere between academic and technical education has been narrowed through the mix of students and programmes within the CEGEP. The provincial curriculum, with its prescribed common core of courses for all students with different fields of specialization and concentration, has been an effective tool to achieve this goal, particularly in the CEGEP, which have made efforts to bring students and faculty from different programmes into close association, despite their diversity of interests. There has been an interesting difference between students of the two language and cultural groups in their choice of programmes. The francophone colleges have been largely successful in bringing about a balance in enrolment between the pre-university and the professional (or career-technical) streams, but anglophone students have persisted in demonstrating a clear preference for pre-university studies. The original expectation that employment-related training should be predominant in all public colleges, in the light of economic realities, has not yet materialized.

Nonetheless, the concepts that general education is desirable for all students, that a comprehensive rather than more specialized curriculum is preferable, and that programme diversity within a single institution is manageable, all seem to have become institutionalized more successfully than in other provinces despite the fact that the CEGEP have not chosen to provide as complete a spectrum of educational offerings as found in some other provincial college systems. Vocational and trades training are under other jurisdictions, as are the wide assortment of credit-free, recreational, and cultural courses found in colleges in other provinces. Education for adults in Quebec colleges is largely an evening and part-time activity, usually an extension of the credit course offerings available during the day for full-time students. While it may appear that the development of the CEGEP has been a fifteen-year saga of success, there are issues still to be addressed.

The early years of operation were characterized by a spirit of idealism, of innovation, and of belief in a great educational experiment in a period of relative economic buoyancy. Administrators were usually inexperienced; the faculty young, aggressive, and idealistic; the students, many of whom were the first in their families to continue their education beyond secondary school, often lacked the maturity to handle a new milieu. The old classical colleges and specialized institutions frequently became parts of the new CEGEP, but in practice they brought their own traditions in curriculum, teaching methods, and institutional goals, and these were not easily set aside within these new colleges. As well, the provincial political climate was volatile, and clashes between college faculty members and college management formed part of the larger industrial turmoil of the entire public sector. College boards, made up of disparate, inexperienced groups of individuals, faced complex management problems in an environment they little understood. The bedlam which characterized the first ten years of the CEGEP certainly required idealism, innovation, and belief that a great educational experiment was in progress.

A more orderly existence for the new college system came, however, with time and experience, and recent years have shown much greater stability. The price for that stability has been a loss of idealism and the willingness to experiment in a whole variety of ways in which the CEGEP had formerly been adventuresome. The CEGEP have gained maturity, but, in the view of many observers, they have also grown old too quickly.

A number of reasons for the apparent inability of the system to retain much of its daring and vitality can be cited, but two have been particularly important. One problem has unquestionably been of a financial nature. Quebec has not escaped economic downturn; in fact, it has been a major victim, and public education generally has lost much of its privileged status. The CEGEP have faced budgetary restraint as much as any sector of public education with the result that with limited budgets assigned to instruction, there has been little flexibility for colleges to explore new programmes, new techniques, or innovative approaches—particulary since instructional budgets for institutions determined at a provincial level have severely hampered institutional desires to continue with creative problem-solving.

The second reason for the CEGEP transition to more conservative operation has been the pervasive impact of collective agreements which have discouraged institutional variation. With province-wide collective agreements, colleges have taken on a provincial rather than community orientation; college education, in a great many respects, has become standardized. At one level, course content is determined for all CEGEP by provincial bodies; at another level, evaluation—of faculty, of institutions and of the system itself—has been seriously hampered by restrictions contained in provincial collective agreements.

As is the case with other provincial systems, the faculty in the CEGEP no longer have much mobility. With no growth in the system, there has been limited personnel turnover, and a procedure by which faculty are assigned to other colleges through a centralized pool limits the entry of new blood into the system. In addition, growth in the student population within the Quebec colleges has been slow if steady. The vast majority of regular students are young (sixteen to nineteen), and so the CEGEP have not benefited from an infusion of part-time adult students, which so often characterized colleges in other provinces. The priority given to programmes designed for full-time students and the fact that programme content and structure have been prescribed at a provincial level have both contributed to a narrower student profile than in provinces with more comprehensive curricula.

The most significant changes affecting the CEGEP occurred as a result of a White Paper published in 1978. The government elected in 1976 was ready to review the status of the colleges in the light of its own priorities. The White Paper reaffirmed the original goals of the system noting that:

> Creation of the Quebec public colleges signalled a major pedagogical innovation, a sort of educational "fourth dimension." We believe that this original experiment, if it can get its second wind with the same fervour that marked its first years, carries our future on its back.[43]

One emphasis of the White Paper was that the colleges, despite a variety of problems, were "indisputable successes." However, it was also seen necessary to restate many of the values which the system had embodied and to propose refinements which would bring such values into better focus. In particular, the White Paper noted that the goal of "equality of opportunity" had not been fully attained and that several groups—adults, handicapped, the aged, and those from lower socio-economic levels—were under-represented in the CEGEP.

Despite reservations which had been expressed about the presence of teachers, administrators and students on the boards of governors, the report stated:

> The government does not agree. In an increasingly pluralistic society, participation in the administration of public services is most assuredly a precarious avenue to follow, but it is essential nonetheless. It is the only approach reconcilable with the government's concept of democracy and the decentralization that it intends to establish in the administration of public services. It is likewise the only way to avoid the disadvantages of technocracy and create collectively local institutions that correspond more and more to the wishes of the people.[44]

The actions which followed extended representation on the CEGEP boards to ensure that the majority of board members would come from within the college. Governance was also amended by the creation of an intermediary body between the colleges and the government. This body, the Conseil des Collèges, while advisory, would devote itself to a continuous study of the needs of the system, review objectives, and engage in evaluation activities. Finally, the government decided to increase access for part-time students by dropping all tuition fees and by encouraging colleges to establish more campuses.

The Conseil des Collèges has since produced a number of papers addressed to contentious issues within the system. Of particular note is a report by Robert Isabelle in 1982 entitled "Quebec Colleges: Provincial Colleges or Autonomous Institutions?"[45] Isabelle outlined the events which led to a "distortion" of the original balance of power between the ministry, which was to "regulate only essential matters necessary for the unity and coherence of the college system," and the individual institutions. Gradually, Isabelle argued, the Ministry of Education had assumed powers in financial, material, and labour relations matters to the extent that the concept of partnership between ministry and colleges in the management process, so explicit in the original CEGEP plan, had been lost. In Isabelle's view "three factors came to paralyze local autonomy significantly: the intervention and the insensitivity of the government, the constraints of collective agreements, and the effects of budgetary constraint."[46]

The Isabelle paper concluded with a discussion of the conditions necessary to return to the original vision of balance of authority and restoration of institutional autonomy. A redefinition of the nature of regulation by the Ministry of Education, some form of block funding, simplified collective agreements, new consultative structures, and a reduction in ministerial control of colleges' financial and administrative affairs were all suggested as courses of action to meet this goal. With respect to governance, Isabelle argued for a reduction in size of college boards and for majority governing board representation from the community served by the college. The Conseil des Collèges was seen as an instrument that could help bring about a return to greater institutional autonomy.

There is little doubt that the system of colleges established in Quebec is an intriguing and complex exercise in post-secondary educational innovation.[47] On the basis of the goals which were originally established, the colleges have been a success. The massive increase in participation through extended access for francophone Quebecers, the melding of academic and technical education within integrated institutions, and the impact of the colleges upon the social and economic life of the province are all testimony to the imagination and perseverance of educational planners at several levels. But Quebec college educators and planners see that they have far more to do than maintain the status quo. Several matters deserve re-evaluation. As examples, the powers of widely representative boards are minimal under rigid provincial budgetary control; the very detailed province-wide collective agreements for college employees are often tempered by local agreements whose status is unclear; the concept of open access for high school graduates is often limited by constraints of space; community involvement in college planning is not significant; the large proportion of internal representatives on college boards has limited efficiency in management, maintained the vexing issue of conflict of interest, and caused confusion about the responsibility of board representatives to their individual constituencies. Above all, the issues of autonomy and control remain unsolved. Common opinion within Quebec colleges is that they are now "branch plants of a central system" and that they are "run by the cahiers (provincial curriculum guides) and collective agreements." The early enthusiasm has been replaced by discouragement, if not outright cynicism, by many people in the CEGEP.

Yet, the CEGEP are still evolving. In February 1984, the provincial government took another step to regenerate the system by adopting new regulations, after broad consultation throughout the province calculated to give focus to the planning of college life for the next five- to ten-year period. The regulations confirm Quebec's commitment to expanding accessibility to post-secondary education and propose rationalization of programme distribution among the colleges as well as greater discretion to individual CEGEP to develop local programmes of distinctive value to their own communities. As well, the recent addition of centres of specialization at several of the CEGEP provides the potential for institutional revitalization. Of particular interest is a new CEGEP emphasis on the development of retraining programmes, an aspect of college activity in which Quebec colleges have not been prominent to date.[48] Finally, the transfer of provincial responsibility for CEGEP from a Minister of Education to a Minister for Higher Education, Science, and Technology in December 1984 could imply new directions and priorities for these institutions.

Despite recurring and debilitating conflicts over labour relations, renewal is still a very real possibility in Quebec college education.

Prince Edward Island

Holland College has remained Prince Edward Island's only college—in fact, the island's only post-secondary institution other than the university. Although it does not face many of the problems which commonly beset systems in other provinces, Holland College has its own challenges and has both inherited and developed a number of unique, noteworthy characteristics.

Holland College has really become the "College of Prince Edward Island." It offers its programmes on nine different campuses located primarily in Charlottetown and Summerside. Many of the campuses provide specialized programme units including Marine Technology, Vocational and Visual Arts, and Police Training. Several factors, including local needs, funding sources, and provincial policies regarding decentralization, contribute to the development of a multi-campus college despite the small population of the province. Holland College began with an emphasis upon applied arts and technology, but a significant change occurred in 1976 when the college absorbed the Provincial Vocational Centres and with them a number of trade and apprenticeship programmes for both adult and secondary school students in vocational training programmes. In this last respect Holland is unique within Canada; it has integrated half-time training for students for occupational streams in grades eleven and twelve with similar training for adults. In 1977, legislation was amended to reflect the broader mandate of the college with the addition of the following:

> The object of the college is to provide a broad range of educational opportunity particularly in the fields of applied arts and technology, vocational training and adult education.[49]

As is often the case, the policy decision to add vocational training to the college's activities had mixed consequences. The college certainly became more comprehensive in its curriculum, provided a more rationalized use of physical and human resources, and offered a stimulus for high school students with vocational interests and aptitudes who had been preciously undervalued in the more traditional academic high school environment. But the addition also brought a new population of instructors to the college who had difficult adjustments to make in the process of becoming integrated into the original Holland College faculty. The classic gulf between academic-technical and vocational traditions has not yet been fully bridged.

The form of financial support to Holland College is also unique in Canada. The college budget is drawn from three primary sources. For the technology curriculum, a grant is received through the Maritime Provinces Higher Education Commission (MPHEC, an interprovincial body which deals primarily with university budgets for Nova Scotia, New Brunswick, and Prince Edward Island). An advantage of this mechanism is its potential for rationalized planning of university-college articulation in these programme areas. All funds for all vocational courses have been provided by the provincial Department of Education since the college assumed responsibilities for vocational training. The third source of funding is the purchase of training places in selected programmes by the federal Department of Employment and Immigration, and these funds are directed to the college by the provincial Ministry of Labour. The college's Board of Governors has freedom to allocate only those funds received from the MPHEC and the Department of Education, but the third—federal—source constitutes as much as one-third of the total funding of the college. A smaller but important fourth funding source is the three Maritime Ministries of Justice which collectively support Holland's Police Academy, which services all three provinces. The total impact is that Holland College must operate on a day-by-day basis as a single institution but maintain clear lines of distinction among its funding sources.

A consequence of the incorporation of vocational training into the college curriculum has been more complex labour relations. The original group of applied arts and technology instructors bargain as a faculty association. The vocational personnel and support staff, however, are organized within the Public Service Association. Faculty association bargaining is not governed by the labour code, while bargaining for the other groups is. Although this arrangement has not yet posed problems in practice, there is a concern that genuine difficulties could arise particularly in the context of financial restraint requiring staff reductions. The majority of the membership of both bargaining groups seems content with separate bargaining units and conditions, in part because of differing attitudes towards the teaching task and working conditions.

The composition of the college's Board of Governors also merits mention. Two faculty members, one from each bargaining unit, and two students serve on the board. Other members are selected from specific groups: three from the Department of Education, three from the business community, and four named by government, of whom two are nominated by the board. In addition, the presidents of both the college and the university are ex-officio members. Despite the size and the mix of representation, the board has been able to function effectively, particularly because it has maintained clear role definition with the board limiting itself to policy development and reinforcing the management responsibility of the president.

Of special interest is the fact that Holland College has maintained the curriculum and instructional model it instituted in its early days in which course content is organized into modules which are completed by students on an individual basis and for which a key component is the DACUM (Designing a Curriculum) chart, which specifies the content of each learning unit. Evaluation of student performance is determined by the competencies acquired by the students, not by the length of time the students have been in courses. The programme format, STEP (Self Teaching and Evaluation Plan), has been retained and has been claimed to be quite successful.[50]

While there is wide support for, and a strong commitment at the administrative level to STEP at Holland College, there are also reservations from some faculty members and students. The technique requires a substantial adjustment for students from their previous experience and practice, and some students understandably have difficulty accepting responsibility for their own learning. To compensate for these students, some faculty members adjust the methodology, particularly in the early stages of a programme, but, in general, Holland's adoption of the unconventional STEP methodology has been enthusiastically supported. In fact, Holland's commitment to this methodology is so strong that an impartial evaluation of its effectiveness is probably difficult. Some thought has been given to exploring the use of other methodologies in programme areas where numbers warrant.

Holland College is also well placed to lead Canadian colleges in developing better liaison and articulation with the university sector, even though co-ordination of college and university sector activity has to date been minimal. Should such liaison be pursued, the place of general education within the college curriculum could be a high priority issue for mutual consideration.

In summary, Prince Edward Island's "system" of community colleges demonstrates that smallness is not an obstacle to innovation. Programme development and delivery have received high priority institutional attention, and the multi-campus arrangement has proved effective on several counts. The college has preserved a high degree of autonomy, a product of continuing confidence from government and effective communication among the three major influential bodies: the MPHEC, The Department of Education, and the Board of Governors of the college. Above all, Holland College has remained faithful to one of the most pragmatic and important roles of a community college: it recognizes and fulfils its role as a major contributor to the economic and social progress of the whole province.

Manitoba

Since the creation of the three Manitoba community colleges in 1969, growth and development have been steady but modest by comparison with other provincial systems. As noted earlier, the change of name from Manitoba Institute of Technology—Manitoba Institute of Applied Arts to Red River Community College was intended to bring a different emphasis to the institution, a recognition of community interest, and a broader curricular base. Similar expectations applied to the two smaller colleges, Assiniboine (Brandon) and Keewatin (The Pas). The anticipated evolution which occurred between 1970 and 1983 was, however, constrained by a number of factors, particularly the continuing tensions between the institutions and the provincial government.

The colleges in Manitoba have been in all important respects branches of the government or local post-secondary arms of the Ministry of Education; and their major function has been the preparation of graduates to enter the Manitoba workforce. With some exceptions, college programmes have fallen into the "vocational-occupational-technological" categories, with emphasis on training. The institutional climates have reflected this purpose.

The colleges have not had their own boards of governors and the chief executive officers, titled directors, have recently been responsible directly to the Assistant Deputy Minister of Education, Post-Secondary, Adult and Continuing Education Division.[51] This form of organization and these relationships imply a bureaucratic rather than traditional educational model and tends to reinforce the "branch plants of government" view of the colleges. Greater institutional autonomy, as exemplified by the establishment of college governing boards with powers to shape the character of these institutions, has been under consideration for some time, in part, because Manitoba has been one of only three Canadian provinces without governing boards for colleges. However, it would be inaccurate to claim that there is anything close to unanimity in Manitoba about the virtues of greater institutional independence. Over the years the centralized structure in Manitoba has encouraged high reliance on government to make difficult decisions and to alleviate the pressure of accountability on individual institutions. The Manitoba college system has been efficient and cost effective, if limited in curriculum scope, and the economies generated by the largest college have been used to offset costs of the necessarily less efficient but equally important smaller colleges.

Still, the ability of the colleges to respond to a greater variety of community needs, to become more innovative in programme delivery and curriculum planning, and, above all, to exercise their own budgetary management have been perceived as advantages which could flow from greater institutional independence from government. It may be the issue of institutional identity which will determine whether Manitoba colleges gain greater autonomy. Despite their names, the colleges have not been seen as forming a separate level or kind of education distinct from vocational schools or universities. Even though the college curricula have expanded from exclusively technological programmes to include socially oriented programmes such as child care and employment opportunities for women, as well as providing a resource centre for handicapped students, these changes have generally been identified with government action rather than institutional initiative.

Nor is there any specific legislation in Manitoba applicable exclusively to the colleges. This further reinforces the direct connection between government and the institutions. As well, college faculty are civil servants and members of the Manitoba Government Employees Association.[52] In the recent period of financial restraint by both the federal and provincial governments, several long-established programmes in the colleges were classified as redundant. The instructors in the programmes were understandably concerned, and a procedure for their retraining was developed between the government and the union, something that probably would have been impossible had these instructors been college rather than government employees.

As is the case in other provinces, the role of the federal government in the initiation and funding of specific training programmes has had a major impact upon Manitoba's post-secondary institutions. As federal priorities have changed, as established programmes are no longer funded, and as long term financial commitments are not made, instability within the system has increased, planning has become a complex and often frustrating enterprise, and development of the institutions has depended upon sensitive and creative negotiations between the two levels of government.

Manitoba has nevertheless made an impressive effort to increase accessibility to post-secondary education of different kinds, particularly for the traditionally disadvantaged native population. A number of programmes with designated funding allocations have been developed in both the colleges and universities. Nursing, social work, and similar programmes have enrolled over 450 students, 80 per cent of whom have been native people, a major feat particularly in times of budgetary retrenchment.

By comparison with other provinces, the non-university post-secondary sector in Manitoba is not large. Three colleges, of which only one enrols more than 1000 students, constitute quite a limited system by contemporary standards. And it is unlikely that additional institutions will be built in the foreseeable future. Alternatives which would increase access, such as forms of distance education and the establishment of satellite campuses of colleges in leased facilities, may be effective ways of expanding accessibility to post-secondary education even in difficult times.

Manitoba may be at another turning point in its development of the college sector. New initiatives to improve the quality of education while enhancing system productivity seem likely to inject new energy into the system. The Manitoba Community College System Goals Study in 1983 may be of particular influence in the immediate future. This study included a survey completed by a number of constituencies and revealed a high level of agreement about the primary goals of the colleges. Job training and improved accessibility were seen as high priority goals; institutional autonomy was consistently found at the lower end of the priorities. As this stage of development, Manitoba's colleges are not community colleges within the general definition of the term. Whether they will be in the future will depend upon many factors: their role as interpreted by government, the priorities set by their own management, and the perception of them held by Manitoba society.

Saskatchewan

Saskatchewan post-secondary education entered a period of stabilization following the growth years to 1972. The period of consolidation has not, however, been without change and reorganization, partly owing to change of government policy and partly through reassessment of the effectiveness of the educational system. The public non-university sector in Saskatchewan has included both community colleges and technical institutes, and while there is a considerable interrelationship between the two, there have been independent developments in each sub-system which have influenced the reshaping of post-secondary education in this province.

Within the institute sector, enrolment doubled from 10,300 to 21,000 between 1972 and 1982. The largest of the three institutes, located in Saskatoon, had been renamed the Kelsey Institute of Applied Arts and Sciences, largely to distinguish it from the Saskatchewan Technical Institute in Moose Jaw. Kelsey developed a number of new programmes, including skills extension courses offered throughout the province and a variety of extended day training programmes in co-operation with the federal Department of Employment and Immigration. As the employment needs of the province diversified, the institutes developed new programmes to supply the necessary skilled manpower.

The long-planned institute for the Regina region came into reality in 1972 with the opening of Wascana Institute of Applied Arts and Sciences. Wascana's programming first concentrated on the health sciences and related technologies in addition to general occupational programmes. Nursing education had been removed from the eleven hospital schools throughout the province in the late 1960's and was henceforth to be offered only by the institutes and the University of Saskatchewan. Wascana Institute also developed new agriculture programmes in co-operation with the community colleges in various locations throughout the province. In addition, it undertook new initiatives in non-sequential student entry and part-time study, both of which contributed to an increasing capacity to accommodate more students.

A significant government policy decision in 1976 resulted in the removal of adult basic education, general upgrading, pre-trades training, and English as a Second Language programmes from the institutes and their later relocation to the community colleges; this action coincidentally relocated a large number of instructors and students from rural settings to the urban colleges. Another consequence of this decision was a more comprehensive college curriculum and an accompanying greater specialization of programmes within the institute sector.

New economic growth in Saskatchewan during the 1970's, particularly in the energy and natural resource areas, stimulated an unprecedented demand for skilled labour. This demand went well beyond the capacity of the institutes and their outreach programmes. The government response was to commission a task force report, Voc-Tech 90,[53] which was to offer advice on future directions for technical and vocational education in the province. The report summarized the concerns of a wide range of interests including business, industry, and education, and noted the need for immediate and decisive action to meet the increased demand for skilled labour. Given the limited capacity of the system, the task force saw the solution to be in the improvement of programme delivery and recommended a modular design for packaging courses so that they could be utilized more efficiently. Further emphasis was placed upon the role of the colleges as vehicles to "service programs in smaller communities," a task that could be made easier with modular and competency-based programming. The task force also considered it essential that all resources available for training be mobilized in co-ordinated fashion to avoid waste and duplication. Flexibility and portability of training programme packages were accordingly necessary ingredients of the plan to address severe labour shortage problems.

Two community colleges, Natonum and Parkland, had already taken action through community groups to improve their ability to respond to community needs in technical-vocational education in Prince Albert and Yorkton. The centre of the Natonum region, Prince Albert, was to receive further attention through a decision to develop yet a fourth technical institute in that city. This new institution was also to utilize modular self-paced learning packages for the same reason that Wascana had adopted this instructional approach.

A change of government in 1982 gave reason to anticipate that an even greater emphasis would be placed upon institute rather than college development. Apart from completing the Prince Albert institution, the government made a commitment to increase training capacity within the province by 60 per cent over a three-year period and to sustain this initiative with an investment of some $100 million during this time frame. Among the many implications of these policy decisions, not the least was the need to educate over 500 new instructors for the technical-vocational sector—a major task for the universities of the province.

Because the institutes are under the direct aegis of a government department and do not have their own governing boards, they remain limited in their ability to respond quickly to specific and urgent newly identified training needs.

Similarly, the fact that their employees form a subset of the Saskatchewan Government Employees Association inhibits attempts by individual institutions to develop their own characteristics.

The issue of greater co-ordination in the post-secondary system, a matter raised in Voc-Tech 90, was also addressed by the new government through the creation of a new Ministry of Advanced Education and Manpower. By abolishing the Universities Commission and by relocating responsibility for the colleges and institutes from the Department of Continuing Education to the new ministry, all segments of post-secondary education were to be co-ordinated within one portfolio of government. The addition of Manpower to the new ministry had the feature of bringing apprenticeship training and labour market planning and analysis into the same fold as education and training.

In the community college sector, the first ten years proved to be an era of remarkable achievement in the area of adult and continuing education. During 1982-83, over 100,000 people were involved in programmes offered through the sixteen colleges and regional participation rates went as high as 20 per cent. Approximately 75 per cent of enrolments were in personal and community development programmes, 15 per cent in training programmes (including those with institute or university credit) and 10 per cent in adult basic education and related programmes.[54] In terms of the original goal of improving quality of life, particularly in rural communities, the colleges had proved to be an unqualified success. Furthermore, the direct involvement of the community in college affairs was evidenced by the active participation of over 600 voluntary "contact" committees as well as by local participation on college governing boards. As community-based institutions, Saskatchewan's colleges had few equals.

Despite their successes, however, the colleges could not be complacent. There were, for example, very real differences in the roles and functions of colleges in rural and urban regions. In the latter, the close proximity of the institutes made employment training more viable as a function for which the college would act only as broker, while Adult Basic Education (ABE) also became a significant aspect of the total programme of the urban colleges. This inclusion of the ABE function also brought with it many full-time instructors, a trend which was to exaggerate their differences from the rural institutions. Conversely, the rural colleges, while attracting large numbers of people into community-oriented courses, also tended to attract a high proportion of socioeconomically advantaged citizens. Over the years, the differences between rural and urban colleges have become even more pronounced. The availability of federal funds became an increasingly significant factor in programme planning in the urban colleges, while provincial government initiatives were also steering programme development towards a more provincial, and less community, flavour. Furthermore, as the emphasis upon occupational training increased, and as more people sought further education because of limited employment prospects, it became evident that the capacity of the colleges to provide sufficient training opportunities was severely limited.

The election of a Progressive Conservative government in 1982 led to a significant change in direction for the college system. The new government, sensitive to a perceived decline in public support for subsidy of education that was not employment-related, called for a committee, including college principals, trustees, and department representatives, to review the mandate of the colleges.[55] While restating many of the original objectives, the committee recommended new priorities for the college system. Adult basic education and upgrading were to be given higher priority in the light of data which indicated that over 170,000 adults in the province had less than grade ten education. Unemployment statistics prompted a recommendation that colleges assume a larger role in career and educational counselling. The brokerage function of colleges, particularly in academic and skill development areas, was re-emphasized. While the committee acknowledged an important role for the rural college as "a mechanism for the maintenance and development of a viable way of life," it also reinforced an earlier ministerial decree that costs of personal development courses should be borne by the student, not by government. The report also restated the role of the colleges to co-ordinate rather than duplicate educational services already available from other agencies in the community. This function was reflected in the following diagram, which identifies examples of four areas of a college's operation.[56]

PROMOTION	BROKERAGE	JOINT PROGRAMMING	DIRECT PROGRAMMING
Calendars	Agricultural	St. John Ambulance	Where college
Local committees	programs	Assoc.	has sole
Information nights	University	Alcohol & Drug	responsibility
Advertising	classes	Commission	for designing
News releases	Institute	Public Legal	programmes, hiring
	courses	Education	instructors,
		Association (PLEA)	arranging
		Recreation boards	facilities, etc.

(Mandate Review, 1983, p. 10)

An even more specific initiative from government to affect the colleges was the 1984 announcement that funding would be provided to them for upgrading programmes for 3500 young "employable welfare recipients," as an alternative to their maintenance on social assistance. This announcement reassured college personnel, particularly in urban areas, of continuing government support for their operations. The indications were that the new government saw the community colleges as important and useful. Their worst fears, that colleges would disappear in favour of more technical institutes, had not materialized.

Several additional aspects of college life in the province are notable. Other than in urban centres, few full-time personnel are employed in the college system, a factor which bears upon the nature of labour relations (see Chapter 7)—yet another manifestation of the independent spirit of Saskatchewan post-secondary institutions.

The provincial funding plan for Saskatchewan colleges is relatively simple. Each college receives a basic grant plus a grant based on the number of residents in the college region. In addition, many programmes are "cost shareable" with various agencies. While the colleges have considerable freedom in the internal allocation of their operating grants, any permanent addition to staff must be approved by the ministry. Although some funding is programme specific, the college boards exercise considerable freedom in allocating non-specific funding, with the result that the programme profile of each college is unique in response to different needs in different regions of the province. Colleges are still restricted to the use of leased facilities for instructional or administrative purposes out of a continuing commitment to avoid the identification of colleges with buildings and campuses.

College students in Saskatchewan also show unusual characteristics in comparison with other provinces. Most are part-time (with the exception of those in ABE and related programmes), and normally well over conventional college age. A significant number are Métis and status Indian. Attendance at college by the traditional eighteen and nineteen year old high school graduates is quite modest in Saskatchewan, in large part as a result of the character of the curriculum.

Given the way in which staff appointments are made and the character of the student population, it is not surprising that participation in college governance by faculty and students is not an issue in the province. At the provincial level, an organization designed to promote the interests of the colleges has been created: The Saskatchewan Community Colleges Trustees Association, which includes the college principals as associate members.

In both the community colleges and institutes of Saskatchewan, staff development, which has not yet received systematic attention, is a matter of major concern. New instructional technologies require professional retraining; in tight financial times professional development budgets seem vulnerable. The data collection and research capacity of the ministry and the institutions will require expansion if evaluation and development activities are to be undertaken on the scale necessary to realize ambitious provincial plans to expand the training capacity of the post-secondary sector. And whatever professional development and evaluation models might be selected by Saskatchewan, the particular characteristics of the Saskatchewan college and institute teaching force will have to be recognized, to say nothing of the distinctive needs of colleges and institutes, and of rural and urban colleges.

Saskatchewan has entered a watershed period in the development of non-university post-secondary education. The original community college ideal for Saskatchewan, and the functional initiatives which flow from it, have been under critical review. There is some possibility that "the great experiment" in community education, with the unique assumptions which sustained it, could be compromised to the point where the original vision could be obliterated. Of course, socioeconomic conditions change and governments with changing priorities are elected with full authority to alter institutional mandates. Saskatchewan seems poised to reassess again in the years ahead the most appropriate role for its community colleges. Several reorganization possibilities have already had at least preliminary exploration. One is that the urban version of the community college could be integrated with its technical institute counterpart to create a broadly comprehensive educational resource, to serve a wider segment of society more efficiently. A more specific example of this design is conceivable in Prince Albert, where the major centre of a multi-campus college to serve a wide rural area will be in close proximity to a new technical institute. As other provincial jurisdictions have indicated, several advantages may be gained by operating single but comprehensive post-secondary institutions in localities of sufficient size.

The rural colleges, on the other hand, see for themselves a different role and different problems. The need to revitalize rural society, so prominent during the early college years, is still seen as an important task for rural colleges, and so they are determined to maintain personal and community development programmes. They seem prepared, at the same time, to accept—somewhat reluctantly—government priority for occupational training by also putting to full use the new modular curriculum packages developed by the institutes for occupational programmes. This step seems necessary to ensure their survival as community-responsive institutions.

The new phase of economic development and a new era of political philosophy make for an interesting stage in educational planning for Saskatchewan colleges. The self-determination, imagination, and industry which have so long characterized prairie society are not likely to change; it is far more likely that Saskatchewan will continue to be an innovator within Canadian post-secondary education.

New Brunswick

New Brunswick, like Manitoba, originally established a centrally managed college system. Indeed, although the original single college multi-campus concept has been converted in law into several campuses, centralized direction is still a dominant feature. In fact, the original college legislation included provision for a quasi-independent provincial board of governors to establish policy and advise the minister responsible. Changes have been introduced since that time which have led deliberately towards a more centralized college system.

From 1974 until 1980, the New Brunswick Community College expanded its services under the direction of the board and five regional advisory committees. This organizational form allowed for both responsiveness to different communities and flexibility of programming. In 1978 the board commissioned the preparation of a Quinquennial Plan, which was to address a variety of concerns: governance, curriculum, financial need, professional development, and faculty performance assessment, among others. A broad data base—composed of opinions from students, faculty, industry, and community sources—was used to analyze the state of the college. The plan supported expansion and proposed structural changes particularly to accommodate the bilingual character of the province. It also reaffirmed the original college philosophy:

> The New Brunswick Community College is a province-wide comprehensive and flexible educational institution designed to offer new learning experiences to all citizens of the Province, and to provide a wide range of educational opportunities in accordance with the existing statutes of the Province of New Brunswick. The basic purpose of the College is to prepare a large majority of its students for the world of work, to provide opportunities for other students to strengthen their educational backgrounds in preparation for subsequent training, and respond to those persons who wish to upgrade or update their present skills and/or acquire new skills and knowledge.[57]

Despite this reaffirmation, in 1980 a dramatic change in the structure of the college was ushered in via an amended College Act (1980).[58] The corporate status of the college was abolished with the removal of the board of governors, and the college became directly dependent upon the Deputy Minister of Continuing Education. In effect, a board of governors structure was replaced by a government structure for the administration of the college network. The five college regions—based upon economic, political, and linguistic realities—were to be retained, as were the advisory boards which were to continue to include faculty and students members nominated by their constituencies and appointed by the minister.

The reasons for these changes were essentially pragmatic. The provincial government had been disturbed by pressures for expansion and increased funding generated by the college board. Further, the college was regarded as primarily a province-wide job training institution essential to the economic development of the province: with government direction, the integration of training with other government activities could take place; planning could become more efficient; and because students in trade and technology programmes were already being fully subsidized by government, the government saw every reason to protect its investment by exercising greater control. One effect of the new legislation was to place the practical functions of chief executive officer for the then eight campuses under the Deputy Minister for Continuing Education.

In 1983 the act was amended once again.[59] The government department responsible was renamed the Ministry of Community Colleges. At the same time the regional advisory boards were dissolved. Shortly thereafter, a local advisory board was put in place for each college, but with a number of adjustments to ensure full representation of the two linguistic communities on these bodies. By this stage there were ten college campuses divided equally between francophone and anglophone. New Brunswick now had what it considered to be a community college which would be truly province-wide in scope. By 1984, the total number of colleges had been reduced to nine—five anglophone and four francophone—without change to the structure of the college system.

Since 1983, a number of important college issues have been under active review, and action on some has been underway. A centralized management has provided for decisive action when and where the need has arisen. Federal funding for occupational training programmes—more recently and more specifically, the National Training Act with its Skills Growth Fund—has continued to play an important role in setting the curriculum priorities of the college. The federal contribution in 1984 was approximately 35 per cent of the total college budget; with such an influence, shifts in federal priorities can create major educational planning problems for the province and the college. To this point, that planning has been indecisive and improvement seems likely only as a result of better communication between levels of government.

The New Brunswick Community College has not yet resolved an identity problem. Much of the old "trade school" connotation remains in the view of many parts of New Brunswick society, although the college has undertaken important initiatives in extending its services and providing community education programmes. As well, a considerable amount of occupational training has been conducted outside the college umbrella by the government departments of Forestry, Health, Fisheries, and Labour, and this practice has made it difficult for the college to be publicly identified as the employment preparation institution for the province. A study in which government is examining ways of co-ordinating its social and economic responsibilities has been undertaken and may prove to be the catalyst for more comprehensive programming by the college.

By comparison with other provincial systems, New Brunswick college development has been limited in areas such as the provision of student services, long range planning, programme and personnel evaluation, and related policy matters. Counselling services for students have been few, mainly restricted to career exploration and programme selection. However, attention has been given more recently to many of these matters as well as to the development of province-wide student application and admission policies, and much greater emphasis has recently been given to professional development for instructional staff.

Although the college is a single organization and although the management of the college has been centralized, there has been considerable variation in programmes among the campuses as well as programme specialization by campus. More than half the students enrol at one of three campuses—Moncton, Saint John, and Bathurst—and these campuses offer virtually the entire range of technology programmes and the greatest amount of apprenticeship training. The other seven campuses are primarily involved in pre-employment and academic upgrading programmes, while all campuses offer a variety of continuing education programmes. Fredericton, the capital city with a population of over 40,000, houses the central administration of the college but has no major campus.

It would be wrong to judge the New Brunswick Community College by standards appropriate to other jurisdictions. For some time the government of New Brunswick has maintained a deep commitment to cultural and regional equality, and this equality was to have both economic and political dimensions with the college as an important vehicle for achieving this goal. The province, while long concerned with higher education of an academic nature, has also recently doubled its financial aid to technical and trades training. From 1963 to 1970, this kind of training had been expanded significantly, but even in 1970 it was still virtually inaccessible to francophone students in their own language.

The college system was quite explicitly designed as an instrument of social and economic as well as educational reform. The first phase, in which the somewhat isolated trade and technology centres were given a community orientation, produced beneficial results. The college campuses began to serve a greater spectrum of students through a broader range of programmes. After some years of operating in this mode, the provincial government decided to take more direct charge of the college and its campuses so that planning and decision-making could become more efficient and so that the major cultural and linguistic groups could be assured of equality of educational opportunity.

New Brunswick has adopted a community college model which, while unconventional, has also been highly functional. Above all, the college system is designed to meet limited needs in a sociocultural and economic environment where co-ordination and integration of government services and resources are seen as absolutely vital.

Nova Scotia

By 1983, Nova Scotia included within its post-secondary sector a unique collection of degree and non-degree-granting institutions, a high level of specialization by function, and an intriguing combination of institutional mandates. Since 1970 the six previously established universities[60] have been joined by seven additional degree granting institutions—the Technical University of Nova Scotia, College of Art and Design, Atlantic School of Theology, Nova Scotia Agricultural College, Université Sainte-Anne, University College of Cape Breton, and the Atlantic Institute of Education (which was discontinued in 1983). The organization of several of these new institutions was, by Canadian standards, unconventional. In both the Agricultural College and the College of Art and Design, for example, the curricula included a number of programmes which led to degrees, diplomas, and certificates; the combination of degree and non-degree streams in the one institution had not been a usual Canadian practice, but neither was it unique.

Even more unusual was the decision to integrate the Eastern Nova Scotia Institute of Technology with Xavier College to form the University College of Cape Breton, where programmes were to range from indentured apprenticeship training to baccalaureate degree studies—a combination with major implications for faculty, students, and institutional priorities. Some have suggested that the University College of Cape Breton displays most of the characteristics of a community college although the conventional wisdom is that degree-granting capability undermines those community college activities which, by tradition, enjoy a lower public status than university-type degree studies.

In the non-university post-secondary sector, Nova Scotia developments in recent years have been atypical. Five institutions are highly specialized: the Nova Scotia Institute of Technology, Nova Scotia Nautical Institute, Nova Scotia Land Survey Institute, Nova Scotia Agricultural College (to be proclaimed a university), and the Fisheries Training School at Pictou. In each case the institution is a creature of a ministry of government which provides the planning and management functions. This form of operation has precluded the evolution of these institutions into ones which are directly responsive to community influences and which may otherwise have evolved into community colleges. They have been, plainly and simply, provincial government institutions to achieve provincial, rather than community or regional, objectives.

While the Nova Scotia Institute of Technology has developed a curriculum which includes vocational, technological, and some extension courses, it has intentionally not developed a broader range of offerings to meet other educational needs.

Continuing education and the education of adults in Nova Scotia are the responsibility of the twenty-one school boards of the province which offer a wide variety of courses at several levels. The Department of Education, through its Adult Education Division, subsidizes courses for adults selectively, such as adult literacy training, upgrading in academic and vocational-technical subjects, and second language studies, most of which are not duplicated by any post-secondary institution. Furthermore, the Adult Vocational Training Centres, located in various regions of the province, also operate under department responsibility and limit their curricula to federally sponsored occupational courses and programmes.

The result of historical developments and government policy has been a large assortment of non-university post-secondary educational institutions with enrolments ranging from less than 100 students to more than 3,000, each with a restricted mandate and a limited range of programmes. The overall pattern has been described in Nova Scotia as a series of "water-tight compartments," which while collectively serving a broad range of needs of the population, falls short of being an integrated post-secondary system.

Nova Scotia has also chosen not to adopt two of the more recent post-secondary practices common to other provinces. One is Nova Scotia's retention of nursing education to the R.N. level in the hospital schools rather than transferring it to a college setting. The other is its continuation of the two-year normal school, or teachers' college, rather than the integration of this form of post-secondary study into the university setting.

For over a century the people of Nova Scotia have displayed a deep commitment to, if not a reverence for, higher education. The sociocultural context of the province has placed a high value on classical liberal education for those who seek and are qualified for such study. The number, size, and character of the established universities bears testimony to values which have been transplanted by generations of immigrants, largely from the United Kingdom.

The record in vocational-technical education at the post-secondary level is, however, somewhat different. The current status of occupational training, within a formal institutional setting, has been achieved only through the leadership of a series of dedicated professional educators and a recognition by government of the need for specialized training for economic and industrial advancement. Further, the administrative separation of adult from technical education, even though both are responsibilities of the Minister of Education, has tended to segregate students into different institutions rather than encourage the heterogeneity which is characteristic of post-secondary education in most other provinces of Canada. Were Nova Scotia to choose a community college approach to post-secondary education, the history and current circumstances of the province would likely suggest a Nova Scotia adaptation of the college of applied arts and technology model of Ontario.

In 1982, a Royal Commission on Post-Secondary Education was established and given a challenging assignment: to recommend a plan for the future.[61] The pattern of higher education in Nova Scotia is an impressive testimony to the past. That past is unlikely to be discarded, but the current requirements of government and industry, the educational aspirations of individual citizens, and the imperatives of the future are likely to compel some redirection of post-secondary education in Nova Scotia.

Newfoundland

In Newfoundland, the evolution of two provincial colleges had taken place by 1970: one was for trades and technology, the other for fisheries and related occupations. As well, there had been the establishment of several provincially operated regional vocational schools. In the next decade a number of significant events occurred which were to have a direct impact upon the province's post-secondary educational system.

The first of these events was the decision to establish a junior college, Sir Wilfred Grenville College, as an affiliate of Memorial University, in the western region of the province at Corner Brook. The choice of location was significant because it was preferred over Stephenville, another community in the same region. The decision to create a junior college, while not prompted exclusively by social and educational considerations, did help to encourage more Newfoundland students to remain in the province for their university education.

In 1977, an interesting initiative by government and the two colleges in St. John's resulted in the tabling of legislation to establish a polytechnical institution through the administrative merger of the colleges.[62] The plan for the capital funding for this institute called for a shared contribution by the federal and provincial governments, an arrangement which contributed to the eventual decision not to continue with the plan. The idea of programme co-ordination by the two colleges was to have little bearing upon future developments.

However, in 1978, the first Newfoundland community college in the conventionally accepted sense of the term was created as a result of the decision to co-ordinate all adult and post-secondary services and facilities in the Stephenville region at one institution, Bay St. George Community College.[63] The college was to be the product of a meld of several established enterprises: the Stephenville Adult Centre, the District Vocational School, and the Heavy Equipment School. But the new institution had the potential to develop well beyond its founding units. Under imaginative and aggressive leadership, the college brought the community into its planning, established a broadly representative board of governors, and began to develop a variety of programmes which reflected the specific needs of its catchment area. The college did not include an academic or university-transfer component in its curriculum partly because of the presence of the university satellite, Sir Wilfred Grenville College, in the same region. In fact, the existence of Sir Wilfred Grenville College seemed not inconsequential in the decision to balance regional interests by the creation of Bay St. George Community College in Stephenville.

Despite the establishment of four colleges (including Sir Wilfred Grenville), a substantial area of the province remained outside any college region. This fact was not ignored in a report, published in 1980, which addressed problems of retention and participation of secondary school graduates in post-secondary education in Newfoundland.[64] Although concerned primarily with the issue of declining enrolments in post-secondary education, the task force had no hesitation in reporting on related issues. The authors addressed problems of organizational structure, education, and labour force needs, and issues related to participation in and accessibility to post-secondary education. A broad analysis of community college patterns in Canada and beyond resulted in a long list of recommendations in support of a major college system for the province.

In summary, the report recommended that six community college regions be defined and that in each a college be assigned responsibility for all post-secondary non-university adult and continuing education. Further, it was recommended that changes be made in the mandates of the College of Trades and Technology and the College of Fisheries. The former should become a technology centre, with "non-post-secondary" programmes then offered at that college to be placed in the St. John's Regional College. It was also recommended that Memorial University offer its regional extension courses in college facilities in the different regions of the province.

The task force, as had a Royal Commission some twelve years earlier,[65] recognized a need for a co-ordinated post-secondary system if the interests of people throughout the province were to be best served. Financial constraints of the time, however, coupled with limited but powerful opposition to the recommendations, constituted a substantial obstacle to further action on these recommendations, and no action has yet been taken.

Some characteristics of college governance in Newfoundland are noteworthy. Each college operates under different legislation. Bay St. George Community College has an extremely broad mandate. The other two institutions are more narrowly constituted, and both have a research function. Board members for all colleges are appointed by government: the Bay St. George board includes a student, a faculty member, and a government official; the older institutions have no designated appointees to their boards, but both boards include ministry staff. In each college, the president and vice-president are appointed by the government rather than by the board.

Newfoundland colleges have no shortage of issues to tackle. One relates to planning. It is recognized that, as the institutions develop new programmes, the prospect of unnecessary programme duplication is real without systematic, co-operative planning. The regional vocational schools have, for example, ventured into some post-secondary diploma programming, which could well erode the mandate of the Colleges of Trades and Technologies and Fisheries. Careful planning might indicate that the small vocational school should develop first-year programmes in sophisticated technologies from which graduates could then transfer to the colleges. This could broaden access to these programmes and maintain quality control over the programmes themselves, all the while reducing the drain on limited resources. Some Newfoundland educators see a solution to the planning problem resting in the creation of an independent, objective, co-ordinating council, composed of disinterested but informed lay members to advise the minister. The Senior Advisory Committee on Post-Secondary Education, as recently proposed, is not widely perceived as meeting these criteria.

A second issue concerns the organizational structure of the Department of Education. Since 1975, two separate divisions of the department, one for vocational education and the other for adult and continuing education, have had responsibility for instructional programming in the regional vocational schools and the communities throughout the province. Recommendations advocating better co-ordination of programmes to serve adults have prompted a proposal to bring these two divisions together under a deputy minister for further (or advanced) education. Furthermore, as Newfoundland has been faced with the problems of conflict between labour and education portfolios in connection with apprenticeship and manpower training, it has been observed that there would be additional value in bringing manpower planning under the aegis of the same deputy minister. By 1985, a Department of Career Development and Advanced Education had been established in response to these concerns.

Labour relations also hold potential difficulties. The faculty from two institutions bargain under the Newfoundland Association of Public Employees (NAPE), but the College of Fisheries faculty remains outside this organization. Common problems such as response to potential financial retrenchment, how to provide incentives for instructors to obtain additional credentials and to pursue professional development activities, and how to encourage college teachers to become a unique and unified group of professionals have all prompted an argument in favour of comparable working conditions in all post-secondary institutions.

Other issues in Newfoundland colleges are shared with many college systems in Canada. Part-time mature students are under-represented in the post-secondary sector, particularly in day programmes. Newfoundlanders see the need to find more creative ways to accommodate part-time students and to overcome current administrative and financial barriers to this objective. Secondly, Newfoundland colleges are particularly susceptible to changes of federal government training priorities. They depend very much on federal funding (65 per cent of Bay St. George Community College funds come from this source) and a minor federal change can have a major institutional impact. Thirdly, professional development and programme evaluation activities have never received priority attention, a condition that cannot be prolonged indefinitely. A fouth concern has been expressed about the inconsistent policy of colleges regarding the required level of counselling for students.

Newfoundland has had a long history of varied efforts to provide for the further education of its youth,[66] but institutional self-interest has deep historical roots. However, the immediate future—limited provincial resources for education, the need for better articulation throughout the entire post-secondary sector, a suitable mechanism for planning—impels future rather than past-oriented problem solving. Newfoundland's tradition of committed individuals working toward common goals at both government and institutional levels provides that province with the most important resource for facing the future realistically.

Yukon Territory

While colleges and college systems were developing rapidly in the rest of Canada, slower but significant educational changes were taking place in the area under the jurisdiction of the Yukon Territorial Government.

In the Yukon, post-secondary education began with the establishment of the Whitehorse Vocational Training School in 1963,[67] with funding made available under the Technical and Vocational Training Assistance legislation of 1960, as was the case in many other parts of Canada.[68] Prior to that time the Territory had relied upon a system of grants to residents to allow them to obtain post-secondary education in the south. The centre, located in Whitehorse, first offered trades training of various kinds under an agreement between the Canadian government through Canada Manpower, and the Yukon Territory Government. In short order, however, the scope of the programme offerings expanded with the addition of courses to train bookkeepers, clerk-typists, secretaries, and certified nursing assistants, and extension services were made available to other communities in the Territory.

In 1977, a university transfer component was added to the centre's curriculum. To combat the high rate of turnover of school teachers in the Yukon, to provide opportunities for teachers to obtain in-service and professional upgrading, and to provide native people with an avenue by which they could influence the education of their own children, arrangements were made with the University of British Columbia to offer a teacher education programme designed specifically for residents of the Territory.[69] This Yukon Teacher Education Programme graduated a total of seventy-three students; however, none were native. The programme was discontinued in 1982 in favour of a university-transfer programme with some courses in Education.

By 1979/80, enrolment at the centre reached 400 full-time and 1,026 part-time students in programmes of various lengths. At the same time, the demand for expanded educational opportunities by a growing population prompted planning with a longer term perspective.

In 1979 the University of Alberta was commissioned to study the educational needs of adults in the Yukon and to advise upon a structure for the delivery of expanded services. The report which followed, entitled *Toward a Yukon College,*[70] recommended the creation of a multi-purpose, post-secondary institution which would include occupational training programmes for unemployed adults, apprenticeship training, vocational upgrading, and first and second-year university-equivalent courses. The report further recommended that the new college should expand its delivery systems through extension courses, mobile learning centres, and other methods.

In 1982, these recommendations were translated into action by the formal establishment of Yukon College, with the mandate to deliver all post-secondary educational services in the Territory. With ready access to a good local supply of highly qualified people available to teach on a full or part-time basis, pro-grammes were to be delivered by college staff. Other services were provided by contract with universities and other post-secondary institutions such as Red Deer College. This approach assured credible programming and certification for Yukon students.

There were additional factors which influenced the decision to create a college. One was the Economic Regional Development Agreement negotiated between the federal and territorial governments, which would provide special funding for several programmes for native people. The Yukon Indian Land Claims settlement was also expected to accelerate demand for specialized training in many of the college's programme areas.

It was now evident that the space limitations of the old centre would inhibit programme expansion. Two further reports, *Toward a Yukon College Education Master Plan 1980-1990* and the *Yukon College Phase One Facilities Programme,*[72] proposed a substantial expansion of capital facilities, including those to accom-modate continuing education and business and applied arts programming.

Administratively, Yukon College has operated under the aegis of the Advanced Education and Manpower Branch, a division of the ministry responsible for education. It has no board of governors, and the chief executive officer, with the title of director, reports directly to the Assistant Deputy Minister of the Advanced Education and Manpower Branch. The college serves a population of 21,000 in an area of 483,000 square kilometres, but over half that population resides in Whitehorse. In addition to the major Whitehorse campus, community learning centres are located in eleven smaller communities in the Territory. Approxi-mately a third of the population is native Indian.

Despite a slowdown in the economic growth of the Yukon Territory, the future for the college seems to be full of challenges comparable to those in the provinces. The Territory must address issues of uneven population distribution with many small and isolated communities, a wide range of educational needs in a society with significant numbers of native and disadvantaged learners, problems of inhospitable climate and difficult travel, and a clouded economic future. New developments in the techniques of distance education may provide an improved basis for efficient and effective delivery of educational services. Whatever the pace and direction of future development in the Yukon Territory, the particular adaptation of the community college concept to that region will be vital to the economic and social, as well as educational, future of the Yukon Territory.

Northwest Territories

The Northwest Territories have a population of 45,000 spread over a land area one-third the size of Canada. While some 15,000 Inuit use nineteen different dialects, there are also 9,000 Dene people who speak eight different languages and 21,000 whites and Métis for whom English is the dominant language.[73] Designing and delivering post-secondary educational opportunities in such circumstances poses problems unparalleled in Canada.

As elsewhere in the country, college education in the Northwest Territories evolved from an Adult Vocational Training Centre.[74] The centre, located in Fort Smith and funded by Canada Manpower, was established in 1968. As one of the major population centres in the Territories, but with only 2,500 people, Fort Smith might not appear to be an appropriate locale for post-secondary education, but as noted in a 1975 study, the lack of any training centre was recognized as the major barrier to higher education opportunities in the Territories.[75]

In its earliest years, the Fort Smith Centre offered programmes in Heavy Equipment Operation, Nursing Assistant Training, Secretarial Training, Academic Upgrading, and Life Skills Education. In each programme, admission standards were intentionally flexible to accommodate the diverse formal educational backgrounds of the native and non-native populations. In fact, the Koenig study[76] noted strong differences of opinion among committee members regarding the minimum admission requirements for students. Problems of inadequate preparation, poor study skills, and difficulties in adjusting to a different educational environment were cited as contributing to student frustration and low programme completion rates.[77] Apart from the centre at Fort Smith, upgrading courses and vocational training programmes for adults were made available in several smaller centres through the centre's extension services. Even a second campus at Frobisher Bay was planned at that time.

A Teacher Education Programme was also established in 1968, affiliated at first with the University of Alberta and later with the University of Saskatchewan. The graduation of qualified bilingual teachers had an immediate impact on the educational system, reflected in increasing school completion rates and expanding demand for further educational opportunities.

Largely as a result of new opportunities for growth in the resource sector with a rebirth in mining and oil exploration, an influx of new immigrants entered the Territories during the early 1970's. By 1974, the school population had reached 12,000, a threefold increase over 1960. The consequences of growth were new programmes in paraprofessions and technologies, an expansion of facilities of the Adult Vocational Training Centre, and in 1981, after a competition for an appropriate name, its evolution into Thebacha College.[78] In 1985, the institution was renamed Arctic College with the campus in Fort Smith retaining the name Thebacha.

Programme development of both range and scope has been an ongoing feature of Arctic College and its predecessors. Renewable Resources Technology, a unique programme with immediate application to the north, was added in 1978. Later, its mandate to give priority to programmes with direct relevance to the evolving economy of the Territories resulted in the addition of diploma programmes in Social Services and in Public and Business Administration. Both programmes were affiliated, the former with the University of Calgary and the latter with the Certified General Accountants Association. The first graduates entered the workforce in 1984.

By 1984, pre-employment training opportunities in carpentry, cooking, electronics, welding, and small engine mechanics were supplemented by more apprenticeship training and a variety of academic upgrading courses. By standards of other Canadian provinces, Arctic College had become a comprehensive institution.

Unlike Yukon College, Arctic College has enjoyed a measure of autonomy through its thirteen-member board of governors, which has included representatives of both faculty and student organizations. Executive personnel include the Deputy Minister of Education and the assistant Deputy Minister of Advanced Education. The college director is the administrator of the college. Because of the population distribution of the north, the college has two residences, uncommon for colleges in Canada, and an extensive student services division. Further expansion of facilities is planned for both Fort Smith and other communities.

While Arctic College has been both an educational and economic success, several problems indigenous to the Northwest Territories remain unsolved. The single campus college may be justified in terms of total population; however, the sociocultural, geographic, political, and economic realities are such that unique approaches to programme delivery, instructional technology, and teaching methods seem necessary. Extensive travel and different environments impede effective learning in almost all circumstances, but relocation of students with language, cultural, and ideological differences makes such problems particularly acute.[79]

Developments are already underway at the government level to develop a college system for the Northwest Territories. A multi-campus college, administered from a central facility, may address current issues more satisfactorily, particularly if the character of the smaller centres reflects the special nature and needs of each community. A second method of development could be to give priority to learning at a distance similar to initiatives of the Open Learning Institute in British Columbia or the Télé-Université of Quebec. In a paper addressed to the feasibility of an open learning system for the Territories, Heeley notes that with approximately 15,300 people between the ages of twenty and forty years in the N.W.T., a reasonable target population for distance education would be 1,500.[80] Television reception is available in most communities of 500 or more, and the CANCOM (Canada Communications) network should soon be in place to serve the remote areas of the North. Since four channels will be available, one could be designated for part-time educational programming by CANCOM and the N.W.T. Department of Education. The Open Learning Institute experience in British Columbia suggests that carefully designed print and audio courses in adult basic learning, technical and vocational programmes, and academic subjects at a post-secondary level can meet many learning needs of people in more isolated environments. As Dickinson noted with respect to the goals of distance education:

> Adult education courses should be designed not only to enable people to read and write, but also to make it easier for them to promote their self-awareness and their grasp of the problems of hygiene, health, household management, and the upbringing of children, and to enhance their autonomy and increase their participation in community life.[81]

Whatever the course of action selected for the provision of post-secondary education in the Territories, the task will demand innovation of a kind different from that expected of other Canadian colleges. It is under such conditions that the flexibility of the community college concept can be put to the test.

At present the mission of Arctic College is twofold:

1. developing and maintaining high quality programmes in the Northwest Territories.
2. preparing and assisting students to attend institutions of higher learning in other southern Canadian centres.[82]

New developments in post-secondary education for the North can be assumed for the balance of this decade, and an expanded mission for Arctic College may well be a product of these developments.[83]

Although these accounts of college developments in each province and territory have been presented separately, they have several common threads. In several provinces, the distinctive character of the college—as separate from other post-secondary institutions—has not yet become evident, and, to some extent, all colleges need to come to grips with their own identity. Perhaps this can be achieved by the development of a common college culture. Throughout Canada, the issue of accessibility has changed from: How many more can we admit? to: Whom shall we not admit? It is quite possible that, before the end of this century, many of these colleges will need to specialize, to redirect their energies to new objectives, or to become something quite different from what they now are. The role of provincial governments in determining the destiny of these colleges has become more pronounced, as has the need for the federal and provincial governments to communicate better if the colleges are to flourish. Clearly, colleges now need a different kind of leadership than was necessary in the formative years. And none of them can any longer put off confronting issues that most of them have not yet seriously addressed: how to maintain quality in times of scarce resources and public as well as governmental demands for accountability; how to establish a labour relations climate which will no longer make it necessary to diffuse energies into crisis management; how to amass and interpret information so that these institutions can plan systematically; and how to provide the necessary dimension of general education in a world fascinated by specialization. Indeed, in tackling these issues, Canada's colleges can become important influences on the development of a new national culture.

The extraordinary circumstance is that these colleges must confront these problems in a world whose dimensions are not yet known except for the likelihood that the future will not be a mere linear extension of the past. These are the matters addressed in Part II of this book.

PART II

Issues for the Future

5

COLLEGES AND THE FUTURE

ISSUES

Canada's colleges and provincial college systems are characterized as much by their differences as by their similarities and it would certainly be inaccurate to refer to a Canadian public college "system." In each province, special circumstances sparked the establishment of new colleges, and even though they all came into being within the same short time span, they were meant to serve different social purposes, to have different priorities, and to operate on a day-to-day basis in quite different ways. The last ten years have seen these differences accentuated as they grew beyond infancy and settled in to serving longer term objectives.

In the years to the end of this century, these colleges and college systems will continue to have differences that will further highlight their individual characteristics. At the same time, they will face a number of common issues and their responses to these issues will shape their individual and collective futures. These common issues are the topics of Part II of this book. Each has been recently identified in most if not all provinces and territories as a matter of current concern. The colleges and college systems do not all see these issues from the same perspective or with the same urgency, but most recognize them as fundamental in their long-term planning. These issues need to be addressed if the colleges are to continue to merit the confidence that was originally expressed in them.

The new colleges were founded in quite specific social, political, and economic circumstances within Canada. With time, circumstances have changed, and the colleges have either reacted to or anticipated these changes. Not only is further change inevitable, but virtually all analysts would forecast that the scale of economic and social change is likely to be far greater toward the end of the century than it has been since the colleges were established and first developed. Walter Light, Chairman and Chief Executive Officer of Northern Telecom Limited, sees Canada's immediate future in these terms:

> And that is our real problem. Canada . . . is facing a potentially crippling shortage in almost every body of knowledge we will need in the next two decades. And, the next two decades could decide whether Canada survives as a modern, viable, international, industrial power in the Information Age.[1]

It is not only the fact of the information age and of the rapid pace and diffusion of technological change—that is likely to be of great significance to Canadians and their institutions; it is also how Canadian society responds to the age of information and technology that is critical to Canada's future. And this response speaks directly to the role of colleges:

> . . . it is part of our obligation to equip our students with the knowledge to survive in the new society. However it is also part of our duty to help them to survive well. This means nothing less than assuring that they leave their colleges with the skills to integrate into modern society but also with the social perspective to make rational and critical judgments about it and, with luck, to work to change it for the better.[2]

An examination of prospects for the future, then, provides the setting within which the major issues facing Canada's public colleges will be addressed.

THE INTERNATIONAL CONTEXT

While these colleges function within provincial jurisdictions, it is not realistic for them to see themselves only in a provincial context. Indeed, even the Canadian context is too limited a perspective for an adequate view of the future if the Science Council of Canada's statement of the problem is to be respected:

> Most advanced nations of the world are preparing to place themselves at the forefront of the information society. Many of the changes described will take place whether we like it or not. The question that remains is whether Canada will be an active or passive participant. Canada has been fortunate in having participated in the early stages of this worldwide technological revolution. But what has been accomplished to date has only been a beginning.

Other countries have backed their initiatives with billions of dollars in public and private sector investment. If Canada's present failure to act continues, Canadians face a bleak prospect and the country will be left even more vulnerable.

Many sectors of our manufacturing industry would be rendered obsolete, virtually overnight. Our trade balance, already precarious, might never recover. Structural unemployment could lead to permanent joblessness for many Canadians, a decline in living standards and, for some, emigration. The personal privacy and integrity of Canadian citizens could be compromised in ways and on a scale never before seen in an independent, democratic country; indeed, our cultural and political sovereignty would be permanently jeopardized. Failure to respond adequately to these clear and present dangers could spell an end to Canada as we know it, precipitating a decline which would bring Canadians inevitably to a condition of pastoral servitude by the middle years of the twenty-first century.[3]

Of the numerous international considerations, a most visible one is Canada's place as an international trader. Quite simply, Canada must improve its competitive position in international trade. Historically, Canada has been a major trading nation of the world, but it is now challenged by developing and developed nations for its share of international markets. Canada's abundant natural resources have been its dominant exports, yet technological advances in other countries have already assured this country of very stiff competition even in the resource sector. Of at least equal importance is that many nations have by-passed Canada in the industrial sector by improving productivity through technological innovation and more advanced management. As well, many nations have acquired a distinct competitive advantage over Canada by having much lower labour costs. This nation is in real danger of losing markets it has been able to hold for decades, at the very time when all nations seek to establish new markets rather than lose old ones.

Between 1981 and 1983 . . . Canada dropped from sixth place to eleventh place among industrial nations in terms of competitiveness. And Canada ranks only fifteenth of twenty-two countries in terms of the technologically-related criteria the [European Management Forum] calls "innovative forward orientation" . . . competitiveness has come to depend upon their technological innovativeness, management skills, speed of reaction, and willingness to forge links abroad to seek new forms of co-operation. Competitiveness has thus come to depend crucially on human skills.[4]

The Science Council of Canada had been even more specific in its sombre if not alarming view of Canada's place in the international economy:

> In four key areas that contribute to international competitiveness, Canada has performed poorly for years.
>
> First, the industrial sector is lagging in improving efficiency. From 1974 to 1982, Canada registered zero productivity growth, the lowest among leading industrial countries.
>
> Second, this country's innovative forward orientation—the extent of R and D and ability to adapt to future technological requirements—remains weak.
>
> Third, the outward orientation—the focus on foreign trade and investments—ranks low among the industrial countries.
>
> Finally, Canada lacks a stable sociopolitical consensus. Conflict rather than agreement and cooperation is the standard approach to setting priorities.[5]

Canada's new colleges are not, of course, expected to lead the charge into an improved foreign market position, but to the extent that they are expected to accept some responsibility for meeting trained human resource needs of the country, and all of them have had at least some share of this responsibility, these colleges must assess their role in maintaining if not expanding the country's international competitiveness.

But that is only one dimension of the international context of Canada's colleges. At least as important is a whole list of long-term problems which cross national boundaries and could develop into major world crises. In 1977, the International Centre for the Study of Social Policy of Stanford Research Institute identified forty-one such problems—ranging from malnutrition-induced mental deficiencies leading to social instability through loss of cultural diversity and the growing sub-culture of the information-poor, to cumulative effects of pollution and potentially catastrophic experiments.[6] And these problems, it is noted, were ones for which few if any governments had policies in place.

The colleges reach more young and older adults than any other educational institutions in the country, and their students represent a wider cross-section of the total society than can be found in other institutions in Canada. To the extent that these colleges have a role to play in the general education of adults, in raising sensitivities to social concerns, and in education for informed citizenship, the reality of world-wide problems cannot be judged to be irrelevant to the future directions that these colleges might take. Essentially, the question boils down to this: should Canada's colleges choose to excel only as training institutions, or ought they accept as well a broader educational mission?

UNEMPLOYMENT AND NEW EMPLOYMENT

International concerns aside, no nation-wide problem has been more topical in the mid-1980's than unemployment. Platforms during the 1984 federal election, the daily newspapers, and the flurry of governmental activity and programmes all point to the Canadian preoccupation with, and virtually dreaded concern about, the state and future of employment. Despite political platforms and promises of full employment, there seems little doubt that there will be major employment dislocations to the turn of the century. Part of the recent increase in unemployment was a result of the 1981-82 recession, during which some 595,000 jobs were lost. But even after a subsequent year of strong employment growth in which 374,000 jobs were created, the previous losses had not been made up and the unemployment rolls had grown by 200,000 people looking for work.[7] Even with major changes of public policy, the unemployment problem seems likely to become more acute, particularly as new technology replaces labour in the race for improved productivity. Old jobs will be lost permanently: new jobs will increase, but for people with new skills.

Faced with the prospect of consistently high levels of unemployment, on a scale and in fields quite unknown to people in their middle years, Canadians may well have to revise their thinking about the nature and value of work to develop new attitudes to unemployment and the unemployed, and to design new social assistance programmes for a society with persistently high unemployment. Traditional notions of welfare, social assistance, and employment may need radical altering to conform to new economic realities.

Of particular significance to post-secondary educational institutions should be two aspects of the new employment and unemployment: the impact on persons attempting to enter the labour force for the first time, and the kinds of employment likely to be displaced.

Indications from the mid-1980's are that the youth of Canada will be especially hard hit by the new unemployment patterns. The Canada Employment and Immigration Advisory Council reported in May 1984 that real unemployment among youth had reached 900,000.[8] Of this number, it was estimated that 200,000 young people—an alarming figure by itself—were without work because they had low levels of education and were unskilled. But the social implications of having 700,000 educated and skilled young people without regular employment, or reasonable employment prospects are even more profound. Schemes to give young people a first employment opportunity by extraordinary government programmes may have short-term benefits, but they do not appear to address the more substantial and long-term problems. The stark fact is that many young people may live in a work world in which the five-day week or the eight-hour day will be the exception rather than the rule. A significantly increased number of young people may seldom have the opportunity to hold a steady job; many may be required to live in a world in which work is unwillingly interrupted regularly by what is now referred to as unemployment. In fact, the term "employment" has recently been replaced by "productive and meaningful activity and attachment" as a euphemistic way of indicating that Canada simply may be unable to come close to a full employment goal through the conventional methods of job creation.[9]

Changes of employment patterns seem likely to take place in most kinds of work, but traditional middle class employment may be hit particularly hard.[10] For those with advanced education, more the style than the substance of work seems likely to change: there will be new cottage industries, work at home, and the office of the future will materialize. For less skilled service-sector occupations, the number of work opportunities is likely to increase, but the rewards from such work are not likely to improve without major changes by employers or governments. Even the prospect of a "techno-peasant" class in Canada cannot be ruled out.[11] But, however unattractive the new employment may be for these people, the work prospects for those "in the middle"—technicians, tradespeople, middle managers, supervisors—are even more bleak and less numerous because technological advances and the processing of information will reduce the number of work opportunities of this kind significantly.

Putting these two patterns together, current indications are that young people, a major share of the students and graduates of colleges, will have more difficulty becoming established in the labour market, and the kinds of work for which most college students have recently been prepared will reduce in quantity faster than other kinds of employment. The less advantaged sectors of the Canadian population, many of whom have looked to the colleges for kinds of education which would improve their prospects, do not face an attractive future if colleges do not keep pace with societal changes.

In addition to the need to educate for a new kind of employment world, colleges will have to give greater attention to the need for effective use of non-working time because most people are likely to spend less time working in the future. How that non-working time can be used in personally and socially constructive ways is a matter which ought to command the attention of all educators. A whole set of cultural and social values are intimately tied to the nature and structure of work life. As that work life changes in the years ahead, new values will develop, new concepts of leisure should emerge, and new social assistance programmes will be required. College planners cannot ignore these prospects.

AGE DISTRIBUTION

A major increase in the school-age population before the year 2000, after the declines of the late 1970's and the 1980's, is expected. That increase will then be reflected at the traditional college-age level as Canada moves into the twenty-first century.[12] However, two other features of Canada's population distribution by age will become even more significant before that time.

First, the twenty-five to forty-four age cohort will be the largest one to the end of this century. This segment of the population will have gone through the traditional school/college/university phase; they will be raising families, trying to get established, and working—or hoping to work. They will have and use the loudest political voice in Canada. They will want and need to continue their education. They will not be satisfied with traditional methods of instructing college-age students.

Second, the percentage of the Canadian population in one or another phase of the retirement years will increase dramatically to the end of this century.[13] The younger retirees will be physically healthy and anxious to do more than merely live out their lives. The middle-old will still be willing and able to make constructive contributions to the development of Canadian society. Only the oldest may fit the current stereotype of retired Canadians, and even they may not! These people will have as much right to education as other citizens, and they should expect to exercise that right.

Should not these changes have some impact on the orientation of Canada's colleges in the years ahead?

CANADIAN DIVERSITY

There is little likelihood that Canada will become a cohesive, happy, united nation in the years immediately ahead. Not even the optimists in Canada dare suggest that current regional tensions within the country will be successfully overcome in the next twenty years. Indeed only optimists, without sensitivity to recent Canadian history would predict that regional tensions in Canada will be a constructive and creative force in the years ahead. It is not likely, for example, that French Canada or English Canada or the numerous groups of other origins in Canada will disappear or allow their distinctiveness to diminish in the years to 2000. Canada, as another example, will be a very far-sighted and daring country indeed—and it has not recently displayed these characteristics—if it adequately addresses the question of the distribution of wealth in the next two decades. Canadians need to gird themselves for the prospect of living in a society in which anything approaching national consensus on any significant issue will be extraordinarily difficult. Canada's diversity is one of its strengths, and that strength, as well as the tensions it encourages, will remain very evident. Helping citizens to deal constructively with tensions in society is a legitimate activity of all educational institutions, particularly those which serve the adult population.

A CHANGED CANADA—CHANGING COLLEGES

Canada of the year 2000 is likely to be a different country, in several important ways, from what it is today. Its place among nations will be better—or worse. Long held values at the very core of society will be challenged. Life for most Canadians in 2000 will not be as it now is.

Community colleges must be as dynamic as the society they serve, but no single model for college development in Canada is advocated in the chapters that follow. Rather, each college or college system must set its own future in consideration of its history, current realities, and the needs of the population to be served in different parts of the country. The issues presented in Part II are the ones which college people in all parts of Canada have recognized as of paramount importance for their futures; options for action in addressing these issues are outlined. There is no universally suitable choice of action, just as there is no ideal college model for Canada. All the issues call for fresh vision, anticipation, and change. Canada's colleges have the people to reassess, to anticipate, and to map better futures.

6

COLLEGES AS INSTITUTIONS

The Early Years

When community colleges first came into being in Canada, questions of identity and image were very low in the order of priorities. These institutions and their leaders were far too busy doing all sorts of things. They designed programmes, hired staff, amassed libraries, and built campuses; they welcomed students in great numbers and organized services; they experimented with governance structures and tested different organizational models. They expanded their activities into more remote and less densely populated areas of the regions they were to serve. Above all, they tried new teaching methods, new approaches to instruction, and new ways of dealing with students.

The first years of Canada's new colleges were almost uniformly exciting, challenging, exhilarating. People working in these colleges were energetic and ambitious, and most of them developed an extraordinary level of commitment to their students, their work, and their institutions. Growth and expansion were the call of the day, and thoughts of consolidation or pauses for stock-taking were very far from most college people's minds. The early days were truly "good old days."

To the communities served by these colleges, the early days were intriguing. Most approached their new colleges tentatively and found them to be unusually friendly and accommodating. Colleges seemed to be less bureaucratic than other educational institutions they had encountered; they appeared to offer—or to be prepared to offer—virtually any educational, social, or recreational activity that adults in their regions wished to try. Many offered services that most people had never heard of, and efforts were made to help all applicants determine how their college might best be of service to them. To the first students, college education was a refreshing change. There was little reason for them to be critical of their new institutions.

Of course, many people simply ignored these colleges. Many citizens, especially in larger urban areas, whose own backgrounds included a university education, had similar aspirations for their children and saw the new institutions as being "for other people." Many teachers and counsellors in secondary schools presumed that these new institutions were really for people who did not have the intellectual maturity or aptitude for university studies and advised their students accordingly. Some people in other kinds of post-secondary institutions reacted negatively to the new colleges as tolerable but hardly significant interlopers. The new colleges faced indifference, suspicion, and faint amusement from some citizens, but enthusiasm from others.

Meanings of College

In retrospect, it may well have been a strategic error to call these new institutions "colleges" because that term had been used to identify so many different kinds of institution; indeed, the term had become so imprecise as to be almost meaningless.

Most people were familiar with the terms "university", "institute of technology", "technical school", "trade school", and "vocational school". And they had at least a general idea of what institutions with these labels did. In contrast, the term "college" was open to several quite distinct interpretations, and institutions with that label did very different things. The medieval term "collegium" had a very precise meaning quite different from what a college is today;[1] the term "college" has in some instances in contemporary North America been used to describe an operating unit of a university; in other cases, the term refers to little more than a residence; in still other cases, it has been a synonym for university. Independent secondary schools are often also called colleges, and it is not uncommon for private sector training institutions to use the label "college" regardless of the kind of training they provide. Further, there are labour colleges, colleges of theology, junior colleges, and other institutions known as "colleges." To add to the imprecision, some of these new institutions were called "regional colleges," others "community colleges," still others "colleges of applied arts and technology"—all terms which were foreign to the Canadian educational tradition and which were only vaguely explained to those who enrolled, or worked, in them.

Why, then, was the term "college" used to identify these new institutions? The prime reason was that this label, in a middle class value system, carried prestige and might provide some public credibility. Instant credibility was important to the founders of new colleges and to legislators who had brought them into being.

Origins and Limitations

It was quite clear in the early years that, to the general public, the new colleges lacked a distinctive identity. To many people, both within and beyond these institutions, it was not at all clear what these new institutions were. Their particular character was difficult to discern. They had yet to establish and project their own persona, and their indistinctiveness was in large measure a factor of their origins. Unlike other educational institutions, most came into being by the quick stroke of a legislator's pen at times when politicians faced the pressure of having to create more space for more students to continue their education. Indeed, in some provinces, whole systems of public colleges came into being almost overnight as legislators and bureaucrats rushed to respond to the greatest population explosion in Canadian history.[2] Instant colleges, necessarily makeshift in several respects, immediately produced the best instant education and instant graduates that they could. Nevertheless, most of these colleges have since not only survived but made significant societal contributions, particularly at the local level.

This creative response was all the more remarkable because Canada's colleges were legislated into being with very modest philosophical or directional underpinnings. It is true that, in almost all provinces, a "study" had provided the public rationale for the creation of new educational institutions; in Quebec, for example, a Royal Commission produced a magnificent five-volume analysis of the state and needs of public education prior to the legislation establishing the CEGEP.[3]

All too often, however, the visions for public colleges were lost in the hard realities of the political processes: first, legislators dealt with the structures and some aspects of the governing apparatus for these new institutions, but they neglected, or shied away from, the substance; next, bureaucrats charged with overseeing the implementation of legislation took predictably cautious steps and, in so doing, dulled the more daring visions of what these colleges might become. In addition, in some cases, universities and other more established educational institutions used whatever influence they had to ensure that the new colleges would not be too threatening to their own existence and plans.[4] Despite these developments, Canada's new colleges did get themselves established and operating, but through the wile and the wit and energy of those people, within and beyond their walls, who made of them what they could.

With flimsy philosophical bases, a skeletal legislative framework, a dubious base for public credibility, often with little political support, and a pressure to produce instant results, the new colleges could reasonably be expected to borrow freely from other institutions. Most of them did so. They transplanted, or attempted to transplant, the organizational and governmental structures of the university, with faculties and departments and deans. They modelled their personnel selection procedures on those of the university or the business corporation. They borrowed the management styles of secondary schools or school boards. They grafted on the student personnel service concept of the large secondary school. They copied the rituals and traditions and mores of other institutions. In all but what they taught and how they taught, they were more imitative than innovative.

However imitative they have been, it is difficult to argue with their initial success. Several of them have become known nationally as superior institutions; college graduates in all parts of the country quickly justified the significant investment in this new form of education.[5] And, to reach that level of success, they shared their perspectives and experiences in a massive exercise in reciprocal help, in addition to going their own separate ways.[6]

The Notion of Public College Culture

Because of its successes, the college movement in Canada has become more sure of itself over the years. It can, of course, rest on its laurels and continue to be a somewhat obscure component of Canadian public education. Alternatively, it can choose now to be creative in ways in which it has previously been imitative; in short, it can decide to develop quite consciously its own culture, just as universities, other kinds of institutions, and school systems did in their developmental years. Under any circumstances, energy directed toward the development of a distinctive college culture in Canada would be well spent. It would allow the colleges not merely to carry on, but to rise to a new level of achievement and thereby claim the greater public credibility they deserve.

The circumstances of the mid-1980's, in particular, encourage the development of a unique Canadian college culture. Financial constraints, demands for greater accountability and relevance, and growing concern about persistently high levels of unemployment almost compel a reassessment of the role of public colleges, and the search for a distinctive and socially significant contribution by these institutions. Furthermore, the deliberate development of a college culture in Canada would not be an artificial fabrication; these colleges already possess characteristics which give them some distinctiveness. What is now necessary is to identify and reinforce, rather than suppress, these components of distinctiveness.

The Public Character of Public Colleges

The first of these distinctive components is their explicit public character. Unlike many contemporary universities which now refer to themselves as public because they now receive the largest share of their funding from the public coffers, Canada's new colleges were originally established unequivocally as publicly supported and publicly accountable. Unlike school systems which are also public organizations, colleges have no captive market; they must perform in such a manner as to have citizens choose to use them, and they must gain public support by their performance and by broad understanding of their performance.

Particularly in times of retrenchment and restraint, the acquisition of active public support is no easy task because it is far simpler for governments to withdraw their support from institutions which serve a relatively small sector of the total population and to insist that the students themselves pay for the college services they receive.[7] Of greater danger, however, is the tendency of some colleges themselves to seek less public accountability and to yearn and strive for a more limited mandate, akin to that of a university.

The university is quite rightly and in subtle ways separate from larger society because the university has a clear and historic role as social critic.[8] The public college, in contrast, has no such mandate; its role is one of service to citizens and to society. College personnel, rather than envy the detachment of their university counterparts, should quite deliberately relish the opportunity to convince, over and over again, their publics of the value of the services they perform. Admittedly, it is frustrating and taxing to have to justify one's existence continually. The advantage of doing so, however, is the gradual broadening of constituency support which results. Canada's colleges will thrive only to the extent that they serve their many publics and give evidence of their commitment to the broadest possible public accountability.

Co-operative Orientation

The second distinctive component of Canada's public colleges is their peculiar status, to varying degrees, as both local-regional institutions and as provincially oriented organizations. Unlike universities, which have a very large measure of autonomy by statute that allows them to ignore, co-operate, or compete with sister institutions, colleges in every province of Canada are now individual components of systems or networks more than autonomous organizations. By definition, public colleges should be co-operating institutions, even more so than school systems. School jurisdictions are intended by law and practice to be all things to all students in their districts; no college, in contrast, is now expected to be all-inclusive in the range of its offerings. Any tendency for colleges to compete, emulating other institutions with other mandates, is simply not in the public or college interest.

Inter-institutional competition is far from absent from the Canadian college scene. Perhaps such competition was inevitable in the early years as individual institutions staked their individual claims and as these colleges had little choice but to follow their entrepreneurial instincts; the systems must now mature to the point where voluntary and cost effective co-operation is the rule rather than the exception.

Voluntary inter-institutional co-operation, in some provinces, is hardly a simple challenge. In British Columbia, for example, the mere existence and mandate of the Open Learning Institute has been viewed as a clear, and government-favoured, threat to the very survival of more than one college because that institution is mandated to do precisely what some colleges see as part of their own mandate. In virtually every metropolitan area of Canada, it is a common practice for several post-secondary institutions to advertise their new offerings in the daily newspapers; however economical it may be, it is perceived by many ordinary citizens as wasteful, indeed shameful, hucksterism at public expense. Surely it is possible for public colleges to be, and be perceived as, institutions which are not competing with one another. The emergence of post-secondary consortia in Alberta to meet the needs of citizens in smaller communities is an excellent example of co-operation among educational institutions and between the government and institutions. If they are to capitalize on their strengths and distinctiveness, Canada's colleges need to give greater emphasis to their status as co-operating units of province-wide networks, even at the apparent expense of their institutional autonomy.

Admissions

Canada's colleges have also been distinctive in being approachable by all citizens. Most of these institutions came into existence at a time when other post-secondary institutions were turning away applicants: in some cases, rejection was based on the fact that the institutions simply could not accommodate any more students; in other cases, universities and specialized post-secondary institutions rightly rejected applications from people who were quite unprepared to undertake demanding further study.

The desire for greater exclusivity and a preoccupation with "standards" has already seeped into some colleges and provincial ministries, particularly in provinces where students have had the choice of different post-secondary institutions to pursue what appeared to be the same programmes. In many cases, public colleges seem to have become as admission-standard conscious as other institutions whose claims to exclusivity are far more rational and mandate-related.

A universal early feature of community colleges common throughout Canada was their openness, in one or another programme, to all who wished to further their education; admissions criteria, when space restrictions dictated that all applicants could not be accommodated, were intended to include factors in addition to prior academic performance, so that all applicants—regardless of age, sex, race, or socioeconomic background—might have an equal opportunity for admission. That feature of community colleges is now threatened by a search for artificial status.

Community colleges were never intended to be exclusive or selective. One of their essential objectives has been to accept all serious applicants, with all their strengths and shortcomings, and to build instructional programmes which allow learners to proceed from where they are to where they wish to go. Universities and specialized post-secondary institutions have had no such mandate or prospects; they must, as they do, require the student to conform to what the institution has to offer. Other post-secondary institutions legitimately require students to meet institutionally determined standards. To be faithful to their origins and purposes, however, colleges must adapt to the individual "standards" of individual students.

The thought that virtually any citizen should be admissible to their college has been of real but often hushed concern to many college personnel. If their institution is truly accessible to all adults, it is claimed, it loses the ability to control programme quality; programmes will only be as strong as the students admitted to them. Unless there are moderately rigorous admissions standards, the argument goes, programme quality and institutional reputation will suffer. And who wants to be part of a second-rate institution?

The "second rate" argument is, of course, based on a hierarchical view of educational institutions: the institution that is the most exclusive must be the best, and the institution that is most accessible must be inferior. College people need to convince themselves and their publics that any hierarchical view of educational institutions is inappropriate to the kind of society in which Canadians live and that a real strength of a college is the heterogeneity of its student population. A community college ought to be a microcosm of the society it serves and it can be such only if it is truly open. Several kinds of educational institutions ought to exist side by side in a pluralist society, each with its own character, none more prestigious than another. Community colleges should relish the opportunity to be first class institutions of a particular kind whose status is acquired in part by an openness to all citizens who wish to continue learning. An open, rather than more restricted, approach to admission ought to characterize Canada's colleges in the years ahead as they help to democratize Canadian society and avoid the emergence of a de facto educational caste system in Canada.

Heterogeneity

A major implication of flexible admission requirements to colleges is breadth of activity: they have, or should have, no predetermined limit on programming, no fixed level at which to operate, and no predictable core of students. Colleges should not be schools: every public school jurisdiction has legally defined responsibilities and must, in practice, meet all basic educational requirements for young people within its territory (and, in many cases, provide some education for people beyond public school age as well). Nor are colleges universities. Universities and specialized institutions have historical and/or statutory constraints; their programmes are prescribed; their level of activity is identifiable; and their student populations are correspondingly homogeneous. College programming and services should, by contrast, be as diverse as the needs that an open admission policy dictate. College programmes and services should be determined and adjusted, as required, by the educational needs of the students; they should accept both the most able and those whose background is far short of potential performance at a post-secondary level; they should be characterized by variability of student body, and in-and-out-and-in mentality by students, and a student population including many for whom formal education is but a part of their daily lives. Community colleges should be, by definition and style of operation, heterogeneous.

Accordingly, many of the traditional features of post-secondary institutions have questionable application to Canada's colleges. A student society as the collective voice of the student population, for example, may well be an anachronism for public colleges—in fact just another special interest lobby—because any heterogeneous college needs many voices to express the concerns of the many different student populations. The traditional exhortations for institutional loyalty by students of a community college are misplaced; "school spirit" is indeed ephemeral when many students have multiple preoccupations beyond the college, when the amenities of residential accommodation do not exist, and when many students are simply at an age when proclaimed institutional identification is no longer a strong personal need. Intercollegiate athletics and other competitions also have a hollow ring for many college students. The general atmosphere of the campus of a college, if indeed the college thinks in terms of campus or campuses, is simply different from that of more traditional, more conventional post-secondary institutions. The differences should be recognized, not regretted, and incorporated into the development of a culture unique to the community.

Continuing Education

In Canada, "college" ought to become synonymous with "centre for the continuing education of adults." In its ideal form, the community college would be open to anyone beyond school age and would permit each "adult" to "continue" learning, frequently with interruptions as required for other than educational pursuits, at an individually appropriate pace, to achieve individually satisfying and socially useful goals. Holland College in Charlottetown is one of several Canadian colleges originally designed with this orientation. It would provide opportunities for all citizens to obtain services which would help them identify personally realistic objectives; it would challenge the able and rebuild the self-confidence of those whose previous educational performance had been hampered by a system which saw education as a sieve through which only a small percentage of people should pass. Many Canadian colleges seem not to have seen the contradiction in creating Adult or Continuing or Community Education departments within their institutions, because this practice suggests that some (indeed, the most important?) work they do does not fall into these categories.

From this perspective, it is interesting to examine some aspects of the history of adult education in Canada.[9] Not long ago, "adult education" was largely provided by committed non-professional volunteers and organizations which saw education outside formal structures as critically important to less advantaged segments of Canadian society who did not reap much benefit from the formal educational system. They worked on the fringe of Canadian education, were experimental and daring, and their formal efforts did much to shape the character of contemporary Canada. A variety of programmes in Saskatchewan, the Farm Forums in Quebec and Ontario, and the "Antigonish Movement" in Nova Scotia are but a few of the most visible successes. Little by little over time, as adult education was viewed as more "legitimate" (or at least could no longer be ignored), it entered the publicly supported sector of education, and much of it became institutionalized—while, some would say, it lost much of its vitality in the process. That it was not funded on an equal basis with more traditional forms of post-secondary education added to its isolation.

Many of Canada's most prominent adult educators provided active leadership to the establishment of community college systems in several provinces of Canada in the hope that these colleges would continue and expand the earlier adult education spirit and avoid the pressures to become simply traditional institutions with traditional objectives and aspirations. It is doubtful that Canada's colleges have yet taken full advantage of this leadership and vision and made these colleges into centres where all "adults" could "continue" their education by "extending" educational opportunity in the interests of the people in "communities" of Canada. In part, this has been the fault of the colleges and of adult educators; in greater part, it has been the fault of public authorities who have seen non-traditional adult education as little more than an inexpensive way of expanding educational opportunity.

All of the characteristics noted above could form a framework for a distinctive public college culture. However, that culture will not simply emerge spontaneously. What these colleges do together and how they conduct themselves collectively in the future will determine whether a college culture actually materializes. An action plan is necessary to develop a Canadian college culture.

Purpose

Canada's colleges should, first and foremost, reaffirm their distinctive purpose. The historic purposes of the university, simply put, are research, teaching, and education for the professions. Debate about the precedence of research over teaching is an arid one; ideally, one complements and enriches the other. The university in all its parts must be a centre for research with teaching growing out of and challenging that research. That many universities have recently gone far beyond these basic purposes into the area of public service and that they may in the future seek to extend themselves beyond their raison d'etre ought not obscure the particular, unique character of the university.

The purpose of the technical or technological institution is to train. While theoretical studies form parts of the curriculum of any such institution, their objective is pragmatic: to produce the well-trained graduate with competencies to do things well. In the years ahead, that training should become far more sophisticated because graduates will have to live and work in a far more complex world. But effective, contemporary training should be the goal and purpose of such institutions.

And what of the community college? It has been popular to contrast these institutions and their purpose by stressing that they are teaching institutions in which quality of instruction is a priority in relation to research; indeed, that research has no place in the college.

To claim that the college's priority purpose is to teach, the university's is to conduct research, and the technical institution's is to train does an injustice to all three kinds of institutions; in fact, all three must give attention to all of these functions. The more significant difference among these kinds of institutions should be their relative emphasis on the learner and what is to be learned. In the case of the university and the technical/technological institution, the constant is what is to be learned; the learner is the variable who must master what the institution declares is to be learned. Historically and quite correctly, universities have had a preoccupation with entrance requirements and standards of performance because they know from experience that students cannot master what is required unless they have been prepared in advance for the level of performance to be demanded at the university. Similarly, universities have placed relatively less emphasis on the art and skills of teaching because they have rightly assumed that the students must rise to meet the institutional requirements rather than that universities must meet the particular needs of the students. Analagously, the technical/technological instructor must produce a graduate who can meet predetermined levels of achievement; the instructor has neither the mandate nor the resources to bring the student up to a level of initial performance and then allow the student to begin the real training.

The community college differs significantly from both other kinds of post-secondary institution because neither the student nor the curriculum content is constant. The range of student competencies in an institution which is open and truly accessible is extraordinarily varied, the variety of "what is to be learned" ought to correspond to the variety of student and societal objectives, and the diversity of learning modes of students will be as broad as the student body itself.

In a college with a student body composed of some students who wish to be trained for some specific tasks or occupations, others who wish to keep open the option to transfer, properly prepared, to another institution, still others who wish to start their formal education a second time, and others simply wishing to learn for personal fulfilment or enjoyment, the real institutional emphasis ought to be on the individual student and the personal learning objectives of that student—this is the essential purpose of the college. College instructors must teach or help students learn, must engage in research (albeit of a different kind in many cases from that conducted by a university professor), must train, must re-educate students, and must make their expertise available to the citizenry as a community resource. The single thread in this whole process is the individual student and the objectives of that student. With a rapid and continuing turnover of students and their objectives, the college instructor can never lose sight of the student any more than university scholars can lose sight of their research responsibilities. The scholar's primary allegiance is to a discipline; the community college instructor's primary allegiance ought to be to the student.

This accent on the student and the student's objectives has several implications for the operation of a college. One of these implications is that the college needs to set its own limits, because no institution can effectively be all things to all people. In some provinces, Ontario, for example, these limits are substantially set by provincial legislation, but even in these cases an institutional assessment of its own limits is desirable. For this reason, a "mission statement" and a regular review of institutional performance are virtually imperative. A college's desire to be open needs to be balanced by the reality of limited resources.

Are not openness to all citizens and institutional limits contradictory or in conflict? They would be, if colleges viewed themselves as independent entities; however, through co-operation with other institutions in the public college networks throughout Canada, and through co-operation with other community agencies with education mandates (YMCA's, school boards, for example), a significant broadening of opportunity can still be possible when individual colleges resist the temptation to bite off more than they can competently chew. The quality of a community college ought to be measured by how well it performs in relation to its purpose and its resources, not by how many students it serves.

In establishing institutional limits, colleges need to remain aware of their need to retain some breadth of programming and service. It would appear far better for a college serving a large community to do a little of many things for many students than to set limits by specializing in only a few programme areas. If essential categories of community college education can be identified as basic education, transfer education, general education, career education, vocational education, and community education, it would be preferable for colleges to offer some of each rather than to specialize in one or two because this range is most representative of the society to be served. Heterogeneity of student population and breadth of programming ought to be preserved as special features of the community college. The college has an explicit or implicit residual responsibility for the education of adult learners and ought to assume this responsibility in the public interest.

If the central purpose of a college is to respond to the particular learning needs of individual students, there are clear implications for determining the appropriate size and organization of these institutions. Simply put, the view that "big is beautiful" need not apply. The argument in favour of multiversities, massive secondary schools, and other large institutions is that there are significant economies of scale to be realized. This argument has much to recommend it where production and return on capital investment are the objectives, but is unquestionably less tenable when development of individuals through learning is the objective.

We now have sufficient experience with large educational institutions and systems to suggest that economies of scale are often offset by less obvious but no less real costs of administration, control, and co-ordination.[10] Colleges are labour-intensive institutions; they do not have the capital requirements of sophisticated research facilities on the frontier of scholarship, as do universities and institutions of applied technology, nor do the principles of mass production apply to the provision of a variety of services to a diversity of learners. Colleges, or at least college campuses, should approximate supermarkets more than assembly lines. In and beyond the 1980's, Canada's colleges might be well advised to scale down rather than expand and, if necessary, provoke the establishment of more colleges or more campuses. The advantages of more personalized education—through smaller classes, more individualized instruction, more direct contacts between learner and instructor—coupled with hidden overhead costs of large-scale operations of colleges and college systems require careful and detailed analysis. Even where scaling down is not practical, greater attention needs to be given to organizational considerations that can increase the personal character of colleges and reduce the psychological distance between learner and teacher. Open learning systems and the use of distance education techniques are particularly appropriate to community colleges and offer genuine opportunities to personalize college education.

A third implication of recognizing student objectives as the focal point for the college is the notion of institution as place. Traditions of our society compel us to think of colleges and universities and schools in terms of campuses and physical locations; indeed, it is almost impossible for many college people not to identify an institution with a "campus," and such identification is appropriate to most universities and most specialized institutions.

The need for a "campus" for a community college is less compelling, if the essential purpose of such a college is taken seriously. Students can indeed meet their own objectives in several different locations: in a classroom or library, in industry, in a meeting room, or in any other place where learner and teacher can come into personalized contact. In fact, for many students much college learning may need only minimal contact with teachers. North Island College in British Columbia is but one practical example of an open learning "system" which puts no emphasis whatever on campus identification.[11] The entire Saskatchewan college system was originally premised on the fact that colleges do not have to have their own space at all.[12] Indeed, the argument that colleges should be distinctive is not a suggestion that they should be peas in the same pod. By their very nature as respondents to different communities, they should have many differences. Colleges in metropolitan areas where universities operate, for example, properly should have a different range of programming and probably a different institutional emphasis in all respects from those in communities where the college is the only centre for post-secondary education. Colleges operating side by side with school districts which have thriving adult education programmes need to adjust their activities to provide, co-operatively with the school districts, the best and most cost-effective joint service to the community. Similarly, outreach and extension activities of universities should influence the programming and services of colleges. In summary, community colleges should retain the degree of flexibility appropriate to the community to be served, in light of all other educational opportunities available to their communities. Anything less in times of scarce resources, indeed at any time, seems socially indefensible.

Governance

The way in which colleges are governed should be a contributing element to their distinctive culture. There has been almost an irresistible pressure in several colleges for employees to seek to govern their own institution. After all, a large measure of self-government is characteristic of other post-secondary institutions, particularly universities wherein the senate has been the de facto institutional government. There are sound reasons for senate-type government of universities. These institutions are intended to exercise full freedom to challenge societal values. Furthermore, the nature of the specialized activities of universities requires an inward-looking perspective that invites self-criticism by and of the community of scholars. To propose any other kind of governance of universities would be to undercut their mission, their social effectiveness, and their historic role on the edge of the larger society.

There is no justification for the same kind of governance for community colleges. On the contrary, the public character of the college in the service of society compels a different approach to government and control. Such colleges are meant to respond to, rather than be critics of, their society and there is no way in which this intent can be realized unless colleges remain, in their objectives and orientation, accountable to external boards whose sole preoccupation should be to ensure that the college operates in conformity with the board members' perception of the public interest. Of course, the employed members of colleges should be able to contribute significantly to the policies of their institutions and should have full freedom to exercise their professional responsibility to their students. The fact remains, however, that the interests of the personnel of community colleges must not take precedence over the judgment of the representatives of the community to be served by the college.

Indeed, community colleges have had a clear opportunity to test new forms of internal governance, but they have tended to forfeit this opportunity. Young as they are, most have moved very quickly to institutionalize their forms of government, their administrative structures, and their organizational patterns. The ambiguity of their role, their lack of public support, and the general insecurity of their status have prompted many colleges to cast in stone their styles and forms of management all too quickly. Nothing is less conducive to the continuing vitality of the college movement in Canada. All of their internal apparatus should be recognized as tentative and experimental with the commitment that, whatever the structures may be, the objective is to retain and foster their outward-looking, public character through final responsibility resting with representatives of the public to be served, not the employees who provide the services. A second commitment must be that the members of the institution will have full chance to play their role in governance experimentation.

Institutional Cohesion

Institutional unity should also be a component of Canada's college culture. Douglas T. Kenny, as President of the University of British Columbia, observed that "the mission of the university should be, in large measure, the aggregation of the missions of its constituent Faculties, which in turn should be aggregates of the missions of their Departments."[13] Appropriate though this statement may be to the university setting, it is diametrically opposed to the community college milieu.

Good universities are indeed loose federations of co-existing faculties and departments; community colleges are not. To be most effective, colleges need to place the greatest possible emphasis on the integration of what they do, rather than on the separateness of their activities. This integration ought to be most obvious in the alignment of programmes or grouping of students with differing objectives. There is seldom a good reason why a student wishing to learn German for enjoyment should not be in the same laboratory or discussion group with another student who wishes to learn German for transfer credit to university. There is seldom a good reason why a student in business management should be segregated from an arts student for the study of introductory economics. There is no reason why a part-time student should be required to attend courses designed exclusively for part-time students. There is every good reason for young and older students to work together when their educational objectives are similar. Many colleges necessarily began with a different perspective on programme development; the advantages of integrated programming, to say nothing of more cost effective instruction, now justify considerably greater attention and a change from traditional programming whose rationale was totally different. The traditional distinctions between credit and non-credit instruction, full- and part-time students, younger and older students, warrant re-examination in the college setting.

If integration of programming based on student objectives merits detailed feasibility study, even more so does the integration of services with programmes. For far too long educational institutions have seen student services as peripheral or subordinate to the direct instructional or learning process, with the result that such services have commonly been viewed as dealing with "student as person" while instruction has been viewed as dealing with "student as learner." Given the heterogeneity of the college student population and the necessary diversity of its programming, traditionally isolated student services ought to be viewed as complementary to, and as important as, instructional programming, all focused on the individual student as learner. Counselling should not be viewed as an ancillary "service" provided as therapy to people who happen to be registered at college; rather, it should be seen as a range of services needed by many students and applicants if they are to be able to achieve their learning objectives. Similarly, financial aid is not really a peripheral fringe benefit for some students; financial assistance and a related financial advising function can well make the crucial difference between student success or failure by helping the student to manage scarce resources effectively, thereby allowing the student to give maximum attention to learning objectives. A women's resource centre is not a high profile luxury in a community college; it may be an essential component as long as women students do not have equal access to the full range of educational and career opportunities. In colleges, an integration of services with programmes is the only logically and psychologically sound approach.

The integration of personnel, the development of a sense of shared task, is clearly the most important form of institutional integration if colleges are to realize their potential. It is legitimate for linguists and biologists to have only passing associations with each other in the university context, but it is antithetical to the purpose of the community college for instructors of physics to be isolated from instructors of geography while they both share in the pursuit of the same student's objectives. In college systems where new institutions were the product of melding other established, disparate institutions and where vocational and academic personnel encountered each other for the first time, the need for personnel integration is still particularly acute.

The integration of college personnel into the distinctive mores of the community college will be a complex task for some years to come. Virtually all college personnel are themselves products of different educational cultures; they are business persons and university graduates and technicians and community people for whom the college was initially an unfamiliar environment. They need opportunities to learn about their college and their students; they need to break habits of thinking and acting more appropriate to other kinds of institutions; they need to become acclimatized to and comfortable with a new and quite different setting. The complexity of the task, however, should only be stimulation to undertake it vigorously.

The complexity of integrating college personnel is made no simpler by the fact that most colleges employ a high percentage of part-time staff whose employment is not solely dependent upon the college and whose personal preoccupations are broader than those of the full-time college employee. If, however, the community college is to remain faithful to its essential purpose, these part-time employees have as much need for integration with their full-time colleagues as do their full-time associates with one another.

Many of Canada's new colleges have tended to shy away from training or orientation sessions for their personnel for a variety of reasons. In many cases, they have simply been too busy; in other cases, the particular character of the community college has not been recognized and therefore has not been an obvious topic for orientation. In yet other cases, orientation to this kind of institution and culture has not been a priority simply because "other institutions don't do this sort of thing"; staff training would be an admission of less than fully satisfactory past performance. Whatever the reason, the successes and failures of the colleges to date provide ample reason for genuine efforts to build greater cohesion and unity of purpose among all employees in every college.

Conclusion

The community college is very much a unique component of Canadian education. The bases for this distinctiveness, both theoretical and practical, are only now becoming evident in any comprehensive way. Once recognized and appreciated, they form the nucleus of a unique culture which needs to be fostered if these colleges are to take their rightful place within society as a whole and within the Canadian educational community.

Perhaps the single most damaging feature of the Canadian college movement has been the tendency for its members and others to evaluate these institutions on bases appropriate to other kinds of institutions. Where colleges prepare students for university entrance or for advanced standing in university, it has commonly been the mores of the university by which the college has been judged. Where the college has prepared students with job-entry skills, it has been the employer market that has sometimes made unwarranted assumptions about what graduates must know and do. Where colleges have provided varieties of education for personal and social development of individuals, comparisons with the work of other institutions in this educational arena have been inevitable.

It is not unreasonable for community colleges to assert themselves now, to display publicly their strengths and limitations, to be themselves—in short, to develop a uniquely appropriate Canadian college culture and to acquire a "parity of esteem" with other components of Canadian education. Once this objective has been achieved, the public credibility of colleges will no longer be an issue. Any allegation that Canada's community colleges may be "overfunded redundancies in the context of the times"[14] will be put to rest.

ACCESSIBILITY

Well into the 1980's, accessibility was one of the buzzwords of Canada's colleges. In every province, one of the prime justifications for establishing new colleges had been to open up post-secondary education to a much broader segment of the general population. Universities, it was said, were by their very nature, quite selective if not elitist (although they too became much more "accessible" throughout the 1970's); technical and technological institutes offered a narrower and more specialized curriculum which had historically been geared to addressing manpower training needs and appealed to only a limited segment of the population. The new colleges were to be the salvation, or at least the avenue of opportunity, for citizens who aspired to other forms of post-secondary education.

Curriculum Breadth

Canada's community colleges responded exceedingly well to the call to "open their doors" by developing curricula previously unheard of in Canada. They offered a deliberately broad curriculum, as broad as their provincial legislation would allow. All of them offered a rich new variety of technical or career programmes intended to lead to immediate employment in new occupational areas, with the expectation that graduates would not require retraining in a few short years because of the breadth and substance of these new programmes. Most colleges also introduced or expanded their shorter term trade and vocational programmes to provide a much broader range of job-preparatory opportunities for many more Canadians—with a significant boost from the federal government which invested heavily in training programmes prompted by the bustling Canadian economy of the late 1960's and the 1970's.

At least as dramatic was the emphasis placed on adult basic education by Canada's young colleges.[15] Thousands of Canadians who did not have the scholastic credentials to study or train at the post-secondary level were given a "second chance"; colleges dipped down well below the traditional post-secondary level to provide upgrading for adults short of basic literacy skills; several levels of basic education (equivalent to years of elementary and secondary schooling) were provided in every province. At first, these programmes were intended to provide students with fundamental literacy skills, largely in mathematics and language, which would allow them to pursue vocational training and then enter the skilled workforce with a much better chance of reasonable and satisfactory employment. Soon, however, these basic education programmes were expanded to include literacy education for its own sake, and, in the bargain, many Canadians for the first time discovered that they could master academic skills which would allow them to pursue a variety of studies beyond the secondary level to which they could not have reasonably aspired without the second chance offered by Canada's new colleges. By the end of the 1970's, optimists in Canada's colleges forecast the eradication of adult illiteracy within years as a result of the emphasis on basic education for all adults.

Closely related to the adult basic education emphasis was a curriculum movement to expand second language training for the many people in Canada for whom English or French was not the first language or the language of the home. Going well beyond the language requirements for immigrants to obtain citizenship status, most of Canada's colleges, again with substantial support from the Canadian government, provided increasing amounts of second language training. With substantial immigration throughout the 1970's, second language training became an important, integral part of the work of many of the new colleges. In the same pattern as developed with basic education, the earliest forms of second language training were justified on the grounds that they provided the language skills necessary for new Canadians then to pursue vocational training required for enhanced employment opportunity. Before the mid-1970's, however, many new Canadians saw second language training as the door which opened up many personal and occupational opportunities that would otherwise have been denied. By the late 1970's, second language training was also eagerly sought by thousands of people who were well-established in business; they simply wanted to improve their ability to speak, work, and live in a society in which English and French were the official languages. By the 1980's, second language training was one of the most popular and most successful components of the programming of several colleges.

In provinces where the new colleges had the mandate to offer general education to a post-secondary level, parallel to or preparatory to the first years of university undergraduate studies, many of these colleges developed this aspect of their curriculum with gusto.[16] Indeed, some of them saw this form of post-secondary education as their special mission if not their raison d'être. In Quebec all of the CEGEP offered "enseigement générale" some of extraordinary quality and range. Even more important, despite the efforts of provincial and many institutional leaders to steer students into occupationally oriented programmes, students (and their parents) insisted on maintaining their opportunity to attend university by enroling in two-year general education programmes in far greater numbers than were anticipated. In British Columbia, most colleges, even those with very small population bases, developed academic studies or liberal studies or arts and science programmes of substance and offered them not only on their major campuses, but also in satellite centres with sparse populations. When resources were plentiful, many of Canada's public colleges truly diversified their curricula; even as resources shrunk, the philosophical, if not always the practical, commitment to a comprehensive curriculum remained one of the predominant features of several colleges. General education through public colleges came in several forms: in standard university-influenced forms and in refreshingly new and imaginatively packaged ways.

This commitment to comprehensiveness as a means of broadening access and creating educational opportunity for more people was most evident in the organization, development, and expansion of continuing or community education.[17] From their very beginning, most of the colleges created bright and attractive short term programmes of extraordinary variety to meet the particular needs of special interest groups or the general population they were to serve. Continuing and community education programmes really allowed the colleges to stretch their curriculum imaginations in the 1970's. They agreed to offer virtually anything of a recreational or social or educational nature desired by even a small group of people; it was not uncommon for them to advertise an almost bewildering array of evening and weekend courses, and then be pleased if more than 50 per cent of these courses should attract sufficient numbers of students to warrant being offered. Colleges dreamed up course ideas almost without limit; their instructors and planners insisted that new courses be advertised as a way of stimulating demand for more education and training. They knew, even if their clientele did not, what was good for Canadian adults. Colleges employed development officers and animateurs and change agents and outreach personnel whose task it was to learn about their communities, to create educational demand, to reach into their regions and communities to determine what courses and community activities they could promote as a way of achieving the goal of more education for everybody. Evening and weekend activities—from gold panning to bicycle repair to Great Books to Esperanto to beginners' bridge to conceptual blockbusting—expanded into "college in a day," summer sessions, and off-campus ventures. Canada's public colleges "did their thing"; community groups found colleges to be convenient if not indispensable resources; individual citizens had the chance to become instructors or create their own courses and offer them to their fellow citizens; education of one's choice on demand was a growing characteristic of many of these colleges. In an era of expansion, governments and colleges gladly invested in all forms of education and social service; citizens were delighted to pay modest amounts to satisfy their thirsts for more learning and the social interaction provided on college campuses and in other community locales. Dipping into public coffers to subsidize even the most unorthodox of learning experiences was quite acceptable to most Canadian citizens and governments.

But these colleges did not stop there. As a logical extension of their expanding training programmes, many colleges quickly seized the opportunity, and were encouraged by governments to do so, to develop educational links with business and industry in the communities they served.[18] In most cases, their initial efforts consisted of making contact with businesses in their communities for purposes of identifying, and then responding to, the training needs. By the mid-1970's, at least several colleges had taken the step of entering into formal contracts with business and industrial corporations to provide at cost some of their training, frequently on-site. By the late 1970's, contracting with business to supply training was a minor part of the work of many Canadian public colleges and a major endeavour of a few. The principle that Canada's new post-secondary institutions should contract with business and industry as a normal part of their activities was well in place in most provinces by the end of the 1970's.

By the late 1970's the more experienced of Canada's public colleges looked for even more outlets for their entrepreneurial spirit. One result was the emergence of international education as a growing and self-supporting component of college programming.[19] From the very start, a few colleges had made it a practice to bring to Canada groups of foreign students during the summer months for language training. However, in the mid-1970's, somewhat later than some of Canada's universities and technical institutions, colleges and organizations such as the Canadian International Development Agency (CIDA) and the Canadian Bureau of International Education (CBIE) began to recognize mutual interests. Spurred on by the enthusiasm and growing influence of the International Studies Bureau of the Association of Canadian Community Colleges (ACCC), several institutions sent exploratory missions first to new African and Caribbean nations and later to countries of the Middle East and those on the

Pacific Rim. More and more Canadian college personnel established or facilitated training programmes in foreign nations, and more and more foreign student groups found their way into colleges in Canada. The initial internationalization of colleges which had been designed to meet provincial if not local or regional needs attracted very little public attention in Canada, but what attention if did receive was largely favourable; Canadians were hardly opposed to the virtues of broadening the horizons of their college students and campuses, particularly when international education initiatives usually covered all their costs and in some cases generated modest profits. By the mid-1980's, international education was a major growth area for several colleges and one of the favoured choices for the exercise of entrepreneurialism and revenue generation.

Interspersed with all these common efforts to broaden the base of programming and services were individualized efforts by several colleges to respond in unique ways to the call for expanding accessibility to "college".[20] Some colleges developed specialized "institutes" to promote one or another cause; others found needs unique to their communities and went about the business of trying to satisfy those needs; some colleges found it appropriate to offer programmes for pre-schoolers and school children, usually in subjects which were considered to be of lower priority within the public school system. Some colleges opened their doors to high school students who were fascinated by computers long before computer education was incorporated into school curricula. Others recognized that senior citizens constituted a major portion of their constituencies who were more than eager to take advantage of whatever educational opportunities their colleges were prepared to offer them. Still others provided community theatre and fine arts activities and became more community educational resource centres than traditional colleges.

In sum, over a period of less than fifteen years, Canada's colleges had pushed the concept of accessibility to the point where the range of courses and community services offered went well beyond what the original planners of public college systems had anticipated. Canada wanted to give more Canadians access to more kinds of education than ever before, and Canada's colleges did an amazingly quick and thorough job of responding. Indeed, by the early 1980's, many Canadians assumed that subsidized access to the kind of education and training they wished to have was their right by practice if not by legislation. Canada's colleges provided curricula as comprehensive as the law allowed, and in some cases, the legal limits were interpreted very generously.

New Students

The call for more access to more kinds of education was not only manifested by the broadening of college currricula. Equally significant was the expansion of opportunity to sectors of the Canadian population which had previously had very limited access to any kind of post-secondary education. The expansion of programming was not for its own sake, but quite deliberately to make public colleges more inviting to more citizens, to give educational opportunity, substantially at public expense, to adults who wished to continue their education but who previously had very limited opportunity beyond that provided as part of the compulsory school systems within Canada.

The first people to take advantage of these new and expanded opportunities were middle class graduates of secondary schools who had not achieved well enough in school to obtain university admission. Joining them were young adults not yet ready or interested in university undergraduate studies but intrigued by the possibilities of the new career and occupational opportunities offered by these institutions.[21]

Canada's colleges did not long remain alternative post-secondary institutions for young, adult, male, middle class Canadians. Soon middle class young women (or their parents) recognized that colleges opened opportunity well beyond the traditional nursing and secretarial training courses which had been almost the only realistic post-secondary choices for women other than university. Despite this early development, it would be some years before the full spectrum of college programmes became realistically available to women students; the push for women in non-traditional jobs surfaced only in the late 1970's. It did not take long for colleges to demonstrate an appeal to less advantaged young men and women. Attracted by low or no tuition fees as well as educational and living subsidies through Canada Manpower (later Canada Employment and Immigration Commission) for many short-term vocational programmes, many Canadians with previously low educational aspirations were knocking on the doors of Canada's colleges. The process of real democratization of Canadian education had begun. And graduates obtained jobs in record numbers, or went on to university or more advanced technical studies. Quite apart from promotional literature of the colleges, the informal grapevine was that Canada's new colleges indeed were accessible to the financially and educationally less advantaged. By the mid-1970's, Canada's colleges were broadly recognized as new avenues of opportunity for the previously disenfranchised.

Several of the new colleges also attempted, from the earliest years, to make a particular appeal to part-time students. Promoting the view that college education could effectively be combined with employment and child-raising, the new colleges attracted more and more older students who wished to re-enter the workforce, to acquire new skills and credentials, or to have the intellectual stimulation of college level work. By the late 1970's, the median age of Canada's college students was well beyond that of Canadian universities, and at least a step toward the "learning society" had been taken by Canada through its new colleges. It would be a mistake, however, to argue that most of Canada's colleges had given parity of esteem and service to young full-time and older part-time students. The truth is that most of Canada's colleges still appealed primarily to younger adults even though older students were accommodated and frequently welcomed.

In short order, new Canadians, young people looking for the opportunity to start their formal education over again, young business people eager to acquire new skills, people who had been failures in school as youngsters but were now determined to make up for lost time, heads of single parent families, senior citizens thirsting for intellectual and social stimulation, university graduates now in search of marketable skills, and simply ordinary citizens wishing to enrich their lives found Canada's new colleges as at least a partial answer. The International Year of the Disabled, 1979, highlighted the need for a broadly based equality of opportunity for Canada's disabled persons, and no Canadian institution responded better to this call than Canada's community colleges. By the late 1970's, these colleges had become "citizen schools" of broad popularity; particularly in non-metropolitan areas without other agencies for voluntary education for younger and older folk, the colleges had made education of many varieties truly accessible to virtually all citizens. Many of them had become microcosms of the communities and regions they served.

Narrowing Accessibility

By a combination of government funding and institutional creativity, Canada's colleges had been able to reduce several barriers to education and training for Canadian adults: financial barriers, through the maintenance of low tuition fee levels combined with substantial government-sponsored student aid programmes; geographic barriers, by becoming established in virtually every major population centre, and by reaching out to smaller communities and individual citizens in more remote areas through distance education and correspondence means; social barriers, by welcoming students of all backgrounds, ages, abilities, and educational interest.

But, by the late 1970's in some places, and across the nation by the early 1980's, universal accessibility could no longer be taken for granted. The downturn in the Canadian economy, declining government revenues, rising unemployment, and associated economic ills influenced these colleges as much as other Canadian institutions. The virtues and values of broad accessibility to post-secondary education came under review.

What are possible responses for Canadian colleges in such circumstances? Many people in Canada, but few of them in government, argue that economic downturns are the very times for heavier public investment in education and training of the kinds provided by these colleges. With high unemployment levels and decreasing job opportunity, poor economic times are presented as those during which colleges should devote their attention to preparing citizens for what is seen as the inevitable upswing in the economy. (In contemporary times, many would argue that Canada's colleges should be preparing people not for an economic upswing but for the new economic age well underway in Canada.) This is a particularly apt response in a country such as Canada, which has historically looked to immigration rather than training to meet new and expanding manpower needs as economic upswings have occurred. Traditionally, Canada's young people have not had increased training opportunities in difficult economic times, and Canada's older workers have had few opportunities to retrain in such times. Instead, Canada has imported skilled workers as its economy has improved, and they have done an excellent job, but the price has been less employment and underemployment for the many Canadians who would have been willing and able to undertake training, if only the training opportunities had been created at the right times in Canada's economic cycles.

A second response in difficult economic times is to hold the line in public financial support to post-secondary institutions. This response, at least maintaining a constant level of support for post-secondary education regardless of the times, has been the strategy of the Canadian government in the mid-1980's and of those provincial governments where even good economic times did not bring great prosperity. It is significant, as one example, that New Brunswick has seen fit to classify college education as a matter pertaining to economic development and therefore favoured for purposes of public support, while wealthier British Columbia has seen college education as a social service, and therefore a costly liability drawing too heavily on the public purse.

But there has been yet another response in the 1980's: to reduce public expenditures on colleges, to demand of institutions that they seek alternate sources of funding, to pass on more costs to the learner/consumer, to require productivity increases, and to limit the "product line" to those activities which are most cost effective.

All of these measures can be defended as legitimate and can be defended in more than economic terms. When times are difficult, it is fair and reasonable to expect colleges to bear their share of the brunt of reduced public revenues. An argument can be forcefully made that Canada's colleges have been excessively dependent upon public support and that a search for alternate sources of funding is desirable if they wish to avoid becoming, in fact if not in name, branch offices of government. Similarly, direct costs of college education of Canadians have traditionally been kept low as a matter of public policy, and it is easy to defend the view that the consumers of education should have to face the same burdens as the consumers of any other product. Many of Canada's colleges have not been models of productivity and efficiency, however these may be measured, and so demands for reasonable improvements in this regard are not outlandish. Finally, most colleges have attempted to be many things to many people and so a call for greater focus to their activities deserves every consideration.

These responses, particularly in combination, have a price, and that price is reduction of accessibility. Every time there is a tuition fee increase, there is some reduction in the number of citizens able to obtain a college education. There is a raising of the barrier of financial accessibility and a partial retreat to circumstances which prevailed before there were public colleges in Canada. One increase is barely perceptible; annual increases, no longer uncommon in Canada, pose a real threat, particularly for those who see college education as one of few solid opportunities for less advantaged Canadians. Every time there is a real reduction of public investment in college education, some service or programme is adversely affected, and normally the first to go are either the most recently established or the ones which do not serve the mainstream of Canadian college students. Special services for older students, programmes and courses for part-time learners, learning support services for students with disabilities, programmes developed to meet particular needs of students who have not traditionally had equal access to public education such as union members or native people, courses which ease the difficulty of returning to education in mid-life (usually for women), and a whole host of activities which have come to distinguish colleges from other kinds of post-secondary institutions are in peril. Admission "standards" become a growing issue, as though it were more important to control who enters college than who graduates successfully. Social barriers to entry rise.

Every time there is pressure to reduce costs of colleges, the temptation to circle the wagons around the major campuses is most inviting. People in smaller communities rarely can marshal the political support available in larger cities. College accountants can quickly point to the higher costs of more remote and sparsely populated satellite operations. Pressure is brought to bear on people to come to college rather than to bring college services to the people. The lone student shut-in or living in more remote parts of Canada is hard-pressed to make the case for equality of opportunity, even through distance education means. Geographic barriers become more evident. Every time there is a call for colleges to pull in their wings and become more cost effective, there is the charge that colleges have tried to do too much for too many. And many colleges have a difficult time deflecting or rebutting these charges, particularly when they cannot demonstrate, for example, that their heavy investment in basic education for adults has had any substantial effect on literacy rates.

It is a fact that the public colleges have not yet become the social equalizers and democratizing agents claimed by their earliest proponents. The vision of the college campus where students of all ages, programmes, and backgrounds rub shoulders together to provide a laboratory of democracy in action is a Canadian rarity. Closer to the common experience is the campus, with a heterogeneous population and comprehensive range of programmes, on which students in different programmes rarely come into serious contact with one another because social interaction has not been actively facilitated, because the workload of students is so heavy that they have few opportunities to meet socially with other students, or because the students have additional responsibilities of earning a living or rearing children or both. In these circumstances, how serious to a college, to a community, or to a student body is the loss of a programme or a service? The answer, of course, is very serious for those denied opportunity, but not critically serious in institutional terms. Several such losses tend to reduce college education to a mere collection of separate courses.

The Choices

It is understandable that government authorities and the general public should expect from their colleges accountability, high standards of performance, successful graduate placement, and quality service to communities. It is even legitimate for them to demand all these without a constant level of public support, given the levels of support in years gone by. But they should understand the price. The price to be paid for these demands in these circumstances may well be reduced opportunity for the very students who might benefit most from a college education. This risk is quite real. Some colleges which formerly accepted all qualified applicants or admitted by lottery to programmes with quotas are now admitting only the best qualified applicants to programmes to which admission must be "rationed," for reasons of insufficient institutional resources or limited employment opportunities for graduates. Indeed, particularly in Ontario, university and grade thirteen graduates are now applying to colleges of applied arts and technology in significant numbers because the graduate placement record of these institutions has been consistently outstanding. For each grade thirteen university graduate admitted, and subsidized, there is one less place available for the students these colleges were originally intended to serve. To ensure that less advantaged citizens will still be able to obtain entry to college and show how well they can perform, is there a college or government in Canada, especially in times of restraint and shrinking job opportunities, prepared to put university graduates at the bottom of the admissions priority list or have them pay the full cost of their college education while other qualified applicants with less prestigious credentials receive favoured treatment?

The mounting pressure on colleges to maintain or improve "standards" yet operate even more efficiently than in the past is a seductive enticement to them to be more selective in other respects as well and to alter the traditional character of the college. If colleges decide to give preference to "good" applicants who can be safely assumed to be able to perform well, there is little reason for these institutions to retain programmes and services that they established years ago precisely because they were mandated to welcome higher risk students.

Professionals in student services in colleges have good reason for feeling insecure.

Should the number of students to be served by colleges be determined more by reduced financial support from public sources than by demand for one or another type of college education? The Canadian educational and social tradition strongly suggests that the historically disadvantaged members of Canadian society will again be burdened with the consequences. The transference of responsibility from colleges to school districts in some provinces for the provision of adult basic education has already revealed that governments are prepared to deny accessibility to colleges for many students whose needs for college services and programmes have been well established. But students in remedial programmes seeking a second chance to improve their lot do not have a high political profile in a society imbued with middle class values.

Colleges have in recent years done much to improve opportunities for women students, but education for women, particularly for non-traditional occupations, does not have encouraging prospects for the future. No one should feel confident about the maintenance of special services for handicapped students despite the prominence finally given to such services since the International Year of the Disabled. Unless they can recover a substantial portion of their costs, programmes for special groups such as trade unionists and native students are almost certain to be among the first to fall by the wayside under the pressures now being felt. The opportunities for older students to upgrade their skills or prepare for a return to the workforce with public assistance can no longer be taken for granted. In provinces like British Columbia where ability to pay has already become a major determinant of who may go to college, an original mission of the community college has been dismissed as inappropriate for these times. The potential that colleges once had to improve the quality of life in smaller and more remote communities now appears to be threatened.

Who and how many will be able to attend colleges in Canada in the years ahead is not yet at all clear. A very real danger is that many of these colleges will, perhaps imperceptibly, take on the characteristics of more exclusive, less accessible American-model junior colleges or second-rate technical schools. Such institutions, however, are neither a priority nor an urgency for Canada. It will take commitment to important social values rather than pragmatic but oversimplified solutions to keep colleges accessible to most citizens, significant to community enhancement, and vital to the economic development of the country. It will take better, more imaginative planning and policy. But it will also take political courage at both institutional and governmental levels.

Post-Secondary Traditions

Canadians still see education as a task for the young. Almost all Canadians have attended school to age seventeen or eighteen and those who have not have been seen as having little long-term likelihood of being productive or successful citizens. The years eighteen to twenty-four have been viewed as the appropriate time for some Canadians to continue their education in technical institutions, colleges, and universities. It has been a tidy system.

Post-secondary education in Canada has also developed in such a way that it now displays some dominant characteristics. First it is a full-time occupation. Part-time students are, of course, now well received on college and university campuses, but all too often they are regarded primarily as people filling spaces not occupied by full-time students. The ambiance of most colleges and universities is still established for full-time students. Other students are encouraged to accommodate to a full-time pace as best they can; if they can cope in that environment, well and good; if not they do not survive. Second, good post-secondary education is not a brief process. Students, so the mystique goes, must spend as much as two to four uninterrupted years, or at least eight months of each of those years, to obtain a worthwhile educational credential. To interrupt that sequence is to reduce its quality. Third, post-secondary education is best conducted in a setting which is cut off from the workplace, museums and galleries, and other everyday components of general society. Post-secondary education is serious business, requiring its own milieu and its own standards.

This description is, of course, a caricature, but not an extreme caricature. Co-operative education, apprenticeship, and other forms of liaison between the worlds of education and work have become more popular, but they have not yet gone beyond the point of being viewed as interesting and innovative appendages to the mainstream of post-secondary education. Adult education has acquired a growing and expanding respectability in recent years, but not quite to the point where students beyond age twenty-five are viewed simply as older students. In the public eye, they are still viewed as bored housewives, fortunate opportunists, or courageous if not brilliant returners—but not quite legitimate. Government funding still favours full-time students. More and more students interrupt their post-secondary education to work or to devote their primary attention to other tasks, but it is normally out of necessity rather than any conviction that interrupted education for some people may in fact be better education. Distance education has established a toe-hold in Canada, and various forms of open learning have become more attractive, but the fact remains that the ways in which most Canadians are educated today at the post-secondary level are not essentially different from those of generations ago.

Far more Canadians now receive some form of post-secondary education, and while there have been a few wrinkles added to the processes and methods, the fabric has remained essentially the same.

To the extent that there have been substantial changes in patterns of post-secondary education, these changes have come from sectors other than the publicly supported institutions. Large industries like Bell Canada and the Insurance Corporation of British Columbia have entered the training business in a significant way and have established their own in-house training programmes; at least in good economic times, they have given stiff competition to institutional forms of training. The trade union movement has also directed more of its resources to the education of its members and has been very flexible in adjusting to their time constraints. Adult educators have been creative in trying to find new ways to bring more forms of education to more people.

In all, Canada has not been on the cutting edge of post-secondary education, despite the massive public and private sums devoted to this endeavour. A conventional, adequate, plodding method of educating for life and work in an industrial society has been developed. The advantaged and the able have received a thoroughly good education; the less advantaged have had opportunities to better themselves, and many have succeeded. The least advantaged and the least able, as in many other more developed nations, have fallen by the wayside. By and large, Canadians have been satisfied with the organization of their educational systems. Until recently, these systems have appeared to work. Certainly no public outcry for basic structural change has been heard.[22]

New Circumstances

But these are different times. Canada will not continue to prosper merely by continuing to develop its economy as it has in the past. More of the same is not the answer.[23] An unacceptably high level of youth unemployment has already appeared, and the prospects for meaningful employment for many citizens are not bright, regardless of initiatives that may be taken by governments or by the private sector.[24] The traditional Canadian practice of filling manpower shortages through immigration of trained personnel is no longer an answer, in part because of the levels of domestic unemployment, but also because Canada is no longer any more attractive than many other countries as a place to live and work.

Canada is now attempting to become a knowledge-based society, recognizing that this is the route to international competitiveness upon which continuing prosperity depends. But the technological changes that are part and parcel of such a society have already generated unprecedented levels of unemployment (or partial employment) and promise to bring about other dramatic social changes. Full employment for Canadians, in the ways in which they have been employed in the past, is simply an unrealistic goal regardless of political rhetoric. There will be different kinds of employment, there will be fewer people employed for the period of time it takes for Canada to make the shift to a new era, and there will be major social dislocations. Under these circumstances, it is hard to imagine that publicly supported educational systems should merely stand by as observers as these changes occur. They should help shape the future.

To complicate the adjustment, more Canadians rightly insist that they too must share in the benefits that further education should bring. Canada long ago passed the stage of being satisfied with a relatively small educated elite. Despite economic vagaries, all citizens claim equal right to reap the benefits of more and better education.

The Evolutionary Response

What courses of action are open to Canada's newest public post-secondary institutions in these circumstances?

One choice is to evolve naturally and gradually from their historical roots. This option would see most of Canada's new colleges remain as comprehensive institutions dedicated to offering a great variety of programmes and courses to satisfy a great variety of community needs as these needs emerge. They would, in this scenario, continue their community and client responsiveness and remain as institutions which do at least a little for a large number of Canadians.[25] They would remain residual institutions, filling voids not met by other educational agencies. In this role, they would continue to be important and accessible to many and they would learn to live with their blurred, unfocused image. Particularly in a world of high technology, this choice has much to recommend it as the need for the human response is as integral to the new circumstances as is the new technology.[26] As Naisbitt points out, there is a counterbalancing human response to the introduction of any new technology, or that technology will be rejected.

The Preparatory Response

A second approach would be for these colleges to limit their role to that of providing the initial post-secondary education of young Canadians before they really assume adult roles and tasks in a Canada of the information age. Should this choice be taken, the basic curriculum of Canada's colleges would undergo major change with the range of college offerings considerably compressed. Canada's colleges would make no pretense of training people for employment; rather, their task would be to provide a contemporary general education for all their young adult students, who would then be sufficiently adaptable for training and later retraining as the demands of the labour market should dictate. In this scenario, who would provide training for work? One obvious answer is Canada's technical and technological institutions which already are mandated to provide work-related education or training. A second answer would be industry, which has long been quietly unhappy about the calibre of the products of Canadian formal education and has consistently urged Canadian educational institutions to produce graduates who have solid basic skills and who are highly motivated to be industrious workers.[27] Big industry would be only too happy to provide job-specific training for young Canadians, provided that Canada's colleges could deliver to them graduates who were anxious to work hard and could read, write, analyze, and exercise critical skills.

This choice has definite attractions. Canada's universities could continue to train scholars and professionals. Colleges could educate young people with the basic skills and attitudes required for all forms of work and citizenship in an information society. Technical institutions and industry could continue to train. Community agencies and school districts could provide a complete range of community and personal educational and recreational opportunities for adults. A division of educational responsibilities along these lines could be manageable and effective.

Retraining Response

The opposite approach would be for the colleges to dedicate themselves to the primary task of retraining for the new information society of rapid technological change. This choice would call for these colleges to focus their activities on people who had already received a basic education or training and prepare them, sometimes over and over again, for new forms of work within Canada. A consequence of this choice would be that other means would have to be found to provide the initial, more general, pre-employment education now being provided by many of Canada's colleges, and to offer the range of continuing education opportunities for personal and community interest now offered by many of these institutions. It is not inconceivable that Canada's public school systems and universities could successfully and appropriately pick up these responsibilities for initial and continuing education which up to now have been part of the Canadian college mission. In an information age, the notion of colleges as retraining institutions could have an attractive ring.

A Specialization Response

Another and more dramatic approach would be to abandon, as inappropriate to an information and technological age, any common model for these new colleges. The premise for this approach is that institutional comprehensiveness and almost universal accessibility are not avenues to either efficiency or effectiveness in post-secondary education at a time when economic necessity and the public will demand both of these qualities from publicly supported institutions. Now that we have provincial college systems in place, the argument goes, it is timely to determine how each component of each provincial system can best play its role. In short, the objective would be to have comprehensive and accessible systems of post-secondary education rather than comprehensive institutions. In this model, each province would re-examine how it could most efficiently and effectively provide the kinds of post-secondary education it requires. Each province would quickly conclude that many of the programmes required for a sophisticated economy could not be efficiently provided by numerous institutions nor could all institutions attract the calibre of instructors to make these programmes effective. The certain result would be increasing programme specialization by most post-secondary institutions and greater mobility of students among institutions. The community-based programme-comprehensive institution could virtually disappear.

Critics of this approach could rightly point out that the logical extension of this model would be to centralize all forms of post-secondary education in one institution in the centre of densest population in each province. In terms of institutional efficiency, this observation would indeed be correct. But in terms of effectiveness and reasonable social planning, anything close to total centralization would have obvious shortcomings. A serious examination of this approach would demonstrate the pitfalls of excessive centralization. It would also highlight the inefficiencies resulting from a commitment to comprehensive institutions in as many localities in Canada as resources would allow. Pursuit of this approach would result in more specialized institutions, particularly in larger population centres, and would increase the differences that now exist among post-secondary institutions. Some colleges would remain more programme-comprehensive than others, with institutions in more remote areas providing at most only the initial preparation required for the more advanced technological education that has already become vital to Canada's economic prosperity. The social cost would be that more students would be unable to pursue many kinds of post-secondary education within their own communities, but the trade-off for them and for the supporting public would be education of higher quality.

Good post-secondary education will be costly in the future simply because the individual, social, and technological dimensions of that level of education will expand. It will be costly whether it is provided by many or fewer institutions. The case for more specialization for most post-secondary institutions is better quality of learning as well as greater cost effectiveness. This is an approach that may well appeal to educational planners at a provincial level, for whom costs and accountability are prime considerations. It would require a major shift in thinking for many college and community people at an institutional level.

The Lifelong Learning Response

An even more dramatic response to the new circumstances would be for the new colleges to convert themselves into catalysts for the development of Canada as a learning society. Many Canadian educators, like their counterparts in other nations, have talked for years about lifelong learning. They have familiarized themselves with the 1972 report of the International Commission on the Development of Education, published by U.N.E.S.C.O., known as the Faure Report.[28] They subscribe to the view that lifelong education is a "master concept," proposing that everyone ought to have "organized and systematic opportunities for instruction, study, and learning at any time throughout their lives . . . to remedy earlier educational defects, to acquire new skills, to upgrade themselves vocationally, to increase their understanding of the world in which they live, to develop their own personalities, or some other purposes.[29] Many of them are sensitive to the notion that "the community (or city or metropolitan region) should be the locus for planning and conducting learning activities.[30] But they are also aware that the master concept of lifelong learning has not been translated into action in Canada, that there are few established organizational models elsewhere for the implementation of the lifelong learning concept, and that there are formidable practical obstacles in Canada to any serious effort to make Canada a lifelong learning society, no matter how noble that concept may be. Regrettably, the majority of Canadian advocates of lifelong learning have been identified only with adult education, and the suspicion has grown that promotion of lifelong learning is merely a skilful way of attempting to expand the scope of adult education in Canada. Many people associated with colleges are barely familiar with the term, but spearheading a lifelong learning movement throughout Canada is indeed a realistic and useful challenge for at least some of these colleges. And the timing is right. Entering a new economic age requires modification of the educational infrastructure to support the new economy.[31]

To advance the lifelong learning concept, the most fundamental need is for a change of Canadian attitude about learning. There is still the widespread view that the years from six to eighteen are the best for learning, despite the richness of educational and general literature which refutes this claim. There is still the common assumption that schooling and learning are virtually synonymous, despite the fact that most adults know that most learning takes place outside the school or college or university. There is still the general stance that improvements in formal educational institutions are the key to a better educated society despite the overwhelming evidence that formal educational institutions at their best have severe limitations in their capacity to meet many learning needs. There remains the popular view that teaching is synonymous with learning, despite the fact that teachers themselves have learned far more through their own devices rather than through formal instruction.

This is not to claim that the rigidity and institutionalization of publicly supported education at all levels has not been challenged. The Canadian Association for Adult Education has championed the lifelong learning cause for many years in many ways,[32] even though its voice within the established structures of Canadian education has frequently not been heard. Employment and Immigration Canada has recently proposed steps in the direction of lifelong learning by its advocacy of skill development (or paid education) leave as a new component of Canadian public policy.[33] And the level of malaise within the general public about the inadequacies of education in this country has created a climate conducive to bold new ventures. But no institution, or group of institutions, has seized the opportunity to lead in the total transformation of Canadian educational institutions that would be required to develop this country into a learning society. Some of Canada's colleges could demonstrate that leadership.

One aspect of that leadership would be to bring about a more co-operative posture among all institutions and agencies within their communities that can assist people to learn—schools, colleges, technical institutions, universities, community organizations, business, labour, informal learning networks, private sector trainers and consultants, libraries, museums, volunteer agencies—to form a new network in support of all citizens, younger and older, as learners. One result of greater co-operation would be the de-institutionalization of learning opportunity and its reorganization in a new form for a new age.

Currently, public educational institutions at all levels guard their mandates jealously and co-operate with one another only to the extent that co-operation is in their self-interest. Private institutions have acquired their own domains. Industry engages in training and subsidizes public education to the extent that it sees an immediate payoff. Voluntary associations fill voids, but sit outside the establishment with all the concomitant disadvantages. Community agencies meet special needs but communicate very little with other, more orthodox components of Canadian education systems. Educational entrepreneurs operate in splendid isolation. Literally thousands of agencies are in the business of education in Canada: at worst they compete with one another, needlessly duplicate service, and incur the silent wrath of cost-conscious citizens; at best, they commiserate with those most akin to themselves and ignore the others. Canadian educational institutions and agencies, including colleges, act as though the consumers of education are a scarce commodity and a small market over which many and assorted agencies of education should compete. Nothing is farther from the truth, and the needs will increase and diversify in the years ahead, not contract, unless Canadians persist in acting as though learning is a task for one stage of a life rather than for all stages. The fact is that the interests of educational institutions and agencies have taken precedence over the interests of learners.

The reinstitutionalization of opportunities to learn would do more than provoke institutional change; it would require personal and professional re-orientation for people who identify themselves as educators. The current fragmentation of education into self-standing programmes and levels would be reduced; greater emphasis throughout schooling would be placed on how to learn rather than on the immediate mastery of specific content; learners could leave "school" once essential skills had been acquired and, over time, the sanctity of compulsory education legislation would be called into question. What is now thought of as post-secondary education could begin at an earlier age, or much later in life, and be viewed as a quite normal feature of contemporary living; even closer working relations between employers and educational institutions would be established; the sharing of resources among community agencies and institutions would increase. "The schools and colleges would become just one—albeit probably the most significant—instrument for learning in the community, subject to the general plans of a co-operative body created to ensure needed, efficient, effective learning opportunities for people for all ages."[34]

Indeed, educational institutions would recognize business, industry, and labour as co-equal partners in the educational enterprise. They would not maintain an arm's length relationship with the employment community but would actively promote the notion of the workplace as a setting for learning. The demarcation line between educational institution and workplace would become increasingly blurred, with the gradual integration of the two as one. In similar fashion, the family and neighbourhood as important venues for learning would be restored. Such changes would be threatening to many career educators, but they ought to be no less threatening than the loss of employment in a more traditional educational institution judged to be irrelevant or obsolete by its society.

The new community learning networks would make a frontal attack on illiteracy, which remains an anomalous legacy of Canadian educational history and which makes it virtually impossible for too large a segment of the Canadian population to become productive employees, effective citizens, or people who can enjoy personally satisfying lives.

As components of lifelong learning networks, most educational institutions in the community would adjust their styles of operation to give greater attention to the needs of older learners. This would mean far more than a change of classroom schedules to more realistic hours for adults who are parents and workers as well as students. It would also mean the provision of those services of highest priority to older rather than younger students: perhaps inexpensive meals, certainly child-minding services, probably the fostering of personal support networks for older students—in preference to the promotion of pub nights or the subsidization of intercollegiate athletic competition, both of which are traditionally more attractive to younger students. In general terms, it would mean making the more mature learner central to institutional life and activity, rather than remaining as a guest in an institution primarily geared to younger, full-time, conventional students.

The college itself would place greater emphasis on results and competencies acquired than on the time spent on the process used to achieve these results. Short, concentrated training rather than conventional "courses" would be a much more visible aspect of college organization than at present. Colleges would learn how to adjust to the pace of students rather than require students to accommodate to their predetermined tempo.

Lifelong learning networks would give special attention to learning opportunities for the traditionally disadvantaged: native peoples, women, the disabled, the economically less favoured. They would ensure a more equitable share of educational opportunity for those who have traditionally had less access for reasons beyond their own control.

The college opting for this mission would take much greater advantage of open learning and distance education techniques to bring more education to more learners in more varied forms. Group instruction would remain a significant method of education, but it would not remain the dominant method it has become. Modularized packaging of curriculum would become commonplace, continuous or multiple entry would become more common, small group tutorials on demand would be more easily arranged, and people learning would generally be more able to tailor their learning activities to their own dynamic needs rather than to the static demands of inflexible institutions. Such a college would recognize that a considerable amount of valuable learning takes place informally and that informal learning is no less legitimate than formalized, institutionalized education. As an outcome of this approach, it would lobby to obtain educational credit for learning that has taken place outside the walls of formal educational institutions. A "credit banking" arrangement would be established to recognize the value of experience and unstructured learning experiences. Indeed, to the lifelong learning society, the acquisition of formal educational credentials would be of far less significance than it is today. The college would become even more entrepreneurial than it has been in recent years. Rather than operate on a factory model, in which variety of approaches to teaching and learning is viewed as cumbersome and administratively awkward, it would subsidize instructors and groups of instructors to develop their own facilitation activities in response to learners, with the college becoming the corporate marketing agency for programmes and activities developed by creative and sensitive assistants to learners. Employee entrepreneurialism would become a feasible and fostered alternative to layoff for employees whose services would no longer be required if only conventional courses and programmes were to be offered.

The college would de-emphasize its teaching function in favour of its "support for learning" function. It would place less emphasis on the institution's preferences, and more emphasis on the individual needs of individual learners. These colleges would become learning centres: centres for learning, in the variety of forms and fashions associated with mature, self-directed individuals.

The colleges across the country choosing or accepting this mandate as catalysts and demonstrators for the lifelong learning society would, in addition to changing public attitudes to learning and their own styles of operation, act as brokers for other learning agencies in their communities, in much the same way as Saskatchewan colleges were originally intended to operate. They would not be in competition for students, but they would be willing arrangers of learning—anywhere in the community, with any agency within or beyond the community—to ensure that all people of all ages anxious to learn would have the opportunities to pursue that goal at minimum cost in the most effective and personally satisfying manner possible.

Possibilities for lifelong learning have always existed and a few people with resources and initiative have taken advantage of these opportunities.[35] In a country like Canada which espouses the ideals of equality of opportunity, transformation to a learning society would increase the number of people who could take advantage of opportunities now available only to the few. Given the nature of current society and projections for the future, such a transformation is a social as well as individual necessity. Some colleges in Canada, singly or in co-operation, could show the way.

A Choice of Directions

By the turn of the century, it is unlikely that Canada's colleges will continue to function as they now do, because the society which they serve is in the process of major adjustment. The colleges have already begun the change, or they will change, or they will be changed, or they will cease to serve. They now have the opportunity to choose or influence the direction of change: they can evolve from their roots, they can become preparatory institutions, they can become retraining institutions, they can specialize, they can become centres for lifelong learning, and they can decide that these choices are not always mutually exclusive. Just as they now manifest many differences, it is improbable that they would all choose the same direction for change. But they can all reassess their future and plan for the change appropriate to their own circumstances.

7

THE POLITICS OF COLLEGES

As in other organizations, the making of decisions has been a crucial and controversial matter in Canada's public colleges. Who ultimately makes what decisions and how those decisions are reached determine the quality of those decisions and the shape of these institutions. The story of the evolution of the colleges reveals that there have been three key decision makers: the governing body of the institution itself, the provincial governments (and a ministry of these governments), and the federal government (and departments of that government). As these colleges look to the future, in virtually every part of Canada the process of decision-making and the interplay that ought to characterize the relationships amongst decision-makers are under review; the results of these assessments will shape the colleges of the future, and it is not at all clear where real power will reside or ought to reside.

College Boards

The status and stature of the governing boards of Canada's colleges may best be appreciated by contrast with other educational governing bodies in this country.

Canadian school districts have been creatures of provincial governments; they have all been subject to provincial legislation through which power has been delegated to school trustees to act on behalf of provincial authorities.[1] There is no doubt, in law or in practice, where power and authority finally lie in matters of public schooling; school boards have functioned only with delegated authority, and provincial governments have been able to alter school legislation to respond to what provincial legislators have seen as right and appropriate.

In a different fashion, most technical and trade institutions have also been provincially oriented. They were established and operated by provincial governments, their employees have been civil servants, their curricula and admission criteria have been set by provincial authorities, and their graduation credentials have been provincial as much as institutional.[2] In a very real way, post-secondary institutions for technical training have been local branch offices of provincial departments of labour or education. Even in instances where technical training has been provided by private or commercial licence, there has been provincial control and, not uncommonly, indirect provincial financial support.

At the other end of the spectrum, universities in Canada have been viewed historically as independent institutions largely unfettered by governments at any level and able to pursue research, teaching, and social criticism without fear of government intervention. Even in recent years when the highest proportion of financial support has come from government sources, Canadian universities have felt little pressure to dance to the tune of governments. While governments have had powers of persuasion and have frequently prevented universities from developing as they have wanted when they have wanted, Canadian universities have nevertheless largely controlled their own academic destinies within the limitations of the resources available.[3] In fact, the separation of town from gown has continued into the 1980's with only periodic public and governmental pressure and with declining financial support from governments. Canadian universities have remained independent centres for scholarship and research, successful to the extent that they have been able to manage declining resources effectively.

As in so many other matters, the relationship of the new public colleges to provincial governments in Canada has been far more ambiguous than has been the case for school districts, specialized technical institutions, or universities. When colleges were originally established, considerable emphasis was placed on their community, regional, or local orientation. Most colleges had boards and—regardless of the manner in which board members were elected or appointed—it was the clear expectation that these boards would govern or share in the governance of the colleges. A priority was placed on the decentralization of power and responsibility for post-secondary education. From this perspective, colleges were expected to have some of the institutional autonomy historically accorded to universities; they were meant to have more discretionary powers than either school districts or technical institutes. With few exceptions, they were not intended to be branch offices of provincial governments.

At the same time, all Canadian colleges and college systems were to operate under provincial legislation and within provincial jurisdiction. They were to be neither autonomous, private institutions nor simply local, community, or regional implementors of provincial policy. Implicitly, the governance of most Canadian colleges was intended to involve a balance of authority and responsibility between institutions and provincial governments.[4] The fact of that balance was spelled out in some cases by legislation or government policy statement, but in other cases it was not made explicit at all. The nature, proportion, and character of that balance could not be legislated, but it was expected that they would develop with time and circumstance.

The Composition of Boards

Much has been written about the need for representation by faculty and students on the governing boards of post-secondary institutions.[5] Unfortunately, there is little to document the advantages and disadvantages of such involvement. In provinces where wide representation occurs, supportive arguments have rested on the issues of power-sharing, democracy in decision-making, and the values of broadly based consultation. Conversely, in provinces where board membership is confined to lay appointees, issues relating to conflict of interest have dominated arguments against such representation. While this matter is not an issue of dominant concern in any province in the mid-1980's, it has been an issue in several provinces and is likely to re-emerge as an issue in the future, particularly if any change to existing patterns of representation is proposed.

The appropriate governance role for college faculty in particular is likely to be an issue of recurring debate, especially in institutions and provinces where substantial numbers of faculty have come from a university milieu. The Canadian university culture has held that financial decisions reside with the university board of governors while academic and curricular decisions fall within the expertise of the faculty. The result of this thinking has been a legislated division of power between the board and the senate, both with statutory authority. This principle has not, however, been applied to the college sector, although in two provinces, Alberta and Quebec, formal "senate-like" bodies have been established in each college by legislation. But in each of these cases, their powers are advisory and the college board has final authority in both financial and academic or curricular affairs.

It would not be difficult to argue that instructional staff in colleges are as competent as their university colleagues in matters of curriculum, organization of teaching, evaluation procedures, and programme structure. Indeed, many colleges have developed informal arrangements whereby faculty committees offer advice to the president and, through that office, to the board. In some cases, collective bargaining has been used as an instrument to ensure that various levels of consultation occur with faculty on academic questions. But the right to advise and the right to be consulted are not the right to decide, and only the last right assures the power that many college people judge to be necessary. This issue has not been put to bed.

The appropriateness of having the chief executive officer as a member of the board has been a common topic of discussion and one which has evoked a number of reactions. Some views were that the chief executive officer could wield greater power as a non-voting participant in board affairs, while others argued that disagreement between president and board on matters of substance would make the former's position untenable. The most common stance in recent years has been that the most satisfactory arrangement would be full participation by the chief executive officer in board decision-making, without the right to vote.

Provincial Governments

There is now no dispute within Canada about the constitutional authority of provinces in matters of education. Under Section 93 of the original British North America Act, education at all levels was within the exclusive jurisdiction of the provincial governments. The Constitution Act of 1982 made no change to this division of jurisdictional responsibility.[6] Consistent with democratic government as practised in this nation, provincial governments are responsible to the electorate for the determination of overall policy, control, and financing of the educational system. The appropriate minister is held accountable to the legislature for management decisions.

In fact, the first major difference among the provinces in the exercise of provincial authority begins at the level of minister. The portfolio of the minister responsible for colleges reveals the particular form of organization of education in each province. Some of the provinces (Quebec until recently, Nova Scotia, and Prince Edward Island) have organized education as a unitary system which places the public schools, technical institutes, universities, and colleges within one portfolio. Alberta and Saskatchewan assign all post-secondary education to a Minister of Advanced Education, who has no responsibilities for the schools sector. Ontario retains two educational portfolios—Education, and Universities and Colleges— but one minister until recently was responsible for the administration of both. British Columbia organizes colleges and institutes under a Minister of Education, but universities had fallen within a separate portfolio. Manitoba and New Brunswick allocate colleges to a Minister of Continuing Education and a Minister of Community Colleges respectively. In Quebec since December 1984, CEGEP and universities have there own minister who has no responsibility for schools but who also includes Science and Technology within his portfolio. Newfoundland has a Department of Career Development and Advanced Education.

There is another ministerial relationship which influences the operation of colleges. It concerns the provincial responsibility for labour, apprenticeship training, and the needs of the workforce. In some constituencies, jurisdictional disputes between ministries of Labour and Education over control of vocational-technical curricula and programme development have proved detrimental to effective college planning. In recognition of the critical role of labour in training, some provinces (Alberta and Saskatchewan) have created structures which include Advanced Education and Manpower within a single ministry. In Alberta, all training and education have been under one minister, a decision which ensured a high degree of co-ordination and a reduction in government conflict over policy. However, a separate manpower portfolio was established in 1982.

Provincial Governments and Intermediary Bodies

Given that elected provincial governments are responsible for overall policy and design of the education sector, a question arises as to the extent to which government should exercise direct control over such matters as the allocation of budgets to institutions, programme approval or discontinuation, and detailed system planning. The concern with the direct exercise of government authority in such maters raises issues of undue political influence in local educational matters and potential violation of the autonomy which has so often been associated with educational institutions.

The conventional manner of dealing with this issue, particularly in the university experience, has been for government to establish a buffer agency or intermediary body identified as an IMB, located between government and the institution. The prototype for an IMB, the Universities Grants Commissions, was founded in the United Kingdom in 1919. The rationale for its establishment, as stated by Robbins, was as follows:

> The evaluation of the performance of particular institutions and the alloca-tion of funds between them is a function which, if it is to be discharged efficiently and without danger to academic freedom, needs to be done in an atmosphere from which political considerations are absent.[7]

In Canada, various provinces have formed intermediary bodies to deal with the university sector, with either statutory or advisory powers, primarily in matters of budget allocation and programme approval. A particularly comprehensive discussion of this subject has been provided by Sibley. The membership of IMB's sometimes excludes scholars or administrators still in active service in their institutions, although practice varies among the provinces. As Sibley notes: "They all have the responsibility of distributing provincial grants to the universi-ties in their jurisdiction . . . all of them are required to exercise fiscal over-sight of their institutions."[8]

Within the Canadian college sector, however, intermediary bodies have been an exception. Alberta had a Colleges Commission from 1969 to 1971, British Columbia had three provincial councils between 1977 and 1983, and in Quebec a Conseil des Collèges was established in 1981. The most enduring and most successful college intermediary body has been the Council of Regents in Ontario, which has been in operation throughout the life of the college system in that province. The question still remains: Are intermediary bodies a desirable feature for college systems in Canada?

The Federal Presence

Although education has always been a matter of exclusively provincial jurisdiction in Canada, Canada's federal government has nevertheless played a crucial role in post-secondary education and in the evolution of colleges within Canada.[9] Most obviously, the Canadian government has defrayed a significant portion of the general costs of post-secondary education everywhere in Canada through the Established Programme Financing (See Chapter 1) arrangement without direct or indirect invasion on the autonomy of institutions or of provincial college systems.[10]

Of lesser but not insignificant importance has been the federal participation with the provinces in the financial assistance programme for post-secondary students and the federal contribution to research. In the latter case, by 1982 some funding hitherto reserved for scholars associated with universities has become accessible to scholars on college campuses.[11] Nor should funding for special programmes such as Labour Education, Canadian Studies, and Second Language Education be ignored in the tally of federal contributions to college educational costs.

None of these federal involvements has seriously hampered the institutional discretion of Canada's colleges. The federal role in vocational training and in adult education has, however, been of a different order. While it has been clear and accepted by both levels of government in Canada that education is exclusively a provincial responsibility, the same could not be said of training; particularly because training or vocational education can be seen as directly related to economic development, an acknowledged federal responsibility, the federal government has been able at different times to fund and influence training. And in characteristically Canadian fashion, the distinction between what is education and what is training has never been sharply drawn.

Similarly, it has been a convenient Canadian myth that only young people are to be educated while only adults need training or retraining. Again, Canadian governments have not seen fit to draw the line sharply between youth and adult for purposes of education or training, and so it has been possible for the federal government to assume some responsibility for costs associated with the training of adults, without clearly stipulating where youth ends and adulthood begins. At different times in Canada's past, the two levels of government have worked out different pragmatic definitions so that they could get on with a job both wanted done without constitutional bickering.

These distinctions between education and training and between youth and adult eventually come to bear on colleges in Canada. Most colleges saw their mandates as including both education and training; most also thought of their clientele as both college-age students (and are they older youths or young adults?) and older, usually part-time, learners. In consequence, colleges in Canada have offered both federally funded training and provincially sponsored education, and the institutions have frequently found themselves beholden to two levels of government as they have tried to operate coherent institutions.

The federal government first became a funder of vocational training under the Agricultural Education Act of 1913. The Technical Education Act of 1919 brought about the first federal-provincial cost-sharing arrangement. The 1937 Unemployment and Agricultural Assistance Act and the 1942 Vocational Training Act involved the federal government even more deeply in training for employment, well before the establishment of Canada's colleges of today.[12] However, it was the Technical and Vocational Training Assistance (TVTA) Act of 1960 that really gave momentum to the contemporary role of the federal government in adult training. (See Chapter 1.) Funding made available with the act was vitally important, but of almost equal importance was its motivation: the serious unemployment levels of the late 1950's were considered to be a direct result of the inadequate education/training systems in Canada; Canada's labour force was simply insufficiently trained to cope with the needs of the industrialized society of that time. It might also be noted that, at that time, education, loosely defined, was coming to be known as the key to the resolution of social as well as economic ills in Canada and elsewhere in the western world.

However ground breaking in federal-provincial relations in education the TVTA Act had been, it really only served as a prelude to the Adult Occupational Training Act of 1967.[13] This act was passed on the explicit grounds that the federal government was well within its jurisdiction in shaping the training of adults to meet national economic priorities. The act permitted the federal government to determine who was to be trained.

Provincial legislation establishing many of the colleges came short on the heels of the Adult Occupational Training Act and, in some provinces, the colleges quickly became centres for adult training using federal funds in what appeared to be provincially funded institutions. In fact, almost all public colleges in Canada depended heavily on Manpower-sponsored training programmes, complete with training allowances provided by the federal government to federally selected trainees. Similarly, British Columbia colleges were officially but not popularly identified as "colleges of technical and vocational education" until 1977, and Alberta colleges developed an extensive apprenticeship training programme dependent upon federal funds and in conformity with federally determined training criteria. By 1980, some 180,000 Canadians were being trained to meet Canada's needs through federal training programmes, and most of them were being trained or retrained in Canada's colleges, under legislation and federal training programmes which had evolved through the 1970's from the Adult Occupational Training Act of 1967. The National Training Act of 1982 merely reinforced and solidified the federal presence in the training of adults, and exercised considerable influence over many activities of colleges throughout Canada. The proper role of the federal government in post-secondary education remains a major issue to that government, the provinces, and post-secondary institutions.

One Pattern: A Priority on Institutional Autonomy

Canadian colleges have substantial experience with both institutional autonomy and institutional control by provincial government. Those experiences merit review.

Most college board members and employees in the early days found the prospect of broad institutional autonomy very attractive. Board members would have the opportunity and the power to shape their colleges to meet the specific needs of the citizens in the regions they served; they would not be mere puppets whose strings were being pulled by provincial authorities. College employees found great favour with institutional autonomy because they would have more professional discretion than their secondary school colleagues and even more professional latitude than they would have received as junior members of a university department. They would have the opportunity to be creative and innovative; they would have the freedom to shape their professional lives and their institutions.

In the early days of the colleges, the grandest vision was one of a loose network of institutions throughout Canada, each shaping its own destiny within broad provincial guidelines, each capitalizing on its own strengths and individual personnel, each responding to its own community or locality or region in its self-determined, unique, and distinctive way. This prospect of heady institutional discretion was an immediate and effective stimulus to action and enthusiasm. Tremendous energy was expended by board members, employees, and students in making colleges "our own." College presidents and administrators were generally entrepreneurial and politely competitive with their neighbouring colleges. Instructors developed fresh programmes, experimented with different teaching techniques, and threw themselves into developing "their own" colleges. Great institutional pride and loyalty were clearly evident.

Citizens as well favoured the notion of having their own colleges. In region after region, community members, many with no previous access themselves to post-secondary educational opportunity, developed a personal identity with their new colleges. They registered for courses, used their new colleges for community activities, and generally took an active interest in college affairs. Many volunteered their services for work on advisory committees of various kinds. Not a few made or sought donations to their new institutions. Particularly in areas outside metropolitan centres, Canada's new colleges became vital, new educational and cultural centres which significantly enriched community life in addition to providing broader access to educational opportunity.

From quite a different perspective, Canada's colleges were also an economic stimulus to many cities and towns. In fact, in several cases, they became major employers. The presence of colleges brought new life to many centres and that new life was indigenous, not like the construction of provincial or federal buildings or the decentralization of senior government services to localities throughout provinces. The sense of ownership of colleges by board members, college employees, students, municipal officials, and large numbers of ordinary citizens was real. Colleges were part of the community, approachable, dynamic, personal.

Another Pattern: A Priority on Government Control

Exciting though local authority and responsibility may have been, Canada's colleges never were as autonomous as Canada's universities. With the exception of British Columbia and Alberta, all provincial governments made it clear from the start that colleges must be in some ways part of a provincial plan for post-secondary education. In Quebec, for example, the local responsibility recommended for colleges by the Parent Royal Commission was never translated into legislation: the first college legislation made it quite clear that the Ministry of Education would have significant influence over the CEGEP and the immediate establishment of a college branch within the ministry (La Direction générale de l'enseignement collégial—DIGEC) was the practical application of this decision. Similarly, in Ontario, the colleges of applied of arts and technology were to have considerable local discretion, but the ministry and a Council of Regents to monitor the separate developments of individual colleges were in evidence from the start. In New Brunswick, the provincial influence in establishing and directing the destiny of all components of the college system was clear and unequivocal even before the colleges began operations. Even in the two most westerly provinces, the provincial governments were more than providers of funds to colleges; the only difference in these provinces was the degree of provincial influence and the provincial commitment to highly decentralized colleges.

Most of Canada's colleges were, of course, established in the euphoria of the late 1960's and early 1970's when decentralization of authority, responsibility, and power was politically fashionable and safe and when public funding for colleges was almost lavish. New patterns emerged in the early 1970's, however, and produced an almost universal pattern of increased centralization of college systems by the mid-1970's.

The Current Pattern

There is no doubt that centralization of power over college developments by provincial authorities was a dominant characteristic of the late 1970's and early 1980's. The reasons for this change in emphasis were rarely made explicit, but common developments were in evidence throughout the country. In the first instance, provincial authorities saw dramatic increases in the costs of post-secondary education, caused in part by a significant increase in the numbers of students and in part by costs of new equipment, facilities, and teaching methods. In fact, the very success of the colleges in attracting students to their varied curricula was a major if subtle reason for their loss of autonomy. Even though it was a political aspiration to expand post-secondary educational opportunity throughout Canada, the colleges and the people served by them succeeded to a far greater extent than most provincial politicians could have anticipated. In most cases, colleges had originally been expected to serve either one of two major population groups: the eighteen to twenty-four year olds, for whom there was expected to be insufficient space at universities, or the adult part-time learners.[14] What actually happened was that students from both groups, in far larger numbers than expected, flocked to the colleges as many of these institutions said in effect to their publics, "Tell us what service or course you want, and we will provide it for you if there are enough of you who want it". From the viewpoint of institutional autonomy, the colleges could be said to have become the victims of their own successes; some control on costs to provincial governments had to be exercised.

This gradually but steadily increasing rush of citizens to colleges from 1975 into the early 1980's was made even easier by the relatively low cost of post-secondary education to students. Increasing accessibility to post-secondary education had been one of the earliest political justifications for the establishment of colleges, and one of the surest ways of increasing accessibility was to keep tuition costs low. The political decision at provincial levels from the start was to fund college operations essentially from the provincial treasuries rather than through local or regional taxation. Once the student populations of these colleges began to boom, it became apparent to politicians that provincial treasuries would be burdened by the colleges to a far greater extent than had been originally anticipated. Recognizing that it was not advantageous politically to call for explicit and direct restrictions on admissions, provincial authorities chose rather to increase gradually their controls over college expenditures and, in doing so, to increase their power over college systems. Quite simply, college education began to cost provincial governments—of all political stripes—too much, and economy took precedence over the principle of accessibility to post-secondary education.

In these same years, inflation in Canada came close to running out of control. As a result, even though costs of college education were mounting as a result of more students and higher unit costs of operations, these increases appeared even more dramatic by the effects of inflation. Real costs were rising, but inflation made the increases appear even greater.

The colleges themselves did little in these years to keep costs under control and to respond effectively to the growing apprehensions of provincial governments. Neighbouring colleges only infrequently concerned themselves with duplication of services, when co-operative measures could have reduced costs and maintained adequate levels of service. College administrators and instructors saw it more desirable to expand curricula and to reach out to new clients than to keep the brakes on corporate expansion. New methods of teaching and new equipment were introduced without due concern for return on investment. In some parts of the country, colleges, universities, technical institutions, and adult education divisions of school districts appeared to the public and to sensitive government officials to be offering many of the same courses and services— competing fiercely, if politely, with one another for students—without stopping to analyze either public reaction to these developments or ways in which satisfactory levels of service could be provided without such a proliferation of courses and activities. Colleges were still thinking and acting in an expansionary mode while politicians and large segments of the general population were looking for tax relief and fewer demands on the public dollar.

With institutions going their own ways and politicians wanting to move in opposite directions, it was inevitable that those with the greater power would have their way. And those with the power, of legislation and of funding, were the provincial governments. Almost without exception. provincial governments took a more active interest in college affairs and in the process permitted more administrative control of colleges by their officials. They then clamped down on funding. In some instances, new legislation was introduced as apparently the only way to ensure greater provincial control of these unruly beasts called colleges. By 1983, the almost nation-wide swing to more conservative governments and governmental measures only strengthened the swing to provincial control of local or regional activities.

Nor was the increasing control by provincial governments always introduced with sensitivity. The institutions, accustomed over the years to processes of consultation—however inefficient they may have been—which universities and school systems had enjoyed for decades, were generally notified by provincial authorities about the need to be more cost effective and more productive but rarely invited to share in determining the process by which these goals should be achieved. Provincial officials, for their part, saw college personnel as unwilling to recognize their problems and arrogantly casual in coming to grips with what their political masters judged important. Furthermore, politicians and government officials saw the need to address college problems urgently, while college personnel, beset first-hand with the repercussions of controls and financial restraint, generally attempted to slow down the processes of change. As a result, the movement towards greater provincial control of colleges not only took place, but took place with not a little acrimony and frustration for all parties.

Canada's colleges have never fully been the master of their own destiny. Since their inception, the degree of their mastery has steadily declined, with the power and influence of provincial and federal governments gradually becoming more dominant. But continuation of that process of centralization is neither inevitable nor obviously necessary.

Directions and Options for the Future

All of the issues relating to the exercise of powers of decision-making affecting Canada's colleges will remain controversial in the future as they have been in the past. Who will be college board members? What powers should college boards have? How should colleges relate to various ministries of provincial governments? What is the suitable role and presence of the federal government in college matters? All these questions still call for answers; they are also questions for which there are no absolute or universal answers.

The first question, that of college board composition, prompts an almost flippant answer. College boards are clearly intended, by both legislation and history, to represent the community of citizens to be served by the college. As such, they should be made up of citizens who can best represent fellow citizens, regardless of the manner in which board members come to be selected. An acceptance of this rationale would imply that college students, as adult community members, should be eligible for boards membership. Indeed, some would argue that students should be even more eligible for membership precisely because they are students, the most actively involved of all citizens in the life of a college. And, particularly if colleges move in the direction of becoming centres for lifelong learning, the argument for board membership eligibility for students becomes even stronger since the objective of such centres would be to assist all citizens to become learners throughout their lives. Yet in most Canadian jurisdictions, students are in fact ineligible for board membership, presumably on the grounds that they have special interests and cannot be as dispassionate as other citizens in policy analysis and decision-making, a difficult position to defend.

To the extent that this matter poses a problem if not a dilemma, the resolution lies in recognizing college students as citizens first and as students second. With this distinction, students could sit as board members representing other citizens, but not as board members representing the current student body of a college. Admittedly this is a fine distinction, but practical politics require many fine distinctions, particularly if colleges in Canada succeed in developing their own culture (See Chapter 6). Then the issue of student membership on college boards could dissolve in both theory and practice.

The appropriateness of assigning college faculty members, in the capacity of faculty members, reserved places on college boards is more complex. Faculty members, as such, are not members of the community served by the colleges and in this capacity should not have reserved board membership. Yet if colleges are viewed as learning and teaching institutions, the professional skills of faculty members ought to be a prized attribute of any college, and only short-sighted legislation should deny to a governing board access to the full extent of the professional expertise of the central group, other than students, within a college. On these grounds, faculty members, as skilled professionals central to the college enterprise, should have college board representation. But the issue is not as simple as presented above, because across the country faculty members are members of unions and in that capacity they collectively are a vested interest rather than a professionally disinterested college party. Until the complexity of faculty member as trade unionist/faculty member as professional is sorted out satisfactorily, or until professional and union matters can be satisfactorily compartmentalized in college operations, only daring legislation would establish board representation for college faculty members. Nor is this complexity beyond resolution: Alberta colleges have been successful with faculty members on boards by making, and respecting, the distinction between faculty members "selected by " but not "representatives of" or accountable to their peers; Quebec colleges have successfully operated with faculty members as college governors by removing from board jurisdiction those union-related matters which would pose conflicts of interest for any employee group. And, as a Canadian college culture matures (see Chapter 6), other methods of capitalizing on the unique expertise of professional employees at a board level should become evident. In the interim, without legislated board membership, colleges can and should be constructively involved in the process of predecision consultation with faculty members on all matters which pertain to their professional expertise.

A second question, pertaining to the powers appropriate to college boards as distinct from those appropriate to government, is at least equally difficult. From the vantage point of almost anyone within a college, a return to that measure of autonomy originally enjoyed by the first colleges would be most welcome. The institutions know their actual and potential clientele far better than do more remote provincial and federal government officials. The creativity and inventiveness of instructors and administrators are fostered best by a minimum of outside regulation. Institutional people are able to regulate their own institutions without bureaucratic procedures that characterize governmental practice, and governments, after all, do not educate or train any students. Many college people would claim that governmental practice and procedure merely constrain, or at best complicate, the flexibility an institution needs to be responsive. To such people, more government funding with less government interference in the internal affairs of colleges would be the preferred direction for the future.

From the vantage point of government officials, a return to the degree of institutional autonomy originally enjoyed by many colleges would be neither appropriate nor effective. Inter-institutional conflict, institutional self-aggrandizement, publicly indefensible overhead costs, the tolerance of mediocrity, and the lack of extra-institutional vision can be presented as documentable consequences of institutional discretion once enjoyed by some colleges. Furthermore, colleges have been designed, some would say, to serve societal not institutional goals, and so the elected representatives of society should indeed fetter all institutions, especially neophyte institutions, which depend upon public funding for their existence. A case can be made for colleges being viewed as local branches of government, dispensing education and training for adults in the amount and of the kinds decided by government. Besides, governments, but not institutions, have the power to rationalize college systems and to counterbalance the non-productive and sometimes esoteric tendencies of institutions.

Clearly, both these vantage points are extremes; a reasonable direction for the immediate future lies between them. Colleges need and merit some measure and some kinds of autonomy if the creativity and inventiveness of their members is to be put to best use. Equally, however, governmental authorities must be in a position to protect public funds and promote the measure of planning and system development that is in the public interest. The balance of power ought to shift from time to time and from province to province, until both college people and government officials acquire experience, establish a basis for mutual trust, and learn more about the particular characteristics of the public college. One of the greatest threats to the future success of Canada's colleges is premature institutionalization. Making immutable the power relationships between college boards and their sponsoring governments would be a particularly unfortunate form of institutionalization.

The third question, pertaining to external governmental organization as it relates to the operation of colleges, is in two parts: one concerns the organization of departments and ministries of government, and the second relates to the value of intermediary bodies for college systems. Much more than in the past, all components of the public post-secondary sector—colleges, specialized institutions, universities—will share common concerns such as programme allocation, credit transfers and articulation, assignment of federal funds, policies on accessibility, and co-ordination. These commonalities virtually require a common ministry for post-secondary education. At the same time, vertical articulation with secondary schools, particularly with respect to vocational training and adult literacy, prompt a single education portfolio without regard to level or kind or sector of education, even though the character of public colleges is fundamentally different from that of the public school or specialized post-secondary institution or university. There is clearly no ideal model of ministerial organization, and the choice of structure is always influenced by more than what would be in the best interests of colleges. The organizational structure which enhances the effectiveness of institutions in meeting the goals they have set or that have been set for them, and that is surely variable in a dynamic educational and social system, is certainly the most appropriate one.

Konrad expresses little doubt about the relationship he saw between colleges and other segments of the post-secondary education system:

> The rapid emergence of non-university institutions in isolation from existing colleges and universities portends problems of articulation, prestige, and governance. In an era of escalating costs and financial stringencies, society can ill afford the wastage of resources through the proliferation and duplication of educational programmes. Whether by governmental direction or voluntary co-operation, societal interests are served best through the development of unitary systems of post-secondary education. Although constitutionally Canadian systems of education must be provincial in nature, nothing prevents the co-operative development of supraprovincial systems of meeting societal needs on a regional basis. Whatever its nature, no institution or institutional type should be allowed to develop outside a post-secondary system proper.[15]

With regard to the value of intermediary bodies for colleges or for the non-university post-secondary sector, the issue rests on an understanding of the particular relation of these institutions to provincial governments in Canada. Unlike universities, Canada's colleges have neither a long tradition nor a legislated base in matters of institutional autonomy. Generally speaking, public colleges have been seen as instruments of government policy implementation for economic development, manpower training, the elimination or reduction of adult illiteracy, and other government sociopolitical priorities; for the most part they have been seen, and they have perceived themselves, as part of an explicit or implicit strategic development plan of their provinces.

Given this relationship and self-perception, Canada's colleges need to be able to respond quickly and efficiently to rapidly changing needs and circumstances, far more so than in the case of other publicly supported educational institutions. Direct government management of college funds, resources, and programmes has been seen as facilitating this kind of responsiveness while intermediary bodies have been portrayed as additional bureaucratic instruments which would only delay institutional responsiveness.

But colleges are also educational institutions in their own right. Not only do they serve as cultural resources in their regions, but they often include an intellectual component which suggests that they must also express values which transcend contemporary political concerns. Decisions regarding the allocation of resources within an educational system directed to such personal and social ends should be based upon a long-term planning perspective for which intermediary bodies can serve a useful purpose in counterbalancing quick change and expediency as the sole criteria for college effectiveness.

Furthermore, programme evaluation and programme allocation among institutions should be immune to direct political influence. Accordingly, intermediary or buffer bodies responsible to, but independent of, both government and the institutions would provide for more dispassionate decision-making. In Ontario, for example, the Council of Regents has been a constructive source of advice to both government and institutions, even though it has also been in an indirect employer role for purposes of provincial collective bargaining. As well, the primary orientation of the Conseil des Collèges in Quebec has been to perform an evaluation function for a college system where neither government nor the institutions themselves are seen as appropriate to undertake this task.[16]

Despite all of the foregoing, the trend in Canada has been away from the utilization of intermediary bodies. In times of economic difficulty, governments have been more reluctant to delegate power, advisory or statutory, to agencies over which they have limited authority. Even in the university sector, the trend of the 1960's to encourage university autonomy in planning and related matters has been reversed as governments seek more direct control over institutional expenditures. The view that no rational system planning can exclude government as a direct instrument of control over the expenditure of public money has received wide support and is tenable. In fact, the issue of intermediary bodies for college systems has become increasingly irrelevant to contemporary circumstances, despite forceful scholarly arguments in support of such agencies.

The final power issue concerns the role that the Canadian government should play in the decision-making processes within the public college sector and, by extension, the relative influence of federal and provincial governments on college activity. The respective roles of federal and provincial governments clearly ought to be the expression of a dynamic rather than bunker relationship; there should be a measure of co-operation between levels of government that would at one and the same time respect constitutional jurisdiction and promote the best interests of post-secondary education. In an ideal world, neither level of government should need to call attention to its constitutional prerogatives:

whatever the dilemma about education in the Canadian federation is, it is not a constitutional one. Indeed, Section 93 (of the BNA Act) is a model of flexibility. Whenever it becomes clear that special education provision is needed to carry out responsibilities undertaken by Parliament in the exercise of its exclusive powers in 5.91, Parliament is entitled to make that provision by whatever means and instrumentalities are required in the circumstances. As so often turns out in this country, obstacles to action that are declared formidable constitutional barriers turn out to be merely political. That may not make the problem any easier to deal with but at least one can make a start by removing the "no trespassing" signs and opening up Federal-Provincial consultations.[17]

However, Canada has not been an ideal world and recent federal-provincial consultations in the field of post-secondary education have not frequently been notably productive. There seems little doubt that in any recent confrontation between federal and provincial governments over post-secondary education, the provinces have had the upper constitutional hand; the federal government had had the access to additional funding and a strong sensitivity to negative public opinion. Particularly as Canada strives to enter the internationally competitive world of advanced technology, it is imperative that the federal government assert its responsibility for the economic development of the country and ensure an educational infrastructure necessary to achieve national economic goals. This direction need not provoke federal-provincial confrontation, but, should that be the result, the federal government would seem to have limited options: leave the orientation of post-secondary education and training to the provinces and their institutions at the risk of thwarting the economic development of the country or establish and fund unilaterally its own institutions to serve its legitimate objectives and priorities. The latter choice, in the years ahead, may be the only practical course of action.

Conclusion

Power and decision-making authority are a serious business to and for Canada's colleges. Both their current effectiveness and their potential are intimately connected to the relationships that will be established between both levels of government and the institutions. However college board membership is determined, and whatever powers these boards may acquire, in the final analysis, the colleges are instruments of governments which have created and supported them. What confidence provincial governments place in college boards, and how the two levels of government work out their relationships as they pertain to post-secondary education, will surely have a major impact on the future direction of colleges in Canada.

MANAGEMENT AND LEADERSHIP

The new imperatives of educational management will increasingly require men and women who are intellectually acute, politically adept, financially astute, and organizationally sophisticated. They will need to be audacious and ready to accept the responsibility of reshaping education's structures in fundamental ways. And they will need to be tough enough, persuasive enough, and sensitive enough to achieve that goal despite the congenital nay-sayers and the uncritical enthusiasts. More than in other institutions, power in an academic institution is a fluid and elusive thing. The person who tries to fix it, free of all ambiguity and shiftings, will find it slipping away like sand in the face of storms and driving tides.[18]

The Starting Point

One of the startling features of the early days of Canada's colleges was the extraordinarily high rate of turnover of senior administrators, particularly the most senior (president, principal, director general). While examples in the late 1960's and early 1970's could be found in all provinces, the outstanding cases were probably Quebec and British Columbia, where the "mortality rate" of college chief executive officers became a standing joke.[19]

Several factors account for this attrition, which was not paralleled in other sectors of post-secondary or higher education where it had been quite common for the tenure of presidents and principals to be measured in terms of decades. One factor was certainly the job itself. The original senior administrators had to be builders and doers. Sheer physical stamina was an unforeseen but quite real prerequisite for the job. High demands were placed on versatility as well; it was not uncommon for almost all institutional and departmental decisions to require the personal imprimatur of the most senior officer, and there were simply too few jacks-of-all-trade available. The demands of students, instructors, governments, community groups, and governors were not only insistent but frequently in conflict to the point where consensus for action could not be reached and unilateral administrative decision-making—even after extended consultation—incurred the wrath of at least one important and vocal institutional power bloc.

At times, strong, personally aggressive decision-making was required, if only to avoid one or another institutional disaster such as the termination of a programme that simply was not attracting sufficient students to warrant its continuation. At other times, and not infrequently on the same day, subtle collegial behaviour had to be encouraged, as in the case of establishing criteria for the evaluation of the performance of personnel. On yet other occasions, postponement of any decision might have been the best course of action, as in a case of finalizing an annual budget. A frantic pace, conflicting expectations, impossible hours, imprecise mandates, and few personal satisfactions or rewards made the life of senior administrators abnormally difficult. Some found it all quite intolerable and chose to leave; others were given a good push by their institutional colleagues; still others were dismissed or invited to resign.

Invitations to resign often came from well-meaning and passionately concerned board members who, not long before, had hired the senior administrator in good faith and often after elaborate search procedures. The fact was that boards did not know what they really wanted, or needed, in a chief executive officer because community colleges were as new to them as to everyone else. Not infrequently, different members of the same board had quite conflicting views as to the attributes that should be given highest priority in the selection of senior administrative personnel. In some cases, boards simply abandoned any pretense of objective criteria and chose whomever they liked most or disliked least. In other cases, boards arrived at selection decisions virtually by intuition after cursory interviews and reviews of credentials. In yet other cases, boards opted for the candidate who could start tomorrow, almost regardless of credentials and background, because so much needed to be done so quickly.

Of course, college boards usually had quite an array of candidates from which they could choose. Applicants varied from school principals, to retired military personnel, to people in business who saw themselves blocked on a low rung of the corporate ladder, to unfulfilled scholars who had visions of playing the role of headmaster, and to bright young teachers. They ranged in age from early thirties to retirees. Some had limited experience of any kind, while others were urbane and worldly. Most were Canadian, but others brought experience from different settings. Some saw themselves as corporate executives; others, as social reformers. Many had quite romantic visions of the role and expected instant respect if not adulation, and a few saw it as just another job with considerable status and reward. What they had in common was a lack of experience with and appreciation of the uniqueness of community colleges, a lack of first-hand knowledge of what to expect, and a lack of role models. Quite literally, like the board-employer, they did not know, and could not know, what they might be getting themselves into.

With boards lacking selection criteria appropriate to colleges, criteria from the corporate world or from post-secondary institutions in other environments or from local schools or universities were tested. With applicants lacking any clear understanding of what might be expected of them, many relied in their search interviews on charm, articulateness, and professed confidence that they could get the job done well, whatever the job was. In the final analysis, several boards did the job of selection over and over again, not quite every year, until they had sufficient background to make better choices.

Who were the better choices? People who could at one and the same time be day-to-day administrator, public relations expert, fund-raiser, resource and finance manager, personnel specialist, building designer, planner, conciliator, director, and teacher. High energy level was the prime requisite, but at least liberal doses of sensitivity to others, humility, decisiveness, self-assurance, compassion, scholarship, and keen business skills were also useful. They were operating in uncharted waters with shifting winds.

The originals did, however, have two conditions operating in their favour. One was the fact that sophisticated management skills were really not necessary. The second and related condition was the freedom the choose their own management styles.

In the early 1970's, a shortage of skilled leadership by senior administrators could effectively be counterbalanced by liberal injections of more money, and more money was not very difficult to acquire. Governments generally looked kindly on the new colleges and frequently accepted uncritically the college argument that more resources—people, equipment, programmes, services, buildings, satellite operations—could resolve whatever the current problem might be. Growth and expansion characterized this early period, and the symbols of growth were largely associated with having more funds at one's disposal. In fact, it would not be totally unfair to refer to this period as the era of "administrator as cheerleader."

In an era of almost unrestricted expansion, college presidents and principals could use whatever management style they preferred or could get away with, because style of management was rarely seen as the source of problems a college might encounter, and a different or better style of management was rarely viewed as a promising method of problem resolution.[20]

Canada's colleges saw both extremes of classic management models in the first days. At one pole, the hierarchical model from the corporate world was in vogue. The chief executive officer sat at the top of the organizational pyramid, with deans and directors responsible for specific administrative areas, instructors viewed as technicians responsible for turning out products called students and diplomas. Where this model was in operation—usually determined by a chief executive officer who had come from the school milieu, or from a technical institution, or from a not very successful private sector business—consultation before decision-making was commonly perfunctory, directions were provided from the top down, official memos were the favoured means of internal communication, board minutes were in immaculate shape, and the maintenance of policy manuals was a high priority. Many college people, particularly those whose university teaching or study was fresh in mind or those who embraced enthusiastically and earnestly the culture developed in the 1960's seethed under regimes of this kind, but the job got done as long as the senior administrators and board members held their ground. Besides, in those days, instructors and other personnel who were disenchanted with their employers did not find it difficult to relocate to more hospitable college climates elsewhere in the country.

The most hospitable climate for such people was provided by the colleges which embraced the other pole of management, the collegial model. In this model, supposedly borrowed from the university milieu, students, instructors, administrators, and board members were portrayed as forming a "collegium" of equal participation in the running of the college. "Those most directly influenced by a decision should have the right to make that decision," "administrators are here to serve the faculty and students," "participation in itself is an essential part of the educational process" were very much part of the rhetoric and reality of some Canadian colleges.[21]

Just as the hierarchical model worked in many colleges, the collegial model worked in others. Meetings were not only the favoured means of internal communication; in a number of cases, they became ends in themselves and attractive pastimes for some college people. Major institutional decisions were taken or, indeed, not taken only after laborious and protracted consultation with every constituent body from within and with the identifiable pressure groups from without. Trust, not written correspondence, was to be the basis for the establishment of internal working relationships; chief executive officers served as conciliators and referees; board meetings were endurance contests, and policy manuals were really quite unnecessary because policy was always subject to change. Many college people, particularly those who had been trainers or who had come from "the real world" of business, spent much of their first years being perplexed at this peculiar way of operating. Frustration at being unable to get the simplest task done without elaborate consultation processes was a common feeling of many college instructors, who were then accused of being task oriented rather than process oriented. Some learned to tolerate if not enjoy the collegial atmosphere, and others simply moved on.

In fact, few colleges were managed in totally hierarchical or totally collegial style. Most had elements of both, with some generally leaning more in one direction than the other. From a management perspective, the new colleges of Canada were a strange and wonderfully "mixed bag."

It might be noted that Canada's colleges were operating in these very different ways precisely at a time when the study of management was developing rapidly in the corporate world.[22] Business and industry were very much preoccupied with improving management of their firms, but colleges (as well as universities, other post-secondary institutions, and schools) were unaffected by these new developments outside their arena. In fact, it seems unexaggerated to claim that educational institutions seemed quite insensitive to the larger social and technological forces in the late 1960's and early 1970's that were in the early stages of reshaping Canadian society. Colleges (like other educational institutions of the time) were discrete, independent domains of their own, responding to their own unique pulls and pushes, largely oblivious to what was going on, at least from a management perspective, in the larger world outside their walls. Styles and theories of management, and managers, were not really very important in the early days. Expansion covered a multitude of weaknesses. Senior administrators came and went. Those who survived and persevered did so largely by being able to reconcile, at least temporarily, the disparate views expressed within their institutions and their communities. And the colleges carried on, some enormously successfully, in these circumstances.

The New Needs

There is now a major body of educational literature about leadership, management, and the needs of educational institutions which wish to cope more effectively with new conditions that are already in evidence.[23] Lists abound of qualities to be possessed or developed by tomorrow's educational managers. Profiles of "good" institutional administrators are plentiful, and hardly unanimous. There is broad concern that institutional management needs reappraisal.[24] It may just be that if these institutions are to continue to flourish, Canada's colleges cannot continue to maintain the variety of management styles that have been in use.

From another perspective, it can be argued that Canada's colleges have directed funds to students, to programmes, to buildings, and to equipment— and they must continue to do so; but to do so without also improving the management of institutions, these investments will not be effective. Colleges now need to reconsider the organization of their organizations. This need for colleges to improve their management is no different from the needs for other organizations and businesses.[25] Modern management philosophies and techniques have been developed largely because the business world has changed from a dominance of small independent corporations to complex webs of major companies and branch operations and the emergence of large-scale business operations.[26]

True as this change is for the business world, it is equally true for Canada's colleges. All are also part of formal provincial educational networks. Any college in Alberta, for example, is not only an institution in its own right but also a part of a provincial post-secondary network. That college must also function as part of another network of local or regional social and educational agencies, probably with some in the public sector and others in the private sector. If that college hopes to do its job well, it must also be plugged into its employer community, and it must also be aware of university and school developments in Alberta. If it really wishes to have an impact, it cannot be oblivious to municipal government initiatives any more than it can ignore what is happening in the rest of Canada. All these linkages, desirable in the past but indispensable in the future, require a different kind of management and place new demands on Canada's colleges. Gone are the days when the senior institutional administrators, regardless of how small the institution might be, can review and endorse every institutional decision; they now are too busy managing their colleges as parts of larger interconnected systems and networks in which they have important stakes.

In addition to active participation in extra-institutional linkages and networks, the college president, principal, or director general is required to manage, or see to the management of, declining institutional resources. That task is complex and requires sophisticated skills. Additional resources will no longer be available to disguise management weaknesses or institutional indecision. Choices that need not have been made in a time of plenty cannot be avoided in times of restraint in spending on education and of growing public skepticism about the effectiveness of public institutions. It is fair to claim that, at one time, a college board or senior administrator could not really make a wrong decision because there were always ways of compensating for error. In the future, virtually every major decision will have negative as well as positive consequences: a programme or service will be cut, employees will face unemployment, and a community group will no longer be able to obtain a service it had taken for granted for years. In this environment of intra-institutional tension, administrators must change from cheerleaders to adept managers of resources.

New Circumstances

No longer will a collegial management model or a hierarchical management model be appropriate for Canada's colleges. Collegiality as a style of management evolved over centuries, but in most circumstances where the pace of change was slow. Often, one of the key objectives of the collegial approach was to slow down the rate of change.[27] Universities, where collegiality was born, were clearly intended to maintain existing conditions unless there were compelling reasons otherwise. As a result, no change was introduced until every important element within the collegium had its say; professors harumphed and contemplated; senates debated at length; university presidents or principals truly presided over exercises in participatory democracy. Decisions were eventually made, but this model was calculated to resist or to defer change and to avoid conflict rather than bring about change internally or respond to it from without. Collegiality may be for dinosaurs.

The only realistic future that colleges in Canada can anticipate is one very different from the casual environment of the traditional university. As others have noted, it is not the fact of technological change that has characterized modern societies in recent years; technological change has been a reality throughout the ages. What is now different is the far more rapid pace of technological change.[28] Similarly, social, cultural, economic, and political changes are likely to continue to characterize contemporary society. In this setting, it would be sheer folly for any institution which wishes to continue to contribute to its society to retain a management model which is inconsistent with its need to bring about or cope with change. As Canada's colleges have clearly witnessed in recent years, some important changes have been forced upon them by external forces, others have been inevitable consequences of being parts of networks rather than simply self-standing institutions, and still others have been prompted by internal conditions. In any event, change is likely to be the single most important phenomenon facing Canada's colleges in the years ahead, and they need an operating mode that is compatible with responding to, and provoking, institutional change.

It is also apparent that the collegial model worked most effectively in small institutions whose members were able to know one another, personally and professionally. They lived, worked, and played together, and, in so doing, developed over time a community of thought and purpose for their institution. Those who did not fit in moved to another collegium.

As universities grew and some became multiversities, they operated as several smaller collegia called departments and faculties, in which the characteristics of smallness, close working and personal relations, and a community of thought could be sustained. Most universities, at least in North America, have come to function as loose federations of quite autonomous departments and faculties which co-operate with one another only to the extent that co-operation with one another is absolutely necessary. Indeed, changes in university structures and organization have already begun to take place to the point where the collegial model often works only at the lowest, departmental level of many universities.[29]

Colleges in Canada do not display the characteristics of successful collegiality. Most are not small enough or concentrated enough to permit their instructors to meet one another, let alone know one another, beyond the ritual college-wide events. These colleges do not have, nor can they expect to have, the internal working relationships essential to collegial operation. In fact, the brotherhood and sisterhood of unionism has become, for some college faculty members, a partial substitute for university collegiality. But unionism is a far cry from real academic collegiality.

Colleges with working forces in the hundreds and in some cases thousands have an additional liability which militates against collegial operation. By their very nature, community colleges operate a great variety of programmes for a great variety of students. Some of these programmes are work-oriented, others lead to further education, and still others are quite clearly for personal or community development. Similarly, students' age range is considerable, as are the ranges of aptitudes, interests, and abilities. As a result, a true, effective community of purpose among all members of a college is much more difficult to achieve than in a less comprehensive, more homogeneous institution.

Are there not colleges in Canada where business management instructors conflict in their basic ideology with instructors of sociology, who in turn share very little (except the same employer) with auto mechanics instructors, who simply do not meet, let alone have anything in common with, instructors in self-hypnosis? Are there not fundamentally different perspectives between many of these instructors and the administrators of their institutions (even those they have helped to select) whose responsibilities transcend individual program-mes and departments? It is circumstances such as these which call into question the suitability of the collegial style of operation for Canada's colleges.

But an even more profound shortcoming of collegiality in the college setting is the existence of clear power blocs within these institutions, many supported by legislation. Effective collegiality requires that all members of the collegium have as their primary goal the institutional good; the purpose of discussion, deliberation, and participation is to come to agreement on what is in the institutional best interest. Co-operation and dialogue are intended to produce consensus upon which action can then be taken with the support of most if not all members of the collegium. In reality, however, compromise as well as consensus has been the result of collegium deliberations, and compromise among differing viewpoints has largely been satisfactory when changes were not crucially important in any case.

Conditions in Canada's colleges have not been, and are unlikely to be, conducive to the search for consensus among people with a community of purpose. Much closer to reality is the existence of power blocs within colleges, with power blocs competing one with another, with diversity rather than unity of purpose, and with adversarial relationships rather than co-operation domin-ating the way in which people function in relation to each other.

The most obvious example of adversarial relationships is the existence of labour unions within Canada's colleges and college systems. For very good and sufficient reasons relating to the manner in which colleges have operated to this point, first college instructors and then other college employees have chosen to unionize. Whatever positive results have come from unionization, and there have been many, it is inescapable that a primary objective of unions is to advance the welfare of their members. These interests are not always coincident with the interests of the college or the interests of students. In these circumstances, the labour-management approach to resolution of difference is the contest between competing interests: union and management are pitted against each other in adversarial relationship, and a bargain is reached. This is a quite satisfactory way of resolving all sorts of institutional differences, and the search for better methods goes on unabated, but it does not contribute to collegiality.

In fact, quite the contrary. By definition, unionism excludes some college members—all those who are not union members—from the collegium, or, stated otherwise, a union is a collegium of its own members which resolves differences with others by adversarial means. Consensus and co-operation, the sine qua non of collegiality, are incompatible with labour-management relations as they have evolved in Canada.

It would be a mistake, however, to isolate unionization as the sole basis for portraying the collegial model as anachronistic for Canada's colleges. Adversarial relationships characterize many facets of Canadian life, the courts and parliament, among others. Canadian society is seen increasingly as composed of special interest groups which compete, not co-operate, to achieve their ends. This societal evolution, hardly unique to Canada, now permeates the college sector as much as other sectors of Canadian life. All too frequently, faculty, staff, students, administrators, community groups, and boards are seen or portrayed as competitors and adversaries, rather than persons of like mind and community of purpose with different perspectives on controversial issues. Under these circumstances, a collegial style of operation is doomed to be ineffective, frustrating, and inappropriate to the current and anticipated needs of Canada's colleges.

If the fluidity required for collegiality is but a romantic illusion as a style of contemporary college management, the rigidity of traditional hierarchical management is equally unsuitable. Only passing reference need be made to current management documentation,[30] particularly impressed with the spectacular success of Japanese approaches to management, which makes the point that hierarchies are inappropriate to almost all kinds of modern organizations, and this observation is indeed applicable to colleges.

Colleges cannot function effectively in traditional hierarchical form or in conformity with traditional bureaucratic regulation primarily because of the characteristics of college people, college students, and the communities served by these colleges. First, college personnel are, or should be, highly trained professionals, not merely technicians, whose expertise cannot be cultivated in a highly regulated environment. Individually and collectively, they need considerable autonomy and freedom to be most effective in their areas of professional competence. College administrators are, or ought to be, equally skilled professionals who frequently have to assume responsibilities which go beyond the formal authority of their positions. They work best in a team framework rather than in the structured relationships associated with bureaucracies or the military chain-of-command approach to management. College students are not components on an assembly line, or merely the "product" of colleges, or the privates in a military-style organization. They are autonomous people functioning in a special and unique relationship with instructors and other highly skilled professional people. Their role is not to absorb, to be submissive or directed, nor merely to obey; part of their task is to challenge themselves, their colleagues, and their instructors. But hierarchies do not look kindly on challenge of any kind. Community groups served by colleges are not problems to be addressed, obstacles to be overcome, or annoyances that must be tolerated. If colleges are to serve them, they must respect people in communities in ways that bureaucracy and hierarchy do not allow.

An Approach to Management

If the ability of a college to resolve conflict and to bring about or respond to change, rather than resist change or to introduce change arbitrarily, is a contemporary requirement, and if colleges are made up of disparate interest groups and idiosyncratic individuals with only a slender community of purpose, there are three keys to effective college management: a clear sense of direction or purpose, openness of communication, and clarification of roles. These provide the balance between consensus and hierarchy.

The appropriate evolution from collegial or hierarchical decision-making requires full and open access to information, all the information upon which decisions must be made. Particularly in a knowledge-based society, wide access to decision-influencing information is essential to effective management. Not unlike other large or complex organizations, many colleges have taken a very guarded approach to the dissemination of information: the board has some information, the chief executive officer has other, and other people within and beyond the college have different and usually less information. In an equally common example, an individual instructor guards his information about departmental matters or at best shares it with departmental colleagues. In both of these situations absence of pertinent information, or incomplete information, can only lead to less effective or less comprehensible decision-making.

While some colleges may have been able in the past to continue to function as though they were part of the small business world, Canada's colleges have almost uniformly reached the size where they have the characteristics of large, complex, intricate organizations. Those that have not reached this size are still more akin in their internal operation to larger corporate bodies, and they need to be managed that way. Gone are the days, if they ever existed, when colleges could be managed effectively on the back of a figurative envelope, particularly if different college people have different envelopes. Nor can colleges operate well in the style of the family business, the corner store, or a government bureaucracy. Only an active stance on information distribution can ensure that college people may understand the basis for decision-making. It is then necessary to ensure that decisions are well made. This requires definition of and accountability for roles within a college because complex organizations function well only when roles are clear and understood by most members of the organization. Similarly, those who are responsible for decision-making need the authority to make the proper decisions and must be accountable for those decisions.

Board Roles

Particularly the role of a college board needs clarification. It is probably true that college boards have taken on whatever roles they have wished to assume, and most college legislation has been less than helpful in determining what roles they should play. In British Columbia, as one example, provincial legislation specifies that college boards are responsible for managing their colleges.[31]

The origin of the difficulty in providing precision to the distinctive roles of the college board is probably the fact that college boards were modelled after boards of school trustees. In the early days of school districts, school boards did in fact manage all affairs except the teaching functions: they hired the staff, selected the "principal" teacher, established school policies, and generally ran the school district in a very direct way[32]; they were the managers and administrators of the school and the school district. School management has come a long way since the earliest days in Canada, and now the management and administration of good schools is largely left to trained professionals, who are accountable to the school board for their actions and decisions. The same evolution is required in the college sector, to the extent that such evolution has not already taken place.

The current textbook role statement for a college board is policy formulation. High sounding as that may seem, it is frequently misunderstood by both board members and other college people alike. It means that boards should set directions and priorities to be achieved by the institution. In theory, that is a sufficiently clear, explicit, and important task. In practice, however, it is exceedingly difficult for many board members to accept because it requires an important discipline on their part. In truth, administering a college on a day-to-day basis is something tangible, concrete, and immediately rewarding; managing a college is considerably more complex but still something that is visible and potentially satisfying. Governing, on the other hand, requires the setting of directions and priorities, a frequently nebulous and remote task, and then leaving the implementation to others. It requires personal detachment and the conscious forfeiting of the satisfactions and rewards which accrue to others. Becoming active in the day-to-day operations of a college has an almost irresistible attraction for some board members who feel that they are not doing their job unless they are deeply involved in college affairs. But in the complex kinds of operations colleges have become, nothing could be less beneficial to the institution because of the role confusion it engenders. Similarly, it is not the role of a board or board member to monitor or second guess its administrators, faculty, or students, although that too is easier than the vital but unrewarding task of setting directional policy for an institution.

To have college boards function effectively, it is not only important for their members to restrict their role to policy formulation; it is equally important that board members be selected on the basis of criteria appropriate to colleges and appropriate to board functions. There has always been some debate about the skills and backgrounds that should be possessed by board members collectively. It is frequently observed, for example, that at least financial and legal expertise should be found on any college board. A much better case, however, can be made for having boards made up of quite ordinary people without necessarily any specialized expertise, but with a commitment to the mission of the institution and an ability to reflect and influence the disparate views of the population in whose trust they act. College board members are trustees of the population to be served by the college (and in some cases trustees of government), and it is people who can collectively best represent this population who should serve as trustees, regardless of the specialized expertise they may or may not individually possess.

Policy formulation—direction setting and the setting of institutional priorities—is the most basic role for a college board. The effective exercise of that function, however, requires a second role, that of evaluation. It is impossible to continue to set directions and rearrange priorities, which any dynamic institution requires, without rigorous assessment of institutional performance against previously established directions and priorities. It is not uncommon for public institutions to invite external auditors to assess the performance of their institution, and this practice has much to recommend it. But no college board can play its role effectively by merely transferring the responsibility for evaluation of institutional performance to external third parties or to its own administrators. Active participation in the assessment of institutional performance is an inescapable direct role for college boards, and one that is substantial, and perhaps even attractive.

A third board role is that of interpreter between the community served by the college and the college itself. As with people in other lines of work, college people develop their own jargon, acronyms, and day-to-day language often quite unintelligible to outsiders. It ought to be a task of lay board members not only to cut through the jumble of college vocabulary but also to explain to outsiders what their college is doing, in what directions it is trying to go, and why it has chosen its directions and priorities. Similarly, it is a task of a good board to interpret the people it represents, their interests and their expectations from the college, to the people within a college. Good boards accept a two-way public information role and do not leave that role entirely to staff.

The fourth basic role for a college board—and the most critical, some would say—is the selection of a chief executive officer, by whatever label, responsible for providing it advice on matters of policy and for managing the college on its behalf.

Instructor Roles

Role clarification for instructors and other professional staff is equally important. The inadequacy of a collegial management model to meet the needs of contemporary colleges does not mean that instructors should be relegated to the status of instructional technicians. College instructors are highly specialized professional experts. That expertise should have its primary outlet in the classroom or with students, but it would be an imprudent college that ignored the contributions that professional experts can make to college policy formulation, to priority setting, and to management and administration. Consultation, the honest seeking of informed advice by experts on matters within their expertise, should characterize the management style of contemporary colleges.

If any term has been abused in colleges in recent years, however, it has been the term "consultation." College faculty members have claimed that consultation has been phony when their advice has been sought but not followed. Administrators have felt slighted when their views have not formed the basis of board action. Board members have expressed amazement and disappointment when in good faith they have sought college-wide opinion on issues and directions only to find that their eventual decision caused internal friction because it did not conform to the views expressed by one or another internal college body. These difficulties can make it tempting simply to abandon consultation as part of the process of institutional decision-making, but that course of action is not in the institutional interest.

For consultation to be useful and effective in the current Canadian college context, several distinctions need to be made and understood. First, consultation is not the power or authority to decide; it is the opportunity to contribute to and influence decisions, and it is quite reasonable to expect decision-makers to seek advice honestly from several quarters without any commitment to follow the advice they receive. Secondly, there is little justification to offering the opportunity of consultation to those who have no particular expertise or specialized information on which they might base their advice; as harsh as it might sound against a history of extensive consultation within Canada's colleges, these institutions can no longer afford the luxury of seeking and assessing amateur advice on professional issues. And the third distinction is between consultation on expert or professional matters and consultation on institutional concerns where a decision might affect the entire life and character of the college. In the former case, only consultation with those who have specialized expertise or knowledge makes sense, just as academic freedom is only properly extended to those with acknowledged expertise and only in the field in which that acknowledged expertise has been developed. There are no universal experts within colleges or beyond. In the case of crucial institutional concerns, broad consultation is not only appropriate but vital to institutional health because what is being sought is not expertise but a polling of views and impressions that may influence the eventual decision. Whether new criteria for the evaluation of the performance of teaching faculty should be introduced, for example, is an issue on which the instructors and other academic professionals, but not the business office professionals, need to be consulted. On the other hand, the change of criteria for admission to a college may well be an issue on which college-wide advice, expert and inexpert, should be sought.

Support Staff Roles

In many colleges, support staff—secretarial and clerical personnel, maintenance people, technical staff among others—are unappreciated and see themselves as on the lowest rung in the status and recognition ladder of the institution to which they frequently have very high levels of loyalty.

That there should exist status and recognition ladders at all in colleges is unfortunate because the work of all people is so intricately interwoven that virtually all employees are essential contributors to institutional performance. As most college people know, to get important and immediate things done, it is rarely a board member or senior administrator or instructor who expedites; it is a janitor or secretary or courier who has learned to cut through institutional red tape unobtrusively and keep the college going. Nevertheless in a community of well-paid, high status, articulate, and aggressive professionals used to the demonstration of deference, support staff do go largely unrewarded and unrecognized for their institutional contributions. It is true that their role is to be of service to others within and beyond their institution. It is not true that their role is to be the servant of anyone.

Student Roles

The essential and common role for college students is to learn. Most of that learning takes place in the classroom, laboratory, shop, library, studio, learning centre—or in front of a television monitor, on the end of a telephone, or in a carrel in a mobile teaching unit. And most of that learning takes place within an instructor-student relationship, which is not a relationship of equals.

Yet there are circumstances where students have significant contributions to make to institutional life, particularly in colleges which enrol large numbers of mature and experienced citizens as students. On virtually all instructional and academic issues, students have and ought to have the opportunity to share their normally frank and dispassionate views, and the institution that takes advantage of student perspectives will do itself a favour, as long as students are not led to believe that consultation is the power of decision-making and as long as instructors do not forfeit their professional responsibilities to their students.

There has been the view within at least a few colleges in Canada that student participation in the larger political life of a college is itself an important part of their education and accordingly ought to be vigorously encouraged if not required. In the glory days of the early 1970's, student parity with faculty in institutional departmental decision-making was a very compelling idea which was implemented with reasonable success in some cases.[33] This approach to student participation warrants further exploration, as long as the heterogeneity of college student bodies is recognized, as long as political participation is not viewed as sport but as serious business, and as long as students are not manipulated by others within colleges who have more sophisticated political skills.

Administrator Roles

Of all the roles that need clarification for the effective operation of colleges in Canada, none is more critical than that of the chief executive officer. Even the title "chief executive officer" has a false and worrisome ring to many college people. For some it conjures up the image of the hard-nosed, uncaring, bottom-line, corporate executive, and surely public colleges ought not to become mere businesses run only for the purposes of fattening shareholders wallets and aggrandizing the incumbent. But, because Canadian colleges do have many of the characteristics of complex, labour-intensive corporations, their chief executive officers do indeed need to have many of the characteristics of the contemporary, not caricatured, business executive. Their essential role is to execute the will of the board, to recommend to the board on all matters of policy and its assessment, to manage the enterprise in the full meaning of that term by setting operational policy, to see to the daily effective administration of all college affairs, to be the continuing public face of the college to both its members and the community it serves, and to act on behalf of the college in its dealings with external bodies and other components of the networks of which the college is a part.

Chief executive officers in Canadian colleges go by three different titles: there are presidents who in only a limited sense "preside," but who reap the benefit (and the liabilities) of a title which grows out of the American college tradition; there are principals who in no way serve in the traditional role of "principal" teacher, but who may have the advantage (and limitations) of being identified as part of the academic component of a college; there are directors general (for which the English translation in law is principal), whose title connotes the sense of general manager in an institution in which the chairman of the board is president and the Directeur des Services Pédagogiques (in law, the English translation is dean) is the senior instructional (or operating) officer.

Whatever the title, the common role is chief executive officer, or the most senior employee charged with executing the policy of the board and acting in all respects on its behalf.

However one may play the role of chief executive officer in a Canadian college—and all of them have their own peculiarities—their common responsibility is to make decisions on a continuing basis, and virtually all of their decisions have impacts that go far beyond themselves. In the final analysis, the chief executive officer decides on behalf of the institution and is accountable for actions and decisions. Others may advise, others may implement, others may act on behalf of a component of the college, others may act through delegation, but it is the man or woman serving in the senior executive capacity who must accept the heat and carry the responsibility.

At an earlier time, in less complex and smaller colleges, it was indeed possible for the chief executive officer to preside, direct, and serve as principal teacher. It was even possible, in the manner of the universities, to appoint inexpert assistants from within the college to serve in capacities which required skills quite different from those required to be excellent instructors. Managing and administering a college could be achieved by a process of "on the job" learning, and to ensure that no one would be saddled with an onerous and thankless job indefinitely, a policy of rotating non-instructional work among personnel trained to be instructors could be implemented without disastrous institutional results. Fumbling through was tolerable when growth or maintenance of the status quo was of paramount importance, when difficult decisions were unnecessary, and when the stakes were not high.

The changed circumstances require different policies and practices. No individual can now both manage and provide daily administrative service to a college without serious adverse consequences for that college, however talented and energetic that individual may be. Canada's colleges are now—like most universities, technical institutions, and school systems—in an era in which trained, expert specialists are required in a variety of non-instructional areas. Instructional administration requires different training and expertise than instruction; financial management for a complex organization requires specialization; in an era of scarce resources, planning and analytical functions take on a particularly critical importance and require distinctive attributes. In short, the view that any reasonably intelligent person who wishes to do so can adequately manage or administer as complex an organization as a college is indeed a myth.

Yet, it is equally mythical that public colleges must develop growing bureaucracies to ensure their proper management and administration. There is no inevitability to growth in administrative complements if these institutions are to take the lead from successfully managed corporate bodies.[34] Increasingly, the use of task forces, special problem groups, and other similar bodies to address one-time issues has been demonstrated to be effective in maintaining a continuity and consistency of management, in obviating the pressure to create additional administrative posts, and in keeping administrative complements lean so that the maximum resources of an organization can be directed to the primary function of that organization.[35]

In all but the rarest cases, the management structure and operation of any organization depends upon the chief executive officer who sets the institutional tone and provides the institutional leadership.

Canada's colleges now need chief executive officers who can articulate clear visions for these institutions and help others to see and seize a vision.

Canada's public colleges now need chief executive officers who understand the nature and distinctiveness of their institutions, and the particular character of adult learning.[36]

Canada's public colleges now need chief executive officers who manage by planning and anticipating; no longer can they just be reactors to situations or mere crisis managers.[37]

Canada's public colleges now need chief executive officers who have feet in both community and college, so that they can be the social analysts required for rapidly changing times.[38]

Canada's public colleges now need chief executive officers who can function well within formal and informal networks of which their institutions are part. Colleges can no longer operate in isolation or in competition; skills in co-operation with other strong-willed and determined people have become essential.[39]

Canada's public colleges now need chief executive officers who are skilled mediators or power-brokers to cope constructively with the tensions and conflicts that are inevitable, and desirable, in dynamic organizations and in communities which demand more and better learning opportunities without unwarranted cost.[40] College chief executive officers must be skilled and humane communicators who can set a positive institutional climate; they must be persons who will take the time to listen to people as human beings as well as competent professionals. It is the quality of communication that provides the credibility upon which leadership depends.

Canada's public colleges need chief executive officers who are forceful advocates, not only for their institutions but also for the college movement, because colleges cannot isolate themselves from sister institutions, from other components of the post-secondary sector, or from other elements of the public sector.

Canada's public colleges need chief executive officers who can make difficult decisions, and who can resist pressures to respond to short term demands in favour of longer term institutional interests.

Canada's public colleges need chief executive officers who have a high tolerance for ambiguity because no organization functions consistently as planned, and no Canadian college need tolerate regimentation as the price for achievement of its goals and objectives.

Conclusion

Canada's colleges have gone through a process of learning and maturation since their earliest days, and Canadian society is now proceeding to a new stage as it becomes a member of the information society. As the pace of change accelerates, it is incumbent upon these colleges to realign their governance, their management, and their administration for the new circumstances. Previously adequate management models need reassessment so that the development of college management can at least keep pace with the developments in learning that are key to the continued success of Canadian colleges. It is characteristic of people in educational institutions to call for change of all kinds so that the world may become a better place for all. It would be ironic and disastrous if their own institutions were to resist changes that could allow them to become the really important educators of and for the future of Canada.

LABOUR RELATIONS

Of all the issues common to Canada's colleges, the ones that stand out as most sensitive for the long-term future as well as for current day-to-day operations are those that fit the category of labour relations. These issues touch every aspect of college life in very immediate, personal, and professional ways. And they provoke emotion as well as thought, action as well as reflection.

It should not be difficult to acknowledge why these issues are so central. The working conditions, security, and roles of most college employees are defined by agreements which, from an employee perspective, are intended to stabilize if not improve their personal and professional status and prerogatives. On the other hand, from a college perspective employee agreements not only result in material and professional improvements for employees, but in that process they also impose restrictions on the ability of a college to be managed in what are perceived as the best interests of the students and community. From an employee perspective, the best protection against management capriciousness is a formalized working contract. From a management perspective, the ability to manage is limited by formal contracts and collective agreements. Working contracts and collective agreements may limit the ability of colleges to evaluate the performance of their employees; they may prevent or delay the introduction of curriculum change; they may limit the numbers of students who may be admitted to a college or a college programme; they may constrain the manner in which colleges provide services to satellite campuses; they may impose limitations on the use and deployment of part-time employees. To many in Canada's colleges, such agreements not only may, but should, curb the unbridled discretion of managers in all these respects; to others, each constraint is a troublesome if not obstructive interference in legitimate management discretion and a denial of essential responsiveness to citizens. Colleges are, and should be, committed to change; employees are committed to change only if change is not unreasonably at their expense and frequently only if they are assured of at least participating in, if not determining, the nature of the change.

Put bluntly, good labour relations have not been a strength of the colleges, nor are the real problems likely to disappear—despite the fact that boards, administrators, faculty, and support staff want many of the same things for their institutions. And if labour relations have been tense and controversial in the past, they have become even more strained in recent years. The mid-1980's are times of financial uncertainty for colleges and job insecurity for employees. Colleges are less able to plan confidently, to offer creative solutions to their problems, and to preserve their client-centred approach to their tasks. They must respond, however they can, to demands for accountability, productivity, cost effectiveness, and rationalization. Yet each one of these demands is perceived by instructors and support staff as an ominous challenge to job security and professional recognition. An examination of how the colleges reached the current state of labour relations will put these issues in context.

The Beginnings

The new colleges grew from a variety of roots. Some began as extensions of public school systems, others from vocational or trade schools or institutes previously under direct provincial government control; some had previously been privately controlled with a heavy academic bias in their values; others were the product of the melding of several disparate post-secondary institutions each with its own specialized curriculum. Some were created from the "ground up."

Similarly, the employees of the new institutions, particularly the instructors and administrators, had joined the colleges from a wide variety of sources: universities, small and large industry, school systems, adult education agencies, vocational institutes, trade schools, private colleges, and government departments. Without established staff functions and status for various employee groups in the college, many of the instructors assumed or hoped they would retain many of the traditions and practices of their previous employment. In some cases this meant a form of public sector unionization, while in others the professional association model as practised in many school districts and universities was the expectation. In rare cases, new employees expected no contractual commitments at all, and some instructors even saw themselves as individual professionals acting as entrepreneurs under an institutional umbrella. From those who saw the need for some form of organization different structures emerged: in some provinces, legislation provided for one provincial organization for all teaching personnel; in others separate associations for academic and vocational instructors was the practice. In all this untidiness, board members and senior managers hoped for a fresh new start and frequently regretted that they had to respect previous employee agreements and employee organizational structures. In all, the variations among the new colleges were reflected as much in their employee relations as in their curricula.

In the seven provinces where colleges were established under the governing authority of local boards, the early years saw relatively trouble-free labour relations. By and large, board members as employers were as inexperienced as their employees within these new institutions, which began as "big happy families" with common objectives. The instructors were not overly concerned about basic labour relations issues and usually formed internal "professional" associations which dealt with college boards and senior administrators in an informal and "gentlemanly" fashion. The favourable economic circumstances during these years when governments funded institutions generously contributed to the absence of either formal bargaining structures or to collective agreements. Problems related to reduction of the work force, lay-off procedures, retraining, or technological change simply did not exist.

However, the rapid growth, expansion of programmes, increase in services, and the accompanying escalation of the financial needs of these institutions had a direct impact on labour relations. Boards were or were perceived as becoming more arbitrary in their management decisions; and instructors, in turn, became increasingly restive about the reduction of opportunity to participate in the decisions which would affect their work styles, their professional roles, and their personal security.

In an era of increased public sector collective bargaining under provincial legislation, professional associations applied for and obtained rights to represent their members as certified bargaining agents. Although the specific conditions and structures which governed the bargaining processes varied considerably by province, a formal industrial model of labour-management relations was introduced into the college systems to regulate matters such as salary, benefits, and working conditions.

In a separate but related action, most provinces adopted legislation, usually in the form of a "Colleges Act," which specified the degree and character of involvement of employees in institutional governance. In most instances, actual participation has gone beyond what law requires, but that has been little consolation to those who claim that more direct participation should be a right of faculty members. Unionization has become a fact of Canadian college life. Advocates of virtually every style of employee relations work in Canada's colleges, and virtually every issue in these colleges has an important labour relations dimension. Although colleges are hardly unique in this regard, their lack of tradition and the heterogeneity of their activities as well as their personnel add a dimension to labour relations concerns that do not prevail in most other Canadian educational institutions. Elsewhere, the debates are theoretical and speculative; in Canada's colleges they have become real and pressing.

Two major objectives on the part of employees are universal: to advance their welfare as employees and to ensure participation in the institutional decisions affecting their employment and professional lives. Similarly, management has had two major objectives; to retain the ability to manage their institutions and to ensure optimum service to students and communities. The lines have been drawn.

Currently, the context for collective bargaining in the college sector is different in each province. The differences reflect the wide diversity in organization, from highly centralized to decentralized structures, from agreements which include college personnel as part of the public service sector to contracts specific to college teachers, and from provincial legislation to separate acts for each institution. Despite these differences, the agreements influence the future of these institutions as much as or more than policies of government, attitudes of board members, and the directives of ministries.

In British Columbia, the Colleges and Provincial Institutes Act (1977) provided for three options under which colleges and institutes could conduct negotiations. The first option provided for collective bargaining in conformity with the terms of the labour code of the province. The second and third options allowed for legal agreements outside the labour code: a "fair comparison" method, by which market comparisons would set the basic conditions of the agreement; and a method of limited bargaining with compulsory arbitration. Primarily because previous negotiations had been conducted with all the protections of the labour code and because there seemed little advantage to forfeiting these rights, the instructors in only two post-secondary institutions chose not to maintain collective bargaining as it had been previously.

There is no province-wide bargaining; rather, each institution bargains separately with each internal association which has been certified to act on behalf of its members. A variety of bargaining arrangements exists within the system. Some colleges have separate bargaining units for academic instructors, vocational instructors, and support staff; in other cases, all faculty of an institution form one unit, with support staff another. One college includes both instructors and staff within the same bargaining unit. A majority of, but not all, faculty bargaining units are members of a provincial organization called The College and Institute Educators Association of British Columbia, which serves as an information clearing house and lobbying agency for faculty interests. Most support staff unions are affiliated with either the Canadian Union of Public Employees or the British Columbia Government Employees Union.

The College and Institute Act currently specifically excludes employees and students from board membership. However, the legislation does have the requirement for colleges to establish a "programme advisory committee," whose terms of reference are not specified, with representation from students and professional staff. The view of students and professional staff is also required on all changes to board by-laws.

Although the history of labour relations in post-secondary educational institutions in Alberta is a long and complex one, as of 1981 a unique bargaining approach had been developed. In legislation enacted in that year all post-secondary institutions—universities, technical institutes, and public colleges—were to bargain in essentially the same manner. Negotiations are now conducted at the institutional level; individual academic staff associations bargain with management under the conditions outlined in the Colleges Act. Bargaining in colleges is not governed by the Labour Relations Act of the province which covers the private sector, nor the Public Service Employee Relations Act which pertains to the public sector. Binding arbitration is used as a method of conflict resolution. The right to strike and lockout may be bargained under the college labour legislation.

The Colleges Act provides for one academic staff member, one student, and one non-academic staff member as board members. As well, an academic council is to be established in each college, largely composed of academic faculty, administrators, and students. These councils advise boards on all matters they deem desirable.

One matter of concern to faculty members in Alberta's colleges has been that aspect of the college legislation which provides for the employer, the College Board, to determine who shall constitute the bargaining unit for professional faculty. In consequence, the Alberta Association of College Faculties (which expanded in 1984 and was renamed the Alberta College-Institute Faculties Association) has lodged a complaint with the International Labour Organization, claiming that the legislation denies them the right of free association.

A variety of arrangements for labour negotiations exists in the Saskatchewan college and institute systems. All instructional staff in the three Institutes of Applied Arts and Sciences are members of one unit of the Saskatchewan Government Employees Union; that unit also includes non-teaching groups such as museum technicians, librarians, and culture and recreational consultants. The institutes do not have individual governing boards, and there is no formal involvement of instructors in governance. The community colleges have staff associations which may choose to bargain as unionized bodies. Nine of the fifteen associations have elected to bargain through the Saskatchewan Government Employees Union, although bargaining is technically conducted with individual college boards. The other six colleges have retained non-unionized professional association status. It is of some significance that the number of full-time instructors in Saskatchewan's community colleges is quite small.

The instructors in Manitoba colleges belong to the Manitoba Government Employees' Association, which contains more than twenty bargaining units. Of these, nine units—including clerical, education, and health workers—are employed directly by the government of the province. The community college instructors bargain an "education component sub-agreement" for provisions in addition to those in the "master" agreement. The "sub-agreement" details working conditions, instructor accreditation matters, and other terms specific to the college enviroment. The three community colleges in Manitoba do not have governing boards but operate under the direct jurisdiction of the Ministry of Continuing Education. College instructors in Manitoba have no formal role in institutional governance.

Although both the support and instructional staff groups in Ontario Colleges of Applied Arts and Technology negotiated with the Council of Regents as separate associations in the early years, they were each recruited into a provincial body, the Civil Service Association of Ontario, in 1967 and 1970 respectively. This organization later became certified as the Ontario Public Service Employees Union (OPSEU).

Each college functions as an individual local of the central bargaining unit. As a subset of OPSEU, the instructional personnel bargain with the Council of Regents, the appointed provincial intermediary body, consistent with terms of the colleges' Collective Bargaining Act (1975). Although the majority of member organizations in OPSEU do not have the right to strike. the college staff and faculty unions retain that right. While faculty members in individual colleges often are involved in informal governing and consultative bodies, there is no legal provision for faculty representation at the board level.

In few provinces have union-management relations and the role of government in these relations reached as high a public profile as in Quebec. Unionization of faculty in post-secondary education was established in Quebec well before the development of the CEGEP. In 1965 an amendment to the Quebec Labour Code extended application to all teachers, including university professors. As a result, in many institutions which were to form the bases for many of the CEGEP—normal schools, technical institutes, even some classical colleges—unions had already been established. After 1967, the personnel of most of the new colleges quickly unionized, within either the Fédération Nationale des Enseignants du Québec (FNEQ) or the Centrale des Enseignants du Québec (CEQ). Generally, three bargaining units were created in each college: for instructors, non-teaching professionals, and support staff respectively. In the last fifteen years a series of legislative acts have brought increasing centralization to the bargaining process and, at the same time, given the provincial government more, and more direct, influence at the negotiating table. The bargaining representative for management is the Fédération des CEGEP, which maintains a large Labour Relations Division. However, the direct influence of government on bargaining stances by the employer have been evident.

Faculty in Quebec colleges have negotiated significant benefits. Their salary, job security, and working conditions are among the most attractive in Canada. However, there have been several periods of major conflict and acrimonious dispute. Particularly since 1982, faculty unions have clashed with the government which, in response to public opinion and a critical economic climate, joined with the employer to take a much stronger bargaining stance than in previous years. Indeed, the demoralization of faculty has become widespread, primarily as a result of the state of labour relations.

Nova Scotia's limited purpose post-secondary training institutions operate under the direct jurisdiction of the Ministry of Education. Instructors in the technical institutes bargain as part of the Nova Scotia Government Employees Union. Vocational teachers of adults in schools throughout the province remain members of the Nova Scotia Teachers Union. The non-degree granting institutions do not have governing boards, but lay advice on curriculum is provided through advisory committees. Instructors are not represented on these bodies.

Since the 1981 Amendment to the New Brunswick Community College Act, the nine campuses of the college system operate as directed by the Ministry of Community Colleges. The instructors are organized as the Education Collective Bargaining Unit represented by the New Brunswick Public Employees Association. Bargaining with the Association is undertaken by a negotiator of the Labour Relations Division of the Treasury Board. The College also has non-instructional employees in seven other bargaining units and a non-union administrator group.[41] There is no provision in the act of formal participation by faculty in the governance of the college system.

On Prince Edward Island, the only post-secondary institution other than the university operates under its own legislation, the Holland College Act. Two faculty members and two student representatives hold positions on the governing board. No other provision is made in law for faculty involvement in institutional governance. The applied arts and technology instructors bargain with the college through their non-union association. The vocational instructors retain their previous status as members of the PEI Public Service Association, as do support staff members. The College Board negotiates directly with each of its three employee groups.

Each of Newfoundland's three post-secondary colleges functions under separate legislation. Instructional staff in two colleges belong to the Newfoundland Association of Public Employees, which negotiates a master agreement as well as sub-agreements for each of its twenty locals. The College of Fisheries has a non-union faculty association which bargains directly with Treasury Board. Each college has a governing board, which is not involved in the bargaining process. At Bay St. George Community College, the faculty are represented on the board.

Despite this diversity, there is general agreement among board members, administrators, faculty, support staff, and government officials in all parts of Canada that labour relations issues need to be addressed more effectively everywhere in the country if the best interests of both employees and institutions are to be well served. Although literature related to the U.S. experience is abundant,[42] Canada has not yet developed a substantial body of information that can be used to sort out and assist in the resolution of the issues. The development of collective bargaining in the university sector has attracted some attention,[43] and a special edition of *College Canada* in 1982 at least opened up the question to broader scrutiny within the college sector.[44] The issues presented in the balance of this chapter are the ones most topical in the mid-1980's.

College Instructors—Unionists? Professionals?

The status that college instructors should have is still an actively debated question throughout Canada. Are they professionals or are they workers? Have instructors compromised their roles as teachers by becoming unionists? Can unionist and professional be two sides of the same coin? The views which follow display the range of concerns. The first, by Porter, is expressed as follows:

> My thesis is simple: a teacher by his very nature and by the nature of the profession he has chosen must behave professionally. But a teacher also needs an organization to represent him in seeking just remuneration, reasonable working conditions and protection against injustice. The challenge of the teacher organization must be to meld successfully these two roles—the development, encouragement, and maintenance of 'professionalism' and the responsible promotion of the teachers' interests.[45]

A quite different perspective is advanced by Barrett:

> Having suffered the ravages of a management bent on devaluing teaching and deskilling teachers, we can hardly be faulted for viewing a union movement dedicated to improving working conditions and expanding the range of teacher responsibility and autonomy as the authentic voice of professionalism. Seen in this way, professionalism is not a dying attitude, subverted by self-interested teachers and an indifferent bargaining agent; it becomes a goal that can be achieved despite, not because of, the working arrangements that management endeavours to force upon us.[46]

The third view, advanced by Thompson, addresses the twofold rationale for professionals to unionize. One reason is clearly a matter of preservation of traditional prerogatives and privileges associated with professional status: the other is a consequence of an economic climate which threatens to place non-organized employees in disadvantageous positions relative to organized colleagues. Thompson summarizes the situation as follows:

> The motivation of professionals for adopting collective bargaining may be classified as defensive or offensive. Although few hard data on the subject exist it is logical to assume that motives are mixed for many persons and groups. However, this classification is meant to highlight the predominant forces causing professionals to undertake bargaining. The change to collective bargaining is defensive when professionals organize themselves to avoid inclusion in a bargaining unit or union dominated by non-professionals. Professionals also have taken defensive positions to avoid being placed in a relatively weak bargaining position in comparison with other employee groups in the same enterprise when fellow employees started bargaining. Although professionals often began with limited enthusiasm for bargaining, they saw little choice but to adopt this mode of relations with management. Professionals' motives are offensive when they organize to achieve their own economic or social objectives through bargaining. Professionals who make such a choice look to the bargaining process as the primary mechanism for the maintenance or improvement of their conditions of work. They are willing to consider strikes or other traditional trade-union tactics and may consider alliances with other public-sector unions.[47]

However college employees have chosen to organize themselves, when in fact they had any choice at all, there are important implications of each choice not only for themselves but also for their institutions. Because no choice in this domain is ever irreversible, each basic model which currently operates in Canadian colleges merits reassessment in the light of circumstances which have changed since the introduction of collective bargaining and unionization.

The oldest form of operating post-secondary institutions in Canada is the collegial model, characteristic of the longer established universities in this country. In this mode faculty members clearly consider themselves, and are considered by others, as academic professionals and they accept both the prerogatives and responsibilities of this status. In fact, collegiality blurs the distinction between employee and employer, because faculty members play full roles in the governance, management, and administration of their institutions as well as of their individual departments and faculties. Collegiality involves self-government, both direct and representative.

In collegial governance, as practised in Canadian universities, faculty members have the final authority on academic decisions and faculty working conditions, usually through statutory powers accorded to senates and through the decision-making structures of departments. In addition, academic professionals choose who their colleagues will be and give special recognition to colleagues who distinguish themselves. A collegially governed institution is a meritocracy. As well, professors agree from to time to take on the onerous burdens of administration on behalf of their colleagues so that academic and institutional administrators remain part of faculty. The "we-they relationship" of management and labour in industry normally does not exist. Boards of Governors have traditionally raised and allocated funds for collegial institutions, not managed them.

In this form of organization and operation, salary and benefit provisions have been established by gentlemen's agreements, with at least the tacit understanding that the institution will continue to operate while these agreements are being worked out. Strikes, lockouts, and similar practices in other environments are foreign to collegial institutions. And when collegial institutions have been unable to resolve their problems, they have turned to other collegial institutions to help them, rather than to other sectors of society.

Factors which have contributed to the success of collegial institutions need emphasis. First, the ethics of collegiality have developed over a long period of time. A collegial "culture" has been developed over centuries so that frequently unspoken conventions concerning institutional operations and professorial behaviour have become well ingrained. More simply, when one grows up in a collegial environment, certain things are done or not done by custom and convention and tradition, and most of these practices need not be codified; they are simply respected as part of being a member of a collegial community.

Secondly, while universities have certainly had their financial ups and downs through the ages, until recently they have been largely spared the impact of the swings of economic cycles because they have functioned aside from, rather than as part of the larger society; they traditionally have not depended entirely on public funding for their maintenance. Parenthetically, it should also be observed that the prerogatives of collegiality have been traditionally extended only to the professoriate, not to support personnel who have had to work in conditions comparable to other unorganized workers in non-university settings.

Chinks in the armour of collegial institutions in Canada began to appear at the very time when the public colleges were coming into existence and there are many universities which now not only retain vestiges of the traditional collegial environment but also regulate many aspects of their operations in more formalized fashion; unionization of the professoriate is a fact of Canadian university life.[48]

But more directly related to colleges in Canada are several facts which distinguish these institutions and their circumstances from traditional universities. They have not had a long history through which collegial conventions and customs could be developed. They have not been institutions deliberately set aside from the larger society; in fact, they have been creations of governments to serve public ends. They have not been designed as collegial institutions in law; publicly elected or appointed boards have been given legislative responsibility to govern and manage these institutions. All the people working in these institutions have been clearly identified as employees rather than colleagues— even those who have been formally or informally recognized as professionals, including instructors, librarians, counsellors, and others.

Many of the colleges came into being at a time when collegially governed institutions were coming under internal and external attack for being unresponsive. In the late 1960's and early 1970's, increased participation of students, faculty, and community members in the affairs of historically collegial institutions was demanded through passionate rhetoric and sit-ins—and more. Not oblivious to the legitimacy of many of these pressures, several new colleges attempted to perform an intricate balancing act: to encourage participation of everybody in virtually everything, but to retain the effective decision-making power by the college board and those appointed by the board to manage and administer the institution. The response of other colleges and governments to the call for greater participation was to point out, not always diplomatically, that colleges were not collegial institutions and that their employees were expected to act as employees.

In both cases, these responses were judged by many college instructors to be, at the very least, inadequate. The participation-without-power response was often seen by instructors as collegiality-when-convenient to the board, with faculty members still subject to the arbitrary or unattractive decisions and processes of board members and administrators who thirsted for power and really did not understand the distinctiveness of the college enterprise. The act-as-an-employee response was seen as an affront, an indignity to people who were quite capable of accepting the responsibilities of being autonomous, independent, and collegial professionals, and a challenge to act like employees outside the college or university setting. As Handel has argued, "as the evidence and the literature suggest, community colleges have never been, in the university sense of the term, collegially governed."[49] And all of this was taking place as public sector unionization—and the prospects of strikes, lockouts and arbitrations— was expanding rapidly throughout Canada.

The reality now is that colleges in Canada are not, in any usual sense of the term, collegial institutions, even though there may be significant levels of faculty, staff, and student participation in the decision-making processes of several of the institutions. And there is no likelihood of a change of this base line in the immediate future, whatever the strengths and limitations of collegiality might be. What then are the strengths and limitations of the alternatives to collegiality? Is there a preferred way for college professionals in Canada to acquire what they have a legitimate right to expect as persons and as professionals and for colleges to be able to achieve their objectives?

One approach has been for college instructors to choose unionization: to form trade unions operating under labour legislation which applies equally to other certified unions in the public and private sectors. With this approach, whatever the union and the college as employer agree to bargain is negotiable: forms and levels of participation, powers and processes for decision-making, as well as the more conventional bargaining issues of salaries, benefits, and working conditions. The rules for bargaining are clear and supported in law, grievance and arbitration procedures exist, and the ultimate weapons of strike and lockout encourage the process of negotiation.

Despite the obvious advantages of this approach to both parties, there is considerable opposition from a number of college instructors and board members. Some of this opposition is superficial or transitory, such as the view that collective bargaining is somehow unseemly for people in educational institutions or that people on both sides of the educational bargaining table are rank amateurs unskilled in the real arts of negotiation, who really only play at the tough game of bargaining. Some of the reluctance is merely unfortunate, such as the concern that college administrators (most of whom have a college teaching background, and on a day-to-day basis work as professional colleagues with faculty members) are perceived as the adversaries of their faculty colleagues not only during the bargaining stage but throughout the year because they serve as collective agreement administrators as well as professional colleagues.

But some of the opposition is substantial. The Canadian college experience with formal collective bargaining reveals that adversarial relationships between management and labour in education have adversely affected the close working relationship and ideological kinship that ought to prevail in an educational setting. College administrators, college board members, and college faculty members are not normally adversaries in the same ways that supervisors and workers may be in other workplaces: they often share similar social philosophies, they hold common institutional objectives, and they want most of the same day-to-day results. Secondly, there is legitimate concern that arbitration hearings and similar appeals to external methods of conflict resolution put the destiny of faculty members and institutions in the hands of third parties who may have no sensitivity whatever to the particular characteristics of the college setting. But the most profound and compelling opposition stems from the view that general labour legislation—covering private and public sectors, industrial and public service and educational workplaces—does not give sufficient recognition to the distinctiveness of the college as a workplace to allow the proper balance of interests between the needs of educational employees and the needs of educational institutions. This view contends that a college is not a shop floor or a government office or a bank or retail store and that labour legislation to deal with one setting is not appropriate for others. It also contends that colleges find it exceedingly difficult, if not virtually impossible, to be responsive to changing community demands for service if through negotiations they find themselves constrained by seniority clauses (in place of the meritocratic tradition of collegial universities) or elaborate processes relating to the introduction of technological change (especially when those clauses have been designed for industrial workplaces). One reality is that the uniqueness of the college as workplace has never been defined with any satisfactory level of specificity; another reality is that most people in colleges would agree that they do indeed work in a unique workplace. Until this matter is adequately addressed, standard industrial model negotiations will have detractors in colleges, from both faculty members and managers.

A second approach is a variation on the trade union model—the public sector model. This approach, as practised in the Canadian college sector for many years in several provinces, sees the instructors in a college as members of a local of a province-wide union of public sector employees. For college instructors, it has the advantages—and the disadvantages—of the trade union model, with the added dimension of size and solidarity with other public sector workers. For colleges and their boards and administrators, it has the advantages—and disadvantages—of removing much of the adversarial conflict from the college itself to a more remote and more detached forum.

Vallance would see distinctions between college instructors and other college employees, and between college instructors and other employees providing other public services, as not only artificial but as part of a long standing strategy of divide and conquer by manipulative college managers. She notes:

> When it comes to basics, we are all employees. Our employment is governed, for the most part, by collective agreements that are hammered out in the necessarily adversarial context of industrial relations. Our employers are the same, and they are committed to the same basic principle: to get as much productivity as possible from us for as little payment as possible. Moreover, they appreciate that teachers are especially vulnerable to the mystique of professionalism (which means working for "psychic rewards" instead of payment) mainly because, no matter how much chatter there may be about commitment and caring, teachers are not professionals.[50]

There is little doubt that the notion of "psychic rewards instead of payment" for professional services is one aspect of labour relations in colleges. But equally a matter of concern in public sector bargaining is the tacit assumption on the part of the employer that a college instructor is merely an educational technician, with the implication that this technician is quite replaceable by another technician. From this perspective, the college instructor who aspires to recognition as a professional will get little comfort from being a member of a public sector union local.

If the college trade union falls short in not recognizing the distinctiveness of the college as a workplace, the public sector union model falls short not only on this count but also in not acknowledging the professional character of college instruction and the professional training of those who provide it.

A third approach is the non-union, professional association model. This approach leaves instructors the most vulnerable to capriciousness because there is no legal status or protection against arbitrary actions and decisions. On the other hand, this approach comes closest to the traditional collegial model of operation, avoids much of the tension of formalized collective bargaining, and accords, at least tacitly, some professional status and rewards to instructors. Most college instructors would find this approach quite unsatisfactory, despite attractions claimed for it, if only because it gives boards an unbalanced opportunity to meet institutional needs without adequate assurance that the needs and rights of employees will be recognized, protected, and enhanced.

There is a fourth approach which has received scant attention, except in Alberta. This approach starts from the recognition that post-secondary education workplaces are indeed unique settings unlike the shop or government office. But it also recognizes that college employees need the protection of law if their rights are to be protected. As a result, special labour legislation designed for and applicable exclusively to post-secondary educational institutions has been adopted. Within this unique legislative framework, college faculty members in each college are then able to bargain collectively with their own boards.

There is no doubt that the current Alberta legislation has imperfections. Yet, to the extent that college boards need to be quickly responsive to changing needs at a rate different from other public service or industrial organizations and to the extent that the fraternity of some forms of collegiality is desired by college instructors, Alberta-type labour legislation for the college milieu has much to recommend it. Instructors can have as much protection of their interests as in the trade union or public service approaches, and the college board has the advantage of having its institution recognized in law as having distinctive characteristics. If the appropriate balance of interests does not now prevail in Alberta colleges, at least the groundwork for improved college labour legislation has been established.

Of course, it would be naive to suggest that any single approach to college labour relations would be realistic for the diverse colleges and college systems of Canada. It would be equally unrealistic, however, to propose that current methods of reconciling college and instructor needs should become entrenched. Government officials, college officials, and college instructors need to approach labour relations issues with the same sense of dynamism and commitment as is required for every other aspect of college life.

Collective Bargaining—Centralized or Decentralized?

Despite the fact that structures for collective bargaining in colleges have been well established throughout Canada, there is still considerable debate over whether bargaining should be conducted at a provincial level or at an institutional level. Indeed, throughout Canada it is possible to elicit strong, often passionate, defences of each approach. But does it really make any difference? The proponents of provincially centralized bargaining extol the virtues of consistency among like institutions within a province and express anxiety about the prospect of one college playing off, or being played off, against another within the same college system. They see additional advantages in that centralized negotiations allow employees to negotiate directly or indirectly with government, the source of funds and legislation for the college systems. Additionally, they argue that province-wide bargaining allows college boards, administrators, and instructors to detach themselves from bargaining processes and to work collaboratively for the common interest of their own institutions.

The advocates of in-house bargaining, on the other hand, see local negotiations, however much they may strain internal relationships, as an essential part of the creation of a real community-based institution where roles, responsibilities, and rights can reflect the uniqueness of each college and the region it serves. Colleges are very different from one another even in the same province, the argument goes, and these salutary differences will be obliterated by centralized bargaining, which at least implicity views all colleges within a single province as peas in a pod.

There is substance to both positions. In fact, the provincial government is the employer in many provinces, and many colleges are provincial rather than local or regional institutions. College boards do not have their own tax bases and, in these circumstances, they are unquestionably constrained when they serve as the employer in collective bargaining. But it is equally true that many colleges were designed to meet the needs of local or regional constituencies, and to achieve this objective, they must tailor their programmes and services to different clienteles. This is exceedingly difficult without at least some determination of working conditions and institutional style at an institutional level.

There seems little doubt that the common tendency throughout Canada is towards more centralized bargaining and more provincially imposed constraints on local bargaining. The inability or unwillingness of provincial governments to maintain the high funding levels that prevailed in the early years of college development, the greater centralization of decision-making, and the institutionalization of provincial networks, if not systems, of colleges weigh heavily against the maintenance of each college bargaining with its own employees to meet its own priorities.

As provincial governments make greater efforts to monitor and control all public sector spending, the constraints which they place upon college collective bargaining increase. In practice, limitations on salaries and benefits are set either by legislation or by pressures upon all employees who bargain with public money. The results are carefully proscribed limits on what is negotiable, whether faculty organizations bargain as unions or as professional associations, and whether they negotiate with college boards, intermediary bodies, or governments. With all these tendencies, the need of colleges to retain maximum operating freedom to develop creative and individual responses to financial constraint is both desirable and consistent with the character of colleges. Unique labour legislation for the college sector may be more than an avenue for improving college labour relations and addressing the professional-unionist issue. It may at the same time provide the route for striking the balance that ought to exist between centralized and decentralized approaches to bargaining.

What is at Stake?

There is little doubt that college faculty members have benefited from unionization, and there is scant evidence that colleges have lost in the process. Nevertheless, anxieties still prevail on both sides of the bargaining table, and it is not yet clear that colleges will be able to marry successfully their need to be client responsive as well as employee-responsive institutions.

If college instructors are to perform effectively in the classroom, workshop, and laboratory, they need to have reasonable teaching loads and class sizes, adequate time for their own development, and avenues to contribute their expertise to the decision-making processes in their institutions. There is no doubt that collective bargaining has helped to achieve these objectives. There is also no doubt that a number of college instructors, while recognizing the benefits that have accrued to them and their colleagues, remain uncomfortable with unionization because they view themselves as professionals. Although many college instructors see no incompatibility between unionist and professional roles and perspectives, for others a definite ambiguity remains.

For their part, colleges need to be responsive to change, particularly to the requirements of the new economy, to the need to develop new programmes and discard others, to change teaching approaches and introduce instructional technologies, and to respond to new students with new objectives. They want to develop greater flexibility of operation, to evaluate performance, and to reward excellence.[51] Many college board members and administrators see collective agreements delaying if not thwarting these objectives.

The labour relations challenge for the future is to bring creative approaches to the organization of college faculty members and to the bargaining table. The protection and enhancement of the personal and professional aspirations of instructors must be reconciled with the structural changes required of these institutions. A joint instructor-management commitment to the search for better approaches to conflict resolution and distinctive labour legislation for the colleges may well provide many answers.

8

COLLEGES AND EXCELLENCE

IMPROVEMENT OF INSTRUCTION

Canada's colleges are teaching institutions. Excellence in teaching has been their universal objective, and virtually every publication relating to these colleges notes their essential commitment to quality of instruction.[1] Despite these claims, it is generally correct to observe that, in their first days, colleges did not pay as much attention to quality of teaching as might have been expected. In many cases, circumstances required colleges to hire new teaching personnel quickly; careful screening of applicants was not always possible. Not only were new college teachers not expected to have had prior educational training, but in some cases such training was considered as much a liability as an asset. In some provinces, novice college teachers were given some initial pedagogical assistance, and in some cases a brief orientation period was required of all new teachers. But, by and large, college teachers did not have to provide prior evidence that they could teach—or that they had the skills to learn how to teach. Of course, many of them had had previous teaching experience at another level or in another kind of institution, and that was at least one useful measure of competence. In many cases, however, new instructors had had no instructional experience and were left very much to their own devices. They may have been experts in their teaching fields, but there was scant evidence that they were proficient as instructors or as facilitators of learning.

The situation was hardly better with respect to opportunities for college instructors to improve their skills. Most colleges invested in professional development, but funds set aside for this purpose were used in highly individualized ways. Instructors were able to attend conferences with their colleagues or with their counterparts in industry or other institutions. They were able to devote time to their own disciplines. They were, in a few cases, able to have extended periods away from their teaching duties and their institutions. They were able to visit other colleges to learn from other people. But in no province was there an organized, planned, systematic programme of development of the art, skill, science, or craft of teaching.

Nevertheless, the mystique was that the forte of colleges was teaching and, at least implicitly, that most college instructors excelled at teaching. As most people in these colleges today know, that mystique is suspect. How good is the teaching in Canada's colleges? It is reasonable to speculate it is as good as teaching in other educational institutions, and it may not be overly optimistic to claim that it is better than in other kinds of institutions. But the plain facts are that college teaching has not been rigorously and systematically evaluated and that few resources have been devoted to improving the quality of instruction. The question of how good college teaching really is has not yet been answered.

The Evaluation of Instruction

In every province, there exists—and there always has existed—some evaluation of instruction. Unsatisfactory college teachers have been dismissed or discouraged from continuing in that role by their peers. But the problem is that most evaluation of instruction has been geared precisely to that objective: to deal with questions of reappointment and retention—or dismissal—of teaching personnel. In the jargon of the professional educator, evaluation has been of a summative rather than formative character.[2]

Indeed, there has been considerable opposition in Canada even to this most crude form of evaluation. For a variety of reasons, including opposition to judgments by management personnel, unions have generally opposed or blunted any serious efforts to evaluate performance. They have also commonly opposed colleague and student assessments of teaching performance—the former on the grounds that good union members do not judge their brothers and sisters, the latter on the grounds that students do not have the competence and detachment to make sound judgments. Kemmerer and Baldridge make the point that these stances are characteristic of higher education in North America and that they fly in the face of one of the cherished principles of academia: the judgment of merit based upon peer evaluation.[3]

But it is not only teachers and their unions or associations that have been wary of evaluation of college teaching. Many college board members and administrators have privately deplored the absence of good evaluation programmes, but probably because they sensed a futility in pressing the point, they have not seen fit to introduce them. Similarly, government officials who have seen their responsibility as one of protecting the public interest have not insisted upon systematic evaluation, perhaps because they realized the sensitivity of the issue at all levels: government, ministries, intermediary bodies, institutions, students, instructors themselves. No one has seemed ready to provide leadership for an admittedly difficult and contentious task, but a task nevertheless that is undertaken in other sectors of education and in other sectors of employment.

The evaluation of college instruction needs to be based on a fresh set of premises. Apart from the novice teachers, and there are now few of them in colleges, evaluation of teaching performance should not be for the purpose of weeding out the unsatisfactory, but rather for the purpose of establishing a baseline from which improvement could be measured and developed. Quite realistically, college teachers who have survived in college classrooms for several years and who have retained their interest and stamina have far more than the minimum competence to maintain their positions. Even more realistically, the ability of colleges to dismiss teachers on the grounds of unsatisfactory performance after several years of apparently acceptable performance is minimal.

If the orientation of teaching evaluation could be shifted from assessment for the purpose of dismissal to evaluation for the purpose of improving performance, there would be a genuine possibility of implementing evaluation plans that would be credible within and beyond the colleges. Formative evaluation of this kind would also address the claim that teaching is a very complex activity conducted in a highly personalized fashion by professionals who view their activities as unique. For them, effectiveness of teaching cannot be measured or quantified by others. Formative evaluation would accept that claim. Evaluation with this emphasis would also address the concerns of those who charge that any evaluation plan has the potential to create such tension, suspicion, and damaged morale that it is better left undone. Formative evaluation does not judge; it provides a point of reference for improvement and contributes positively to the growth of those whose performance is being evaluated.

In the college context, there is no doubt that any imposed scheme to evaluate the performance of instructors would be doomed to failure. College instructors rightly consider themselves to be professionals for whom a hierarchical evaluation model—by institutional managers or, worse still, by government officials or inspectors—is totally inappropriate. Similarly, to entrust the evaluation of instructors to students, however mature they may be, is undesirable even though the contribution of students to any sound college instructor evaluation plan should be considerable.[4] The correct approach is for the instructors themselves to design and implement their own plan of evaluation, in an open and frank fashion, and to ensure that such a plan is used for purposes of improvement of performance rather than for retention or dismissal of their colleagues.

A largely self-administered performance evaluation plan is feasible and practical. There is an abundance of published materials on the design and implementation of objective procedures.[5] There are colleges in Canada which not only use such procedures but also incorporate evaluation guidelines into a collective agreement in such a fashion as to ensure that they are not merely ritualistic and self-serving.[6] Such guidelines can document that the evaluation of college instruction is indeed seriously undertaken and provide the baseline from which an organized professional development programme for the improvement of instruction may begin. Colleges and their instructors can choose to ignore or pay mere lip service to evaluation of instruction. But it will be only a matter of time before their credibility is challenged in the public arena and their ability to demonstrate improvement is lost.

Professional Development—The Need

The concept of professional development flows from the hypothesis that growth and improvement do not occur simply as a consequence of experience— and that they are possible and desirable. Programmes of professional development for colleges—systematic and continuing strategies to assist in the development of staff members—are particularly necessary because many colleges have allowed staff members to assume their teaching responsibilities without any recognition of their need for orientation and further assistance. This problem is particularly acute for the many part-time college instructors from industry whose contributions are unquestionably an asset to colleges but who, nevertheless, have little in their own background or experience that has prepared them for excellence in teaching.[7]

Whenever the issue of professional development for college instructors has surfaced among instructors or administrators, a common scenario emerged. Virtually everyone has agreed that there is a vital need for effective staff development programmes and that institutions must place a high priority on this aspect of the work of colleges. As well, there is genuine and deep concern that because of the diminished mobility of instructors, college instructors need that revitalization from professional development activities that might otherwise have come from moving to a new or different college. There has emerged the real danger that without a new emphasis on professional development, the colleges will end up with complacent teaching staffs with little incentive or opportunity for improvement: a danger for the instructors themselves, their institutions, and the students and public they serve.

The Reality

Agreement though there may be on necessity, there has been much less concurrence on the orientation and ingredients of a comprehensive development programme. Indeed, colleges in Canada have generally tended to take a scattergun approach to this sphere of activity. Nevertheless, there are currently several examples of positive efforts to involve instructors in programmes designed to improve instructional competence and to broaden the general background of college instructors.[8] In colleges where there is strong commitment to non-conventional instruction, such as Prince Edward Island's Holland College, there are organized efforts to provide instructors with opportunities to upgrade or acquire skills essential to specific methodologies.[9] As another example, most colleges which introduced the self-paced TRAC Programme (TRaining ACcess Programme) in the early 1980's in British Columbia put particular effort into retraining veteran instructors for this unfamiliar approach to vocational training.

In Saskatchewan and New Brunswick, programmes designed to prepare instructors from business and industry for their new roles have been ongoing and have been planned to utilize the resources of universities as well as of the colleges themselves. In Ontario, where responsibility for undertaking professional development has often been assigned to specific offices or positions, several quite extensive programmes have been launched. Ottawa's Algonquin College, for example, provides a broad array of activities to broaden the skills and knowledge of employees[10]: courses or activities in computer literacy, academic disciplines, international education, administrative skills, and a variety of general interest topics are available to Algonquin staff and to instructors at other colleges. In Quebec colleges, the role of the animatuer is undergoing continuous change, but one of the tasks for this position has consistently been to identify problems which require attention by staff members; as one example, the new multicultural character of urban colleges in Quebec has prompted some colleges to adapt their counselling services to their new clientele and to develop an active interest in intercultural education. Other specific examples of professional development activities in various parts of Canada have also been reported.[11] Indeed, the Association of Canadian Community Colleges has recently seized the initiative to document the current state of the art.[12]

A partial picture of the emphasis within faculty development practices is provided by a recent study by Smith of patterns in British Columbia colleges.[13] She surveyed activity within five categories: orientation of new instructors, instructional improvement, general professional development, organizational development, and miscellaneous practices. Her findings revealed that British Columbia colleges showed a decided preference for activities within the category of general professional development: attendance at professional meetings and released time for educational or professional study in business and industry, including some limited paid leave for this purpose. Some reference was made to short orientation sessions for new instructors, released time to develop instructional materials, guest lectures by various specialists, and training in the use of new instructional technologies. Scant reference, however, was made to the provision of incentives for good teaching, to the establishment of a staff development function within colleges, or to the development of the interpersonal skills of instructors. A reasonable conclusion, not inconsistent with what is known about practices elsewhere in Canada, is that professional development has been viewed as support for individual instructors with special interests or as occasional special events. Some professional development has taken the form of academic study for a few individuals; other has been one-time specific in-service upgrading. Staff development positions are scarce; specialized staff libraries are even scarcer.

Canada has not yet attempted to create organizations analagous to NISOD (National Institute for Staff and Organizational Development) or POD (Professional and Organizational Development in Higher Education) in the United States. Nor is there a national staff college such as Coombe Lodge in the United Kingdom.[14] Several Canadian college staffs have, however, taken advantage of the resources of such organizations. Some ministries in Canada have provided leadership and resources for instructional skill development, and one model allows for the training of the trainers who can then provide in-house, in-service training for their peers.[15] Despite all these activities, professional development in Canada's colleges has not been systematic and sustained; it has been allowed to make its own way on skeptical campuses, constantly seeking support and respectability, constantly avoiding suspicion and indifference.

Current Circumstances

Sporadic and unco-ordinated professional development events and activities do not constitute a programme. Yet programmes of professional development are required if their objective, the continuing improvement of instruction, is to be realized.

One reason why organized development programmes have not yet taken hold anywhere in Canada is the absence of leadership. Board members and administrators have made some positive gestures, but—particularly in the context of financial restraint, programme reductions, and personnel layoffs—these gestures have not been warmly received. In fact, professional development opportunities are sometimes viewed as penalties to be endured rather than occasions to develop or refine expertise. It is also true that colleges have not been receptive to substantial investment in programmes that do not have immediately measurable benefits. But the real obstacle to better programmes has been the reluctance of college instructors to allow administrators to dominate matters that pertain to the quality of education, matters which relate directly to the professional responsibilities of instructors. Mintzberg makes the point that colleges are human service organizations which can be described as professional bureaucracies in which operational control is decentralized:

The professional's power derives from the fact that not only is his work too complex to be supervised by managers or standardized by analysts, but also that his services are typically in great demand. This gives the professional mobility, which enables him to insist on considerable autonomy in his work.[16]

In this interpretation, when professional development efforts have been given strong direction by board members or administrators, there has been a tendency on the part of instructors to interpret such initiatives as attempts to impose control over faculty responsibilities. On the other hand, where instructors have sought to initiate and manage, particularly through collective agreements, there has been the suspicion or assumption that professional development activities are predominantly, if not exclusively, self-serving and not in the interests of the institution. Where professional development activities have been most successfully implemented, they have typically been the result of co-operative action between instructors and administrators pursuing common causes of improvement of the quality of education and of enhancing the educational capacity of the college.[17] Even when co-operation is assured, it is not certain that good professional development programmes will result. "Control over his own work means that the professional works relatively independently of his colleagues, but closely with the clients he serves."[18] It is certainly true that college instructors have tended to resist the idea of organized, formal programmes designed to improve general performance. Most instructors have preferred to attend to their own development in their own ways to achieve their own professional satisfaction. Individual initiatives may provide the gist, but not the grist, of professional development.

Direction for the Future

The first responsibility for academic and professional growth undoubtedly rests with the individual instructor. Each much recognize the necessity to remain current, to refine skills, and to contribute to the effective operation of the college. But individual efforts do not constitute a programme which will improve the total institution. Similarly, institutional improvement requires that development programmes not be restricted only to instructors because board members, managers and administrators, and support personnel also influence the degree of success or failure of each college.

One key to success, then, is that professional development programmes be institution-wide in scope; every sector of the college community should be involved in their design and planning, in the establishment of priorities, and in the implementation phases. To have sustained value, programmes need to be co-ordinated and monitored; as in many colleges in Ontario, the designation of a staff development officer has much to recommend it, provided that the officer recognizes the individual needs of different individuals and groups within the college and is prepared to act as catalyst and co-ordinator, but not director.

In recent years, British Columbia has provided an interesting example of co-ordination at the provincial level. Recognizing that some professional development activities can effectively function at an institutional level but that the best use of resources prompts other activities at a provincial level, the colleges and institutes of British Columbia asked the Ministry of Education to provide the co-ordinating service for a variety of province-wide development activities. Since 1978, voluntary programmes for board members, administrators, instructors, and support staff have been funded and organized on a continuing basis by personnel of the Post-Secondary Branch of the Ministry of Education within guidelines provided by a provincial steering committee with representatives from all the constituencies for whom the programmes are developed. Province-wide professional development has been effective and expanding, if low key, and there has been no suggestion that the ministry is either imposing upon college personnel or dominating their activities. More recently, personnel of the ministry have also acted on behalf of the B.C. institutions in the development of national plans for professional development.

The major components of a college professional development programme also merit comment. Unlike institutions with longer histories and traditions, colleges need to provide regular opportunities for staff members to understand the particular characteristics of the college culture (see Chapter 6). They need to develop a deeper appreciation of their individual roles, of the distinctive qualities of college students, of student needs and backgrounds and aspirations, and of the relationship between college and community. College instructors need to understand colleges, their ethos, and their values.

Of course, college instructors also need to be students of learning. In terms of age, experience, attitudes, motivation, academic background, and intellectual abilities, college students represent a widely diverse gathering of human learners.[19] Similarly, new techniques in instructional design, new teaching techniques, different ways of organizing learning, and technological developments applicable to learning abound. This conjunction of a diversity of learners with a diversity of teaching methods cries out for more detailed and scholarly examination, particularly in times when appeals for improved productivity and increased effectiveness compel fresh approaches to old issues. Without doubt, the ability of all instructors to stay abreast in their own disciplines and areas of teaching is of paramount importance. Instructors need the opportunity to remain current, to reflect, and to grow individually, if they are not to reduce themselves—or be reduced—to mere educational technicians repeating day after day and year after year their first year of experience.

A Matter of Priorities

In 1973, the Task Force on Post-Secondary Education in Manitoba recommended that 3 per cent of the total operating budget for colleges be allocated to professional development.[20] It is doubtful that any recommendation to increase investment in professional development would be well received at this time anywhere in Canada. But recommendations of this kind and scope should not be dismissed because they reflect the importance that professional development programmes must assume if Canada's colleges are to achieve their potential. After all, many colleges in Canada still spend less on personnel development than they do on building maintenance.

With few new dollars and a realignment of the use of funds now allocated to the evaluation and improvement of college instruction, the construction of continuing, comprehensive, and co-ordinated development plans is indeed possible. Initiative and leadership are required. Planning and organization are required. Inspiration and the education of others in new ideas are required.[21] Above all, commitment and recognition of the stakes are required.

GENERAL EDUCATION

While the general topic of curriculum invites spirited debate within colleges across the nation, the aspect which receives most attention is the question of general education. In virtually every province concern has recently been expressed about the lack of emphasis assigned to general education and the need to find ways and means of increasing the general education component of the curriculum, particularly within vocational programmes. Despite the enthusiastic support expressed for this aspect of the curriculum, it is evident that some confusion also exists with respect to the actual meaning of general education, its content, or the most productive way of incorporating it into the overall curricular structure. Indeed, the entire issue has been something of a contradiction: an almost unanimous level of support for an idea which, at the same time, has seemed clouded as to its essential nature, purpose, and design.

This impression has been reinforced by the results of a study conducted by Sorensen[22] commissioned by the Association of Canadian Community Colleges, which assessed the current status of general education in a substantial sample of community colleges in all ten provinces. The study concluded that while there was widespread agreement on "the high value of general education as a preparation for lifelong learning," there were major discrepancies over the aims, design, organization and subject areas which should fall under the rubric of general education.

Despite the ambiguities which surround the issue, however, one concern is widely shared. As Canadian society enters a new stage, general education will assume a new level of relevance. The full implication of the new technological age has yet to be realized but its effects will be felt not only in the workplace but in every dimension of life:

> The current innovation in societal technology, however, is not concerned with the productivity of material goods, but with information productivity, and for this reason can be expected to bring about fundamental changes in human values, in trends of thought, and in the political and economic structures of society.[23]

Post-secondary educational institutions can no longer take responsibility for merely preparing students to enter the world of work. Not only will job skills, no matter how finely honed, not guarantee a secure future of gainful employment, but labour itself may assume a subsidiary role in a world where the task of economic and spiritual survival will have a new meaning. The challenge for educators in the third millenium will be to fashion a curriculum which provides the basis for a lifetime of learning, for adjustment to technological change, for emphasis upon quality of life, and for multi-dimensional literacy. The heart of the curriculum of the future should be whatever will sustain the individual in a world of unprecedented change and complexity.

In this light, it is useful to explore some of the major questions which surround the issue of general education in Canada's colleges. First, a brief historical analysis of the evolution of general education will be presented. This will be followed by a review of what is currently happening in the name of general education in Canada's colleges, together with an attempt to explore the difficulties, both theoretical and practical, which colleges face in dealing with this issue. Finally, several proposals for the future, designed to bring general education into a more productive relationship with other areas of curriculum, will be outlined.

The Meaning of General Education

Debate over the value of general education is by no means a twentieth-century phenomenon, nor is it peculiar to the college sector. The roots of contemporary general education are deeply embedded in the culture of Athenian society. A curriculum, generally referred to as the liberal arts, was fashioned by the Greeks and founded on two particular concepts: the "paidea" (a reference to education or, more broadly, culture); and the associated practice of "arete" (the ability to fulfil one's life). Education became synonymous with the ideal of the "good" life, rather than simply with the preparation for life.[24] The education which formed the moral code of humanism in Athenian life was measured by two criteria: a repository of ideas and knowledge which would remain viable in any age and a basis for, and precursor to, vocationalism, the practical business of living. "It provided an ideal for education that was flexible enough to adjust to changing times and circumstances, but concrete enough to remain potent and tenacious for 2,500 years."[25]

The Romans refined the structure of liberal education by creating a system which incorporated nine liberal arts to form a curriculum based upon unity and order.[26]

In the Christian era, further refinement of the Greek ideal of culture was expressed in the medieval curriculum of the trivium (grammar, rhetoric, and logic) and the quadrivium (arithmetic, geometry, astronomy, and music). In the universities of the twelfth and thirteenth centuries—Paris, Bologna, and Oxford—the liberal arts formed the basis for professional studies, although the sanctions imposed through the prevailing philosophy of anti-rationalism limited its scope to interpretation by the Christian thinkers of the period. It was not until the age of discovery and intellectual rebirth which characterized the Renaissance that the earlier Aquinian reconciliation of classical Greek idealism with Christian philosophy gave new scope to liberal studies with the addition of the works of Aristotle and the languages and literature of pre-Christian culture.[27]

Liberal education flourished in the European centres of higher learning in the seventeenth and eighteenth centuries, where it was considered an essential ingredient of a full life. Similarly, the tradition was enthusiastically adopted in the colonial colleges in the new world, where a four-year general education curriculum constituted the baccalaureate degree. The number of subjects which formed the core was limited, twelve in the original Harvard Curriculum, but they were required of all students as a mandatory preparation for further professionalism and vocationalism.[28] It was not until the end of the nineteenth century that the monopoly of the liberal arts curriculum faced challenges from the new order of knowledge: science, technology, the practical arts, and contemporary problems in politics, economics, and the social sciences.[29] In North America, in particular, the twentieth century ushered in a revolution in higher education which was to question the value of the past and challenge traditional curriculum designs. The result was a reformation of the entire structure of advanced learning.

A combination of factors—economic, political, and sociocultural—contributed to the restructuring process. Higher education was no longer to remain the privilege of the elite. Economic growth demanded a labour force with technical and intellectual skills which could no longer be gained from the established practice of prolonged exposure to the workplace. Institutions of further education grew rapidly in number and diversification in response to the pressures of government, business, industry, and the new student clientele.[30] Provincial universities, agricultural colleges, technical institutes, and community colleges developed specialized curricula which reflected both their practical mandate and the vocational needs of their students and of industrial society. In most of the new institutions, the twin pressures of specialization and vocationalism spelled the demise of a traditionally defined liberal education and the eventual erosion of the idea of a core curriculum for all post-secondary learning.

While the traditional universities and university colleges attempted to preserve the essence of liberal education, they too faced new circumstances. In particular, the growth of the elective system and the notion that degrees could be attained by an accumulation of credits tied to hours of instruction became forces which fragmented the curriculum. However, the literature of higher education in the twentieth century is filled with arguments, based on both theoretical and practical considerations, for a new consensus on curriculum issues. As Conrad notes:

> While the practice of liberal education had been seriously corroded, the idea of liberal education persisted. Supporters of liberal education were increasingly identified more in terms of their general point of view toward education—what Laurence Veysey (1965) called "liberal culture"—rather than by their commitment to a particular course of studies. In the twentieth century, a series of reforms, known collectively as the "general education movement," were introduced to reinstate and reinvigorate the tradition of liberal education.[31]

Despite the efforts of those committed to reform, there appears to have been very little agreement on fundamental issues. There was no clear agreement, for example, on the meaning of general education. Definitions, of which there are now many, include the following: "We take general education to be education aimed at the cultivation and refinement of intellect, the acquisition of knowledge and culture and the development of the whole person."[32] "General education appears to be the preparation of youth to deal with the personal and social problems with which all men in a democratic society are confronted."[33] "The universals of human culture."[34] "An antidote to barbarism."[35]

In essence, the operational definitions of general education range from those described in terms of content—as a series of courses common to all programmes—to others expressed as understanding of major concepts, principles, and methodologies of broad fields of knowledge.[36] To still more observers general education has a behavioural connotation, as that experience which prepares one "to live more fully as a person and more effectively as a citizen."[37]

The task in the last two decades has been to bring the traditional values of liberal studies into a more contemporary focus by recognizing the changing nature of modern society, the heterogeneity of the student population, and the need to accommodate to the inevitable pressure for vocational requirements. In the process, the dichotomy between those views of liberal studies as theoretical and unchanging ideas and general education as a more practical application of knowledge to life's issues has eroded to the point where the terms are essentially synonymous. As Brubacher states,

> The task of undergirding liberal education with a pragmatic base has been approached in two ways. In one direction there has been an attempt to overhaul the liberal arts and bring them to bear more directly on contemporary problems. The idea of a timeless curriculum, as invariant as human nature, has been replaced with an elective system more responsive to individual differences. One determines whether items in the curriculum are true by noting their consequences when they are tested in the social crucible. Intelligence is regarded as a means instead of an end. Hence, there are no longer any perennial truths in the curriculum of liberal education, but only varying degrees of certainty and conviction.[38]

It is also useful to consider one more detailed description of a general education curriculum which meets the criteria for a comprehensive approach to intellectual survival in contemporary society. It was developed by Sidney Hook in *The Philosophy of the Curriculum* and provides a basis for interpreting general education in the discussion which follows:

> 1. Every student has an objective need to be able to communicate clearly and effectively with his fellows, to grasp with comprehension and accuracy the meaning of different types of discourse, and to express himself in a literate way.
> 2. He must have an appreciation of the impact of science and technology on nature and society.
> 3. There must be a focus on the conflict of values and ideals of our time, the presence of values in every policy, the relation of values to causes and consequences and the difference between arbitrary and reasonable value judgments.
> 4. Every student should acquire some methodological sophistication that should sharpen his sense for evidence, relevance, and canons of validity.
> 5. Students should be aware of how society functions, of the great historical, economic, and social forces shaping its future.
> 6. Every student needs to be inducted into the cultural legacies of his civilization.[39]

A Case for General Education in Colleges

Why should Canada's colleges be concerned about the inclusion of general education within their curricula? It could be argued that given the heavy emphasis upon occupational training, general education may be viewed as either an impractical or luxurious component of the college curriculum. The traditional view has been that a highly skilled workforce is the product of a concentrated emphasis upon specialized training. Funding agencies, particularly governments, tend to measure return on their investment by cost-benefit analyses, job placement statistics, and the relevance of the training function. While some observers recognize that work is only one part of the life of any citizen, they often argue that more generalized education should be a personal responsibility which can and should be sought after the acquisition of marketable skills acquired at public expense.

Even programme planners in colleges experience frustration in their efforts to promote liberal education. Many academic programmes consist of individual courses and emphasize the accumulation of credits which are then transferable to meet university degree requirements. In turn, universities exercise either a direct or indirect paternal influence on college curriculum development. In many cases the essentially conservative and increasingly specialized nature of the university prevents colleges from developing their own innovative courses or course combinations which could enrich students' college experience.

In spite of these obstacles, there are cogent arguments for including a general education component in all college programmes. One argument stems from the nature of the students. Colleges attract a widely diverse student population in age, experience, socioeconomic background, aspirations, career goals, and attitudes.[40] For many students, colleges will represent their only formal educational experience after secondary school. They form a substantial segment of the body politic who will carry a responsibility for the future condition of society in its many aspects—political, financial, legal, industrial, and sociocultural. In a very real sense, the success or failure of democratic institutions will be influenced by those who obtain a college education. It is they who, in large part, will directly deal with problems of unemployment, the technological society, the limitations of the political process, and the value conflicts which threaten to erode the foundation of Canada's social institutions. They also become a large segment of middle management in business and industry, and, as such, they need a general as well as technically specialized education. While it would be unrealistic to expect the colleges to accept responsibility for providing universal general education, they do form one of the few potential instruments for instilling sociopolitical maturity in a broad cross-section of society.

More practical arguments for general education in colleges are associated with the original design of the college concept. The colleges often subsumed a plethora of other institutions: vocational schools, technical colleges, schools of art, music, agriculture, adult learning centres, and later, hospital schools of nursing, police academies, and evening colleges. It was assumed that the new institutions would enrich the previously isolated milieu of the specialized institution. Students and faculty would gain from the formal and informal encounters with those from fields of endeavour unrelated to their own. In effect, training would become education, and specialized education would become more liberal. In the light of the original rhetoric, it seems appropriate to examine the current reality.

Even the concept of work specialization, per se, is under review within Canada. The rapidly evolving nature of the job market and the accompanying need for worker adaption to change indicates a requirement for greater emphasis upon the acquisition of generic skills, particularly those associated with communications, science, and technology.[41] Further, these same conditions suggest that young people need a broader education so that they can make a more intelligent choice of area of specialization. More careful choice of programme options by students might well lead to more prolonged satisfaction with later vocational choices. This issue is highlighted by Hook in a discussion of philosophy of curriculum: "The notion that the generality of students . . . can make an informed and intelligent decision about their abiding educational needs before being exposed to the great subject matters and disciplines of the liberal tradition is highly questionable."[42]

As well, it is instructive to examine one other dimension of the case for general education in the colleges. As part of her study, Sorensen[43] invited college personnel at various levels to rank twenty-one aims of community college and institute education. The results showed a high degree of consensus on three aims: "desire and ability to learn," "effective reading and writing," and "ability to problem solve," all of which were ranked in the "essential" category and above "career skills." Further, there was very little divergence of opinion from various programme areas of the colleges. The real discrepancy which emerged, however, was between "what is" and "what should be" with regard to curricular priorities: the overwhelming view was that "career skills" were in practice far better achieved than those more generalized skills which were ranked so much higher as desirable outcomes of a college education. The inevitable conclusion is that, despite the strength of the case for general education in colleges, rhetoric is rarely translated into reality. To defend this conclusion it is necessary to assess the extent to which general education is provided in Canada's colleges and to isolate the factors which have inhibited its impact.

The Status of General Education

Although there is an abundance of literature in the United States[44] which extols the values of general education in the community college curriculum, there is a little written on the subject in Canada. Comment which does exist is usually buried in statements of purpose, objectives, and goals or included incidentally in institutional literature and "position papers" from government agencies. Some illustrative examples follow.

In British Columbia, an early statement of role for the new institutions, published by the Academic Board, included the following:

> Every field of education has its discursive and contemplative aspects as expressed in its historical, social and aesthetic components. Within a college programme they may be merged in ways that will enable students to comprehend their fields of study not merely as academic or technical but as powerful social and intellectual forces that are deeply and widely influential in human affairs.[45]

In the same province some years later, the vocational schools were melded with the community colleges, partly to give an even greater degree of comprehensiveness to the college curriculum. One of the potential advantages promoted by government to justify the meld contained the following:

> The opportunities which will be afforded to technical, trades-training, and other career programme students to gain exposure either directly or indirectly to general education offerings—an important concept in a world as complicated as ours—and the opportunity for students of academic bent to gain some exposure to the world of technology and business.[46]

In the province of Saskatchewan, the community colleges were designed primarily as centres of lifelong learning where improvement of the quality of life was to be the overriding priority. An essay by a prominent architect of the system included this claim:

> The college's aim is to provide opportunities to meet learning needs to perform all of life's roles in a satisfying way. Within any one phase of a person's life he is likely to be filling several roles . . . . The college staffs undertook to identify needs arising from these new roles and to facilitate programmes that would contribute to the competence of people in all of their endeavours.[47]

Ontario established a structured system of tertiary institutions in a brief period between 1965 and 1968, and their primary mandate was unequivocal: to meet the need for skilled manpower to sustain the economic future of the province. Nevertheless, the minister recognized a responsibility for the colleges well beyond training:

> There has long been a deficiency in our educational system in regard to the training of technical personnel beyond the high school but short of the university level . . . . An adequate general education is the best basis on which to build and to rebuild the particular work skills which the future will require.[48]

And, while references to general education in other provinces may vary in detail, the general intent is shared. The selection which follows serves to illustrate the common sentiment:

> [Colleges will] . . . provide educational opportunities for the continuing development of individuals in their careers, and within this general framework, for personal growth and development. (Manitoba)
> All programmes of studies should include the study of general education subjects and specific vocational subjects. (Prince Edward Island)
> [The college must] . . . promote and provide opportunities for continuous learning for the personal enrichment of the citizens for New Brunswick. (New Brunswick)[49]

Despite the noble sentiments reflected in these statements, practice has been a different story. With the notable exception of Quebec's colleges, few of Canada's non-university institutions have installed a coherent approach to a general education curriculum core.

One of the few attempts to assess the general education curriculum on a province-wide basis was conducted in 1980 by a study group in Ontario acting under the auspices of the Committee of College Presidents. Data supplied by the colleges led the group to conclude that there is no common working definition of general education throughout the college system and there is confusion and disparity within individual colleges about the definition and administration of general education.[50] Further evidence indicates that fourteen of nineteen colleges were offering less than the 33 per cent general education component specified as a requirement for Ontario colleges by the Council of Regents.

An individual analysis by college of curricular content in various diploma and certificate programmes in Ontario reveals a situation which is also characteristic of other provinces. In applied arts, health, and various technology programmes, some provision is made for support courses, usually mathematics, science, computer studies, or communications. The proportion varies by programme and usually consists of one course for every four programme specific courses. In addition, some programmes provide for a limited number of electives, which may be chosen from "liberal studies" departments.

Specific examples of support or elective courses, which might be classified under the rubric of "general" education, include:

> Communications (language, interpersonal skills, reading, technical writing, preparing reports, assertiveness, communicating on the job, business communication, speaking, conducting interviews, correspondence).
> Human relations (social psychology, behavioural science, social behaviour, personal development, human behaviour).
> Unclassified (business ethics, recreation skills, consumer economics, labour relations, criminal law in Canada, learning for leisure, political science).

In virtually all provinces, the opportunity for study outside of specific skill training in trade and vocational programmes is extremely limited. Technical writing is usually required, but most general courses fall into the elective category. There are rare exceptions such as one small prairie college which encourages students in all programmes to elect courses with titles such as Modern Society, Marriage and Family, Canadian Issues, Environmental Concerns, or Consumer Problems.

A statistical analysis of relative ratios among curriculum areas has been carried out in British Columbia. The results indicate that in technology programmes, the skill specific content ranges from a high of 100 per cent (Journalism, Communication Arts) to a low of 17 per cent (Criminal Justice). Conversely, the percentage of the humanities-mathematics component ranges from 67 per cent (Library Technician) to 0 per cent (Early Childhood Education, Sonography).[51] In fact, British Columbia's record of general education into career programmes is generally more impressive than in other provinces. Part of the explanation lies in the history of the colleges of British Columbia, where the university transfer component of the curriculum has enjoyed major emphasis. The development of university equivalent courses, with specialist instructors in the humanities and social sciences and natural sciences, has facilitated curriculum planning with an emphasis beyond skill specificity.

The results of the Sorensen study also reinforce the impression that general education has received only spasmodic attention in most provinces. Almost 10 per cent of the respondents stated that there was no general education component in their programmes, while only 20 per cent of the group claimed that general education represented more than one-third of their curriculum.

The study also revealed that the most common method of incorporating general education into college programmes was through introductory courses in traditional disciplines, rather than through courses which were interdisciplinary, theme based, tailored to professional objectives, or designed to develop critical thinking or communication skills. When asked to indicate why general education did not receive the support and encouragement which most respondents felt was desirable, respondents cited three major reasons: budget constraint, the high demand for skill training, and a reduction in the number of hours available for each subject. In each case the responsibility for the decision to reduce the general education component was attributed to senior managers, a charge which they predictably rejected.

Indeed, after reviewing the evidence there appeared to be only one province in which general education has been made available in systematic fashion so that all college students, in all programmes of study, may acquire a broad educational experience. That exception is Quebec.

Quebec—A Unique Experiment

Quebec's CEGEP form a mandatory level of education between secondary school and university for those who seek further education, or between school and work for those who wish to earn a credential in a technical career field. CEGEP were designed to have both traditional curriculum streams, general and technical, which would share a common curriculum core with up to 50 per cent of each in each programme of study.[52] The Quebec colleges were very much an integral part of that government's plan to bring sociocultural reform to the province. The objectives were economic and political as well as educational; a goal was the preparation of the francophone majority for leadership roles in the future centres of power.[53] Hence, the education provided in the CEGEP was to be far more than the mere acquisition of skills and knowledge; it was to include the development of a sociopolitical ideology for that province's most important resource, its young people.[54]

After ten years of a formidable experiment in educational reform, the Ministry of Education reviewed the state of the system in 1978. The report which followed reaffirmed and strengthened the original objectives and paid particular attention to general education as a key factor of educational quality:

> Basically, the quality of education will be better assured as colleges attach more importance to the 'general education' or if you will, 'formation fondamentale' of their students . . . .
> The term "formation fondamentale" alludes to teachings which promote the integral development of the person and which are indispensable for anyone who wishes to live his life to the fullest.[55]

The content of the "formation fondamentale" in the CEGEP now includes language and literature (four courses), philosophy or humanities (four courses), Quebec civilization (one course), Quebec economy (one course), and physical education (four courses). Where feasible, these required courses are offered over a period of two years to classes which include students from a mix of academic and technical programmes.

The Quebec curriculum with its commitment to general education and a required core curriculum is unique in Canada. In no other province are the purposes of a college education so clearly articulated. At the same time, unlike other provinces, students enter CEGEP after only eleven years of schooling. As well, the CEGEP curriculum does not include trades, apprenticeship, or short-term vocational programmes which are usually found in college systems in other provinces. Both factors, the early entry age of students and the absence of trades training, woven within the special role for the colleges, strengthen the case for general education in CEGEP, or at least remove some of the more common obstacles to its inclusion in college curricula.

An examination of the curriculum outlines in several Canadian colleges, supplemented by discussions of general education with college personnel in all ten provinces, prompts a summary of the extent to which college students have access to courses beyond those specific to the skills and competencies required in their specialized programmes. The evidence indicates that, with the exception of Quebec, there is a wide variation in the course components which may be described as general education. The variations occur by province, by institution, and by programme within individual institutions. Programmes in applied arts, health, business, and advanced technologies usually require about 20 per cent of the courses outside the speciality. Vocational, trade, and apprenticeship programmes rarely include general education components. University transfer programmes are bound by the requirements set by receiving universities. It must be noted, however, that this summary conclusion is based solely upon the labelling of college courses in calendars and from discussion with college administrators. It does not take into account the emphasis or orientation of teaching as it occurs in the laboratories, shops, seminars, or classrooms of the colleges. It is conceivable that a great deal of general education is provided informally through the attitudes, styles, and emphases of individual instructors.

Proposals for the Future

Whatever the reasons for the inadequacies and inconsistencies in provision of general education in the colleges across the nation, fresh approaches to addressing the issues of general education are desirable. Because the values of general education are worth retaining and because the character of society in the next century compels change, new designs in curriculum organization must be explored.

Several colleges have already developed innovative general education strategies. Grant MacEwan Community College in Alberta has designed an approach which merits particular comment. Following an internal study, the college made a deliberate commitment to general education as part of the total curriculum and sought ways to ensure its implementation. The committee charged with the latter task identified a number of approaches and recommended the "functional course model." The latter was defined as follows:

> In this approach students may take courses with content that closely reflects the problems, the cultural, social, economic, and political environment in which they live. Stress may be placed on the understanding and the integrating of the various parts of a complex society. The concept of individual choice, social adjustment, adaptation, interdependence, and global community may be reviewed. In addition, course modules on the aesthetic and spiritual nature of man may be included.[56]

The next step was to identify specific general education course content: the committee proposed that courses be placed under four headings: Generic Learning Skills, Life and Learning, The Global Community, and Culture in the Value System. The courses in these categories became the core curriculum.

In the light of the Grant MacEwan approach, it is useful to consider recommendations advanced in the Sorensen study. Noting the significant discrepancies between what currently exists and what the great majority of respondents from all provinces felt should exist for general education, Sorensen recommended that each college examine the general education component of each of its own programmes to determine if reform and development are needed. More specifically, Sorensen proposed that the curricula in the various programmes offered by each college reflect those aims of college education judged of highest priority by that college. If "learning skills," "critical thinking,"and "lifelong learning" are, as college personnel suggest, the most important aims of a college education, devices to achieve those aims should be specifically incorporated into all programmes. The most popular approach to providing general education, from an organizational standpoint, was to provide an integrative seminar of at least a semester's duration through which students would be assisted to assimilate the various elements of their total college experience.

If reform of general education is to succeed, it is evident that a commitment to reform must be college-wide and supported at all institutional levels. If reform is to begin at an institutional level, each college should assess its human and material resources and the characteristics and needs of its students and then adapt its curriculum organization and instructional methods to these elements. As Sorensen also suggests, a monitoring system in each college would be crucial to the continuing development of the general education curriculum. If other provinces were to adopt the Quebec approach and effectively establish a core curriculum for all students, more than a government policy pronouncement to this effect would be required. Basic financial resources specifically designed to support a required core of studies would be a necessary adjunct to policy. Given the current financial conditions of most provinces and the common priority to employment training, heavy provincial investment in general education seems quite improbable in the immediate future. The more realistic source of innovation in general education is far more likely to be individual colleges. And there is one proposal for reform that does not depend upon changes of course, programme, or curriculum content; it emphasizes the impact that individual instructors may have, regardless of the subjects they teach.

The proposal is that the major focus for reform should shift from content to instructor. In effect, the cultivation of ideas, concepts, and broader understandings which are essential for survival should become the specific responsibility of every college teacher independent of the field or discipline of teaching. Stated otherwise, all college teachers should accept a unique additional charge which would distinguish them from their counterparts in other post-secondary institutions.

Every content area includes knowledge and ideas which extend well beyond the relatively narrow scope of the curriculum and which can contribute to a broader, more general education:

Communication skills, oral and written, are required in all subject areas. Technical reports, laboratory observations, artistic projects, and simulated job interviews are all examples of themes which fit the category.

Broadly based moral and ethical issues, whether in the health sciences, industrial technology, business practices, or environmental studies are effective and legitimate extensions of the acquisition of skill competencies in these areas.

Contemporary questions involved in labour-management relations, which include an appreciation of the history, role, and legal structure of organized labour, are integral to almost any occupational programme.

The challenges to economic and spiritual survival in an era of reduced or uncertain employment are relevant subject matter in any course which prepares individuals for the workplace.

It would seem indefensible to engage in the teaching of gas and oil technology, or of environmental control, independently of the reality of national energy policy or the politics of pollution, respectively.

The human dimension of decision-making, in the context of ethical judgment, seems equally appropriate within the teaching of humanities, social sciences, or business practices.

These examples are not exhaustive; in fact, they merely touch the conceptual argument, but they should serve as a stimulus to the imagination.

This approach to general education would bring a new dimension, although not a universally acceptable one, to college teaching. College faculty members, particularly those from traditional trade and vocational fields, often lack both the background and conviction to assume so broad a teaching responsibility. The strategy which is vital to receiving their support rests not so much on the need for expanded course content but on the philosophical case which must be argued, based very much on the distinctive role of a college teacher. Exploration of this approach to general education could bring a new meaning and a new purpose to professional development which has long suffered from a confusion or diffusion of objectives in colleges.

It seems appropriate to conclude this section with two quotations. The first is by Dr. Bette Stephenson, as former minister responsible for universities and colleges in Ontario:

> Not everyone, even at the post-secondary level, has a precise idea of what he or she will do in life. Our research further tells us that the average young person today will pursue five or six careers before his or her working life is over.
>
> The point is balance. For these people, who are, I suspect, increasing in number, often it is not the 'training' part of post-secondary education which is the most important, but the general skills acquired—the analytical abilities, the logical thinking, the research methods, and ability to synthesize, the writing skills, and ability to communicate.
>
> These will be at the heart of everything else in any field of endeavour through which they finally choose to earn, to live, and to contribute to society.[57]

The second reflects the perspective of most employers in the mid-1980's:

> Generally speaking, I think most employers are interested in college and university graduates who have a proven record of achievement in their academic background, their work experience, and their extra-curricular activities, on the basis that the best indicators of future potential are achievements in the past.
>
> Obviously, employers recruit people from a variety of academic disciplines to match their skill needs. Additionally, they look for people with analytical and communication skills, as, in an era of growing complexity, they want people who can understand complex issues and have the ability to simplify these issues, problem-solve, and formulate practical action plans.
>
> Equally important, they look for employees who will contribute to the effective operation of the business and try to improve it. Basically, they look for people who are energetic, self-confident, imaginative, thorough, and who have a questioning attitude about things.[58]

The views expressed above—one from government, the other from the business community—agree on a common concern for the workplace of the future and for those who will enter it. College planners in Canada should pay heed.

INSTITUTIONAL EVALUATION

Accountability was not a frequently used term in the early days of Canada's colleges. The emphasis at that time was on expanding access to post-secondary education as the improvement of accessibility was a dominant goal of virtually all colleges, technical institutions, and universities. While the term accountability was not used, colleges were implicitly accountable for making it possible for more students to obtain more kinds of post-secondary education. And they did the job well: more than 300,000 full-time students now attend Canada's colleges, and although there are no accurate records for part-time students, their numbers are more than double the full-time enrolment.[59]

Declining public confidence in all forms of publicly supported education, financial restraint, and increasing provincial government influences on the course of college development have formally introduced the term accountability into the Canadian college lexicon. Colleges are no longer judged on their openness and accessibility, but on how good they are and on how well they use the public resources available to them. Return on investment in college education, much more than its quantity, is now at issue.

Most colleges are well aware of the need to be identified as institutions of quality and efficiency. They need to prove their calibre to themselves and to government as well as to the general public. They know that if they are not or are not seen to be solid and substantial institutions, they will lose whatever public support they have developed over the years; and if they lose that public support, they will lose the public dollars on which they are so dependent. The obvious and common way to acquire the kind of reputation now sought by colleges is to submit to public scrutiny, to be evaluated in terms of performance and in terms of resource utilization.

> Evaluation and accountability, as applied to education, are interrelated concepts. Both imply a determination of the effects (planned or fortuitous) of educational programs and institutions. But whereas evaluation, as traditionally practiced, has been concerned solely with impact or outcome (effectiveness), accountability adds efficiency—the relation between outcomes and resource utilization.[60]

There is little dispute about the need to evaluate the performance of colleges or the need to demonstrate effective use of resources. All colleges espouse this cause. On the other hand, the evidence indicates that good intentions have rarely been translated into action and that few colleges are confident that current evaluation practices are useful or effective. When issues related to evaluation and demonstration of accountability are raised, all too often colleges respond defensively or acknowledge with regret that they have not yet been able to find satisfactory ways of carrying out proper studies. In many cases, the real reason for not conducting thorough performance evaluations has been the fear that institutions would not measure up to tests of external scrutiny.

Studies conducted in several provinces confirm that evaluation and accountability issues are now serious, complex, and nation-wide in scope,[61] even though they also record some notable efforts in several provinces to bring a systematic, thorough, and rigorous approach to the processes of institutional evaluation.

How can colleges demonstrate that they provide quality education efficiently? Most Canadian colleges have not yet found satisfactory answers to this question. And satisfactory answers are urgently required.

Why Evaluate?

What should colleges be trying to achieve by reviewing the performance of their programmes, their services, and their institutions? To what ends or for what purposes should performance evaluations be conducted? Strangely enough, there is no unanimity of response to these questions. Some authorities see evaluation as a means by which colleges can renew, revitalize, and improve their own performance; to these colleges, evaluation is primarily an introspective activity. Others portray evaluation primarily as an exercise in documenting past performance to constituencies the institution has served or wishes to serve. Still others see evaluation as a strategy to justify one's existence, usually to government or the public, or to argue one's case for continuing support.

These distinctions of purpose are not merely academic niceties. In fact, evaluation to achieve renewal might take a very different form from evaluation to consolidate public or governmental support. However, the current reality is that both institutional revitalization and public credibility are required by colleges, and the task is to find appropriate and efficient methods of achieving both. That task is not simple. Evaluation for renewal must be an open and exposing process including an honest appraisal of both strengths and weaknesses.[62] But the exposure of weakness, it is feared, makes colleges vulnerable to public and governmental criticism, which is not conducive to continuing support. As a result, some colleges have gone through the formalities of evaluation but have neither done an honest and dispassionate assessment nor made the result of their evaluation public. Neither institutional renewal nor public credibility have been products of such processes; the exercise has largely been a sham and a waste.

In the current circumstances, sham and waste are foolhardy. Colleges must use institutional evaluation to assess and revitalize their performance; they must risk exposing their deficiencies to public scrutiny. Any other choice can lead at best to the withering of institutions with great promise and the legitimate charge that colleges are merely self-serving institutions which do not merit public support.

Expectations and Evaluation

It is axiomatic that it is not possible to determine whether an institution or a system is performing effectively until it is possible to identify precisely what that institution is trying to accomplish. The first step in evaluation, then, must be to determine what individual colleges and college systems are attempting to achieve.

Throughout Canada, it is normal practice for colleges to express their intentions and expectations through institutional statements of missions, goals, and objectives. Mission statements are commonly summary pronouncements relating to the philosophical and directional emphasis of the institution, such as:

> _____ College subscribes to the philosophy that all people should have as great opportunity as possible to pursue educational programs in keeping with their economic, cultural, and social aspirations; that career-oriented educational programs satisfy the needs of individuals as well as the collective needs of a productive society; and that it must be committed to excellence in programs designed to satisfy the needs of the students and the community it serves.[63]

Goals commonly focus more directly on specific ends to be achieved as evidence of the continuing commitment of the college. As such, they are long-term statements of intent, such as "A major goal of the college is to provide equity in access to post-secondary education for a wide cross section of the community," or "The college will provide training opportunities which reflect the needs of employee groups in the community." Objectives are usually more measurable plans to achieve specific outcomes within specific time periods in specific ways such as "the college will establish a continuous 20 student intake program in marketing by 1987," or "the college will have community advisory committees in place for all programs by 1982 as a result of initiatives taken by each department under the leadership of the Dean of Instruction."

Mission, goal, and objective statements by colleges are excellent starting points for evaluation. Quite clearly, however, to the extent that evaluation is expressed in clearly defined and accurately described terms, only objectives —not mission or goal statements—include sufficient detail to allow anything close to precise measurement. Several shortcomings of mission, goal, and objective statements merit comment.

First, mission and goal statements, in particular, can take on the aura of public relations releases which sound attractive but are so generalized as to be meaningless for the purposes of evaluation. To counterbalance this tendency, some institutions have included in these statements references to what they are not or what they do not hope to accomplish as well as their positive aspirations and ideals.

Secondly, the mere statement of institutional mission, goals, and objectives is no necessary assurance of institutional commitment. All colleges are made up of programme or departmental units which have their own priorities, and hence it is not uncommon for an institution to express goals to which relatively few people within the institution subscribe. Nor is it uncommon for goals and objectives of different groups within a college to be at variance if not contradictory. In fact, the only productive way to develop a meaningful mission and goals in a complex organization such as a college is to make the process an all-institutional one. To those who have participated in such an exercise, the resulting statements can have meaning and can produce commitment. To those who have not shared in the process, the results are usually seen as tired platitudes. It is for this reason that the review of mission, goals, and objectives ought to be a recurring process with broad participation from all elements of the college community.

If there is sometimes a lack of congruence between statements of an institution and statements of actions of its component parts, there is an even greater danger from lack of congruence between institutional statements and system mission, goals, and objectives. And this is the third shortcoming.

All colleges in Canada are parts of systems or networks as well as self-standing institutions, and provincial government ministries are integral elements of these systems or networks. While the distance in the relationship between institutions and government varies considerably from province to province, provincial ministries and governments do have major impacts, not always deliberate and not always coherent, on colleges everywhere in Canada. Indeed, to greater or lesser extents, government policies have made colleges instruments for the implementation of governmental economic and social policy. As a result, colleges should not develop their missions and goals independently; lack of congruence between governmental priorities and goals and institutional missions can only lead to conflict and unfulfilled expectations. The matter of government influence on college functions has recently been of major significance in several provinces—Manitoba, Saskatchewan, and British Columbia, to name only three—where changes of government have resulted in abrupt shifts of political philosophy which have prompted new and quite different expectations for colleges and other social institutions.

In college systems in which governments play so central a role, expectations that governments have for colleges need to be as clear and as comprehensible as institutional plans. Without such clarity, system cohesion is almost impossible, and the risks are contradictory planning, erosion of morale, and waste. Unfortunately, governments in Canada are not well known for the precision or permanence of their policy statements; nor are they well known for their use of participatory processes for policy development and articulation. As a result, colleges have no choice but to be sensitive to the vagaries of political reality if they are to function effectively within provincial systems.

By way of illustration, it is useful to analyze a report done in 1981 by the Ministry of Education in British Columbia.[64] This report followed the publication of a system-wide mission, goals, and objectives statement by the ministry, which outlined a framework within which each institution was expected to determine its own five-year plan. The 1981 study included a summary of the annual reports of fifteen of the twenty-one colleges and institutes in the province with respect to perceived congruence between institutional objectives and "system-wide" objectives. The study revealed a combination of related, unrelated, additional, and sometimes contradictory sets of goal statements, though grouped roughly under comparable categories. The conclusion was that many of the institutions were pursuing goals at considerable variance with those articulated by the ministry. Under these circumstances, it would be hard to imagine any process of institutional and programme evaluation that could have satisfied both the ministry and the institutions, because of the divergence about what the colleges should be trying to accomplish. Clarification of expectations must be a starting point for evaluation.

Establishing Criteria

Against what standards should colleges and their programmes be evaluated? Who should establish the criteria for evaluation? These are questions on which there is not yet general agreement, yet the credibility of evaluation programmes are contingent upon satisfactory answers.

Wyman and DeMetra take the position that the quest for accountability has focussed almost exclusively on structure, to the detriment of more important questions such as procedures and identification of the major parties to be served by the process. They identify four distinct groups which have an interest in the quality of college programmes and which, in consequence, should qualify for a role in the determination of the criteria to be used in evaluation.

Commerce and industry, including employees, occupational associations, professional colleagues, and unions, are directly concerned with programme quality for two main reasons. They are accountable to their clients—often the public—for the quality of professional services. This is particularly important in the health and transportation fields where public health or safety is an issue. High, consistent standards of practice mean public confidence. This confidence is reflected in status and bargaining power.

Students are concerned that their programmes provide sufficient skill and experience to help them acquire a job which meets their expectations.

The College mandate is to meet the needs of the community in non-university, career-oriented training and the concern is that programmes continue to reflect these needs.

Finally, government is accountable to the public for the cost of education and is concerned that the college system function effectively and efficiently within its mandate.[65]

While each of the four groups has an interest in programme quality, the standards which each adopts will normally differ. As an illustration, colleges may set criteria for graduation, but employers sometimes expect different competencies for work performance. Government expectations of efficiency are sometimes seen to be in conflict with institutional emphasis on quality; students may have their own standards which can be out of phase with both the college and potential employers. Wyman and De Metra argue that clearly identifiable, precise, and measurable standards of performance must be set in concert by all groups with a stake in the outcomes. The technology currently exists by which performance objectives can be set for any programme by which student progress may be measured before, during, and after completing the period of training or education. Job competencies can be set by industry representatives and institutional personnel jointly. The role of government in evaluation should be to ensure that the evaluation process is conducted fairly and dispassionately, and to ensure that the public interest is well served—not merely the interests of institutions, employees, and students.

The methods used to apply these principles to the performance evaluation of public colleges require additional elaboration. The diversity of programming in such institutions indicates that no single body can responsibly evaluate all aspects of college operations. In fact, specific programme evaluation is a necessary component of any college evaluation programme. A university transfer programme evaluation, for example, requires the expertise of university personnel in specific disciplines as well as more general information on transfer success rates. In non-credit programming pursued by students for personal development, the students themselves should play major roles in setting standards and evaluating performance. In para-professional and technical programmes, professional associations should carry major responsibilities for evaluation of institutional performance.

On the other hand, it is critical for evaluators to appreciate that a college is more than a collection of discrete programmes and services; each college is or should be a coherent institution with operating interrelationships between programmes and services. It is for this reason that an all-institution evaluation, as well as individual programme and service evaluations, should constitute part of the overall assessment programme. An evaluation programme of this scope is one that can help institutions to renew themselves, and that can give the public the confidence that colleges are not merely carrying on uncritically year by year.

Whose Responsibility?

A variety of expectations must be met in any credible evaluation programme, and a variety of criteria and agencies must be involved in the processes; nevertheless, there is still concern in many colleges and provinces over initiative and responsibility. Many college people in Canada are wary about any evaluation scheme initiated by government, even though governments have responsibility for public policy and public funding for public institutions. The source of this caution, plainly and simply, has been suspicion of motives. In several parts of Canada, that suspicion has been converted into cynicism. Government officials are accused of wanting to use only simplistic quantitative methods of evaluation to satisfy their needs to respond to questions of accountability, production, and efficiency without due regard for the more qualitative, and less measurable, concerns of institutions and employees. In some cases, the cynicism goes as far as presuming that governments will decide on the results of evaluation in advance, and then structure an evaluation process to produce the predetermined results.

Despite the suspicion and cynicism, there is no doubt that government must visibly support, if not give leadership to, any college evaluation plan that wishes to claim public acceptance. Governments should ensure that a sound process is in place, but government officials should not take charge of implementing the process. While legislation related to evaluation in colleges is uncommon in Canada, it is instructive to note one clause in the College and Institute Act of British Columbia:

> A corporation shall by March 31, 1982, and by the end of each subsequent five-year period, report to the Minister setting out the reasons, if any, why the corporation should continue to exist and, on receipt of this report, the Minister shall advise the Lieutenant Governor in Council about the measures that should be taken to remedy or improve the situation disclosed by the report.[66]

It is interesting to note not just the direct responsibility assigned to the institutions under this legislation but that the onus of proof rests with them, not government.

Two approaches to style of government initiation and leadership in college evaluation merit comment. The first is where government transfers responsibility to a provincial "intermediary body" (IMB) which has direct connection to neither government nor institutions. Normally, the members of such bodies are government appointed with no direct institutional allegiance. The assumptions which flow from this model are that the IMB will act objectively, hold a longer term non-political view of institutions being evaluated, and retain credibility with all parties. The detached position of the IMB, however, may be its greatest weakness as well as its greatest strength; detachment may be less a virtue than informed, highly motivated, active involvement. Two provinces, Ontario and Quebec, provide examples of ways in which intermediary bodies may play initiating roles in institutional evaluation. In Ontario, the Council of Regents has recorded a "regulation reference" which places responsibility for evaluation upon individual college boards.

At least once in every three-year period, a board of governors shall cause to be conducted in a manner approved by the Council of Regents an operational review of the college and the board of governors shall submit to the Council of Regents a copy of any report, study, or document received by the board of governors as the result of such evaluation and review.[67]

In Quebec, the Conseil des Collèges is expected to play a central role in institutional evaluation. In British Columbia major responsibility for initiating the evaluation process has been assumed by a committee of chief executive officers who, with support from their ministry, have developed more detailed processes than in other provinces.[68] In Alberta, a ministry-initiated evaluation process for vocational centres has been developed.[69]

Regardless of the role that governments and intermediary bodies might play in the evaluation of colleges, it is obvious that the colleges themselves must play more than merely co-operating roles. To meet the objective of institutional renewal through evaluation, only the institutions themselves can effect their own renewal. To meet the objective of impartiality and public credibility, the institutions must be seen as far more than reluctant participants. Colleges can and should control much of their own destiny by active collaboration with government and agencies external to themselves in all aspects of college evaluation.

The Process

Several processes and techniques for evaluation are reported in the literature. In Canada, handbooks of policies and procedures have been developed in some provinces to guide or direct the processes.

Two levels of evaluation are common. At one level, each programme is evaluated. At another level, the entire institution—programmes, services, governance, support functions, institutional issues—is subject to review. Within an institutional evaluation, two stages are common: a self-study by each component of the institution to produce a comprehensive all-institution self-study, and an audit by an external team primarily to validate the findings of the self-study.

Particularly for purposes of renewal, the self-study—open, honest, and analytical—is the key to successful evaluation. For this reason, the self-study needs to include a variety of people and agencies—instructors, students, advisory committee members, external agencies—in its planning, implementation, and follow up. As one provincial manual notes:

> An institutional self-study facilitates co-ordination of all activities in a college—with the goal of increased institutional effectiveness and efficiency. If properly carried out, it should produce a renewed commitment of all its members to the institution as well as a concise, relevant document which serves as the basis for the external audit.[70]

Donald[71] and Krakana[72] both note that a self-study can be a source of anxiety and mistrust as well as an instrument of renewal. Small summarizes the problem in these words:

> In a post-secondary institution which had not yet reached the state of continuing self-renewal it is a function of leadership to create a climate wherein institutional personnel regard purposive change as a desirable and valued characteristic of an organization.[73]

As important as a self-study may be for purposes of revitalizing a college, it is at least equally important that no evaluation process be perceived as merely self-serving. It is for this reason that external audits of institutional self-studies should be undertaken and that the results of both the self-studies and the external audit reports enter the public domain quickly.

For a variety of historical reasons, Canadian college systems do not have institutional accreditation mechanisms and procedures similar to those which exist in the United States. In practice, the right of a public institution, such as a community college, to exist with credibility and to offer particular programmes is the prerogative of governments in Canada, not accreditation associations. On the other hand, professional associations with licencing authority and many other associations can be helpful to colleges in their programme evaluation activities and are more than accessible to these institutions. Formal programme accreditation by external agencies is already a feature of the Canadian college scene in several programme fields and is likely to expand in the future. Indeed, given the imperatives of the world of employment and the need for employment mobility in the years ahead, a national system of graduate certification if not programme accreditation in some programme areas seems virtually certain in the immediate future.

In all, institutional evaluation, programme evaluation, and programme accreditation have become as essential to the activities of colleges as planning, learning, and teaching. How all of these activities can be organized efficiently and in the interests of both institutional quality and public acceptance is a major challenge for Canadian colleges. Too often, administrators want to shield their institutions; too often, instructors view review as a challenge to their security; too often, college people are unwilling to accept, and act upon, negative comment. And, to be effective, evaluation processes are time-consuming and complex. Even evaluation of evaluation is warranted.[74]

Value and Evaluation

In *Investment in Learning*, Bowen referred to education as a process by which resources are transformed into a variety of products, all of which may be measured. The relationship between resources and products in the educational enterprise is the measure of efficiency. "The greater the benefits with given resources, or the fewer the resources with given benefits, the greater the efficiency."[75] The determination of efficiency is one task of institutional and programme evaluation.

Bowen asks the question: Is higher education worth the cost? And surely the Canadian public and their governments have the right to ask the analagous question about the colleges they fund and have supported.

To date, most of Canada's colleges have not supplied adequate answers even for the more measurable activities they have undertaken or the more tangible objectives they have set for themselves. But there are also other benefits less easily measured—growth in cognitive learning, emotional and ethical development, improved quality of community life—which must be subject to evaluation if colleges are not to sell themselves short. Bowen notes outcomes such as changes in values and aspirations, aesthetic sensitivity, tolerance, citizenship, and social criticism among the less quantifiable but no less important potential outcomes of higher education that must be included in any cost benefit analysis. His conclusion is forceful:

First, the monetary returns from higher education alone are probably sufficient to offset all the costs. Second, the non-monetary returns are several times as valuable as the monetary returns. And third, the total returns from higher education in all its aspects exceed the cost by several times. In short, the cumulative evidence leaves no doubt that American higher education is well worth what it costs.[76]

The same may well be true of Canadian colleges. But neither the colleges themselves nor the publics they serve will be able to document the value they add to the education of their students or to the quality of life in their society without rigorous, regular, public, and objective evaluation of institutional performance.

RESEARCH

Research has not been a central activity of Canada's community colleges. Indeed, as part of their effort to distinguish themselves from other post-secondary institutions, particularly universities, these colleges have emphasized over and over again that they are not research-oriented institutions. While it would be an exaggeration to claim that colleges were anti-research, it can be fairly asserted that few institutions and few individuals in colleges have been engaged in any serious way in what would generally fit into the category of research.

It is interesting to note that Canada's colleges have no scholarly publications. *College Canada* has had a continuing history as the voice of colleges throughout Canada, but this publication has largely been a descriptive newspaper: it has provided college news for people throughout the country, and different issues have at different times explored issues or themes or championed causes, but it has consistently adopted the style of a newsletter rather than a research-oriented journal.[77] *The Journal of the Association of Canadian Community Colleges*[78] has had a spotty existence and is no longer produced; it came close in several issues to a scholarly format, but the persistent objective of this publication has been to inform, to argue, or to discuss but not to report serious research. In 1984, the Canadian Association for the Study of Adult Education compiled a list of publications and authors for the period 1977 to 1984;[79] despite the fact that adult education has been central to the mission of most colleges in Canada, few names of people actively involved in colleges are included in this compendium. *The Canadian Journal of Higher Education* has published very little by college authors.[80] In truth, little more than a handful of college people have been in any way actively involved in scholarly research within their own disciplines or in research related to instructional techniques, even though instruction has been their central focus, or in the various forms of institutional research. The research activities related to Canada's colleges have been undertaken largely by a small band of university professors of higher education with particular interests in the college sector.

The reason for this lack of priority to scholarship and research is not merely the raison d'être of the college as a teaching rather than research institution. In part, it has been a factor of the rate at which colleges have developed, which has left precious little time and energy for the more reflective and analytical activities associated with research. To some extent, it has simply been the result of the kinds of people who have been employed by colleges. These institutions have quite consciously sought out doers or activists rather than trained researchers. And to some extent it is the result of a lack of a research tradition. Apart from the reality of the college as a teaching institution, the chief reasons for the lack of scholarly output have been both the meagre resources and the time that these institutions have invested in this kind of activity. College instructors and managers have worked long days and long years at their teaching and administrative functions. Allowances have rarely been made for release time to conduct serious research; so, whatever research has been done has been largely a personal rather than institutional pursuit. Few people can sustain a personal research agenda for any length of time under these conditions.

College instructors have, of course, had time for professional development but, with the hectic pace of their more central activities, this time has often been absorbed with administrative chores and with trying to remain abreast of their fields. Administrators and government officials have participated in the development of scores of position papers, policy documents, and similar endeavours but these have commonly had such a narrow focus and such short time lines that the more in-depth analyses that are associated with other forms of scholarly research have been rare indeed. And, some colleges have employed institutional research officers or recognized in some other form the need for an institutional research function, but all too frequently institutional research in colleges has not been able to go much beyond data gathering and assembly to respond to data requests from government sources. Canada's colleges have simply not placed a high priority on research functions.

The New Need

In recent years, however, several factors have prompted an interest in developing the research capacity of colleges.

The first factor has been totally pragmatic. With the financial problems facing all governments in the early 1980's, college personnel correctly recognized that they were in direct competition with other public sector activities for scarce public dollars. And equally correctly, they observed that they were particularly vulnerable because they had neither the political muscle of the longer established and more prestigious universities nor the mass appeal of health and social services. College people came to realize that they could not succeed in their claims for more substantial financial support from government unless they could substantiate their claims with solid evidence of graduate employability, improved productivity, economic impact on their communities, or similar indicators of successful performance. They recognized that the days of academic argument and rhetoric were over. Hard data, not merely tables of numbers, became an inevitable requirement and the process of gathering and interpreting these data in a systematic, useful, and organized way was initiated.

Second, many colleges recognized the need to go beyond their own rhetoric to satisfy their own need for more information about performance, largely because people outside the college movement were no longer prepared to accept their rhetoric uncritically. Were colleges really expanding access to post-secondary education? Very few colleges had data on the backgrounds of their students, much less on those adults in their communities who were not attending college, and so they were not able either to demonstrate their case or to develop new strategies to broaden the socioeconomic base of their student population. Were colleges really offering the programmes that their communities wanted or needed? Were they simply providing what their administrators and instructors wanted to offer? Few colleges had developed systematic techniques for assessing needs and priorities, and intuitive decision-making had many limitations. Colleges began to recognize that they could provide scant evidence of achievement and that they needed systematic methods for gathering, processing, and evaluating relevant information about what they were doing.

Third, there has recently been a growing concern that college instructors might not be performing well even in those matters related to the central purpose of colleges. If colleges pride themselves on the excellence of their teaching—presumably in comparison with the calibre of teaching in other post-secondary institutions—where is the evidence that college instructors analyze their teaching performance, break new ground in instructional models, or develop and evaluate new programmes and curricula? Where is the evidence that most college instructors understand the nature and difficulties of excellent instruction, that they study the art and craft of learning and teaching, and that they are any better or any worse than other teachers? Consideration, however preliminary, of these issues led to the conclusion that college instructors might need the opportunity to maintain contact with their own disciplines and with new developments in the employment areas in which their graduates would work: the very kinds of research activity that stimulated and sustained the intellectual life of their university counterparts. And particularly with the phenomenon of an aging instructional corps and a sharp decline in mobility amongst colleges, the need for intellectual stimulation for college instructors became more evident if these colleges and their personnel were to retain the vitality essential to the well-being of these institutions.

Information to justify continuing support, analyses to enable institutions to know themselves better, and scholarly pursuit to reinvigorate teaching personnel have become rationales for a new emphasis on serious research as an integral function of Canada's colleges.

A Case for Institutional Research

Like many other institutions, colleges in Canada do a great deal of data collection, but data and information are not the same; data without meaning are not information, and the collection and processing of data is not, of itself, research. There are several examples in Canada where agencies—government, private, or institutional—routinely gather data concerning the characteristics of college students, programme costs, class sizes, faculty qualifications, job placement rates, and a variety of similar variables. In many cases the data are collated, standardized, and distributed with limited analysis and often without apparent purpose.

Research, on the other hand, initiates from within a specific problem and becomes a process by which a resolution to the problem is sought. How may participation rates within a community be increased? In what ways may student services be made more effective? What techniques should be utilized to improve the quality and effectiveness of an instructional programme? These are research questions or problems; answers or solutions will help colleges to attain their goals and objectives. This kind of activity is institutional research, and colleges require institutional research to be effective.

Absence of research of this kind is a major omission on the part of colleges. It leaves a college with no real insights into its operation, no appreciation of the heterogeneity of its students, no understanding of its impact upon the workforce, and no valid basis for assessing its style of operation. A blind repetition of established practices—in admission policy, in instructional methodology, or curriculum organization—based upon untested assumptions carried from the past will neither enhance the quality of the institution nor justify its continued existence before government or public. Based upon these considerations, the case for institutional research activity is easier to make in the college sector than in the universities, where the relationship to society is less direct. Yet, largely because of a lack of understanding of the concept of institutional research, this kind of activity is rarely associated with the responsibility of a public community college.

Responsibility

Even where the values of institutional research are understood and appreciated, enthusiasm for it has been at best muted. One obvious rationalization has been that it is not productive, in the sense that it has no immediate and direct benefit for students. Particularly in times of financial restraint, institutional research is sometimes viewed as a poor investment, if not a luxury. But the more profound basis for skepticism and hesitation is related to responsibility for research. On the one hand, many college people doubt the objectivity of college research conducted by government officials. On the other hand, people outside colleges commonly view studies done by college personnel as too limited in scope—and in some cases, too self-serving—to have any useful application beyond the researching institution. These concerns merit comment.

It is true that much of the research directly concerned with colleges is currently being produced within government departments. And, in general, the interests of government focus upon issues of financial accountability, productivity, and relatively narrow and high profile aspects of college operations, such as the number of students who find employment after completing specific programmes. Data gathered on these topics are used to support arguments by ministers for funding college activities and to provide a basis for allocating operating budgets to different institutions.

When government agencies are so intimately involved in such an exercise, questions of objectivity and political agendas naturally arise. Gathering of data of these kinds, regardless of the care with which they are collected, is commonly regarded by institutions and external agencies as a process by which governments rationalize their own policies, or departmental bureaucracies justify their own existence. The source of data collection hence becomes a critical element in the credibility of its results.

A further difficulty which arises when research programmes are under government aegis is the tendency for the research to start from the assumption that all institutions under study are alike and comparable. Even within the same provincial systems, however, Canada's colleges are in many respects idiosyncratic. As communities differ in historical development, size, geography, demographics of population, patterns of employment, attitudes to and expectations from post-secondary education, to name just a few differences, colleges which attempt to respond to specific communities also vary. The type of training which a nurse requires, for example, may vary considerably from rural to urban colleges in the light of expectations from small hospitals where a wide range of competencies will be preferred to the specialization necessary in large urban health centres.

But data gathering and research conducted independently by colleges are also suspect because they are often viewed as not being applicable beyond the context in which the data are gathered. College planning offices, institutional researchers, or budget analysts devote the majority of their attention to graduate placement, participation statistics, or preparation of internal reports for institutional reviews. Again, the objectivity of studies conducted by college personnel relating to institutional performance criteria is sometimes questioned.

A third source of college research activity is independent research organizations. In cases where such agencies are engaged by contract to undertake college research, the question of objectivity tends not to arise. And the results are made available to the contracting agency but are also usually released for wider distribution. Studies of issues such as the evaluation of institutions, management systems, programmes, and operational units, are particularly appropriate for independent agencies. Government departments may view productivity in terms of class size, instructional hours, or utilization of staff and facilities. Institutions may search for more qualitative measures. An independent agency is generally able to consider divergent views of productivity measures in seeking to assess programmes and policy decisions.

The answer to the question of responsibility for college institutional research really lies with the nature of the data to be gathered, their purpose, and the ways in which they are to be used. Above all, the three criteria for effective research—validity, reliability, and objectivity—must not only exist but also be seen to exist. Consideration of these factors will identify the agencies appropriate for different research studies.

Not to be ignored is the particular contribution that federal agencies such as Statistics Canada and the Department of the Secretary of State can make to college research. Statistics Canada, and its predecessor the Dominion Bureau of Statistics, has been responsible for the collation of data in the community college sector for over two decades.[81] Despite the useful data base which has been generated, Statistics Canada faces a number of difficulties. As a federal agency its role in education is limited. It cannot initiate policy studies and its capacity to gather data depends upon the co-operation of the provinces. Even basic terms such as "post-secondary," "part-time student," "technical programmes," "continuing education," and "student aid" have had different definitions in different provinces. The end result has been a data base which has limited comparability among provinces. Furthermore, Statistics Canada has been slow to respond to new realities in programme development in community colleges. Until recently, data on part-time students and faculty, distance education students, and credit-free continuing education has not been collected, and so the national profile of colleges has been far from complete.

The Secretary of State has conducted valuable surveys of post-secondary students and follow-up studies of students after graduation.[82] Data on reasons for attending college, fields of study, financial support, socioeconomic status of students, and related college characteristics are useful and important bases for comparison of programmes by province.

It is critically important for college researchers to have access to data on a national scale as a means of comparing college programmes in different provinces. If Statistics Canada is to be the source of these data, and no other agency has the capacity to do so, it must consult with, and be responsive to, the particular features of the colleges and different college systems. In areas such as distance learning, part-time studies, co-operative programmes, and technological education, Statistics Canada must recognize new directions in post-secondary education and update data bases accordingly. Effective responses to this need seem imminent.

An Agenda for Research

The agenda for research which is reproduced in appendix C is wide ranging. It represents the aggregate of recent responses by college personnel across Canada to the question: "What are the aspects of your college (or college system) for which research studies are most needed at this time?" It was evident that the priorities varied considerably and were conditioned by many factors: the specific role of the college (or college system), the current relationship with government, the basis for financial support, the areas where retrenchment was being considered, recent developments in organization of post-secondary education in the province, and present expectations for the colleges, particularly from industry. All the priorities identified are reflected in the agenda, so that it might reflect the diversity of institutional needs throughout Canada.

Further, the preliminary agenda has been supplemented by an analysis of the objectives, aspirations, or claims of colleges as reproduced in calendars, mission statements, annual reports, white papers, and government commissioned studies. In each case selection of agenda items is based upon the question: "How can it be known if the colleges are accomplishing the tasks which have been set for them?" or "How can one assess whether college services are producing these changes in this clientele at these costs?"

The categories of research items, while incomplete, represent immediate questions which must be addressed in research programmes of colleges if they are to document their performance, establish accountability, and interpret their contribution to an often skeptical government and confused public. In essence, the items in the research agenda meet at least one of two criteria. The first items relate to accountability and credibility and examine the extent to which institutions serve individuals, society at large, and specialized groups such as employers, industry, and the job market. They also pertain to the economic returns which society may expect from investment in college education and which may be applicable to the individual, the immediate community served by the college, and to provincial and national constituencies. The second set of items explores the performance of the institution with regard to such matters as productivity, service to students in formal instruction and support activity, quality of teaching, counselling, and administration, as well as in more measurable areas such as cost effectiveness, efficiency, and unit costs.

Priorities in Institutional Research

The simple enumeration of items for a comprehensive research agenda does not address the question of priorities. Indeed, left to their own devices, the various interests in college education would select different priorities: governments would focus on cost effectiveness and productivity; institutional personnel, on quality of education and extent of contribution to society; business and industry, on the adequacy of graduate performance in the workplace; and external research agencies, on specific, probably more academic, questions and problems. The need is to have all agenda items researched by the agency most appropriate for each item. Fortunately, in some provinces, much of this research is already underway.

Should a college or a province wish to initiate a research programme, the obvious starting point is with those items which relate most directly to the educational function of the college—to learn more about the students, to determine who might best benefit from the college experience but do not yet participate, and to assess the contribution that a college makes to its society—because these issues are the essence of college education. In short, colleges and provinces need to be able to document the value that colleges add to their students and to their communities.

To undertake or complete such an agenda, colleges need to establish and support an institutional research function, most conveniently in the form of an office or centre for institutional research. Such an office should not only undertake its own research studies but also initiate appropriate studies in collaboration with other colleges and with government, and contract out research work that can be most credibly undertaken by external agencies. In this fashion, a comprehensive but co-ordinated research programme can provide the assurances of quality and competence desired by governments and public, as well as the objectivity required by the institutions themselves. Colleges and college systems simply can no longer neglect institutional research. It is as important as learning, teaching, and evaluating; it ought not be seen as an expensive frill that is justified only in good times.

A Case For Scholarly Research

Institutions need to know themselves better, and the public need to be assured that colleges are in fact achieving their goals prompt a new emphasis on institutional research. However, Canada's colleges have an equally pressing need for scholarly research as well for the same reasons that scholars in other post-secondary institutions conduct research. Research has always been justified in universities as a means of sustaining intellectual life and of keeping teaching on the cutting edge. The same justification holds for college personnel, despite the essential differences between colleges and universities.

Historically, the need for a research component within the college sector was understandably given a low priority. The novelty of getting colleges off the ground, the intellectual stimulation of creating new courses, and the challenges associated with learning to cope effectively with new kinds of post-secondary students were more than sufficient stimulation for instructors in the early college days. For the more adventuresome, the opportunities to move to other institutions on a temporary leave basis, or permanently, were plentiful. If anything, there was so much stimulation that the opportunities for reflection and analysis were all too few.

But these conditions have changed significantly. A great many college teachers have been at their tasks for ten years or more. Mobility between institutions has slowed to a trickle. Many people are still teaching courses similar to those they originally taught. Instructors find themselves defending themselves and their work rather than exploring new activities as the threat of layoffs and course deletions mount. And many instructors have simple lost, or had cut out of them, the idealism that they had at the beginning of their college career. They are bright, energetic, and capable but the spark is no longer there. As with people in other institutions and organizations, a substantial core of people in Canada's colleges need renewal if they are to continue to make useful contributions to their students. Opportunities to do research are a key instrument of renewal. In fact, many college instructors have sought outlets for their own professional regeneration, and involvement in international education has been one of the exciting consequences of this search. Other colleges and The Association of Canadian Community Colleges have encouraged exchange programmes between institutions as another source of renewal. But the potential of research activity as an instrument of renewal, for some college instructors, has not really been tapped.

This is not to suggest that colleges should model themselves on universities or that a priority of research over teaching is justified. It is to suggest that many college teachers are interested in scholarly research, are capable researchers, and would receive new professional challenges from scholarly research opportunities. It is also to suggest that more research would be useful for the colleges themselves.

Two kinds of scholarly research are particularly appropriate to the college sector. The first is discipline-related academic research. Particularly in colleges which provide university-equivalent programmes, there are instructors in virtually all disciplines whose teaching could benefit from a prolonged immersion in the university research environment. Over their years as college instructors, they have lost, or deliberately turned away from, the active research work of their university counterparts. Initiatives to encourage universities to offer adjunct professor status to college instructors, which would provide them access to research facilities and to other active researchers, could be of substantial benefit to colleges. Short-term exchanges between university professors and college instructors are also a practical method of accommodating research needs and could be of mutual benefit, just as exchanges between college instructors in occupationally related programmes and people in the field could produce substantial returns for both industry and education.

The second kind of research warranted in the college sector is that related to learning and teaching. The charge is commonly whispered outside colleges that many instructors are simply not very good teachers: they have not been trained to teach; they have not examined their own teaching; they have very little support or incentive to improve their teaching; their teaching performance has been assessed at best in superficial and cursory ways. And that charge, warranted or not, is a particularly serious one because of the nature and orientation of colleges in Canada.

Even if all college instructors were quite outstanding, there is more than sufficient reason for colleges to devote time and resources to the examination of learning and teaching. Given the range of ages and backgrounds of students who attend Canada's colleges, it would be hard to claim that most aspects of adult learning have received sufficient study; indeed more adult education research within the college milieu may well challenge if not upset some of the conventional wisdom within the field of adult education. Of equal merit is research related to newer methods of educational delivery: the use of television in education, methods of learning at a distance, self-paced learning, continuous entry learning, and a host of other ways of teaching and learning.

The early days of colleges in Canada saw a great deal of experimentation with new courses and new forms of institutional organization. For reasons of institutional age and external constraints now facing colleges, much of this experimentation has evaporated. At no time have colleges given serious research attention to the ways in which people learn. The time is now ripe, however, for colleges to move in this direction, and such a move not only will provide the kind of intellectual stimulation sought by many instructors but also will reaffirm the basic responsibility of colleges to excel as teaching institutions.

Conclusion

It was appropriate for Canada's colleges to leave the research function to the universities and to research agencies in the first years of the college movement.

To achieve their early objectives, the colleges had to be planners and doers rather than analysts. These colleges have now reached to point where they must document their performance and find solutions to new problems. To develop a modest research capacity at this time would not be a denial of their raison d'être as teaching institutions. Rather, it would give supporting governments and the public the assurances that they need, particularly in difficult times. It would give these institutions themselves a sounder and more systematic basis on which they could plan their future. And it would provide for some college people the incentive and the opportunity to renew themselves and their teaching.

In difficult times, it is tempting for colleges and other organizations to focus their investments on short-term opportunities: more classes, competitive rewards for employees, better marketing. To follow this course of action at the expense of the benefits of a research capacity could place the long-term future of these institutions at risk.

9

COLLEGES AND CANADA

Several years before the college movement in Canada was to take clearly identifiable shape, steps to "Canadianize" this movement had already been taken. It was in 1965-1966 that the Canadian Association for Adult Education anticipated the developments that were to take place in the years immediately ahead, and began to discuss the potential of the "community colleges" as a new thrust in the area of adult or continuing education.[1] In the background was legislation and planning in several parts of Canada—Alberta (1958), British Columbia (1962), Ontario (1965)—which called for the establishment of post-secondary non-degree-granting institutions. On the horizon were similar developments in other provinces—Quebec (1966), Prince Edward Island (1968), and Manitoba (1969). Yet it was evident to key adult educators in Canada that college planners in the different provinces were not even talking to one another.

The Canadian Association for Adult Education held an exploratory National Conference on the Community College in June 1966. The objectives of this conference were straightforward: these new colleges were likely to provide opportunity for thousands of adults to continue, or to begin again, their learning; true to their historic role and concerns, the leaders of the association saw these new colleges as agencies which could bring further learning opportunity to the many adults in Canada who had had very little or no access to publicly supported post-secondary education. This conference could be really little more than an animating session, but it did attract the attention of adult educators who had long felt themselves, and adult learners, only on the fringe of Canadian education. The major impact of this first conference was to confirm that indeed a community college movement was taking shape in Canada.[2].

A second national conference took place in June 1967 when the Canadian

Association for Adult Education was joined by five more national education associations: The Canadian Teachers' Federation, The Association of Universities and Colleges of Canada, The Canadian Association of University Teachers, The Canadian Education Association, and the Canadian Association of Secondary School Inspectors.[3] This conference was more substantial, but still tentative. Differences in policies, structures, and organization of this new kind of education in several provinces were identified and discussed. There was the beginning of information sharing about the new institutions across the country.

It was the Canadian Association for Adult Education under the leadership of Alan Thomas which also took the third step towards a Canada-wide initiative relative to these new institutions. Shortly after the second National Conference on the Community College, this association approached the Kellogg Foundation, an educational foundation formed by an American corporation with corporate holdings in Canada, for funding "to explore, with the colleges of Canada, the possibility of a national organization if the circumstances warranted." The Canadian Association for Adult Education argued that these new colleges would be heavily engaged in adult education and proposed to the Kellogg Foundation that there was an obvious relationship between adult education and national development.[4]

The Kellogg Foundation agreed to provide a three-year grant of $202,000 to fund a Canadian Commission for the Community College, which was to conduct hearings in several major cities of Canada. In addition, national seminars were conducted on staff development, college finance, and transferability and exchanges; a publication called *College Canada* was distributed to colleges; and the commission generally served as a clearinghouse for information distribution among colleges, some ninety-six of which were visited personally by commissioners.[5]

The Canadian Commission for the Community College had provided the impetus. By 1969, the decision was taken that the new colleges of Canada should now decide for themselves whether a national association was in fact warranted and, for this purpose, an Assembly of Colleges was convened in Ottawa in 1970. The assembly very much endorsed the idea of a national college organization and formation of the Association of Canadian Community Colleges was the product of that assembly.[6]

It is of significance to note the rationale for a Canadian organization of post-secondary non-degree-granting institutions (for obvious but not entirely precise reasons, the less cumbersome "community college" label was preferred even though several institutions which could hardly be identified by that name were represented at the assembly). Apart from the evident roles as clearinghouse for information among institutions, as a national and international representative of the institutions, collectively, and as a facilitator of student and personnel exchanges among institutions, the Canadian Commission for the

Community College identified two functions as particularly appropriate to a national college organization: it could "become a major force for new and improved concepts of citizenship in Canada",[7] and it could be a significant contributor to national unity. In addition, it could be a "growing stimulus to the concept that continuous learning is a basic prerequisite to enlightened partici- pation in the democratic processes at all levels of government".[8] This blending of strong commitments to fundamental concepts about adult learning and to national educational interests, through inter-regional and intercultural dia- logue within Canada as well as on the international scene, set very high sights for the new Association of Canadian Community Colleges.

VISION TO REALITY

The Association of Canadian Community Colleges and indeed the individ- ual colleges were not originally up to the tasks set for them, and understandably so. The mere job of getting the association firmly in place consumed much of the energies of the first years. The original executive directors, Robert Gwilliam and Jacques Fournier, faced an almost impossible task. Equally important was the fact that the new colleges, institutes of technology, and technical institutions—125 of them in 1970—were in their formative years, and precious little time and energy could reasonably be devoted to the more esoteric activities of a national body, especially when provincial organizations of colleges were also being formed in most provinces at the same time. And, once the new association was in place, the Canadian Association for Adult Education rightly redirected its energy and imagination elsewhere, but in the process deprived the fledgling association of the drive and leadership it had provided, directly and indirectly, since 1965.

There were other and more profound reasons for the slowness with which the association found its feet. Originally the Ontario colleges showed no great enthusiasm for the national association. Later, reluctance of Quebec colleges to retain membership in an organization for which they had originally been very supportive emerged. This reticence was in part a product of Quebec nationalism, which expressed itself in an aversion to being publicly identified with anything that smacked of federalism or with any organization suspected of promoting "national unity." It was also partly the result of the association acquiring within Quebec in the mid-1970's the reputation of being an "English" organization despite its early history of bilingual national conventions.

Colleges in other parts of the country were neither quick nor uncritical in jumping on the national organization bandwagon. Several college boards in the west questioned the institutional benefits of a national body to the point where there was an annual pull and tug to determine whether they would remain paying members, let alone participating members. In addition, several colleges in Ontario, where much of the drive for national activity should normally emanate, acted as though they had little to learn from colleges in the rest of Canada and retained an obvious detachment from the association. With the exception of Holland College in Charlottetown, the college movement in Atlantic Canada had not even begun by the early 1970's.

Besides, other post- secondary organizations at a national level were attracting some attention of people within Canada's colleges and competing with the Association of Canadian Community Colleges. The older Canadian Vocational Association included in its membership administrators and trainers in governments, post-secondary institutions, secondary schools, and industry; the relatively narrow orientation of this organization was more attractive to many college people from one coast to the other. As well, the Association of Canadian Community College Administrators—again with nation-wide participation—was not numerically a major force, but it was more attractive to many college leaders than the Association of Canadian Community Colleges, which persisted in attempting to be not only national in scope but also attractive to every major constituency of post-secondary institutions: board members, students, faculty, and administrators. In seeking this range of participation, the association was unique and imaginative, but it also diffused its meagre energy and resources by trying to be all things national for all colleges.

But the association persisted and, by the late 1970's, definite signs of a renewed sense of mission and energy were apparent. A series of strong presidents was one sign; the employment of a new executive director committed to making the association viable was a second. More attractive activity by the association was evident even in non-participating colleges. Institutions which had not been vigorous members renewed their involvement. More Quebec colleges revived their memberships, more Ontario colleges became actively involved, and the new presence of Atlantic Canadian institutions added an important and enthusiastic dimension.

The Association of Canadian Community Colleges turned the corner in 1983. For the first time in years, it was debt free and operating on a sound business basis. It had an active Canadian Studies Bureau which held regional as well as national meetings; although the bureau's appeal was not broad, it had firmly established a nation-wide network of instructors committed to improving the amount of Canadian studies in college curricula and to encouraging colleges to expand the number of courses in which a Canadian context would be recognized. With a special Quebec office, the Canadian Studies Bureau was also instrumental in attracting more Quebec colleges into the national fold without losing their own distinctive identity as Quebec institutions. The association also had a thriving international education bureau. Cultivated over several years, this bureau was of particular appeal to many college personnel—people

with an international outlook, administrators who saw the personal and institutional benefits of international involvement, and instructors who yearned for
new challenges and the excitement and opportunity that had characterized the
early days of the colleges.

A publications bureau was also a growing part of the association's activity,
and the quality of dialogue across Canada through the association improved
markedly. Quiet efforts to organize a student bureau were also underway in
recognition of the fact that students had not played much more than a token
role in the affairs of the association despite having full powers of participation.
Representations to federal authorities by the executive on a number of national
policy issues such as a new training policy had raised the public profile of the
association to the point where requests for participation in any debate over
post-secondary educational issues of national consequence could now be taken
for granted. Support for studies of the state of general education and of the
need for professional development further enhanced the association's credibility throughout Canada. Annual national conventions, consistently well attended
since 1970, rounded out the growing state of major activities of an association
now on the move.

While the national body of the non-degree-granting colleges and other
post-secondary institutions was struggling during the 1970's, few colleges on
their own initiative did much to raise their sights beyond their own provinces, if
not their own institutions. Quite simply, they were busy getting themselves
established "back home." From time to time, Gordon Campbell of the University of Lethbridge used his initiative and ingenuity to bring together some chief
executive officers of community colleges to discuss issues of common interest,
because he believed that the Association of Canadian Community Colleges was
too formal and structured an organization to generate the vitality he considered
so important. Several administrators and faculty members built their own
cross-Canada contact networks, but by and large the vision of colleges as
instruments of interregional and intercultural dialogue remained far from
realization.

Furthermore, apart from the activities of the relatively small band of Canadian Studies enthusiasts, colleges did little in the 1970's to promote a sense of
pan-Canadianism in their curricula. If public schooling could be viewed as
parochial in Canada—and it could—most colleges did very little to restore the
balance. These colleges had been established primarily with a local focus or
orientation, and had some community of interest with like institutions in their
own provinces. This rather limited perspective was reflected in their instructional life and student activities. With some notable exceptions such as Seneca
College in Toronto and Dawson and Vanier Colleges in Montreal, any move
towards a national perspective in college programming was quite peripheral.
Curiously enough, it was in intercollegiate athletics in the late 1970's that the

first visible evidence of a national perspective became apparent. Throughout this decade, Canada's public colleges were largely community, or regionally, oriented. The vision of an active national network of public colleges pursuing national as well as more limited objectives simply did not exist.

But the greatest disappointment to the leaders of the Canadian Association for Adult Education, who had originally stimulated nation-wide activity among colleges, must have been the indifference displayed by the colleges to the concept of continuous learning as a national strategy. No organization had worked more vigorously on behalf of the many Canadian adults who had not had the advantages of formal education; no organization had tried harder to promote the principles of lifelong learning; no organization had done more to encourage Canadians to pursue learning as a self-motivated activity; no organization had expressed greater respect for adults as learning beings; no organization had faced such difficulty in having its views on adult learning respected by other sectors of Canadian education. The hope was that Canada's community colleges would now take on these causes and move Canada more and more toward becoming a true learning society in the sense advocated by U.N.E.S.C.O.

In the 1970's, this hope was ill-founded. Canada's new colleges, in their search for respectability, took on the appearance of more traditional institutions, and organized themselves in more traditional ways to pursue more traditional goals. It is true that these colleges were more hospitable to older and part-time students than other institutions for adults, but in the main they required students to meet their demands. Few were prepared to adjust their requirements to the more revolutionary views advocated by frontier adult educators around the world. Few of the new colleges were learning centres for adults; most were teaching institutions to which many older and part-time students were admitted.

REALITY TO VISION

The concept of public colleges as potential centres for adult learning, rather than as more traditional institutions who would admit older as well as younger adults as students, is addressed elsewhere (see Chapter 6).

But what of the notion of community colleges as forces for "new and improved concepts of citizenship" and as "contributors to national unity"? Was the original vision of the leaders of the Canadian Association for Adult Education unrealistic? Was it wrong-headed? Was it simply a victim of poor timing? Is that vision now more appropriate? Ought it to be pursued in the years to the end of this century as part of the process of renewal of Canada's colleges?

Certainly, if practical realities of the early 1970's militated against the realization of this vision, many of those realities are still present. Canada's colleges are still not mature institutions and continue to face all the problems of getting organized and firmly established. Equally certainly, much of the energy and enthusiasm of the early years has been knocked out of many college people by a variety of realities which have emerged over the years: many college students are not as bright or as enthusiastic as instructors had romanticized, and teaching in many colleges is hardly fun for most teachers; many of the grand schemes for curriculum reform have been dashed on the rocks of conservative administrators and board members, less daring students and timid teaching colleagues, as well as on the reef of insufficient revenue. Many college people are simply tired from the years of high energy, frustrated by personal or professional dreams unrealized within the college milieu, and, in some cases, cynical about their own futures and those of their institutions. It would be unrealistic not to admit that a portion of Canadian college staff members are doing little more than putting in time to retirement, even though they are still quite young.

There is, however, another concern that is an even bigger obstacle to any nation-wide push for greater Canadian consciousness by Canada's colleges. That is financial restraint. Few colleges in Canada have the financial resources that they once had, and it seems likely that the passage of time will not be the solution to this problem. With fewer resources and a national spirit of retrenchment and accountability, colleges face strong internal and external pressures to preserve what they already have rather than embark on new ventures, particularly ones that could become costly or that stray from the core of their legislated mandates.

Nor is Canadian society any more cohesive than it was in the late 1960's and early 1970's. The relationship between Quebec and the rest of Canada is still at best tenuous, and many Quebecois have already psychologically separated from the rest of the country.[10] Regionalism is still as pronounced in Canada as it was in the late 1970's when attention to the New West was so vigorously demanded. The existence of "have" and "have not" Canadians is even more evident in times of persistently high unemployment. Nation-wide consensus on any major issue remains very difficult.

Acknowledging all these and other negatives, three factors suggest that a renewed effort toward pan-Canadian consciousness by Canada's colleges is realistic, timely, and desirable: the Canadian need for greater cohesion, the college need for renewal, and the appropriateness of the task for the colleges of Canada. As long as Canada remains a political entity, the need to strike the proper balance between national and other equally legitimate interests is still present. The view that tensions within any society can be a constructive force, depending upon how the tensions are addressed, is and will continue to be valid.[12] It is in the interests of all Canadians that the tensions existing in a Canada of enormous diversity be addressed now.

Similarly, Canada's colleges, as do other social institutions, need to be renewed if they are to retain or expand their influence. To call for renewal is not to criticize unjustifiably; it is simply to acknowledge that no institution can remain effective simply by continuing to do what it has previously done. The concept of "continually adjusting colleges" is as apt today as it was in the formative years.[13] Renewal, bringing new imagination to old and new issues, is urgently required, not merely desirable.

But what makes Canada's colleges particularly suitable for the advancement of Canadian consciousness? The most obvious answer is that these colleges reach more adults in Canada than any other educational agency in the country[14] and that the task is essentially an educational one. The public schools of Canada are a favourite whipping boy for those who express dissatisfaction with the quality and quantity of knowledge of and attitudes to Canada,[15] but it just may be that the sophistication of knowledge required for a politically healthy Canada is beyond the reach of young Canadians. Schools can and should provide a basis for mutual understanding and respect among diverse Canadians, but active citizenship requires a continuous cultivation beyond the school years.[16] If Canadians are to express their citizenship beyond the ballot box, it will be the result of understandings they develop, attitudes they form, and actions they take as adults, not as youths.

There is probably little constraint on the number of ways in which Canadian colleges might contribute to development of "new and improved concepts of citizenship." One contribution might be the development of pan-Canadian consciousness within their student bodies and within their communities. Evidence of this contribution might be manifested several ways. Within colleges, centres for Canadian Studies are one obvious possibility; curriculum revisions which encourage students to examine issues of significance to all Canadians, or of significance to Canadians other than themselves, would be another. Ensuring that the Canadian context of all courses, where applicable, would receive due attention is yet a third. Several colleges have already developed or considered still other ways.

The precise formula, however, is not as important as maintenance of the objective because new formulae can always be found. But if Canadian society from sea to sea is to give serious attention to causes of alienation in the West; to bilingualism; to the legitimate aspirations of francophones within a predominantly anglophone society; to a renewed sensitivity to local cultures and history in Atlantic Canada; to fundamental human rights for all Canadians; to the persistent preoccupations of native people; to equality and opportunity to contribute to the mainstream of Canadian society by members of the many ethnocultural groups in a legally established multicultural society; to the plight of the chronic poor and unemployed; to the recurring American influence on Canadian political, economic, and cultural life; to questions of energy and resource conservation; to Canada's responsibilities to the developing world;

then Canada's colleges can properly spearhead within their own institutions and throughout their regions practical, informed programmes in all these and other areas of Canadian public concern.

Canada's universities will continue to engage in scholarly examination of public policy and issues of broad public concern. Canada's schools can lay important foundations through an emphasis on "Canadian" studies.[17] Canada's community colleges are the only agencies, however, which have the platform and access to a full cross-section of Canadian society to bring Canadian public affairs right into the public arena for Canadian adults, the people who are in position to influence political, economic, and social change directly and immediately.

It should not be surprising that Canadian college instructors have shown in recent years significantly more interest in international affairs than in national concerns. With many instructors raised in the university environment and wishing to compete with their university counterparts rather than create their own culture (see Chapter 6), Canadian Studies are seen as too narrow or too parochial for some Canadian colleges. Nevertheless, the call to help Canadian adults "to know ourselves"[18] is a challenge particularly suited to the broader mandates and missions of Canadian colleges.

Modifying the format of programmes of Canadian colleges will not by itself either substantially enhance pan-Canadian consciousness or generate new concepts of citizenship. A critical component of any strategy to maintain such consciousness is enhancement of dialogue among colleges. The creation of provincial networks of colleges and the recent activities of The Association of Canadian Community Colleges have been a good start. But, without obstacles that deter schools from a more Canada-wide perspective, the colleges are well-placed to make inter-institutional activities an integral, continuing part of the Canadian college approach to adult learning.

Inter-institutional activity to achieve the objective of greater Canadian consciousness should not be centred on administrators and their institutional problems nor on impressive but dubiously productive annual national conventions. Large numbers of teachers, instructional administrators, and students need to meet regularly—and the use of newer communications technologies should facilitate such meetings without unreasonable cost—if individual colleges are to remain sensitive to the diversity of Canada and to pay more than lip service to Canadian public issues. Apart from the obvious benefit to students and to Canadian society as a whole from having large numbers of adult Canadians engaged in dialogue that is pan-Canadian (and therefore international as well) in scope, a programme of less formal professional activities combined with more structured, more focused national and interregional meetings could serve as the catalyst for the continuing renewal of the colleges themselves. College personnel and students do not generally have access to the energizing international community of scholars to which Canadian university people need access, and it is highly improbable that they will be able to renew themselves without creative sparks emanating from beyond their own institutions. Canada's colleges should decide to learn all they can from one another, and a focus on national consciousness throughout the college network of Canada could be the trigger for that learning.

Canadian educational institutions at all levels have expressed considerable reticence about being used—manipulated, many might say—to further the cause of national unity. Canadian educators rationalize that their institutions should not be used to achieve political ends, even though consideration of specific political issues of other kinds is part of the daily routine of schools, colleges, and universities. Perhaps more to the point is the view that national unity is a subtle—or not so subtle—attempt, usually on the part of central Canadians, to homogenize a stubbornly heterogeneous Canada. Of course, this kind of national unity deserves no place in Canadian society or education. However, a concept of national unity which advocates respect for diversity, the use of political and economic institutions to make Canada and the world better places for all, and the use of tension as a constructive method of social problem-solving deserves active pursuit. New concepts of citizenship in Canada can indeed result from this kind of national unity.

In 1977, Roger Lemelin, publisher of *La Presse* in Montreal, expressed forcefully the kind of vision that could captivate Canadian colleges and Canadian society: "The real urgency is to give Canada, this abstract country, a high collective national passion, a set of accessible goals towards which, over and above language, racial, or religious prejudices, our young people could strive, whether they are from Vancouver or Toronto or Quebec or Saint John."[19]

IMPLICATIONS OF CHOICE

The original vision of a national role for Canada's colleges has been blurred by more pressing realities of the first years, and by the abrasiveness of Canadian society during this period. The vision of greater Canadian consciousness as a result of a deliberate strategy taken on by Canada's colleges can remain subdued. These colleges can point to enormous problems which confront them and retreat from such a strategy with a solid rationalization. The other choice is for the colleges to subscribe to the original vision, renew their efforts to realize that vision, and in the process renew themselves and the Canadian society which prompted their coming into being. Opting for this second choice on a Canada-wide scale will not sit well with those in Canadian colleges who publicly or privately yearn for the academic, professional, or social status achieved long ago by professionals in other post-secondary institutions. This choice would imply that Canada's colleges remain mavericks within Canadian education, with all the shortcomings of that status. But playing the maverick to the hilt could be the way to become a unique, significant educational force.

And, if ever mavericks were needed in Canadian education, they will certainly be necessary in the years ahead. Roger Elmes, at the time Director of the Canadian Studies Project of the Association of Canadian Community Colleges, captured the sense of the maverick and the potential of Canada's colleges in 1980 when he wrote:

> In post-secondary education we have a special role which can no longer be ignored. Draftsmen, auto mechanics, surveyors, nurses, plumbers, child care workers . . . are all eligible voters as are university-transfer students, biology majors, philosophers . . . . We must dedicate ourselves to the proposition that no community college student will graduate without a realistic level of exposure to critical thought on Canada's political, economic, and social culture. Nothing less is acceptable if we are to survive as a nation.[20]

Perhaps it is this vision that will allow Canada's colleges to revive the original notion that collectively they could become "a major force for new and improved concepts of citizenship in Canada."

Appendix A

POST SECONDARY
EDUCATIONAL INSTITUTIONS IN CANADA
(Other than Universities and University Affiliated Colleges)

A. PUBLIC COMMUNITY COLLEGES

British Columbia

1. Camosun College, Victoria
2. Capilano College, North Vancouver
3. Cariboo College, Kamloops
4. Douglas College, New Westminster
5. East Kootenay Community College, Cranbrook
6. Fraser Valley College, Chilliwack
7. Kwantlen College, Surrey
8. Malaspina College, Nanaimo
9. College of New Caledonia, Prince George
10. North Island Community College, Campbell River
11. Northern Lights Community College, Dawson Creek
12. Northwest Community College, Terrace
13. Okanagan College, Kelowna
14. Selkirk College, Castlegar
15. Vancouver Community College, Vancouver

Alberta

16. Fairview College, Fairview
17. Grand Prairie Regional College, Grand Prairie
18. Grant MacEwan Community College, Edmonton
19. Keyano College, Fort McMurray
20. Lakeland College, Lloydminster
21. Lethbridge Community College, Lethbridge
22. Medicine Hat College, Medicine Hat
23. Mount Royal College, Calgary
24. Olds College, Olds
25. Old Sun Community College, Gleichen
26. Red Deer College, Red Deer

Saskatchewan

27. Carlton Trail Community College,
    Humboldt
28. Coteau Range Community College,
    Moose Jaw
29. Cumberland Community College,
    Nipawin
30. Cypress Hills Community College,
    Swift Current
31. La Ronge Region Community College,
    La Ronge
32. Mistikwa Community College,
    North Battleford
33. Natonum Community College,
    Prince Albert
34. North East Community College,
    Sandy Bay
35. Parkland College, Melville
36. Prairie West Community College,
    Biggar
37. Regina Plains Community College,
    Regina
38. Saskatchewan Indian Community
    College, Saskatoon
39. Saskatoon Regional Community
    College, Saskatoon
40. South East Region Community
    College, Weyburn
41. Westside Community College, Beauval

Manitoba

42. Assiniboine Community College,
    Brandon
43. Keewatin Community College, The Pas
44. Red River Community College,
    Winnipeg

Ontario

45. Algonquin College, Ottawa
46. Cambrian College, Sudbury
47. Canadore College, North Bay
48. Centennial College, Scarborough
49. Conestoga College, Kitchener
50. Confederation College, Thunder Bay
51. Durham College, Oshawa
52. Fanshawe College, London
53. The George Brown College, Toronto
54. Georgian College, Barrie
55. Humber College, Rexdale
56. Lambton College, Sarnia

57. Loyalist College, Belleville
58. Mohawk College, Hamilton
59. Niagara College, Welland
60. Northern College, South Porcupine
61. St. Clair College, Windsor
62. St. Lawrence College, Brockville
63. Sault College, Sault-Ste-Marie
64. Seneca College, Willowdale
65. Sheridan College, Oakville
66. Sir Sanford Fleming College,
    Peterborough

Quebec

67. Collège de L'abitibi-Temiscamique, Rouyn
68. Collège Ahuntsic, Montréal
69. Collège d'Alma, Alma
70. Collège André-Laurendeau, La Salle
71. Collège Bois-de Boulogne, Montréal
72. Champlain Regional College, Lennoxville
73. Collège de Chicoutimi, Chicoutimi
74. Dawson College, Montréal
75. Collège de Drummondville,
    Drummondville
76. Collège Edouard-Montpetit, Longueuil
77. Collège Francois-Xavier-Garneau,
    Sillery
78. Collège de la Gaspésie, Gaspé
79. Collège de Granby, Granby
80. Collège de Hauterive, Hauterive
81. John Abbott College,
    Saint-Anne-de-Bellevue
82. Collège de Joliette, Joliette
83. Collège de Jonquière, Jonquière
84. Collège de Lévis-Lauzon, Lauzon
85. Collège de Limoilou, Québec
86. Collège Lionel-Groulx, Ste-Thérèse
87. Collège de Maisonneuve, Montréal
88. Collège de Matane, Matane
89. Collège Montmorency, Laval
90. Collège de la Pocatière, La Pocatière
91. Collège de L'Outaouais, Hull
92. Collège de la Région de L'Amiante,
    Thetford Mines
93. Collège de Rimouski, Rimouski
94. Collège de Rivière-du-Loup,
    Rivière-du-Loup
95. Collège de Rosemont, Montréal
96. Collège de Saint-Félicien, Saint-Félicien
97. Collège de Sainte-Foy, Sainte-Foy
98. Collège de Sainte-Hyacinthe,
    Saint-Hyacinthe
99. Collège Saint-Jean-Sur-Richelieu,
    Saint-Jean-Sur-Richelieu

100. Collège de Saint-Jérôme,
     Saint Jérôme
101. Collège de Saint-Laurent, Saint-Laurent
102. Collège de Sept-Îles, Sept-Îles
103. Collège de Shawinigan, Shawinigan
104. Collège de Sherbrooke, Sherbrooke
105. Collège de Sorel-Tracy, Tracy
106. Collège de Trois-Rivières, Trois-Rivières
107. Collège de Valleyfield, Salaberry-de-
     Valleyfield
108. Vanier College, St. Laurent
109. Collège de Victoriaville, Victoriaville
110. Collège du Vieux-Montréal, Montréal

New Brunwick

111. N.B.C.C. Moncton, Moncton
112. N.B.C.C. Saint John, Saint John
113. N.B.C.C. Woodstock, Woodstock
114. N.B.C.C. St. Andrews, St. Andrews
115. N.B.C.C. Miramichi, Chatham
116. C.C.N.B. Bathurst, Bathurst
117. C.C.N.B. Cambellton, Campbellton

118. C.C.N.B. Edmundston, Edmundston
119. C.C.N.B. Sud-Est, Moncton

Prince Edward Island

120. Holland College, Charlottetown

Newfoundland and Labrador

121. Bay St. George Community College,
     Stephenville

Yukon Territory

122. Yukon College, Whitehorse

Northwest Territories

123. Arctic College, Fort Smith

B. OTHER PUBLIC POST-SECONDARY INSTITUTIONS

British Columbia

124. British Columbia Institute of Technology,
     Burnaby
125. Emily Carr College of Art and Design,
     Vancouver
126. Justice Institute of B.C., Vancouver
127. Open Learning Institute of B.C.,
     Richmond
128. Pacific Marine Training Institute,
     North Vancouver

Alberta

129. Northern Alberta Institute of
     Technology, Edmonton
130. Southern Alberta Institue of Technology,
     Calgary
131. Westerra Institute of Technology,
     Stoney Plain
132. Alberta Vocational Centre, Calgary
133.   "   "   "   Edmonton
134.   "   "   "   Grouard

135.   "   "   "   Lac La Biche
136. Alberta Petroleum Industry Training
     Centre, Edmonton

Saskatchewan

137. Kelsey Institute of Applied Arts and
     Science, Saskatoon
138. Prince Albert Technical Institute,
     Prince Albert
139. Saskatchewan Technical Institute,
     Moose Jaw
140. Wascana Institute of Applied Arts and
     Sciences, Regina

Ontario

141.* Ryerson Polytechnical Institute, Toronto
142. Ontario College of Art, Toronto
143. Toronto Institute of Medical Technology,
     Toronto

144. College de Technologie Agricole et Alimentaire d'Alfred, Alfred
145. Centralea College of Agricultural Technology, Huron Park
146. Kemptville College of Agricultural Technology, Kemptville
147. New Liskeard College of Agricultural Technology, New Liskeard
148. Ridgetown College of Agricultural Technology, Ridgetown

Quebec

149. Collège Marie-de-France, Montréal
150. Collège Stanislas, Montréal
151. Institut de Technologie Agricole, Saint-Hyacinthe
152. Institut de Technologie Agricole de la Pocatière, La Pocatière
153. Institut de Tourisme et d'Hotellerie, Montréal
154. Conservatoire de Musique de Chicoutimi, Chicoutimi
155. Conservatoire de Musique de Montréal, Montréal
156. Conservatoire de Musique de Québec, Québec
157. Conservatoire de Musique de Trois-Rivières, Trois-Rivières
158. Conservatoire de Musique de Hull, Hull
159. Conservatoire de Musique de Rimouski, Rimouski
160. Conservatoire de Musique de Val d'Or, Val d'Or

New Brunswick

161. Ecole des Pêches du Nouveau-Brunswick, Caraquet
162. Centre Universitaire Saint-Louis-Maillet, Edmundston
163. Maritime Forest Ranger School, Fredericton
164. New Brunswick Craft School, Fredericton
165. Institut de Memramcook, Sainte-Joseph
166. School of Medical Laboratory Technology, Saint John
167. School of Radiological Technology, Saint John
168. School of Radiological Technology, Moncton

Nova Scotia

169. Canadian Coast Guard College, Sydney
170. Nova Scotia Agricultural College, Truro
171. Nova Scotia Institute of Technology, Halifax
172. Nova Scotia Land Survey Institue, Lawrencetown
173. Nova Scotia Nautical Institute, Halifax
174. Nova Scotia Teachers College, Truro
175. University College of Cape Breton,* Sydney
* Also grants degrees

Newfoundland

176. Newfoundland and Labrador College of Trades and Technology, St. John's
177. Institute of Fisheries and Marine Technology, St. John's

C. PRIVATE POST-SECONDARY INSTITUTIONS

British Columbia

178. Columbia College,** Vancouver
179. New Summits College,** New Westminster

Alberta

180. Alberta College,** Edmonton

181. Camrose Lutheran College, Camrose
182. Canadian Union College,** College Heights
183. Concordia Lutheran College, Edmonton
184. The Kings College,** Edmonton
** both secondary and post-secondary

Quebec

185. Collège d'affaires Ellis, Drummondville
186. Collège André-Gasset, Montréal
187. Collège Bart, Québec
188. Collège Francais Inc., Montréal
189. Notre Dame Secretarial College, Montreal
190. O'Sullivan College, Montreal
191. Petit Séminaire de Québec, Québec
192. Séminaire Saint-Augustin, Cap-Rouge
193. Séminaire de St-Georges, Saint-George-de-Beauce
194. Collège St-Jean-de-Vianney, Montreal
195. Séminaire de Sherbrooke, Sherbrooke
196. Institut Téccart Inc., Montréal

197. Ecole de Musique Vincent-D'Indy, Montreal
198. Conservatoire Lasalle Inc., Montréal
199. Collège Jean-de-Brébeuf, Montréal
200. Collège Lafleche, Trois-Rivières
201. Collège Lasalle Inc., Montréal
202. Collège de L'Assomption, L'Assomption
203. Collège de Lévis, Lévis
204. Marianopolis College, Montréal
205. Collège Marie-Victorin, Montréal
206. Collège Mérici, Québec
207. Ecole Supérieure de Musique de Nicolet, Nicolet
208. Campus Notre-Dame-de-Foy, Cap-Rouge

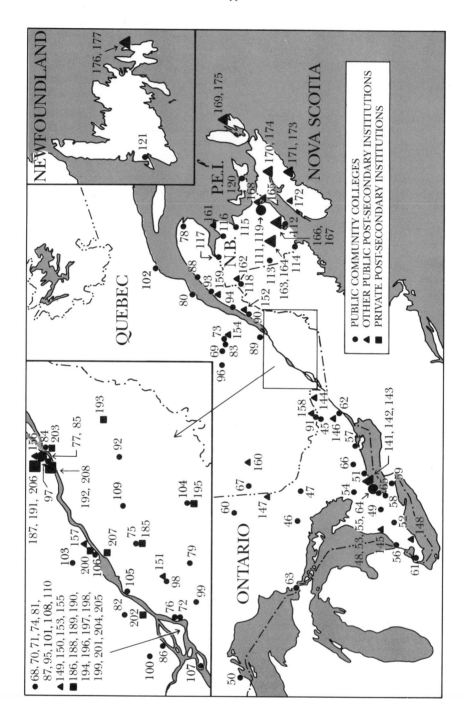

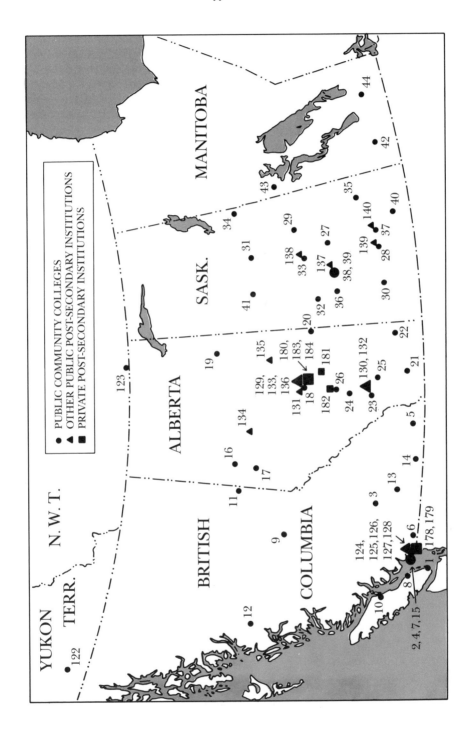

Appendix B

STATISTICAL INFORMATION—
COLLEGES IN CANADA

The three tables which follow have been presented to achieve two purposes. First, they provide a broad statistical picture of important aspects of post-secondary education in Canada. Secondly, they illustrate the relatively primitive national data base on non-university post-secondary institutions which has existed to 1985, and reveal why Statistics Canada has now decided to develop a much more complete data base for post-secondary education in Canada.

Table 1 provides full-time enrolment data by province and by programme category. Comparable data for part-time students and for the many college students not pursuing a college diploma or certificate were not compiled for 1982-83 or earlier years. In this table, community colleges refers to all non-university institutions, both public and private.

Table 2 provides a longitudinal perspective, in rounded figures, on enrolments by province in post-secondary programmes offered by all non-university post-secondary institutions in Canada. It should be noted that Trades, Vocational and Pre-Vocational enrolment data are not included in this table.

Table 3 provides a snapshot of full-time administrative and instructional personnel in the non-university sector of post-secondary education. It should be noted that one of the major characteristics of community college staffing in Canada is the very high proportion of part-time instructional personnel on whom no national data have been compiled.

TABLE 1

FULL-TIME ENROLMENT IN COMMUNITY COLLEGES, BY PROGRAMME
1982-83

	British Columbia	Alberta	Saskat-chewan	Manitoba	Ontario	Quebec	New Brunswick	Nova Scotia	Prince Edward Island	New found-land	Northwest Terri-tories	CANADA
POST-SECON-DARY LEVEL												
Career	11761	17418	2445	3609	89326	74547	2162	2834	905	2576	63	207651
University Transfer	8849	3372	27	-	-	75687	-	-	-	-	-	87935
TRADES OR VOCATIONAL												
Pre-Employment	14471	1811	2760	3311	33093	-	3192	273	573	3766	248	63498
Apprenticeship	6268	21048	914	2613	27154	-	2277	2591	218	894	226	64203
Skill Upgrading	7024	717	1190	1699	827	-	367	277	27	1224	-	13352
PRE-VOCATIONAL												
Acadmic Upgrading	7367	4572	316	1808	12215	-	999	-	169	448	103	27997
Second Language	2197	829	19	399	7789	-	69	-	11	-	-	11313
Other	-	210	101	617	-	-	1085	-	95	85	39	2232
TOTAL	57937	49977	7772	14056	170404	150234	10151	5975	1998	8993	684	478181

*SOURCE: *Statistics Canada Report Catalogue 81-222*

TABLE 2

FULL-TIME FALL ENROLMENT IN POST-SECONDARY PROGRAMMES,
BY PROVINCE AND YEAR *
(*in thousands*)

PROVINCE	1976	1977	1978	1979	1980	1981	1982
			Career Programmes				
Newfoundland	2.0	2.0	2.0	2.0	2.0	2.5	2.5
Prince Edward Island	1.0	1.0	1.0	1.0	1.0	1.0	1.0
Nova Scotia	3.0	2.5	2.5	2.5	2.5	2.5	3.0
New Brunswick	1.5	1.5	1.5	2.0	2.0	2.0	2.0
Quebec	55.0	61.5	66.0	66.5	67.0	69.0	74.5
Ontario	59.0	61.0	64.5	70.0	76.0	80.5	89.5
Manitoba	3.5	3.0	3.0	3.0	3.5	3.5	3.5
Saskatchewan	2.5	2.5	2.5	2.5	2.5	2.5	2.5
Alberta	14.0	14.5	15.0	15.5	15.5	16.0	17.5
British Columbia	9.0	9.5	9.5	10.0	10.5	11.0	12.0
CANADA	149.5	159.0	168.0	175.0	182.5	190.5	207.5
			University Transfer Programmes				
Quebec	66.0	72.5	71.5	67.5	68.5	72.5	75.5
Alberta	2.5	2.5	2.5	2.5	2.7	2.5	3.5
British Columbia	8.0	7.5	8.0	7.0	7.5	7.5	9.0
CANADA	76.5	83.0	82.0	77.0	78.5	83.0	88.0

*Source: *Statistics Canada Report Catalogue 81-222*

Appendix

TABLE 3

FULL-TIME COMMUNITY COLLEGE STAFF BY PROVINCE, PROGRAMME LEVEL, STAFF POSITION AND SEX*
1982-83

PROVINCE AND SEX		POST-SECONDARY Teaching	Administrative	TOTAL	TRADES-LEVEL Teaching	Administrative	TOTAL	Senior Administrative	Other Administrative
Newfoundland	M	103	16	121	89	4	94	2	-
	F	24	-	24	21	-	21	-	5
	T	127	16	145	110	4	115	2	5
Prince Edward	M	27	8	35	4	2	6	2	1
Island	F	12	1	13	6	-	6	-	1
	T	39	9	48	10	2	12	2	2
Nova Scotia	M	122	23	145	49	5	54	7	4
	F	33	5	38	1	-	1	1	2
	T	155	28	183	50	5	55	8	6
New Brunswick	M	108	12	123	171	7	179	16	5
	F	20	3	25	59	2	56	-	1
	T	128	15	148	225	9	235	16	6
Ontario	M	3036	550	3586	1543	45	1588	128	170
	F	1993	258	2252	412	11	423	50	169
	T	5029	808	5838	1955	56	2011	178	339
Manitoba	M	116	38	160	321	29	350	4	4
	F	71	10	89	94	12	106	1	6
	T	187	48	249	415	41	456	5	10
Saskatchewan	M	148	42	193	166	25	191	7	7
	F	154	11	170	23	2	25	1	4
	T	302	53	363	189	27	216	8	11
Alberta	M	1064	364	1458	544	91	637	30	26
	F	387	59	464	61	10	72	1	22
	T	1451	423	1922	605	101	709	31	48
British Columbia	M	1022	285	1354	366	62	428	36	45
	F	403	76	518	257	40	298	1	36
	T	1425	367	1872	623	102	726	37	81
CANADA	M	5746	1338	7175	3253	270	3527	232	262
	F	3097	423	3593	927	77	1008	55	246
	T	8843	1761	10768	4182	347	4535	287	508

* Adapted from Statistics Canada Report Catalogue 81-254.
  Does not include Quebec.

Appendix C

NATIONAL RESEARCH AGENDA QUESTIONNAIRE

1. Preparation for Employment
   a. Do graduates find jobs in fields related to their college programme?
   b. What is the relationship between skills specific to programmes and the reality of the workplace?
   c. In what geographic regions are graduates employed?
   d. What are income levels, by programme, by gender, and by location of job?
   e. What measures of quality of performance in the work place are obtainable?
   f. What is the relationship between a college diploma and long-term success in the workplace?
2. Preparation for Further Education
   a. To what extent do college students transfer to university, technical institute, or other post-secondary institutions?
   b. To what extent do students progress within levels of college education?
   c. What measures of success by transferring students are available?
   d. To what extent are college credits transferable to other institutions?
   e. What comparable measures of success exist between college transfer and non-transfer students?
3. Colleges and Community Life
   a. What evidence is available to indicate that colleges contribute to the quality of life in their communities?
   b. Are college personnel involved in cultural, intellectual, and recreational activities in the community?
   c. What degree of integration exists between the college and its community?
   d. To what extent are college facilities used by the community?
   e. What community projects involve college personnel?
4. Colleges as Agents for Democratizing Educational Opportunity
   a. Do colleges attract students from "new" segments of society?
   b. What data are available to indicate that colleges remove traditional barriers to further education?
      -educational/academic
      -geographic
      -socioeconomic and sociocultural

  -demographic, age, gender
  -ethnic
  -psychological
  -financial
   c. What are the aspirations of students entering the post-secondary education sector via the community college route?
5.   Organization of Instructional Time
   a. To what extent are college programmes, credit and credit-free, available on a part-time basis?
   b. What is the extent of part-time participation?
   c. What evidence of non-traditional timetabling of programmes is available?
   d. What are the barriers to part-time attendance?
   e. What variations in student progress exist between part-and full-time study?
   f. May all programmes be completed on a part-time basis?
   g. Do admission policies discriminate against part-time study?
6.   Access to College Programs
   a. What percentage of the community participates in college programmes?
   b. What programmes involve high or low community participation rates?
   c. What differences exist in participation rates by region, age, sociocultural, and ethnic criteria?
   d. What differences exist between participants and non-participants in college programmes?
   e. What are effects of employment opportunities upon participation rates?
   f. What are effects of decentralized college faculties, i.e., satellite campuses, upon participation rates?
   g. What are the characteristics of students who engage in college distance learning formats within a community?
   h. In which ways does the college encourage lifelong learning?
7.   Service to Community Agencies
   a. In what ways does the colleges serve the needs of hospitals, penitentiaries, senior citizen groups, social welfare agencies, cultural and recreational groups, native groups, and other groups within the community?
   b. To what extent is co-operative programming conducted with community agencies?
   c. How do community agencies view the college?
8.   Provision of New Learning Models
   a. To what extent does the college provide non-traditional learning opportunities, e.g., distance education, self-paced learning, tele-learning, satellite campus studies, other non-traditional opportunities?
   b. What is the success of non-conventional versus conventional models?
   c. What measures of cost effectiveness exist with regard to non-conventional models?
9.   Cooperation with Industry
   a. What barriers exist to improved co-ordination of training between the college and industry?
   b. What regulations, procedures, and practices exist in either industry or college which impede co-operation?
   c. What barriers to co-operation are presented by trade unions, provincial associations, or provincial statutes?
10.   Colleges as Teaching Institutions
   a. What evidence of professional development of personnel is available?

b. What measures of success of professional development programmes are available?

c. What techniques exist for the improvement of teaching?

d. What techniques exist for the evaluation of teaching?

e. What incentives exist for the improvement of teaching?

f. What is the evidence of the college's commitment to teaching?

g. How does the college assess the qualities of good teachers?

h. Do qualities of good teachers vary by programme?

11. Governance Issues

a. What is the range of community representation on the college governing board?

b. How do board members rank priorities in governance?

c. What measures exist of community input to the college board?

d. What differences in perception exist between government-appointed and "other" board members?

e. What are the advantages and disadvantages of broad participation on boards, i.e., faculty, students, and support staff?

f. What are the real powers of college boards?

g. What advantages, if any, accrue from the chief executive officer's full participation on the board?

h. What are the most critical roles of college boards?

i. Is there documentable evidence of "conflict of interest" on the college board?

j. What advantages or disadvantages accrue from a "senate-board" structure in a community college?

12. Community Orientation of Colleges

a. What evidence exists of community involvement in college planning?

b. What measures exist as to effectiveness of programme advisory committees?

c. What are the characteristics of members of programme advisory committees?

d. What channels exist for community input into college decision-making?

13. The Provision of General Education

a. What is the extent of general education in college programmes?

b. How is general education defined by the college?

c. What measurable benefits from a general education curriculum exist?

d. What are the attitudes of the board, administrators, faculty, and students towards general education?

e. What are the views of employer groups towards general education in a college curriculum?

f. Is there a "common core" within the curriculum of all programmes?

14. The Provision of Remedial Education

a. To what extent are learning assistance centres, adult literacy, basic remedial education and adult learning disability programmes integrated into the college curriculum?

b. What evidence exists of the progress of students from remedial programmes?

c. What priority is assigned by the college to remedial education programmes?

d. How do students in these programmes view their college experience?

e. What co-ordination exists between the school board and college board relating to adult basic education?

15. Counselling and Student Services

a. To what extent and for what reasons do students use student service programmes?

b. What are the effective qualifications of student services personnel?

c. How effective are counselling and similar services?

d. What are the expectations held by students of counselling services?

    e. What forms of evaluation of student services have been conducted?

    f. What is the extent and content of professional development programmes for student service personnel?

    g. What evaluation of the organization of student services has been carried out?

16. Collective Bargaining and Labour Relations

    a. What measures of the advantages and/or disadvantages accrue from faculty bargaining within the labour code of the province?

    b. What alternatives to labour code bargaining have been evaluated?

    c. What effects of labour code bargaining exist with regard to faculty and programme evaluation, programme and instructional innovation, and governance issues?

    d. What evaluation of centralized, decentralized or "two-tier" bargaining methods exist?

    e. What advantages and/or disadvantages accrue from placing all college personnel, academic and vocational teaching faculty and support staff, under one single bargaining unit?

17. Predictors of Success in Post-Secondary Education

    a. What student characteristics are predictive of success in various college programmes?

    b. What student characteristics are predictive of success in the workforce?

    c. What are the legitimate criteria for the selection of students for various programmes?

    d. Which pre-college experiences are predictive of success in various programmes?

18. Cost Variables for Different Programmes, Institutions, and Regions

    a. What are the operating costs for various programmes by institution?

    b. What are the administrative costs, instructional costs, support costs, and variable costs?

    c. What developmental, capital, and operating expenses are involved in the implementation of new programmes?

    d. What would be the financial impact of eliminating certain programmes?

19. Productivity and Efficiency Measures

    a. How many students, course enrolments, faculty, support staff, and administrative personnel are associated with each programme?

    b. What are the graduation, discontinuation, and failure rates for each programme?

    c. What are the workloads, student contact hours, hours of work, general working requirements, salaries, and fringe benefits for personnel involved in each programme?

    d. What is the financial impact of part-time student participation in a programme?

    e. What are the ratios between administrative, teaching, and support staff in each programme?

20. Return from Investment in Community Colleges

    a. What financial benefits accrue to the community from the presence of a college, e.g., wages, goods and services, lease and rent of facilities, taxes?

    b. What financial benefits accrue to the community from public and private funding of college programmes, e.g., co-operative programmes?

Appendix D

CANADA'S "FIRST" COMMUNITY COLLEGE

Although the answer to the question as to which institution could claim the distinction of being the first community college in Canada will depend upon the definition applied, there are two outstanding claimants to the title.

The Port Arthur Junior Chamber of Commerce, concerned over the lack of post-secondary educational facilities in that community, prepared a brief to the Minister of Education in Ontario in 1944. The institution requested was to be a Technical Institute, largely to serve the needs of the expanding industrial sector in the region. After an extended planning period, the Lakehead Technical Institute opened in January 1948 to accommodate grade twelve graduates. The curriculum consisted of diploma courses in mining, forestry, and industrial chemistry, first year courses of university equivalency, and advanced technology in the evening division.

In 1956, the Ontario legislature passed an act to establish the Lakehead College of Arts, Science, and Technology with its own board of governors. The curriculum continued to incorporate a variety of post-secondary programmes. In 1962, however, the college was awarded the right to confer degrees in the arts and sciences. The formal title of Lakehead University was awarded in 1965, but the institution continued to offer many diploma and certificate courses of a technical nature. The announcement of the creation of a system of colleges of applied arts and technology in Ontario in May, 1965, however, marked the formal termination of the facility as an institute of technology, under the terms of the Education Act.

Reference has been made (Chapter 2) to the circumstances which led to the creation of Lethbridge Community College in Alberta in 1958. In this case the inclusion of local funding argues for the status of a "community" college, in the strict sense of the term.

Cases can be made for both Lakehead and Lethbridge as the "first" community college in Canada. Both offered comprehensive curricula and responded to regional needs. Both were publicly funded and governed by regional boards—Lakehead by 1956, Lethbridge from its opening in 1959. Ironically, both provided the nucleus of future university-level institutions. By Canadian standards of non-university post-secondary education, Lakehead probably earns the title of the nation's first community college.*

*An excellent reference is an unpublished doctoral dissertation by Frederick Hamblin at The Ontario Institute for Studies in Education, 1984, entitled "An Analysis of the Policy Formulation Process Leading to the Establishment of the Colleges of Applied Arts and Technology of Ontario."

Notes

NOTES TO INTRODUCTION

1. Donald J. Wilson et al., *Canadian Education: A History* (Toronto: Prentice-Hall, 1970). See also C.E. Phillips *The Development of Education in Canada* (Toronto: Gage, 1957).
2. John Porter, "The Democratisation of the Canadian Universities and the Need for a National System," in *The Best of Times—The Worst of Times*, ed. Hugh A. Stevenson et al, (Toronto: Holt Rinehart Winston of Canada, 1972), p. 88. See also John Porter "The Economic Elite and the Social Structure of Canada," in *Canada: Sociological Profile*, ed. W.E. Mann (Toronto: Copp Clark, 1968), pp. 126-36.
3. David Munroe, "Post-Secondary Education in Canada: A Survey of Recent Trends and Developments," in *Post-Secondary Education in a Technological Society* ed. T.H. McLeod (Montreal: McGill-Queen's University Press, 1973), pp. 33-34. See also Ian Montagnes, *An Uncommon Fellowship: The Story of Hart House* (Toronto: University of Toronto Press, 1969).
4. Norman Henchey, "Quebec Education: The Unfinished Revolution," *McGill Journal of Education* 7, no. 2 (1972): 195.
5. Murray G. Ross, *The University: The Anatomy of Academe* (Toronto:McGraw-Hill, 1976), p. 51.
6. Sid Gilbert, "The Selection of Educational Aspirations," in *Education, Change, and Society: A Sociology of Canadian Education*, R.A. Carlton et al. (Toronto: Gage, 1977), pp. 284-85.
7. T.R. Morrison, "The Illusion of Education: Learning and Bureaucratized Schools," in *Options: Reforms and Alternatives for Canadian Education*, ed. T.R. Morrison and A. Burton, (Toronto: Holt Rinehart Winston, 1973), p. 234.
8. Phillips, *Development of Education in Canada*, pp. 106-9; 296-97.
9. S.D. Clark, "Canada and the American Value System," in *The Canadian Political Process*. Rev.ed. ed. O.M. Krulhak et al, Rev. ed. (Toronto: Holt Rinehart and Winston, 1973), p. 61.
10. Munroe, "Post-Secondary Education in Canada," p. 33.
11. "Reviews of National Policies for Education: Canada" (Paris: Organization for Economic Co-operation and Development, 1976), :72
12. Commission to the Association of Universities and Colleges of Canada, *Financing Higher Education in Canada* (Toronto: University of Toronto Press, 1965), p.11.
13. Ibid., pp. 6-7.
14. Ibid., pp. 56-66.
15. Gordon Campbell, *Community Colleges in Canada* (Toronto: Ryerson Press McGraw-Hill, 1971), pp. 1-10, 21-64.
16. "Reviews of National Policies for Education: Canada," 20.
17. Ibid., pp. 65-66.
18. Campbell, *Community Colleges in Canada*, pp. 75-76. See also Joseph Couture, "Conference Raises Call for Action," *College Canada* 2, no. 1 (1977): 1-2.
19. René Levesque, *An Option for Quebec* (Toronto: McClelland and Stewart, 1968), pp. 13-27.
20. Ludger Beauregard, *Le Quebec, vedette du*

regionalisme Canadien. Canadian Issues/Themes Canadiens (Ottawa: The Association for Canadian Studies, 1983).

21. Committee on the Future of Multicultural Education in Canada (Peter L. McCreath, editor). *Mainstreaming Multiculturalism in Canada: Challenges and Opportunities.* (Ottawa: Multiculturalism Canada, 1984).
22. Barry Lesser and Bruce Roald, *Canadians and Their Economy* (Halifax: Lighthouse Publications, 1982). See also Raoul Anderson, "Millions of Fish," *Canada and The Sea. Canadian Issues* 3, no. 1 (1980).
23. *Northern Frontier, Northern Homeland.* Report of the Mackenzie Valley Pipeline Inquiry, vol. I Mr. Justice Thomas Berger, Commissioner. (Ottawa, Supplies and Services, 1977).
24. Michael Jenkin, *The Challenge of Diversity: Industrial Policy in the Canadian Federation. Background Study 50* (Ottawa: Science Council of Canada, 1983).
25. M. Lamontagne, "The Loss of the Steady State," in *Beyond Industrial Growth*, ed. A. Rotstein (Toronto: University of Toronto Press, 1976), pp. 1-21.
26. Paul Anisef et al. *Losers and Winners* (Toronto: Butterworth, 1982).
27. "Reviews of National Policies for Education: Canada," p. 93.
28. George S. Tomkins, "Canadian Education and the Development of a National Consciousness: Historical and Contemporary Perspectives," in *Canadian Schools and Canadian Identity*, ed. A. Chaiton and N. McDonald (Toronto: Gage, 1977), pp. 6-28.
29. J. Killeen, "Address to the 1983 Annual General Meeting of the Canadian Teachers' Federation." Supplement no. 4 to *News.* Canadian College of Teachers. (Ottawa, 1984).

NOTES TO CHAPTER 1

1 .E.F. Sheffield, *Education in Canada* (Ottawa: Statistics Canada, 1962) pp. 64-66, and Z.E. Zsigmond and C.J. Wenaas, *Enrolment in Educational Institutions by Province, 1951-52 to 1980-81* (Ottawa: Economic Council of Canada, 1970).
2. P.M. Leslie, *Canadian Universities 1980 and Beyond* (Ottawa: Association of Universities and Colleges of Canada, 1980).
3. A.V. Pigott, *Education and Employment* (Canadian Conference on Education, Study 9, 1962).

4. E.F. Denison, *The Sources of Economic Growth in the U.S. and the Alternatives Before Us,* (New York: Committee for Economic Development, 1962); T.W. Schultz, "Investment in Human Capital," *American Economic Review* 51 (1961), no. 1:1-17; G.S. Becker *Human Capital: A Theoretical and Empirical Analysis* (Princeton: Princeton University Press, 1964); Economic Council of Canada, *Report, 1964.*
5. *The Land-Grant Act, 1862,* known as the Morrill Act in honour of its sponsor.
6. A.E. Soles, "Development of the Two Year College in British Columbia" (M.A. thesis, University of British Columbia, 1968), p.21.
7. Discussion of this point will be found in A.M. Cohen and F.B. Brawer, *The American Community College* (San Francisco: Jossey Bass, 1982).
8. Soles, "Development of the Two Year College."
9. American Association of Community and Junior Colleges, *Directory* (Washington, DC AACJC, 1981).
10. Soles, "Development of the Two Year College."
11. David Stager, *Federal Involvement in Post-Secondary Education for Highly Qualified Labour* (Ottawa: Supplies and Services Canada, 1981).

NOTES TO CHAPTER 2

1. D.E. Berghofer and A.S. Vladicka, "Access to Opportunity 1905-80," (Alberta: Advanced Education and Manpower, 1980).
2. Mount Royal, Saint-Jean, St. Joseph's.
3. Gordon Campbell, "History of the Alberta Community College System: 1957-69," (Ph.D. Dissertation, University of Calgary, 1972).
4. John C. Long, "The Transferability Issue in Alberta: A Case Study in the Politics of Higher Education," (Ph.D. Dissertation, University of Alberta, 1979).
5. S.V. Martorana, *A Community Plan for Lethbridge, Alberta* (Lethbridge: Lethbridge Collegiate Institute, 1951).
6. W.H. Johns, quoted in Campbell, "History of Alberta Community College System."
7. The School Act, Section 128 (1931), Province of Alberta.
8. The University of Alberta Calendar, Forty-Third Session 1950-51 (Edmonton: The University of Alberta, 1950).
9. "An Act to Provide for the Establishment of Public Junior Colleges" (Edmonton: Queens Printer, 1958).
10. Ibid., section 5.

11. Royal Commission on Education in Alberta, *Report*, (Edmonton: Queens Printer, 1959).
12. "The University and College Assistance Act, 1964."
13. Andrew Stewart, *Special Study on Junior Colleges* (Edmonton: Government of Alberta, 1965).
14. "An Act Respecting a Provincial College System" (Edmonton: The Queens Printer, 1969).
15. Victoria College, later the University of Victoria (1963).
16. Trinity Junior College, now Trinity Western College.
17. W.W.D. Knott, "The Junior College in British Columbia," (M.A. thesis, Stanford University, 1932).
18. Ibid., p. 46.
19. Ibid., p. 86.
20. Frank Beinder, "The Community College in British Columbia: The Emphasis is on Community," *Creating Citizens*. (Vancouver: Pacific Association of Continuing Education, 1984), p. 66.
21. Province of British Columbia, *Manual of School Law and Rules of Public Instruction*, (Victoria: Queens Printer, 1958), Chapter 42, Section 17 (O).
22. Ann Dawe, "The Kelowna Junior College Survey," (Kelowna: Kelowna Printing Co., 1959).
23. *Report of the Royal Commission on Education* (Vancouver: Queens Printer, 1960).
24. Dawe, "Kelowna Junior College," p. 129.
25. John B. Macdonald, *Higher Education in British Columbia and a Plan for the Future* (Vancouver: University of British Columbia, 1962), p. 8.
26. Ibid., p. 9.
27. B.C. School Trustees Association, "Brief to the Macdonald Committee," (Vancouver: B.C. School Trustees Association, 1962), p. 11.
28. Ibid., p. 14.
29. Senate of the University of British Columbia, "A Report of the Problem of Higher Education in British Columbia," 1962.
30. Ibid., p. 17.
31. Macdonald, *Higher Education*, p. 6.
32. Ibid., p. 19.
33. Ibid., p. 87.
34. Province of British Columbia, *Public Schools Act* (Victoria: Queens Printer, 1963).
35. Extensive discussion of these procedures may be found in A.E. Soles, "The Development of the Two-Year College in British Columbia" (M.A. thesis, University of B.C., 1968).
36. Beinder, "Community College in British Columbia," p. 65.
37. Royal Commission on Education in Ontario, *Report*, J.A. Hope, Chairman. (Toronto: King's Printer, 1950).
38. E.F. Sheffield, "Canadian University and College Enrollment Projected to 1965" (Ottawa: NCCU Proceedings, 1955), p. 44.
39. R.S. Harris, "The Evolution of a Provincial System of Higher Education in Ontario," in *On Higher Education: Five Lectures*, ed. D.F. Dodson (Toronto: University of Toronto Press, 1966).
40. Committee of Presidents of Provincially Assisted Universities. *Post-Secondary Education in Ontario 1962-70*. (Toronto, 1963).
41. Committee of Presidents of Provincially Assisted Universities and Colleges of Ontario. *The Structure of Post-Secondary Education in Ontario*. Supplementary Report No. 1, (Toronto, 1963).
42. Ibid., p. 16.
43. Ibid., p. 29.
44. *Report of the Grade 13 Study Committee*, F.A. Hamilton, Chairman. (Toronto: Department of Education, 1964).
45. The "Robarts Plan" had introduced into the secondary schools parallel academic and technical/vocational streams, partly as a means of obtaining federal funding through The Technical and Vocational Training Assistance Act of 1960.
46. Committee of Presidents of Provincially Assisted Universities and Colleges of Ontario. *The City College: Supplementary Report No. 2* (Toronto, 1965).
47. Ibid., p. 11.
48. Murray G. Ross, "Community Colleges and Adult Education," *Conference on Adult Education in Community Colleges: Report*. ed. John Cornish, Toronto: CAAE, 1965 (mimeograph). p. 29.
49. P.E. Bartram, "The Ontario Colleges of Applied Arts and Technology: A Review and Analysis of Selected Literature", (Ph.D dissertation, University of Toronto, 1980), p. 29.
50. Ontario Department of Education, *Colleges of Applied Arts and Technology: Basic Documents* (Toronto: Queens Printer, 1966), p. 4.
51. "Text of Ross Proposal for Dual Curriculum at Community Colleges," *Globe and Mail*, 19, March 1965.
52. Government of Canada, "An Act Respecting Technical and Vocational Training Assistance," (Ottawa: House of Commons, 1960).
53. G.T. Page, "Canada's Manpower Training and

Education: Federal Policy and Programmes," *Canadian Education and Research Digest*, 7, no. 4 (1967).

54. Ross, "Community Colleges.".

55. N. Sisco, "Canada's Manpower Training and Education: A View from Ontario," *Canadian Education and Research Digest*, 7, no. 4 (1967): 303.

56. Royal Commission of Inquiry on Education in the Province of Quebec, *Report*. Alphonse Marie Parent, Chairman. (Quebec: Les Presses Des Marais, 1963), 1:8.

57. Ibid., p. 11.

58. Quebec, Department of Education *College Education and the General and Vocational Colleges* (1968), p. 10.

59. Royal Commission on Education in Quebec, *Report* p. viii.

60. Ibid., Chapter 1.

61. Ann Denis and John Lipkin, "Quebec's CEGEP: Promise and Reality," *McGill Journal of Education*, 7, no. 2: 119-34.

62. C.W. Dickson, "Post-Secondary Education in Quebec," *The Teachers Magazine*, (January 1968): 8-12.

63. Royal Commission on Education in Quebec, *Report*, vol. 2, p. 159.

64. Ibid., p. 160.

65. Ibid., p. 161.

66. Ibid., p. 163.

67. Ibid., p. 166.

68. Ibid., p. 173.

69. Ibid., p. 180.

70. Quebec, Department of Education, *College education and the general and vocational colleges.*

71. D.A. Burgess, "The English Language CEGEP in Quebec," (Paper delivered at the CAPE Convention, Manitoba, 1970).

72. J.A. Whitelaw, "Quiet Revolution in Technical Education," *Canadian University*, 3, no. 4 (June 1968):18.

73. Patry et al. *Si CEGEP M'etait conte . . . Les Presses cooperatives.* (Sherbrooke, 1972). See also Paul Gallagher and Gertrude MacFarlane, *A Case Study in Democratic Education: Dawson College* (Montreal: Dawson College Press, 1976).

74. Mary Olga McKenna, "Higher Education in Transition," in *The Garden Transformed.* ed. V. Smitheram et al. (Charlottetown: Ragweed Press, 1982), p. 203.

75. Royal Commission on National Development in the Arts, Letters, and Sciences. *Report* (Ottawa: Queen's Printer, 1951).

76. Royal Commission on Higher Education for Prince Edward Island, *Report*. W. LaZerte, Chairman. (Charlottetown: Queen's Printer, 1965).

77. Department of Regional Economic Expansion. *Development Plan for Prince Edward Island* (Ottawa: Queen's Printer, 1969).

78. "Policy Statement on Post-Secondary Education," Hon. Alex B. Campbell, Premier, (Legislative Assembly, Prince Edward Island, 2 April 1968).

79. Ibid.

80. Holland College, *Diary of Holland College 1968-1979.*

81. *Post-Secondary Education in Manitoba: Report of the Task Force on Post-Secondary Education in Manitoba* (Winnipeg: Queen's Printer, 1973).

82. "A History of Community Colleges in Manitoba," *Review and Development* (Community Colleges Division, Department of Colleges and Universities Affairs, 1978).

83. Ibid., p. 7.

84. R. Faris, "Colleges without Walls but with Foundations: Integrated College and Communications Development in Saskatchewan," (Unpublished Speech, Lambton College, Ontario, 1974).

85. Royal Commission on Agriculture and Rural Life. *Report No. 6: Rural Education*, W.B. Baker, (Regina: Queen's Printer, 1956).

86. Ibid., p. 282.

87. E.A. Davies, Unpublished paper on History of Vocational Education in Saskatchewan, undated.

88. Government of Saskatchewan. Joint Committee on Higher Education, J.W. Spinks, Chairman. (Regina: Queen's Printer, 1967).

89. Special Provisional Committee on Higher Education, *Report to the Minister of Education* (Regina, 1970).

90. Province of Saskatchewan, *Report of the Minister's Advisory Committee on Community Colleges*, R. Faris, Chairman. (Regina: Department of Continuing Education, 1972).

91. Ibid., p. 7.

92. Province of Saskatchewan, *The Community Colleges Act* (Regina: Queen's Printer, 1973).

93. Faris, R., "Colleges without Walls," p. 12.

94. Royal Commission on Higher Education in New Brunswick, *Report*. John J. Deutsch, Chairman. (Fredericton: Queen's Printer, 1962).

95. Ibid., p. 20.

96. Ibid., p. 51.

97. Ibid., p. 52.

98. Ibid., p. 11.

99. Committee on the Financing of Higher Education in New Brunswick, *Report*. John J. Deutsch, Chairman. (Fredericton, New Brunswick, 1967).

100.New Brunswick Higher Education Commission, *First Annual Report, 1967-68*, pp. 1-2.

101.Higher Education in the Atlantic Provinces for the 1970's. John F. Crean, Chairman. (Halifax: Association of Atlantic Universities, 1969).

102.Ibid., p. 71.

103.*New Brunswick Community College: A Statement of Policy and Intent*, (Government of New Brunswick, 1974).

104.W.B. Thompson, "The New Brunswick Community College," *Canadian Vocational Journal*, 10, no. 4 (February 1975): 28-32.

105."*New Brunswick Community College: A Statement of Policy and Intent,*" p. 5.

106.Province of Nova Scotia, *Royal Commission on Education, Public Services and Provincial-Municipal Relations* (Halifax, Queen's Printer, 1974, chapter 61:5).

107.E.F. Sheffield, "The Post-War Surge in Post-Secondary Education" in *Canadian Education: A History*, ed. J.D. Wilson et al. (Scarborough: Prentice-Hall, 1970), p. 4,6.

108.Nova Scotia, *Royal Commission*.

109.Ibid., chapter 63:43.

110.Ibid., chapter 63:45

111H.P. Timmons, "Adult Education Services: 1945-76," *Journal of Education*, (Fall/Winter 1978):13.

112."History of Vocational Education in Nova Scotia," (unpublished paper, author unknown).

113.D. Glendenning, "A Review of Federal Legislation Relating to Technical and Vocational Education in Canada," (Unpublished manuscript, July 1965).

114.Jeffrey Holmes, "The Atlantic Provinces" in *Systems of Higher Education: Canada*, ed. E. Sheffield et al (New York International Council of Educational Development, 1978).

115.Frederick W. Rowe, *The Development of Education in Newfoundland*, (Toronto: Ryerson Press, 1964), p. 3.

116.Ibid.

117.Ibid., p. 170.

118.Dorothy Halleran, "History of Vocational Education in Newfoundland," (Unpublished paper, Education 4370, Memorial University, 1976).

119.Frederick W. Rowe, *Education and Culture in Newfoundland* (Toronto: McGraw-Hill, 1976), p. 126.

120.Royal Commission on Education and Youth, *Report*, (St. John's: The Commission, 1967-68), 2 v.

121.Ibid., p. 97.

NOTES TO CHAPTER 4

1. Paul Axelrod, "Higher Education, Utilitarianism, and the Acquisitive Society: Canada, 1930-80." (Paper presented at the Canadian History of Education Society Meeting, Vancouver, 1983). pp. 31-37.

2. David Dodge, *Returns to Investment in University Training: The Case of Canadian Accountants, Engineers and Scientists* (Kingston: Queens University, 1972).

3. Economic Council of Canada: *Annual Reviews 1964, 1971*. (Ottawa: Information Canada); Canadian Chartered Accountant. "Education and Training Power," October, 1963; *Imperial Oil Review*, September 1959; Kenneth Wilson, "The Business Community's Responsibility of Higher Education," *Monetary Times*, September 1964.

4. Axelrod, "Higher Education," p. 36.

5. "Secretary of State Launches Formal Consultations on Post Secondary Training Funding," (News Release. Secretary of State, Ottawa, 13 July 1982).

6. "Reviews of National Policies for Education—Canada," (Paris: Organization for Economic Co-operation and Development, 1976).

7. News Release, Secretary of State.

8. Parliament Committee, House of Commons, "Work for Tomorrow—Employment Opportunities for the 80's," Warren Allmand, Chairman, n.d.

9. Task Force on Labour Market Development, "Labour Market Developed in the 1980's," (Ottawa: Employment and Immigration Canada. 1981).

10. Bill C-115. The House of Commons of Canada. An act to establish a national programme for occupational training, as passed by the House of Commons 22 June 1982.

11. D.E. Berghofer, "Access to Opportunity 1905-1980," (Edmonton: Ministry of Advanced Education and Manpower, 1980).

12. Department of Advanced Education, *Statistical Report, 1982-83* (Edmonton: Province of Alberta).

13. Province of Alberta, *Colleges Act* (Edmonton: Government Printer, 1980).

14. Province of Alberta, *Technical Institutes Act 1981*, Edmonton, Alberta.

15. *Colleges Act 1980*, Section 4 (I) and (II).

16. *Colleges Act 1980*, Section 24.

17. Historical data on the topic has been compiled in a series of reports by Statistics Canada, Catalogue number 81-220.

18. UNESCO Statistical yearbook, 1980-81.
19. Frank Beinder, "The Community College in British Columbia: The Emphasis is on Community," (Nanaimo: Quadra Graphics, 1983).
20. Andrew Soles, "The Melding of the British Columbia Provincial Vocational Schools with the British Columbia Public Colleges,"—unpublished (Victoria, 1971).
21. Department of Education, Research and Development Division, "Towards the Learning Community," Hazel L'Estrange, Chairman (Victoria, 1974).
22. Government of British Columbia, "Institute of Technology (British Columbia) Act," (Victoria: Queen's Printer, 1974).
23. Ministry of Education, "Report of the Commission on Vocational, Technical and Trades Training in British Columbia," Dean Goard, Chairman. (Victoria, 1977).
24. Ministry of Education, "Report of Committee on Continuing and Community Education in British Columbia," Ron Faris, Chairman. (Victoria: 1976).
25. Government of British Columbia, "Colleges and Provincial Institutes Act," (Victoria: Ministry of Education, 1977).
26. Ministry of Education, "Integrated Five-Year Planning for the British Columbia College and Institute System: System Objectives 1983-87," (Post-Secondary Department [Operations and Planning], 1982).
27. Ministry of Education, Integrated Five-Year Planning, p. 5.
28. Paul Gallagher, "Community Colleges in British Columbia," CEGEPROPOS, vol. 85 (Montreal, 1983).
29. John D. Dennison et al., "A Study of Students from Academic Programmes in British Columbia's Community Colleges," Canadian Journal of Higher Education, 12, no. 1 (1982): 29-37 and "A Follow-Up Study of Career-Technical Students from British Columbia's Colleges and Institutes," Canadian Vocational Journal, 17, no. 4, (1982):18.
30. Students in the colleges in Ontario fall into the following categories: Post-secondary studies—i.e., technology programmes; National Training Act (Manpower) students—i.e., retraining; Apprenticeship Programmes; Part-time—continuing education students.
31. The term "parity of esteem" was first used in the "Report of the Commission on Post-Secondary Education in Ontario," D. Wright, Chairman. (Toronto: Queen's Printer, 1972).
32. G. Campbell, "Some Comments on Reports on Post-Secondary Commission in Relation to Community Colleges in Canada," The Canadian Journal of Higher Education, 3, no. 2 (1975).
33. W. Clark and A. Zsigmond, "Job Market Reality for Post-Secondary Graduates," (Ottawa: Statistics Canada, 1981); College Affairs Branch, Ministry of Colleges and Universities, "Multi-Year Plan Analysis," (Toronto, 1982); Commission on Post-Secondary Education in Ontario, The Learning Society, D. Wright, Chairman. (Toronto: Ministry of Government Services, 1972).
34. Government of Ontario, "Chapter 74: Colleges Collective Bargaining Act," (Toronto, 1972).
35. Ministry of Colleges and Universities, "Continuing Education in the Schools, Colleges and Universities of Ontario," (Toronto: Ministry of Education, 1983).
36. Association of Colleges of Applied Arts and Technology of Ontario, "Background Papers on Colleges Issues," (Toronto, 1982).
37. C.O. Klemp, "Three Factors of Success" in D.W. Vermilye ed., Relating Work and Education (San Francisco: Jossey Bass, 1977), pp. 102-9. J.S. Mill reported in Dissertation and Discussions: Political, Philosophical and Historical, Vol. 4 (London: Longmans, 1875), pp. 334-35.
38. Additional sources in support of this argument are: D.S. Goard, "General and Vocational Education," Discussion Paper (Ministry of Education, British Columbia, 1979); T.H. McLeod ed., Post-Secondary Education in a Technological Society (Montreal: McGill University Press, 1973); J. O'Toole, Work, Learning and the American Future (San Francisco: Jossey Bass, 1977); D.S. Saxon, "Liberal Education in a Technological Age," Science, 218, (1982); G.O. Klemp, "Three Factors of Success," in Relating Work and Education ed. D.W. Vermilye (San Francisco: Jossey Bass, 1977); E. Mumford, Values, Technology and Work (Boston: Maritimes Nyhoff, 1981); S. Serafina and M. Andrieu, The Information Revolution and its Implications for Canada, (Ottawa: Communication Economics Branch, 1980).
39. The comments made by Dr. Bette Stephenson, Minister of Education, in her closing address to the CMEC Conference on Post-Secondary Education reflect the issues which faced Ontario's colleges in 1982. Her observations are quoted, in part, in Chapter 8.

40. Ministry of Education: Province of Quebec; "Colleges in Quebec: A New Phase," (Government of Quebec, 1978), p. 13.
41. Ibid., Ch. 2.
42. Research and Development Service, DGEC.
43. "Colleges in Quebec," p. 5.
44. "Colleges in Quebec," p. 42.
45. Robert Isabelle, "Quebec Colleges: Provincial Colleges or Autonomous Institutions," (Quebec: Council of Colleges, 1982).
46. Ibid., p. 9
47. Interesting comment on this point is included in "Review of National Policies for Education," (Paris: Organization for Economic Co-operation and Development, 1976).
48. Ministere de l'Education (D.G.E.C.), *Le Réglement sur Le Régime Pedagogique du Collegial. Version Commentée.* (Quebec, 1984).
49. Government of Prince Edward Island, An Act to Amend the Holland College Act, (Charlottetown: Queen's Printer, 1977).
50. Lawrence Coffin, "In STEP with Holland College" in *Clientele and Community, A Yearbook of the Association of Canadian Community Colleges* ed. A.G. Konrad (Willowdale, 1974), pp. 51-57.
51. There are also three "branch" directors to which the chief executive officers report in specific circumstances. These three are responsible for Adminstration, Finance, and Programming, respectively.
52. While the Manitoba Government Employees Master Agreement covers all employees of the colleges, there are seven sub-agreements which apply to different groups, such as, instructional staff, secretaries, janitors, and A-V technicians.
53. Ministry of Continuing Education, *Tech-Voc 90*, (Regina, 1979).
54. Enrolment data based upon student count may be deceptive. If reported in terms of participant hours, the pattern is quite different, for example, adult basic education forty-five per cent, occupational training and university credit thirty per cent, and personal development twenty-four per cent.
55. Saskatchewan Community Colleges Trustees Association, *Saskatchewan Community Colleges Mandate Review*, (Saskatoon:. SCCTA, 1983).
56. Ibid., p. 10.
57. New Brunswick Community College, "Quinquennial Plan 1978-1983," (Fredericton, 1978), p. 361.
58. Government of New Brunswick, "New Brunswick Community College Act," (Chapter N-4.01), (Fredericton, 1980).
59. Government of New Brunswick, "An Act to Amend the New Brunswick Community College Act," (Fredericton, 1983).
60. Dalhousie, St. Mary's, Mount St. Vincent, Acadia, Kings College, St. Francis Xavier.
61. Royal Commission on Post-Secondary Education, 1982.
62. Government of Newfoundland, "Polytechnical Institute Act," (St. John's, 1977).
63. Government of Newfoundland, "An Act to Establish Bay St. George Community College," (St. John's, Newfoundland, 1977).
64. Newfoundland, Task Force on Education, "Improving the Quality of Education: Challenge and Opportunity," (St. John's: The Task Force, 1980).
65. Newfoundland, Royal Commission on Education and Youth, *Report*, (St. John's, The Commission, 1967-68), 2 vols.
66. D. Halleran, "History of Vocational Education in Newfoundland," (Paper, Education 4370, Memorial University, 1976). See also S. Alexander et al., "Vocational Education in Newfoundland and Labrador," *Canadian Vocational Journal*, 17, no. 2, 1981.
67. Much of the material for this section came from a report published by Pyramid Facilities Planning Ltd.
68. Government of Canada, "An Act respecting Technical and Vocational Training Assistance," (Ottawa: House of Commons, 1960).
69. Department of Education, Yukon Territory, "Yukon Teacher Education Programme," H.J. Weigal, Chairman. (Paper, dated March, 1982).
70. E.T. Ingram, A.G. Konrad and J.M. Small, "Toward a Yukon College. Continuing Education Opportunities in the Yukon," (University of Alberta: Department of Educational Administration, 1979).
71. The mandate for Yukon College reads as follows:

As the singular post-secondary institution funded directly by the Yukon Government, and as the operational matrix for all major post-secondary training and education for Yukon, Yukon College assumes primary responsibility for post-secondary delivery services to the adult peoples of Yukon. Within this mandate, Yukon College offers programming in various formats ranging from part-time to full-time; from centrally-delivered to community-based, mobile, and independent study; from short courses to programmes of one or more years' duration;

and from non-credit to credit and credit transfer. Programme and course disciplines include academic upgrading, Trades and Technical, Business and Applied Arts, and University Transfer.

72. Pyramid Facilities Planning Ltd. "Development Plan: Yukon College," (Calgary: Pyramid Facilities, 1984).

73. F. Heeley, "Thebacha College Should Decentralize Its Services to Allow Greater Accessibility for Students in the Northwest Territories." A position paper, (Department of Administrative, Adult and Higher Education, University of British Columbia, 1982).

74. Thebacha College Calendar, p. 3, 1984.

75. See Koenig, "Northern People and Higher Education," (1975).

76. Ibid.

77. Ibid.

78. Thebacha means "Below the Rapids" which refers to the condition of the Slave River at Fort Smith.

79. Koenig, "Northern People and Higher Education."

80. F. Heeley, "Distance Education Should Become an Integral Part of the Offerings from Thebacha College, N.W.T." A position paper (Department of Administrative, Adult and Higher Education, University of British Columbia, 1982).

81. See Dickinson on the potential roles for the Open Learning Institute.

82. Thebacha College Calendar, 1984.

83. An idea raised in discussion in the Thebacha Calendar, 1984.

NOTES TO CHAPTER 5

1. Walter Light, "Speech to the 1984 annual meeting of the shareholders of Northern Telecom Limited," *University Affairs.* (June/July 1984): 23.

2. Ralph Barrett et al., "Education, Technology and Labour," *College Canada,* vol. 9, no. 2, (1984): 6.

3. Fraser Mustard, "Advanced Research and Technology in Canada: Some Problems, Some Solutions," *Access* 2, no. 1, (1984):7-8.

4. "The Painful Realities of the new Technology— Annual Report on the Canadian Economy," *Saturday Night* 99, no. 7, (1984):24.

5. "Canadian Industrial Development: Some Policy Directions," Summary of Report 37. (Science Council of Canada, Ottawa, 1984), p. 1.

6. E.F. Roots, "Major Problems Confronting Society," *Social Sciences in Canada* 12, no. 1 (1984):7-10.

7. *Challenges and Choices,* Report of the Royal Commission on the Economic Union and Development Prospects for Canada, (Ottawa, 1984), p. 31.

8. Canada Employment and Immigration Advisory Council, "Youth Employment," (Ottawa, May 1984), p. 2.

9. Celine Hervieux-Payette, *Focus on Youth* (Ottawa: Employment and Immigration Canada, 1984), p. 27.

10. Bob Kuttner, "The Declining Middle," *Atlantic Monthly* (July 1983):60-72.

11. Skill Development Leave Task Force, "Learning a Living in Canada," 1. (Ottawa, 1983), p. 67.

12. Michael McCracken, Speech Presented at Canada Employment and Immigration Commission Workshop, Charting the Course to 1990, (Vancouver, 10 May 1984).

13. Ibid.

NOTES TO CHAPTER 6

1. Christopher Jencks and David Riesman, *The Academic Revolution* (New York: Doubleday, 1968). p. 28.

2. See Chapter 2.

3. *Rapport de la Commission Royale d'enquete sur l'enseignement dans La Province de Quebec.* Quebec: l'Imprimerie Pierre les Marais, Tome I, 1963; Tome II et III, 1964; Tome IV et V, 1966).

4. Douglas Lawr and Robert Gidney, eds., *Educating Canadians—A Documentary History of Public Education* (Toronto: Van Nostrand Reinhold, 1973). pp. 242-43, 264. See also The Ontario section of Chapter 2.

5. Margaret Gayfer, *An Overview of Canadian Education,* (Toronto: The Canadian Education Association, 1974). See also John Dennison, "The Canadian Community College in the 1980's: Strategies for Survival." *Canadian Journal of Education* 9, no. 2. (1984).

6. *College Canada* 1. no. 7. (1970/1971).

7. Paul Anisef, Norman Ikihiro, and Carl James, *Losers and Winners* (Toronto: Butterworth, 1982).

8. Keith Goldhammer, "Higher Education: Beacon or Mirror." Proceedings of the Pacific Northwest Conference on Higher Education at University of Calgary. (Corvallis: Ore-

gon State University Press, 1978).

9. Gordon Selman, "The British Columbia Division of The Canadian Association for Adult Education 1961-1971." Occasional Paper No. 7. (Vancouver: Pacific Association for Continuing Education, 1980). See also Audrey M. Thomas, "Adult Illiteracy in Canada—A Challenge, (Ottawa: Canadian Commission for UNESCO, Occasional Paper 42, 1983).

10. Thomas E. O'Connell, *Community Colleges—A President's View* (Chicago: University of Illinois Press, 1968).

11. "Learning at a Distance and The New Technology," (Vancouver: Educational Research Institute of British Columbia, 1982). pp. 22-24.

12. See Chapter 2 (Saskatchewan).

13. Douglas T. Kenny, *The Mission of the University of British Columbia* (Vancouver: University of British Columbia, 1979).

14. Brian Buchanan, Letter to the Editor, The Vancouver *Sun*, 19 June 1984.

15. Audrey M. Thomas, "Adult Illiteracy in Canada—A Challenge." (Ottawa: Canadian Commission of UNESCO, Occasional Paper 42, 1983).

16. Bill Turney, "Living with CEGEPS—As Assessment Ten Years After," *Montreal Review* 9, (September, 1981). See also Association of Colleges of Applied Arts and Technology of Ontario, "Ontario's Community Colleges—A Success Story Worth Knowing," n.d.

17. "The CAAT's Next Decade: A View From the Top," An interview with James Colvin, Laurent Isabelle and Dorothy Rowles by the Editor of OCLEA. 7, Toronto, (1976). See also "Post-Secondary Education in British Columbia—An Investment in Our Future," (Victoria: Ministry of Education, Science and Technology, 1979).

18. Ibid.

19. "ACCC Awarded $70,000 in CIDA Funds for International Office," *College Canada* (February, 1977).

20. David Williamson, "Introduction." *Journal of the Association of Canadian Community Colleges* 2, no. 2. (1978). See also Carol Vander Well, "Alberta Colleges: A Product of Their Times," *College Canada* 2, no. 7 (1977).

21. Elena M. Smith, "Equal Access to College: A Case Study," *Journal of the Association of Canadian Community Colleges* 2,no. 4. (1978). See also Claude Escande, "Les Classes Sociales au CEGEP. parti Pris," (Montreal, 1973).

22. "Reviews of National Policies for Education—Canada," (Paris: O.E.C.D, 1976), p. 20.

23. Leonard Shifrin, "Redistributing the Work,"

The Sun, 14 July 1984, p. A6.

24. Celene Hervieux-Payette, "Focus on Youth," Ottawa, 1984.

25. Frank Beinder, "The Emphasis is on Community: The Community College in British Columbia" in Frank Cassidy, *Creating Citizens*. (Vancouver: Pacific Association of Continuing Education, 1984), pp. 65-83.

26. John Naisbitt, *Megatrends* (New York: Warner, 1982), pp. 39-54.

27. "Youth Employment," Report to the Minister of Employment and Immigration Canada by the Canada Employment and Immigration Advisory Council (Ottawa, May 1984), p. 3.

28. Edgar Faure et al., *Learning to Be. The World of Education Today and Tomorrow* (Paris, UNESCO, 1972).

29. A.J. Cropley, *Lifelong Education. A Psychological Analysis* (Oxford, Pergamon Press 1979), p. 21.

30. Richard E. Peterson et al., *Lifelong Learning in America* (San Francisco: Jossey-Bass, 1979), p. 5.

31. Report of the Royal Commission on the Economic Union and Development Prospects in Canada, "Challenges and Choices," (Ottawa, 1984), pp. 46-49.

32. *From the Adult's Point of View*, (Toronto: Canadian Association for Adult Education and L'Institut canadien d'education des adultes, 1982). See also *Learning a Living in Canada*, Report of the National Advisory Panel on Skill Development Leave (Ottawa: Supplies and Services Canada, 1984).

33. Skill Development Leave Task Force, *Living a Learning in Canada* 1 and 2. Report to the Minister of Employment and Immigration Canada. Ottawa, 1983.

34. Peterson, *Lifelong Learning*, pp. 8-9.

35. Per Himmelstrup et al., eds., *Strategies for Lifelong Learning*, Esbjerg, 1981, p. 22.

NOTES TO CHAPTER 7

1. Frederick Enns, *The Legal Status of the Canadian School Board* (Toronto: Macmillan, 1963), p. 5.

2. Margaret Gayfer, *An Overview of Canadian Education* (Toronto: The Canadian Education Association, 1974). pp. 23-25.

3. David J. Bercuson et al., *The Great Brain Robbery* (Toronto: McClelland and Stewart, 1984).

4. Gordon Campbell, *The Community College in Canada* (Ottawa: Universities and Colleges of Canada, AUCC), 1971).

5. A.G. Konrad, ed., *Clientele and Community* (Willowdale: Association of Canadian Community Colleges, 1977).

6. Constitution Act, 1982.

7. L.C. Robbins, *Higher Education Revisited* (London: MacMillan, 1980), p. 90.

8. W.M. Sibley, "The Role of Intermediary Bodies in Post-Secondary Education," *Post-secondary Education Issues in the 1980's* (Toronto: Council of Ministers of Education, 1983), p. 144. See also John Calder, "Lessons from the Death of a Quango," *The Canadian Journal of Higher Education.* 14 (1984): 2.

9. David Stager, *Federal Involvement in Post-Secondary Education for Highly Qualified Training* (Ottawa: Supplies and Services, 1981).

10. A comprehensive reference on this issue is D.M. Nowlan and R. Bellaire, eds., *Financing Canadian Universities: For Whom and By Whom?* (Institute for Policy Analysis, University of Toronto, 1981).

11. Access to research grants by the Social Services and Humanities Research Council and by the Canadian Studies Programme in the federal Secretary of State are two examples.

12. D.R. Young and A.V. Machinski, *An Historical Survey of Vocational Education in Canada* (Ottawa: Canadian Vocational Association, n.d.).

13. Ibid., p. 53.

14. Gayfer, *Overview of Canadian Education,* p. 24.

15. Konrad, *Clientele and Community,* p. 35.

16. Robert Isabelle, "L'autonomie. Il faut redefinir les relations entre l'Etat et les colleges, *Le Devoir.* (27 janvier 1984): 24.

17. J.A. Corry, "Jurisdiction Under the Constitution in Education in Canada," as quoted in *Reviews of National Policies for Education—Canada.* (Paris: OECD 1976), p. 96.

18. Ernest L. Boyer, "Managing Tomorrow's Education." *Challenge to Leadership—Managing in a Changing World.* Edward C. Bursk, ed., (New York: New York Free Press, 1973), pp. 170-71.

19. Barry D. Moore, "A Matter of Principal," Paper prepared for the British Columbia Council of College and Institute Principals. (Abbotsford, B.C.: Fraser Valley College, 1980.)

20. Paul L. Dressel, *Administrative Leadership* (San Francisco: Jossey-Bass, 1981). See also James Hammons, ed., *Organization Development: Change Strategies* (San Francisco: Jossey-Bass, 1982).

21. G.O. Kelly, "Participation in College Governance," (Ph.d. dissertation. University of Alberta, 1973).

22. William G. Ouchi, *Theory Z* (Reading, MA: Addison-Wesley Publishing, 1981.)

23. Arthur M. Cohen and Florence B. Brawer, *The American Community College* (San Francisco: Jossey-Bass, 1982). See Chapter 4, "Governance and Administration," in particular.

24. Boyer. "Managing Tomorrow's Education," p. 157.

25. Thomas J. Peters and Robert H. Waterman, *In Search of Excellence* (New York: Harper and Row), 1982.

26. Boyer, "Managing Tomorrow's Education," p. 151.

27. Christopher Jencks and David Riesman, *The Academic Revolution.* (New York: Doubleday, 1968).

28. Robert Arnold Russel, "Toward 2000—Economic History Revisited," *Executive* 26, no. 1 (1984).

29. G.B. Kilcup, "Collegiality: A Twentieth Century Myth," (Paper, University of British Columbia, 1982).

30. Peters and Waterman, *In Search of Excellence,* pp. 200-35.

31. College and Provincial Institute Act. (British Columbia, 1979).

32. Charles E. Phillips, *The Development of Education in Canada* (Toronto: Gage, 1957).

33. Kelly, "Participation in College Governance," p. 46.

34. Peters and Waterman, *In Search of Excellence.*

35. Ibid.

36. Robert A. Gordon, "Leadership: A Personal Perspective," *Journal of the Association of Canadian Community Colleges* 4, no. 1, 2. (1980): 53-65.

37. Mike Sasges, "Fighting the Battle of the Budget." *Alumni UBC Chronicle,* (Summer 1984).

38. Roald Campbell, "The Emerging Role of the Educational Leader," (Paper prepared for Symposium on Educational Leadership for the Eighties, Simon Fraser University, British Columbia, 1979).

39. Gordon, "Leadership: A Personal Perspective."

40. Campbell, "The Emerging Role."

41. B. Barlow, "Labour Relations in New Brunswick," *College Canada,* (Nov./Dec. 1981):17.

42. References on this point include Tice and Holmes (1973), Millett (1978), Carr and Van Eyck (1973), Corson (1975), Kemerer and Balridge (1975), Birnbaum (1980), Ladd and

Lipset (1973), Feller and Finkin (1977).

43. B.I. Adell and D.D. Carter, *Collective Bargaining for University Faculty in Canada*, (Kingston: Queens University, 1972).

44. College Canada, (Nov./Dec. 1981), published by the Association of Canadian Community Colleges.

45. J.M. Porter, "Is Professionalism Possible in a Union Setting?" *College Canada* (Nov./Dec 1981): 4-6.

46. R.V. Barrett, "The Union Makes Us Strong . . . Professional?" *College Canada* (Nov./Dec 1982): 6-7.

47. M. Thompson, "Collective Bargaining by Professionals," in J. Anderson and M. Gunderson, *Union-Management Relations in Canada* (Don Mills: Addison Wesley, 1982), p. 382.

48. Bercuson et al., *Great Brain Robbery*.

49. J. Handel, "Faculty Versus Board: The Influence of Provincial Legislation in Alberta College Governance and Labor Relations," (Manuscript; The Department of Educational Administration, The University of Alberta, 1982).

50. S. Vallance, "Across the Great Divide" *College Canada* (Nov./Dec. 1981): 9.

51. F.R. Kemerer and J.V. Baldridge, *Unions on Campus*, (San Francisco: Jossey-Bass, 1985).

NOTES TO CHAPTER 8

1. Publications in which discussion of this question occur include Dennison (1971 and 1974); Konrad (1974); Campbell (1971); and Burgess (1971).

2. N.S. Glasman and W.H. Gmelch, "Purposes of Evaluation of University Instructors: Definitions, Delineations and Dimensions," *Canadian Journal of Higher Education*, 6, (1976): 37-55.

3. F.R. Kemerer and J.V. Baldridge *Unions on Campus* (San Francisco: Jossey-Bass, 1975).

4. J.D. Dennison, G. Jones, and G. Forrester, "A Study of Students from Academic Programmes in British Columbia's Community Colleges," *The Canadian Journal of Higher Education*, 12, no. 1 (1982): 29-41.

5. See Bausell and Magoon (1972); Centra (1977 and 1979); Dwyer (1973); Gessner (1973); Glasman and Gmelch (1976); Kulek and McKeachie (1975); Miller (1975); Smock and Crooks (1973); Wood and De Lorme (1976); and Patterson (1980).

6. Capilano College in North Vancouver is but

one example of an institution whose instructional performance plan is incorporated into the collective agreement between the college and its faculty association.

7. For a discussion of the problem of part-time faculty refer to Ruth McLean, "Professional Development and the Part-Time Faculty," *Journal of the Association of Canadian Community Colleges*, 2, no. 1 (Spring, 1978): 105-14.

8. See Reindeau (1977), Stone (1981), Campbell (1977).

9. STEP (Self Training and Evaluative Process) is discussed in L. Coffin "In STEP with Holland College," in *Clientele and Community, The Yearbook of the Association of Canadian Community Colleges*, (1974).

10. *Professional Development* (Algonquin College, Ottawa, 1984).

11. References on this topic include McLean (1978), Shore (1974), Galowtiz (1979), Stone (1981), and Konrad, Long and Small (1976), Riendeau (1977), Campbell (1972), Konrad (1973), Morphy (1979), Blake (1980).

12. Contacts for the project include M. P. J. Kennedy (Kelsey Institute, Saskatoon) and Grant Kelly (Vancouver Community College).

13. Ruth Smith, "Professional Development Activities in British Columbia Colleges," (Unpublished Paper, The University of British Columbia, 1984).

14. The Coombe Lodge experience is discussed by Gerald Kelly in "College Management Development in the Coombe Lodge Experience," *Journal of the Association of Canadian Community Colleges*, 4, no. 1 (Winter 1980): 67-76.

15. Programmes developed by Diane Morrison, Coordinator of Programme and Professional Development, Ministry of Education, British Columbia.

16. Henry Mintzberg, ed., "The Professional Bureaucracy," in *The Structuring of Organizations* (New Jersey: Prentice Hall, 1979), p. 357.

17. Comments on this point provided by Grant Kelly, Vancouver Community College, in a personal communication.

18. Mintzberg, "Professional Bureaucracy," p. 349.

19. References on this point include Dennison (1974) and Barman Sidorenko (1979).

20. M. Oliver et al., Post-Secondary Education in Manitoba: Report of the Task Force," (Winnipeg: Department of Colleges and Universities Affairs, Government of Manitoba, 1973).

21. Excellent examples of the utilization of individual faculty are in *Revitalizing Teaching*

Through Faculty Development, Paul Lacey, ed., *New Directions for Teaching and Learning* (San Francisco: Jossey-Bass, 1983).

22. Nathalie Sorensen, *General Education in Canada's Community Colleges and Institutes* (Toronto: Canadian Studies Bureau, Association of Canadian Community Colleges, 1984).

23. Y. Masuda, *The Information Society* (Tokyo: Institute for the Information Society, 1980, 57).

24. C.F. Conrad, *At the Crossroads: General Education in Community Colleges,* (Washington: American Association of Community and Junior Colleges, 1983).

25. C.F. Conrad and J.C. Wyer, *Liberal Education in Transition,* Research Report No. 2. Washington, D.C. American Association for Higher Education/ERIC Clearing house on Higher Education, 1980.

26. W. Boyd, *The History of Western Education* (New York: Barnes and Noble, 1966).

27. R.F. Butts, *The College Charts its Course* (New York: McGraw Hill, 1938).

28. A. Levine, *Handbook on Undergraduate Curriculum* (San Francisco: Jossey-Bass, 1979).

29. C.R. Monroe, *Profile of the Community College,* (San Francisco: Jossey-Bass, 1976).

30. J.S. Brubacher and W. Rudy, *Higher Education in Transition,* (New York: Harper and Row, 1968).

31. Conrad, *At the Crossroads,* p. 6.

32. Ibid., 56.

33. C.H. Faust, *Ideas and Practice of General Education,* (Chicago: University of Chicago Press, 1930), p. 6.

34. R.M. Hutchins, *Some Observations on American Education* (Cambridge: Cambridge University Press, 1956). p. 59.

35. E.J. McGrath, *General Education and the Plight of Modern Man* (Indianapolis: Lilly Endowment, 1976), p. 25.

36. Levine, *Undergraduate Curriculum.*

37. L.L. Medsker, *The Junior College: Progress and Prospect* (New York: McGraw-Hill, 1960), p. 37.

38. J.S. Brubacher, *On the Philosophy of Higher Education* (San Francisco: Jossey-Bass, 1982), p. 85.

39. S. Hook et al., *The Philosophy of the Curriculum* (New York: Prometheus Books, 1973).

40. J.D. Dennison et al., *The Impact of Community Colleges: A Study of the College Concept in British Columbia* (Vancouver: B.C. Research, 1975).

41. Discussion on this point may be found in a variety of sources, e.g., D.S. Goard, "General and Vocational Education," Discussion Paper, Ministry of Education, British Columbia, 1979; T.H. McLeod, ed., *Post-Secondary Education in a Technological Society* (Montreal: McGill University Press, 1973); J. O'Toole, *Work, Learning and the American Future* (San Francisco: Jossey-Bass, 1977); D.S. Saxon, "Liberal Education in a Technological Age," *Science* 218 (Nov. 1982); G.O. Klemp, "Three Factors of Success," in D.W. Vermilye, ed., *Relating Work and Education* (San Francisco: Jossey Bass, 1977); E, Mumford, *Values, Technology and Work* (Boston: Maritimes Nyhoff, 1981); S. Serafina, and M. Andrieu, *The Information Revolution and its Implications for Canada* (Ottawa: Communication Economics Branch, 1980).

42. Hook, *Philosophy of the Curriculum,* p. 29.

42. Sorensen, *General Education.*

44. References on this topic include J.P. Bogue, *The Community College* (New York: McGraw-Hill, 1950). J.W. Thornton, "Why General Education?" *Junior College Journal,* May 1955, p. 25. G.B. Vaughan, *Issues for Community College Leaders in a New Era* (San Francisco: Jossey-Bass, 1983). J.G. Rice, ed., *General Education: Current Issues and Concerns* (Washington, D.C., National Education Association, 1964).

45. Academic Board for Higher Education in British Columbia, "The Role of District and Regional Colleges in the British Columbia System of Higher Education," (Vancouver: The Academic Board, 1965).

46. A.E. Soles, "The Melding of the British Columbia Provincial Vocational Schools with the British Columbia Public Colleges," (Unpublished paper, Victoria: Ministry of Education, 1971), p. 6.

47. W.B. Whale and L.A. Riderer, "Colleges that Encourage Life-Long Learning" in *Clientele and Community,* ed. .A.G. Konrad, (Toronto: Association of Canadian Community Colleges, 1974).

48. W. Davis, *Basic Documents: Colleges of Applied Arts and Technology* (Toronto: Ontario, Department of Education, 1965).

49. Sources from which these quotes come are: The Role of Holland College, a position paper produced by the Administration of the College, Prince Edward Island, 1969. Objectives for Manitoba's Colleges, produced by the Department of Continuing Education, Manitoba, 1979. Quinquennial Plan, Ministry of Continuing Education, New Brunswick, 1978.

50. Association of Colleges of Applied Arts and

Technology of Ontario, "Background Papers on Current Issues," (Toronto: ACAATO, 1980).

51. Management Services Division, "Formula Funding for Colleges and Universities in British Columbia," (Unpublished Report, Victoria: Ministry of Education, 1983).

52. Education Documents: College Education and the General and Vocational Colleges, (Quebec: Quebec Department of Education, 1968).

53. Report of the Royal Commission of Inquiry on Education in the Province of Quebec: Alphonse-Marie Parent, Chairman (Quebec: Province of Quebec, 1963).

54. Government of Quebec, "Colleges in Quebec: A New Phase," (Quebec: Ministry of Education, 1978.

55. Government of Quebec, "Colleges in Quebec," p. 39.

56. Grant MacEwan Community College, "General Education; A Plan for Implementation," Report, T.C. Day ed., (Edmonton, 1983), p. 12.

57. B. Stephenson, "Closing Address: CMEC Conference on Post-Secondary Education," (Toronto: Council of Ministers of Education, Canada, 1982), p. 254.

58. P. Dawson, "The Employer's Perception: CMEC Conference on Post-Secondary Education," (Toronto: Council of Ministers of Education, Canada, 1982), p. 108.

59. Max Von ZurMuehlen, Letter to the Editor, *Maclean's* 97, no. 42 (15 October 1984) See also Appendix B.

60. P.L. Dressell, *Handbook of Academic Evaluation,* (San Francisco: Jossey Bass, 1976), p. 175.

61. Studies in this category include those from Ontario: King, (1977); Van Nest and Warren, (1979); Wyman and De Metra, (1980); Geroux and Franklyn, (1978); Krakana, (1978); Gates, (1979); Klein, (1978); Quebec: Gingris, (1979); Donald, (1970); Hamil, (1978); British Columbia: Fisher, (1978); Isbister, (1979); Gallagher, (1979); Fraser, (1979); Cousineau, (1983); and Alberta: Konrad, (1981); Souch and Fahy, (1979).

62. Comment on this point is presented in Walter Stewart, "The Capilano College Self Study," unpublished paper.

63. This statement is taken from a college calendar. The name of the college is irrelevant.

64. Department of Post-Secondary Education: Operations and Planning "Comparison of Post-secondary Department Mission and Goals with Institutional Goals Extracted from the Five-Year Educational Plans" (Unpub-

lished Report, Victoria: Ministry of Education 1981).

65. W. Wyman and G. De Metra, "Who Controls Programme Quality?" *College Canada,* 5, no. 7 (October 1980): 4.

66. Government of British Columbia. College and Institute Act, (Victoria: Queens Printer, 1977).

67. Ontario Council of Regents for the Colleges of Applied Arts and Technology, *Basic Documents* (Toronto, January 1983).

68. British Columbia Council of College and Institute Principals. "Institutional Evaluation Process for British Columbia Colleges and Institutes: Policies and Procedures Manual," Kathleen Bigsby, ed., (Vancouver, 1984). See also D.K. Dary, "An Analysis of Institutional Evaluation in the British Columbia College and Institute System," (Unpublished report, Victoria: University of Victoria, 1982).

69. S. Souch and P. Fahy, "Self-Study in Alberta: Preliminary Report," *Journal of the Association of Canadian Community Colleges,* 3, no. 3 (Autumn 1979): 34-36.

70. British Columbia Council of College and Institute Principals. "Institutional Evaluation Process."

71. J.G. Donald, "The Psychodynamics of Evaluation," *Journal of the Association of Canadian Community Colleges,* 2, no. 1 (Spring 1978): 34-37.

72. M. Krakana, "Participatory Evaluation and the Decision Making Process," *Journal of the Association of Canadian Community Colleges,* 2, no. 3 (Autumn, 1978): 106-10.

73. J.M. Small et al., *Renewal in Post-Secondary Institutions: An Analysis of Strategies* (Edmonton, University of Alberta, 1976). p. 23.

74. N.E. Gleadow, "An Evaluation and Meta-evaluation of the Malaspina College Self-Study," (Unpublished Manuscript, Nanaimo: Malaspina College, 1980).

75. H.R. Bowen, *Investment in Learning: The Individual and Social Value of American Higher Education* (San Francisco: Jossey-Bass, 1977), p. 18.

76. Ibid., p. 448.

77. Issues of Vol. 1 of *College Canada* were published in 1969-70 prior to the establishment of The Association of Canadian Community Colleges. It has been published continuously since that year by the association.

78. Vol. 1, no. 1 of the *Journal of the Association of Canadian Community Colleges* was published in Spring 1977. Vol. 5, no. 1 was published in Winter 1981 as a report on the Association's

national conference of 1980. Some ACCC Yearbooks (the first in 1974) also attempted to meet the need for scholarly publication within the college sector in Canada.

79. John R.A. Dobson, ed., *The Study of People, Programmes, Places and Processes: Canadian Adult Education Literature 1974-1984*. Canadian Association for the Study of Adult Education. (Antigonish: St. Francis Xavier University, 1984).

80. *The Canadian Journal of Higher Education* has listed all articles related to community colleges from Vol. 1 (1971) to Vol. 13 (1983). Only two authors are identified as community college staff members.

81. See Statistics Canada Reports 81-222 and 81-254: "Enrolment in Community Colleges and Educational Staff of Community Colleges or Vocational Schools."

82. Particular references to the work of the Department of the Secretary of State include: "Job Market Reality for Post-Secondary Graduates," by W. Clark and Z. Zsigmond, and "Post-Secondary Student Survey" both conducted by Statistics Canada.

NOTES TO CHAPTER 9

1. B.E. Curtis, 'The Developing Colleges—A Background Paper," *College Canada*, 1, no. 6, 1970.
2. Ibid.
3. Ibid.
4. "The Canadian Commission for the Community College," Press Release of the Canadian Commission for the Community College. (Toronto: Corbett House. n.d.)
5. Ibid.
6. "The Colleges Assembly—Verbatem Report". *College Canada* 1, no.7, (1970/1971).
7. Curtis, "Developing Colleges," p. 3.
8. Ibid.
9. Edgar Faure, et al., *Learning to Be—The World of Education Today and Tomorrow* (Paris: Unesco, 1972).
10. Graham Fraser, *PQ: Rene Levesque and the Parti Quebecois in Power* (Toronto: Macmillan, 1984).
11. The platforms of all political parties in the 1984 federal election paid particular attention to the perceived aspirations and grievances of the western Canadian provinces.
12. *Challenges and Choices*. Report of the Royal Commission on the Economic Union and Development Prospects for Canada, Donald S. Macdonald, Chairman, (Ottawa: Supply and Services, 1985).

13. Sally Nelson, "Literacy and the Aims of Community Colleges," *Journal of the Association of Canadian Community Colleges*. 3, no. 3, (1979). The term "continually adjusting colleges" was frequently used at Dawson College, Montreal in the early 1970's to describe the character that community colleges should assume. See G.O. Kelly, "Participation in College Governance," Ph.d. dissertation, University of Alberta, 1973.

14. See Appendix B. Statistical information on post-secondary education in Canada has consistently been weak. Enrolment figures have only recently included part-time students, who make up a substantial portion of the college enrolments. No collection of data on the thousands, if not hundreds of thousands, of adults who pursue courses for their own purposes, without credit toward any diploma or certificate, has been yet attempted, yet these people are also college students. See Chapter 8 as well.

15. A.B. Hodgetts, *What Culture? What Heritage?* (Toronto: The Ontario Institute for Studies in Education, 1968).

16. Thomas H.B. Symons, and James E. Page. *Some Questions of Balance: Human Resources, Higher Education and Canadian Studies* Ottawa: The Association of Universities and Colleges of Canada, 1984).

17. A.B. Hodgetts, and Paul Gallagher, *Teaching Canada for the 80's,* (Toronto: The Ontario Institute for Studies in Education, 1978).

18. T.H.B. Symons, (Commissioner), *To Know Ourselves—The Report of the Commission on Canadian Studies,* Vol. I and II (Ottawa: Association of Universities and Colleges of Canada, 1975).

19. Roger Lemelin, "An Ill-Fitting Imported Ideology Won't Suit Canada," From an address to the Liberal Party of Canada, as reported in the *Globe and Mail,* (Toronto, 26 March, 1977).

20. Roger Elmes, "Editorial," *Canadian Studies Bulletin*. (Toronto: The Association of Canadian Community Colleges, June 1980).

Canadian Bibliography on Colleges in Canada

This bibliography is a comprehensive listing of items whose major focus is a college, colleges, a college system, or a major aspect of college activity in Canada.

The *Basic Bibliography in French* is a selection of books, reports, articles, and theses written in French which collectively provide a rounded picture of developments in college education. Citations that relate to individual colleges have not been included although there is a substantial body of literature of this kind in French. Special acknowledgement for this bibliography is due to André Le Blanc, Director of Student Services at Champlain Regional College—St. Lambert-Longueuil Campus and Jean-Luc Roy of Centre d'animation, de developpement et de recherche en education (CADRE), Montreal.

BOOKS IN ENGLISH

Anisef, Paul et al. *Losers and Winners.* Toronto: Butterworth, 1982.

Bryce, R.C., et al., eds. *The Community College in Canada.* Edmonton: University of Alberta, 1970.

Campbell, Gordon. *Community Colleges in Canada,* Toronto: Ryerson Press, McGraw-Hill, 1971.

Campbell, Duncan D. *The New Majority—Adult Learners in the University.* Edmonton: University of Alberta Press, 1984.

Dennison, John D.; Tunner, A.; Jones, G.; and Forrester, G.C. *The Impact of Community Colleges: A Study of the College Concept in British Columbia.* Vancouver: B.C. Research, 1975.

Dupré, J. Stefan, et al. *Federalism and Policy Development: The Case of Adult Occupational Training in Ontario,* Toronto: University of Toronto Press, 1973.

Fisher, Grant. *The Community College.* Calgary: University of Calgary, 1967.

Fleming, W.G. *Ontario's Educative Society. Vol. 4. Post-Secondary and Adult Education.* Toronto: University of Toronto Press, 1971.

Gallagher, Paul and MacFarlane, Gertrude. *A Case Study in Democratic Education, Dawson College.* Montreal: Dawson College, 1976.

Garry, Carl. *Administrative and Curriculum Change in a Canadian Community College.* Montreal: The Canadian Sociology and Anthropology Association, 1975.

Jacobs, Dorene E. *The Community Colleges and Their Communities.* Toronto: Ontario Association for Continuing Education, 1970.

Konrad, Abram G., ed. *Clientele & Community.* Toronto: Yearbook of the Association of Canadian Community Colleges, 1974.

Macdonald, John B. *Higher Education in British Columbia and a Plan for the Future.* Vancouver: University of British Columbia, 1962.

McIntosh, R.G. ed. *The Community College in Canada: Present Status, Future Prospects.* Edmonton: University of Alberta, Department of Educational Administration, 1971.

Magnuson, Roger. *A Brief History of Quebec Education.* Montreal: Harvest House, 1980.

Porter, John, et al. *Towards 2000: The Future of Post-Secondary Education in Ontario,* Toronto: McClelland and Stewart, 1971.

Sen, Joya. *Unemployment of Youth.* Toronto: OISE Press, 1982.

Sheffield, E.: Campbell, D.D.; Holmes, J.; Kymlicka, B.B. and Whitelaw, J.H. *Systems of Higher Education: Canada,* New York: International Council for Educational Development, 1978.

Ray, Douglas et al. *Values, Life-long Education, and an Aging Canadian Population.* London: Third Eye Publications, 1983.

Watson, Cicely. *New College Systems in Canada,* Paris: Organisation for Economic Co-operation and Development, 1973.

REPORTS AND DOCUMENTS IN ENGLISH

Academic Board for Higher Education in British Columbia. *The Role of District and Regional Colleges in the British Columbia System of Higher Education.* Vancouver: The Academic Board, 1965.

Academic Board for Higher Education in British Columbia. *College Standards.* Vancouver: The Academic Board, 1966.

Academic Board for Higher Education in British Columbia. *A Guide to Post-Secondary Education in British Columbia.* Vancouver: The Academic Board, 1967.

Adams, Michael J., et al. *College Co-op Review: A Study of Co-operative Education in Colleges of Applied Arts and Technology.* Toronto: Environics Research Group Ltd., 1977.

Analysis of the Statistics Canada Adult Education Survey of January 1984. Toronto: Canadian Association for Adult Education, 1985.

ARA Consultants Ltd. *A Review of the Two-Year Diploma Nursing Programme in Colleges of Applied Arts and Technology in Ontario.* Toronto: ARA Consultants Ltd. 1978.

ARA Consultants Ltd. *A Review of the Arts, Crafts and Design Programmes in Community Colleges in the Province of Ontario.* Toronto: ARA Consultants Ltd., 1980.

Association of Universities and Colleges of Canada. *Some Questions of Balance: Human Resources, Higher Education and Canadian Studies.* Ottawa: AUCC Publications, 1983.

Alberta Colleges Commission. *The Alberta College System: First Annual Report: 1969-1970.* Edmonton: Alberta Colleges Commission, 1971.

Alberta, Commission on Educational Planning. W.H. Worth, Commissioner. *A Choice of Futures: Report of the Commission,* Edmonton: Queen's Printer, 1972.

Atherton, Peter J. *Financing Junior Colleges in Alberta.* A Study Prepared for the Board of Post-Secondary Education for the Province of Alberta. Edmonton: Department of Educational Administration, University of Alberta, 1969.

Barbeau, Maurice et al. "The Role of the University With Respect to Enrollments and Career Opportunities, Admission Policies, Continuing Education and Community Colleges." Ottawa: Association of Universities and Colleges of Canada. December 1977.

Beagle, Peggy and Bennett, Cliff. *Project Comparison—CAAT/CEGEPs.* Toronto: Ontario Institute for Studies in Education, 1970.

Beinder, Frank. *The Community College in British Columbia: The Emphasis is on Community.* Nanaimo: Quadra Graphics, 1983.

Berghofer, D.E. and Vladicka, A.S. *Access to Opportunity: 1905-1980.* Edmonton: Ministry of Advanced Education and Manpower, 1980.

Bosetti, R. *Developing a Master Plan for Alberta Post-Secondary Non-University and Continuing Education.* Master Planning Monograph No. 1. Edmonton: Alberta Colleges Commission, 1971.

Bryce, R.C. and McIntosh, R.G. *Report of the Manitoba Colleges Student Services Study.* Edmonton: University of Alberta, 1974.

British Columbia. *A Student Services Model for British Columbia Community Colleges, Provincial Institutes and Universities: A Discussion Paper.* Victoria: Department of Education, 1981.

British Columbia. *Longitudinal Follow-up Survey of Students from Career Technical Programmes in British Columbia Community Colleges and Institutes.* Vancouver: B.C. Research, 1983.

British Columbia. *Towards the Learning Community: Report of the Task Force on the Community College in British Columbia.* H. L'Estrange (Chairman). Victoria: Queen's Printer, 1974.

British Columbia: Ministry of Education. *Integrated Five-Year Planning for the British Columbia College and Institute System,* Victoria: Ministry of Education, Post-Secondary Department, 1982.

British Columbia Association of Colleges. *College and Provincial Institute Board Members Handbook.* Vancouver: BCAC 1984.

British Columbia Institute of Technology. *B.C.I.T. 1984 Outlook Report.* Burnaby: British Columbia Institute of Technology, 1984.

British Columbia School Trustees Association. *Establishing Regional and School District Colleges in British Columbia: A Guide for Trustees.* Vancouver: B.C.S.T.A., 1964.

British Columbia School Trustees Association. *Regional College Handbook.* Vancouver: B.C.S.T.A., 1967.

British Columbia Teachers Federation. *Community Colleges for British Columbia?* Vancouver: B.C. Teachers' Federation, 1963.

Cameron, David M. *The Northern Dilemma: Public Policy and Post-Secondary Education in Northern Ontario.* Toronto: Ontario Economic Council, 1978.

Campbell, Alexander B. *Policy Statement on Post-Secondary Education.* Charlottetown: Office of the Premier, April 2, 1968.

Canada Tomorrow Conference-Commissioned Papers. Ottawa: Supply and Services Canada, 1984.

Canada. Trade and Vocational Enrolment Survey. Ottawa: Government of Canada, 1984.

Canada Department of Manpower and Immigration/Ministère de la Main-d'Oeuvre et de l'Immigration. Canadian Community Colleges: Programme Groupings and Projected Outputs to 1980/81/Colleges communautaires du Canada: categories de programmes et inscriptions prevues d'ici 1980/81. Ottawa: Department of Manpower and Immigration/Ministère de la main-d'oeuvre et de l'immigration, 1976.

Canadian Association for Adult Education. The Community College in Canada. National Seminar on the Community College in Canada. Toronto: Canadian Association for Adult Education, 1966.

Canadian Facts Company, Limited. Roles and Responsibilities of the Secondary and Post-Secondary Institution, II: College of Applied Arts and Technology, Educators—Detailed Tables. Toronto: Canadian Facts Company, Limited, 1976.

Canadian Facts Company, Limited. Roles and Responsibilities of the Secondary and Post-Secondary Institutions. Toronto: Canadian Facts Company, Limited. 1976.

Card, B.Y. Post-Secondary Educational Planning and Leadership in the Developing West: The Challenge of New Frontiers. Red Deer: Red Deer College, 1984.

Centre for Special Services for Handicapped. A Report on the Accessibility and Services for the Physically Handicapped at the Universities and Community Colleges of Ontario. Toronto: Centre for Special Services for Handicapped Students, York University, 1978.

Chant, S.N.F., et al. Report of the Royal Commission on Education. Victoria: Queen's Printer, 1960.

Changing Economic Circumstances: The Challenge for Post-Secondary Education and Manpower Training. Toronto: Council of Ministers of Education, Canada, 1985.

City of Kelowna. A Regional College for the Okanagan Valley. Kelowna: City of Kelowna, 1964.

City of Nanaimo. The Impact of Malaspina College on the Local Economy. Nanaimo: City of Nanaimo, 1983.

City of Toronto. Evaluation of the Occupational Therapy Programme at Mohawk College of Applied Arts and Technology. Toronto: City of Toronto, 1983.

College Council of New Caledonia. The Need for a College in the Central Interior. Prince George: College Council of New Caledonia, 1968.

Cordell, Arthur J. The Uneasy Eighties: The Transformation to an Information Society. Background Study 53. Science Council of Canada. Ottawa: Supply and Sources Canada, 1985.

Council of Ministers of Education, Canada. Review of Education Policies in Canada. (Four regional reports—Atlantic, Quebec, Ontario and Western) Toronto: 1975.

Commission on Post-Secondary Education in Ontario. Post-Secondary Education in Ontario: A Statement of Issues. Toronto: The Commission, 1970.

D'Costa, R.B. Post-Secondary Educational Opportunities for the Ontario Francophone Population. Toronto: Queen's Printer, 1972.

Dennison, John D. and Jones, Gordon. The Community College Transfer Student at the University of British Columbia—A Three Year Study. Vancouver: Vancouver City College, 1970.

Dennison, John D. and Jones, G. A Socio-Economic Study of College Students. Vancouver: Academic Board for Higher Education in British Columbia, 1971.

Dennison, John D. and Tunner, Alex. The Impact of Community Colleges. 11 vols. Vancouver: B.C. Research, 1971-1974.

Dennison, John D. et al. "Transfer Rates: A Study of Student Flow from the Academic Program in B.C. Community Colleges. Vancouver: B.C. Research, 1980.

Devereux M.S. *One in Every Five—A Survey of Adult Education in Canada*. Ottawa: Supply and Services Canada, 1984.

Devlin, Laurence E. And Jeffels, Ronald R. "Partners in Promise: A Perspective on Continuing Education in British Columbia." Victoria: British Columbia Department of Education, 1975.

Downey, Lorne W. *The Proposed College for the West Kootenays—A Preliminary Report*. 1964.

Draper, James A. and Clark, Ralph J. *Adult Basic and Literacy Education: Teaching and Support Programmes Within Selected Colleges and Universities in Canada*. Toronto: Ontario Institute for Studies in Education, 1980.

Dudgeon, Paul J. et al. *The CAAT Student Survey: An Affect Assessment Questionnaire for Ontario College of Applied Arts and Technology's Adult Training Students*. Ottawa: Department of Manpower and Immigration, 1977.

Dupre, J.S. et al. *Federalism and Policy Development: The Case of Adult Occupational Training in Ontario*. Toronto: University of Toronto Press, 1973.

Dutchak, P.E. *College with a Purpose: Kemptville*. Belleville, Ontario: Mike Publishing, 1976.

Economic Council of Canada. *Canadian Higher Education in the Seventies*. Ottawa: Queen's Printer, 1972.

EDU-CON of Canada, Ltd. *A Study Re Community College Needs in Three Areas of the Province of New Brunswick*. Saint John: Edu-Con of Canada, Ltd., 1981.

Ellis, J.F. and Mugridge, I. *The Open Learning Institute of British Columbia: A Case Study*. Vancouver: Open Learning Institute of British Columbia, 1983.

Evans, Peter J.A. and Northey, Margot. *Writing Test: Recommendations for Ontario's Colleges of Applied Arts and Technology, Appendix A*. Sudbury: Ontario Institute for Studies in Education, 1978.

Fast, R.G. *Red Deer College: The Critical Years*. Red Deer: Red Deer College, 1974.

Fenske, Milton R. "Present Status and Future Prospects of the Community College in Alberta." Conference on Community Colleges, Banff, 1970.

Ferrett, Barbara A. "The Administrative Structure of the CAAT System, as Originally Defined, as it Evolved and its Affect on the Development of the Colleges 1965-76." Toronto: Ontario Institute for Studies in Education, 1976.

Fisher, Grant L. "Major Issues in Community College Organization." Paper prepared for the Department of Educational Administration, University of Calgary, 1967.

Fisher, Grant L. *Post-Secondary Education Needs for Medicine Hat and Area*. Medicine Hat: 1967.

Fisher, Grant L. *The Preparation of College Instructors*. College Administration Project Occasional Paper. Edmonton: Department of Educational Administration, University of Alberta, 1970.

Fisher, Grant L. *The Community Service Program*. Edmonton: Department of Educational Administration, University of Alberta, 1971.

Fisher, G.L. *A Study of Non-University Post-Secondary and Continuing Educational Services in Alberta, 1970-71*. Master Planning Monograph No. 3—Program Service Inventory, Edmonton: Alberta Colleges Commission, 1971.

Giles, F. *A General Site Location Study for a Regional College for the Okanagan Area of British Columbia*. Seattle: University of Washington, 1965.

Gillespie, Edgar D. *Study on Community Colleges*. Saskatoon, 1967.

Goodings, Sidlofsky, Goodings and Associates Ltd. *The Engineering Technician*. Streetsville: Goodings and Associates, Ltd., 1977.

Gregor, A. "University-College Relationships: The Manitoba Experience." Paper presented at the *Conference of the Society for the Study of Higher Education*, London, Ontario, 1978.

Gregor, A. "University-College Relationships: The Manitoba Experience." Paper presented at the *Conference of the Society for the Study of Higher Education*, London, Ontario, 1978.

Hanson, E.J. *Population Analysis and Projections College Areas in Alberta*. Edmonton: Provincial Board of Post-Secondary Education, 1968.

Hamblin, Fred., ed. *Critical Issues in College System Management*, Toronto: The Association of Colleges of Applied Arts and Technology of Ontario, 1982.

Hardwick, Walter G. *Regional College Study*. Vancouver: Tantalus Research Ltd., 1967.

Hardwick, Walter G. and Baker, R.J. *North Shore Regional College Study*. Vancouver: Tantalus Research Ltd., 1965.

Harvey, Edward B. *Education and Employment: Expectations and Experience*. Toronto: Ontario Institute for Studies in Education, 1973.

Harvey, Edward B. and Goodyear, Stewart. *Education and Employment of Post-Secondary Graduates: A Longitudinal Study*. Toronto: Ontario Institute for Studies in Education, 1975.

Harvey, Ray F.E. *Middle Range Education in Canada*. Toronto: Gage Educational Publishing Co., 1973.

Hervieux-Payette, Céline. *Focus on Youth*. Ottawa: Employment and Immigration Canada, 1984.

Johnson, A.W. *Giving Greater Point and Purpose to the Federal Financing of Post-Secondary Education and Research in Canada*. Ottawa: Secretary of State, 1985.

Kehayas, E.C. and Katz, S.M. *Administrative Computing at the Colleges of Applied Arts and Technology in the Province of Ontario*. Toronto: Thorne Stevenson and Kellogg, 1980.

Kehayas, E.C.; Katz, S.M.; and Oliver, William R. *The Computer as a Professional Subject and a Teaching Tool at the Colleges of Applied Arts and Technology of Ontario*. Toronto: Thorne Stevenson and Kellogg, 1980.

Kennedy, Michael P. J. and Williamson, David. *Report of the Task Force on Professional Development Opportunities and Advancement Policies*. Toronto: Association of Canadian Community Colleges, 1985.

Knowledge Network of British Columbia. *Working Model for a Canada-Wide Information Service for the Post-Secondary Sector—A Feasibility Study*. Kathleen Forsythe, Chairman. Victoria: Learning Systems, Knowledge Network, 1983.

Kolesar, Henry. *Post-Secondary Education in Alberta: Toward the Development of a System*. Mimeographed. Edmonton: The Provincial Board of Post-Secondary Education, 1968.

Kolesar, Henry. *College Boards of Governors*. Mimeographed. Edmonton: The Provincial Board of Post-Secondary Education, 1968.

Kolesar, Henry. *Institutional Control in Post-Secondary Education*. Mimeographed. Edmonton: The Provincial Board of Post-Secondary Education, 1968.

Konrad, A.G. and Small, J.M. *Transfer Arrangements in Alberta Post-Secondary Education*. Edmonton: University of Alberta, 1976.

Lacey, Frances M. *A Review of Admissions Policies, Standards and Selection Procedures for Ontario Colleges of Applied Arts and Technology*. Toronto: Ontario Ministry of Colleges and Universities, 1978.

Learning a Living in Canada. Report of the Skill Development Leave Task Force. 2 Vols. Ottawa: Employment and Immigration Canada, 1984.

Learning at a Distance and The New Technology. Vancouver: Educational Research Institute of British Columbia, 1982.

Letts, Alex. *The Characteristics of Students in Alberta Agricultural and Vocational Colleges*. A report prepared for the Provincial Board of Post-Secondary Education. Edmonton: n.p., 1967.

Lewis, Lesley V. *Women and the Colleges of Applied Arts and Technology.* Toronto: Ontario Ministry of Colleges and Universities, 1975.

Manitoba Department of Education. *Intentions of Grade 12 Students, 1983.* Winnipeg: Department of Education, 1983.

Manitoba Department of Education. *Post-Secondary Accessibility of Frontier Students.* Winnipeg: Department of Education, 1983.

Manitoba Department of Labour and Manpower. *Handbook of Labour Market Experiences of Community College Graduates.* Winnipeg: Manitoba Department of Labour and Manpower, 1980.

Manitoba Department of Labour and Manpower. *Assessment of Labour Market Outcomes of 1976 to 1980 Community College Graduates: Detailed Summaries by Community College Program and Course.* Winnipeg: Department of Labour and Manpower, 1981.

Manitoba Department of Labour and Manpower. *Community Colleges Longitudinal Graduate Follow-up: A Study of College Graduates Five Years After Graduation.* Manitoba: Research and Planning Branch, Manitoba Department of Labour and Manpower, 1982.

Manitoba Department of Labour and Manpower. *1982 Manitoba Community Colleges' Follow-up Survey of 1981 Graduates: Summary Report.* Winnipeg: Research and Planning Branch, Department of Labour and Manpower, 1982.

Manitoba Department of Labour and Manpower. *1982 Manitoba Community Colleges Follow-up Survey: Detailed Summaries by Community College Program and Course.* Winnipeg: Research and Planning Branch, Department of Labour and Manpower, 1982.

Manitoba Educational Research Council. *Report on Post-Secondary Education Needs and Training in Manitoba. Part 1: The Social and Economic Structure.* Winnipeg: Manitoba Educational Research Council, 1967.

Manitoba Post-Secondary Research Reference Committee. *Post-Secondary Plans, Aspirations and Profile Characteristics of Grade Ten and Eleven Students in Manitoba, 1977-78.* Winnipeg: March 1978.

Manitoba Task Force on Post-Secondary Education. "The Community Colleges." *Position Papers.* no. 3. Winnipeg: Manitoba Task Force on Post-Secondary Education, 1973.

Marsh, Leonard. *A Regional College for Vancouver Island.* Vancouver: University of British Columbia, 1966.

Marsh, L. *Learning Community for the Lower Mainland: Report of the Survey Committee on Community Colleges in the Lower Mainland, British Columbia.* Victoria: B.C. Department of Education, 1975.

Martorana, S.V. *A Community Plan for Lethbridge, Alberta.* Lethbridge: Lethbridge Collegiate Institute, 1951.

McIntosh, G. et al., eds. *The Community College in Canada: Present Status/Future Prospects.* College Administration Project Monograph. Edmonton: Department of Educational Administration, University of Alberta, 1971.

Mowat, G., et al. *Transfer Arrangements and Practices in the Public Colleges of the Province of Alberta.* College Administration Project Monograph. Edmonton: Department of Educational Administration, University of Alberta, 1971.

Munroe, David. *The Organization and Administration of Education in Canada.* Ottawa: Information Canada, 1974.

New Brunswick. *Report of the Royal Commission on Higher Education in New Brunswick,* J.J. Deutsch, chairman. Fredericton: The Commission, 1962.

New Brunswick. *New Brunswick Community College: A Statement of Policy and Intent.* Fredericton: Government of New Brunswick, 1974.

New Brunswick. *Report on Post-Secondary Education.* Saint John: The Task Force, 1980.

New Brunswick Community College. *Annual report/Rapport annuel.* Fredericton: New Brunswick Community College, 1975.

New Brunswick Community College. *Quinquennial Plans 1978-83.* vols. 1 and 2.

Newfoundland and Labrador. *Report of the Royal Commission on Education and Youth.* P.J. Warren, chairman. St. Johns: Queen's Printer, 1967-1968.

Newfoundland, Task Force on Education. *Improving the Quality of Education: Challenge and Opportunity,* St. Johns: The Task Force, 1980.

Ohliger, John. *The Integration of Continuing Education in Community Colleges.* Castlegar: Selkirk College, 1968.

Ontario: Committee of Presidents of Provincially Assisted Universities and Colleges of Ontario . . . *Post-Secondary Education in Ontario 1962-1970, 1963. The Structure of Post-Secondary Education in Ontario, Supplementary Report # 1,* 1963. *The City College: Supplementary Report # 2,* 1965.

Ontario: Commission on Post-Secondary Education in Ontario, *The Learning Society,* D.T. Wright, chairman. Toronto: Ministry of Government Services, 1972.

Ontario Ministry of Colleges and Universities. *Annual Survey of 1971 Graduates of the Colleges of Applied Art and Technology.* Toronto: Ministry of Colleges and Universities, 1974.

Ontario Ministry of Colleges and Universities. *A Study of the Communication Arts Programs in Colleges of Applied Arts and Technology: Source Development.* Toronto: Ministry of Colleges and Universities, 1973.

Ontario Ministry of Education. *Secondary—Post-Secondary Interface Study: Summary Report.* Toronto: Ontario Ministry of Education, Ontario Ministry of Colleges and Universities, 1976.

Ontario Department of Education. *Colleges of Applied Arts and Technology: Planning for Change.* Toronto: School Planning and Building Research Section, Department of Education, 1971.

Ontario. Ministry of Education. *Basic Documents: Colleges of Applied Arts and Technology,* Toronto: Queen's Printer, 1965.

Ontario: Ministry of Colleges and Universities. *1981 Multi-Year Plan Analysis of the Ontario Colleges of Applied Arts and Technology.* Toronto: College Affairs Branch, 1982.

Ontario: Ministry of Colleges and Universities. *Multi-Year Plan Analysis of Selected Variables from the 1973-74 to 1979-80 Multi-Year Plans.* Toronto: Special Projects Office, 1981.

Ontario Universities: Access, Operations, and Funding. Toronto: Ontario Economic Council, 1985.

Ontario Universities: Options and Futures. Report of the Commission on the Future Development of the Universities of Ontario. (Edmund C. Bovey, chairman). Toronto: The Commission, 1984.

Organization for Economic Co-operation and Development. *Innovations in Higher Education: A Canadian Case Study.* Cicely Watson, ed. Paris: OECD, 1971.

Orme, Michael E. *Teaching Analysis Laboratory Project: Final Report.* Toronto: Ontario Institute for Studies in Education, 1980.

Ostry, Sylvia, ed. *Canadian Higher Education in the Seventies.* Ottawa: Economic Council of Canada; Information Canada, 1972.

Pascal, C.E. *The Year of the C.A.A.T.* Toronto: Committee of Presidents, Association of Colleges of Applied Arts and Technology of Ontario, 1980.

Peat, Marwick and Partners. *Organization of Educational Programmes for Allied Health Disciplines in Downtown Toronto:* Toronto: Kates, Peat, Marwick and Co., 1973.

Peat, Marwick and Partners. *An Evaluation of Training Programs for Correctional Workers in the Colleges of Applied Arts and Technology.* Toronto: Peat, Marwick and Partners, 1975.

Picot, G. *Changing Education Profile of Canadians, 1961 to 2000: Projections of Educational Attainment for the Canadian Population and Labour Force.* Ottawa: Projections Section, Education, Science and Culture Division, Statistics Canada, 1980.

Post-Secondary Education Issues in the 1980's. Proceeding of the CMEC Conference on Post-Secondary Education, Toronto, Oct. 19-22, 1982. Toronto: Council of Ministers of Education, Canada, 1983.

Price Waterhouse Associates. *Study of the Incremental Costs of Bilingualism In Ontario Colleges of Applied Arts and Technology.* Toronto: Price Waterhouse Associates, 1976.

Prince Edward Island. *Diary of Holland College, 1968-1979.* Charlottetown: Holland College, 1979.

Prince Edward Island. *Policy Statement on Post-Secondary Education.* Charlottetown: Legislative Assembly, 1968.

Prince Edward Island. *Royal Commission on Higher Education.* Charlottetown: The Commission, 1965.

Quebec. Department of Education. *College Education and the General and Vocational Colleges.* Quebec: Queen's Printer, 1968.

Quebec. Government of Quebec. *Colleges in Quebec: A New Phase.* Quebec: Minister of Education, 1978.

Quebec. *Royal Commission of Inquiry on Education in the Province of Quebec.* Alphonse-Marie Parent, chairman. Quebec: Government of Quebec, 1963-1966.

Quebec. Superior Council of Education. *The College: Report on the State and Needs of College Education.* Jean-Guy Nadeau, chairman. Quebec: The Council, 1976

Queen's University. *Who Goes to College.* Kingston: Queen's University, 1983.

Review of Policies for Education-Canada. Paris: Organization for Economic Co-operation and Development, 1976.

Rockley, James W.; Farnham, John G.; Lewis, John J.; and Stratton, Peggy A. *Evaluation of Salary Administration Program for CAATs.* Toronto: Towers, Perrin, Forster and Crosby Ltd., 1980.

Rockley, J. *Evaluation of the Salary Administration Program for CAATs.* Toronto: Ministry of Colleges and Universities of Ontario, 1981.

Royal Commission on the Economic Union and Development Prospects for Canada. *Report.* vol 2. Donald Macdonald, chairman. Ottawa: Supply and Services Canada, 1985.

Royal Commission on Post-Secondary Education in the Kootenay Region. *Report.* Nelson, 1974.

Russell, H. Howard, et al. *Programs and Student Achievement at the Secondary-Post-Secondary Interface: Interproject Analysis.* Toronto: Ontario Institute for Studies in Education, 1976.

Saint Onge, Hubert. *Training for Middle Level Skills.* Toronto: Ontario Ministry of Education, 1981.

Sakamoto, Evannah J. and Carroll, Mary Pat. *The OISE-CAAT Project: CAI Courses in the Community Colleges: Prerequisite Mathematics Skills, Technology Mathematics, Mathematics of Finance, Electricity, Chemistry, Accounting, Metric Games.* Toronto: Ontario Institute for Studies in Education, 1978.

Saskatchewan Community College Trustees Association. *Saskatchewan Community Colleges Mandate Review,* Saskatoon: SCCTA, 1983.

Saskatchewan. *Employment Statistics for Institute Graduates.* Regina: Government of Saskatchewan, (produced annually).

Saskatchewan. Ministry of Continuing Education. *Tech-Voc 90.* Regina: Queen's Printer, 1979.

Saskatchewan Department of Continuing Education. *Report of the Minister's Advisory Committee on Community Colleges.* Regina: Saskatchewan Department of Continuing Education, 1972.

Saskatchewan Department of Continuing Education. *Annual Report.* Regina: The Department of Continuing Education, (published annually).

Seger, J.E. and Mowat, G.L. eds. "The Junior College." *The Lecture Series of the Banff
Regional Conference of School Administrators.* Edmonton: University of Alberta, 1966.

Selleck, Laura. *Manpower Planning and Higher Education Policy.* Toronto: Council of
Ontario Universities, 1982.

Sheehan, Bernard S., et al. *A Financial Plan for Alberta Colleges and Universities: Recommendations and Research Results.* Calgary: University of Calgary, 1977.

Sheffield, Edward. *Research on Post-Secondary Education in Canada: A Review for the Canadian Society for the Study of Higher Education and the Social Sciences and Humanities
Research Council of Canada.* Ottawa: Canadian Society for the Study of Higher Education,
1982.

Sisco, N.A. *Review of Program Advisory Committees in the Colleges of Applied Arts and Technology.*
Toronto: Ontario Ministry of Colleges and Universities, 1981.

Skolnik, Michael L. *Research in a Cold Climate.* Toronto: Ontario Institute for Studies in
Education, 1980.

Skolnik, Michael L. and Tracz, G.S. *Technology, Education and Employment—A Study of
Interactions. Part II: A Micro-Model of the Production and Use of Technicians.* Toronto:
Ontario Institute for Studies in Education, 1971.

Skolnik, Michael L. *Diversity in Canadian Higher Education.* Toronto: Ontario Institute for
Studies in Education, 1983.

Skolnik, Michael L.; Marcotte, William A.; Sharples, Brian. *Survival or Excellence? A Study
of Instructional Assignment in Ontario Colleges of Applied Arts and Technology.* Toronto:
Instructional Assignment Review Committee. Government of Ontario, July 1985.

Small, J.M. *College Co-ordination in Alberta: System Development and Appraisal.* Edmonton:
Alberta Colleges Commission, 1972.

Small, J.M. and Konrad, Abram G. *Survey of Post-Secondary Consortia in Canada.* Edmonton:
University of Alberta, 1984.

Smallwood, J.R. ed. *The Book of Newfoundland Volume 4,* St. Johns: Newfoundland Book
Publishers, 1967.

Sorensen, Nathalie. *General Education in Canada's Community Colleges and Institutes.* Toronto:
Association of Canadian Community Colleges, 1984.

Stager, David. *Accessibility and the Demand for University Education.* Toronto: The Commission on the Future Development of the Universities of Ontario, 1984.

Statistics Canada. *Highlights of the Survey of 1974 Ontario Graduates.* Toronto: Ontario
Ministry of Colleges and Universities, 1976.

Statistics Canada. *Survey of 1975 Ontario College and University Graduates: Highlights Report.*
Toronto: Ontario Ministry of Colleges and Universities,1978.

Statistics Canada. *Survey of Federal Government Expenditures in Support of Training and
Education.* Ottawa: Education, Culture and Tourism Division, Statistics Canada, 1984.

Statistics Canada and Secretary of State. *Post-Secondary Student Survey.* Ottawa: Statistics
Canada and Secretary of State, 1984.

Staton, P.A. *Planning in the Colleges of Applied Arts and Technology of Ontario.* Toronto:
Ontario Institute for the Study of Education, 1982.

Sterling Institute Canada Ltd. *Manpower Retraining Programs in Ontario.* Toronto: Queen's
Printer, 1972.

Stewart, Andrew. *Special Study on Junior Colleges.* Edmonton: Queen's Printer, 1956.

Stinson, Arthur, et al. *Community College Outreach in Rural Eastern Ontario: Toward Appropriate Rural Education: A Study of the Rural Outreach Project of St. Lawrence College,
1976-1978.* Kingston: St. Lawrence College of Applied Arts and Technology, 1978.

St. John, C. *Ontario Study of Vocational-Technical Training: A Preliminary Report.* Toronto: The Ontario Institute for Studies in Education, 1967.

Swirsky, Ronald and Van Arragon, John. *Proctorial Versus Lecture Instruction in Part-time Education: An Examination of Student Performance, Student Acceptance, and Costs with Implications for Full-time Education.* Toronto: Ryerson Polytechnical Institute, 1975.

Systems Research Group. *The Ontario Colleges of Applied Arts and Technology.* Toronto: Queen's Printer, 1972.

Thiemann, Francis C. and Mowat, Gordon L. eds. *Report of the Hearing by the Canadian Commission for the Community College.* Edmonton: The Department of Educational Administration, University of Alberta, 1969.

Tolley, G. *Community Colleges in Canada: Report of a Visit . . . March 1978.* Sheffield: Sheffield City Polytechnic, 1979.

Tolsma, Catherine. *Relationships Between Two Methods of Vocabulary Instruction, Vocabulary Achievement, Reading Attitude, and Locus of Control in a Community College Reading Course.* Vancouver: Educational Research Institute of British Columbia, 1982.

Uhl, N. and Murphy, J. *Predicting Those Students Likely to Change College Major as Well as Those Likely to Drop Out.* Halifax: Mt. St. Vincent and Dalhousie Universities, 1980.

University and College Placement Association. *Ontario Community College Fact Sheets, 1978-79.* Toronto: University and College Placement Association, 1979.

Vanier College. *Vanier College, a Place to Learn, a Statement of Goals.* Montreal: Vanier College, 1974.

Weinstein, E.L.; Brown, I.; and Wahlstrom, Merlin W. *A Review of Admission and Selection Procedures for Diploma Nursing Programs in Colleges of Applied Arts and Technology, Phase A: Programme Survey and Recommendations.* Toronto: Ontario Institute for Studies in Education, 1976.

Welch, G. *Estimates of the Variations in the Operating Costs of Business and Secretarial Post-Secondary Programs in the Colleges of Applied Arts and Technology in Ontario from 1972 to 1975.* London Fanshawe College of Applied Arts and Technology, 1976.

Weleschuk, Marian and Eaton, John. *Models for Articulation and Transfer Between Colleges and Universities.* College Administration Project Monograph. Edmonton: Department of Educational Administration, University of Alberta, 1971.

Wheeler, G.W.B. *Centennial College: The Early Years.* Scarborough: Centennial College, 1977.

White, A.D. *Financial Study Report.* London: Fanshawe College of Applied Arts and Technology, 1977.

Wilson, P.L. *Study of the Social Service Worker Programs in Ontario Colleges of Applied Arts and Technology.* Toronto: Urwick, Currie and Partners Ltd., 1973.

Woods, Gordon and Company, *Planning and Statistical Systems for Colleges of Applied Arts and Technology.* Toronto: Woods, Gordon and Company, 1975.

Youth Employment. Report to the Minister of Employment and Immigration by the Canada Employment and Immigration Advisory Council. Ottawa: Employment and Immigration Canada, 1984.

Zaharchuk, Ted and Palmer, Jane. *A Report of Accreditation in the Colleges of Applied Arts and Technology.* Toronto: Decision Dynamics Corporation, 1978.

ARTICLES IN ENGLISH

ACCC. [Association of Canadian Community Colleges] "B.C. Colleges Experience Era of Rapid Growth." *College Canada* 3 (1978):1.

_____."Cambrian College: Serving the Sudbury District." *College Canada* 4 (1979):12.

_____."Governance and Administration in Canadian Community Colleges: Theory and Practice. *Journal of the Association of Canadian Community Colleges* 4, nos. 1 and 2 (1980).

_____."Grant MacEwan Community College." *College Canada* 2 (1977).

_____."Mount Royal College." *College Canada* 3, no.4 (1978):1.

_____."New Brunswick Community College Unveils Mobile Hospitality Training Unit," *College Canada* 2, no. 2 (1977):10.

_____."Old Sun College." *College Canada* 3, no. 4 (1978):1.

_____."Red Deer College: Serving Central Alberta." *College Canada* 2, no. 8 (1977):1.

_____.Special Issue on Distance Education. *College Canada* 7, no. 4 (1983).

_____.Special Issue on Educational Marketing. *College Canada* 5, no. 8 (1980).

_____.Special Issue on Labour Relations in Canadian Colleges. *College Canada* 6, no. 7 (1981).

_____.Special Issue on Student Services in Community Colleges in Canada. *Journal of the Association of Canadian Community Colleges* 3, no. 1 (1979).

_____.Special Issue on Technology in Canada. *College Canada* 6, no. 8 (1982).

Ali, E. Intab. "The Advisory Committee in Vocational Education." *Journal of the Association of Canadian Community Colleges* 5, no. 1 (1981):11-26.

Allgaier, Hans. "Brave New World?" *College Canada* 5, no. 4 (1980): 10-11.

Anden, T. "A National Body for Community Colleges, but Vive les Differences." *Canadian University and College* 5 (1970).

Anden, T. "Time to Take Perspective View of CAAT Aims and Services," *Canadian University and College* 5 (1970): 30-31.

Andrew, Geoffrey C. "What Kind of Colleges Do We Need?" *University Affairs* 6 (1965): 3-4.

Arbuckle, Joe. "The Phoenix Strategy." *Journal of the Association of Canadian Community Colleges* 2, no. 1 (1978): 96-104.

Arine, A. "Demographic and Social Accounting: A Follow-up on the Withdrawals from Quebec Colleges." *Canadian Administrator* 13 (1974).

Arnett, John. "B.C. Colleges—Closer to Needs of Community." *Canadian University and College* 5 (1970): 22.

Arnett, John. "What is a Community College?" *Information* 13 (1965).

Avendon, Lisa. "Taking the Non Out of Non-Traditional," *College Canada* 6, no. 1 (1981): 8.

Baker, Harold R. and Howard, Thelma M. "The Process of Identifying and Assessing Learning Needs." *Journal of the Association of Canadian Community Colleges* 5, no. 2 (1981): 25-31.

Bannan-Sidorenko, Catherine. "Follow-up Study on John Abbott Students," *Journal of the Association of Canadian Community Colleges* 3, no. 1 (1979): 77-84.

Barber, Jackie. "Legalities, Learners and Learning," *Journal of the Association of Canadian Community Colleges* 1, no. 2 (1977): 47-55.

Barrett, Ralph and Doughty, Howard. "Education in the Iron Cage," *College Canada* 6, no. 5 (1981): 25.

Barrington, G.V. "Do Community College Presidents and Government Officials Show the Same Perspective?" *The Canadian Journal of Higher Education* 12, no. 1 (1982): 43.

Bayley, C.M. "Vancouver's City College: Education Indurance." *School Progress* 34 (1965): 38-39.

Beach, Horace D. "Higher Education and Student Employment Needs." *The Canadian Journal of Higher Education* 7, no. 3 (1977): 1-22.

Beinder, Frank. "The Community College—Is There a Future?" *College Canada* 2, no. 3 (1977): 4.

Beinder, Frank. "The Emphasis is on Community." *Edge* 4, no. 3 (1976): 1.

Beinder, Frank. "Federal and State Legislatures vs. Trustees; A Struggle for Local Control." *Trustee Quarterly* 2, no. 1 (1977-78): 6.

Belanger, Charles H. "Managerial and Disciplinary Constrains Applied to Faculty Staffing." *The Canadian Journal of Higher Education* 60, no. 2 (1979): 51-62.

Bennett, W. "B.C.'s Community Colleges: The Democratization of Education." *UBC Alumni Chronicle* (1973): 19.

Bicknell, Ted. "Counselling Evaluation: Friend or Foe?" *Journal of the Association of Canadian Community Colleges* 3, no. 1 (1979): 23-26.

Bissel, C.T. and Ross, Murray G., et al. "Two Year Colleges: Are They Ends in Themselves or Gateways to University?" *Financial Post* 54 (1965).

Blackwood, T. "Teaching Reading at the Community College." *English Quarterly* 8 (1975).

Blake, Larry J. "The Development of B.C. College Administrators: Problems and Prospects." *Journal of the Association of Canadian Community Colleges* 4, no. 1,2 (1980): 77-86.

Boignon, I.D. "Making a College out of a Warehouse." *Canadian University* 2, no. 6 (1967): 42-43.

Bortolazzo, J.L. "Junior Colleges: Bridging an Educational Gap." *The Alberta School Trustee* 37 (1967).

Breuder, Robert L. and King, Maxwell C. "The Canadian Connection." *Community and Junior College Journal* 47, no. 8 (1977): 28-29.

Brown, M.J. "Capilano College: A Study in the Development of a Regional or Community College." *B.C. Studies* Number 17, Spring 1973, pp. 43-56.

Browne, Gordon. "SRCC: College Responsiveness With a Non-Traditional Look." *College Canada* 2, no. 4 (1977): 3.

Buchar, Frank. "Training Forestry Filers the Modern Way at Northern College." *College Canada* 4, no. 3 (1979): 8.

Burgess, D.A. "The English Language CEGEP in Quebec." *McGill Journal of Education* 6, (1971): 90-100.

Burns, John. "Community Colleges Have to Alter Some of Their Cherished Notions." *Globe and Mail.* September 7, 1968.

Buteau, M.R. "Retrospective on the Parent Report." *McGill Journal of Education.* Ed. VII, 2 Fall 1972, pp. 189-204.

Calder, Berry. "Paras and Pros." *Journal of the Association of Canadian Community Colleges* 3, no. 1 (1979): 67-76.

Callaghan, Terry. " 'Fit to Live' A Low Budget, Minimum Facilities, Mass Participation, Do-it-yourself Consciousness-Raising Life-Style and Fitness Programme . . . or 'Fit to Live' A Multi-Discipline Approach to Student Well-Being." *Journal of the Association of Canadian Community Colleges* 3, no. 1 (1979): 85-90.

Cameron, Ralph. "The STEP System: A Step in the Right Direction." *Canadian Vocational Journal* 8, no. 2 (1972): 19-21, 36.

Campbell, Donald S. and Johnston, C. Fred. "The Part-Time Teacher as Learner," *College Canada* 6, no. 5 (1981): 5.

Campbell, Gordon. "Balancing Control and Independence in College Government." *Canadian University and College* 6, no. 1 (1967): 43-45.

Campbell, Gordon. "Canadian Community Colleges: Progress and Problems," *Convergence* ,4, no. 3 (1971): 78-85.

Campbell, Gordon. "Community Colleges in Canada." *CAUT Bulletin* 23, no. 3 (1974): 8-12.

Campbell, Gordon. "Professional Development in Canadian Colleges: A National Perspective." *New Directions for Community Colleges* 5, no. 3 (1977): 19-33.

Campbell, Gordon. "Some Comments on Reports of Post-Secondary Commissions in Relation to Community Colleges in Canada." *The Canadian Journal of Higher Education* 5, no. 3 (1975): 55-68.

Canadian University and College. "Bubbling Enthusiasm, Temporary Facilities Mark Opening of Second Community College." *Canadian University and College* 2, (1967): 43-45.

Canadian University and College. "College Growing Faster Than Universities in Alberta." *Canadian University and College* 6 (1971): 5.

Canadian University and College. "George Brown's Modular System: Room to Grow in a Crowded City." *Canadian University and College* 6 (1971).

Canadian University and College. "Ontario's Emerging CAAT's—A Survey and Progress Report." *Canadian University and College* 2 (1967).

Canadian Vocational Journal. "Manitoba moves to Community College System." *Canadian Vocational Journal* 6, no. 1 (1970): 21-22.

Canadian Vocational Journal. Community College Division, Manitoba Department of Colleges and University Affairs. "What's a Kayjay? Does KJ stand for Killjoy? *Canadian Vocational Journal* 10, no. 4 (1975): 10-17.

Celowitz, Arnold Charles. "Training Needs for College Student Personnel Professionals in Western Canada." *Journal of the Association of Canadian Community Colleges* 3, no. 1 (1979): 109-120.

Chouinard, N. "The Present Physical Education Programs in the Community Colleges of Ontario," *Journal of the Canadian Association for Health, Physical Education and Recreation* 47 (1980).

Christiensen, Philip. "St. Lawrence Learning Centre: A Model for the Future." *College Canada* 2, no. 5 (1977): 10.

Clark, Hilary. "Retail Fashion Programme at Capilano College Meets Needs of Vancouver Clothing Industry." *College Canada* 4, no. 5 (1979): 10.

Clark, Kathie. "Unique Health Education Centre Established by Douglas College." *College Canada* 4, no. 2 (1979): 14.

Clarke, John Cecil and Young, Darius R. "Alberta Community Colleges: Ten Years in Review." *Canadian Vocational Journal* 19, no. 3 (1983): 8-11.

Cocking, Clive. "B.C.: Are Regional Colleges Growing Fast Enough?" *Canadian University and College*, 4 (March 1969).

Cocking, Clive. "Whatever Happened to the Community Colleges?" *UBC Alumni Chronicle* 20, no. 3 (1968).

Coffin, Lawrence. "In STEP with Holland College." *Yearbook of the Association of Canadian Community Colleges.* Edmonton, The University of Alberta, 1974.

Colvin, James. "Centralism: Threat to Colleges." *College Canada* 1, no. 1 (1976): 4.

Colvin, James A. "Colleges and Universities: The Odd Couple." *Journal of the Association of Canadian Community Colleges* 3, no. 2 (1979): 39-59.

Colvin, James A. "More Local Autonomy College President Urges," *College Canada* 1, no. 2 (1976): 4.

Continuous Learning. "Community College for the Ottawa Region." *Continuous Learning* 4 (1965): 228-232.

Cooke, R.H. and Harper, D.C. "College-University transfer: Evolving a Province-wide Solution." *CAUT Bulletin* 23, no. 3 (1974): 21-22.

Cornish, D.J. "Expanded Admissions Challenge," *Education Administration* 22, (1972-73): 18-19.

Cotton, Frances R. "Staff Development Needs Budgetary Priority." *Canadian Vocational Journal* Vol. 20 No. 4 and Vol. 21 No. 1 February-May, 1985.

Cousineau, John G. "Program Evaluation at V.C.C." *Canadian Vocational Journal* 19, no. 3 (1983): 18-21.

Cousins, W.J. "The Community College Movement." *School Trustee* 17, (April 1968).

Craighead, D.H. "Futures-Casting: The Georgian College Project," *Canadian Vocational Journal* 11, no. 3 (1975): 21-25.

Cranton, Patricia A. and Hillgartner, William. "The Relationships Between Student ratings and Instructor Behavior: Implications for Improving Teaching." *The Canadian Journal of Higher Education* II, no. 1 (1981): 73-81.

Creet, Mario and Trotter, Bernard. "Statistics for Policy and Planning in Canadian Higher Education: An Ontario Perspective." *Canadian Journal of Higher Education* 8, no. 1 (1978): 47-59.

Creigh, Jocelyn. "Stepping Through the Open Door: The Underprepared Student and His Problems." *English Quarterly* 10, no. 4 (1977-1978): 37-44.

Cullen, Connie. "Smallest Province . . . A Big View: Canada's Smallest Community College." *Canadian Vocational Journal* 6, no. 1 (1970): 8-9.

Curtis, David W. "Counseling in a Manitoba Community College." *Canadian Counsellor* 8, no.3 (1974): 152-155.

Davis, W. "Ontario: Colleges of Applied Arts and Technology." *School Progress* 34, no. 7 (1965): 48.

Davis, William G. "Statement Regarding Colleges of Applied Arts and Technology." *Argus* 25, (May 1966).

Day, William L. "Cost Benefit and Cost Effectiveness in Education—and Especially Adult Education." *Journal of the Association of Canadian Community Colleges* 5, no. 2 (1981): 33.

Dean, Geoffrey. "Encouraging Intellectual Development." *Journal of the Association of Canadian Community Colleges* 2, no. 2 (1978): 47-67.

Dellamattia, Gerry and Sharpe, Steve. "Minimum Threshold Requirements at Douglas College." *Journal of the Association of Canadian Community Colleges* 3, no. 1 (1979): 55-58.

Demetra, George and Wyman, Bill. "Who Controls Programme Quality? A Look at the Problem." *Journal of the Association of Canadian Community Colleges* 2, no. 3 (1978): 52-60.

Demicell, J.A. "The Problem of Student Diversity in Community Colleges." *English Quarterly* 12, (1979).

Denevi, Donald. "The Growing Canadian Community College Movement." *The Educational Record* 47, no. 2 (1966): 199-202.

Denis, A. and Lipkin, J. "Quebec's CEGEPs: Promise and Reality." *McGill Journal of Education* 7, (1972): 119-134.

Denis, Ann B. "Some Social Characteristics of CEGEP Graduates," *The Canadian Journal of Higher Education* 5, no. 2 (1975): 39-56.

Dennison, John D.; Forrester, Glen C.; and Jones, Gordon. "An Analysis of Students Enrolling in Career Technical Programs in the Colleges and Institutes of British Columbia." *Canadian Vocational Journal* 18, no. 4 (1983): 24-25.

Dennison, John D. "B.C. Colleges Act Heralds New Era." *College Canada* 2, no. 8 (1977): 3.

Dennison, John D.; Forrester, Glen C.; and Jones, Gordon. "A Follow-up Study of Career and Technical Students from British Columbia Colleges and Institutes." *Canadian Vocational Journal* 17, no. 4 (1982): 18-20, 27-29.

Dennison, John D. "Characteristics of Community College Students." *Yearbook of the Association of Canadian Community Colleges.* Edmonton, Alberta: The University of Alberta, 1974.

Dennison, John D. "The Colleges of British Columbia: Some Basic Issues." S.T.O.A. *The Journal of the Canadian Society for the Study of Higher Education* 1, no. 1 (1971): 27-33.

Dennison, John D. "Community Colleges in Canada: the Challenge of the 1980s." *Journal of the Association of Canadian Community Colleges* 4, no. 1, 2 (1980): 1-16.

Dennison, John D. "The Community College in Canada: An Educational Innovation." in *Canadian Education in the 1980s* J.D. Wilson, ed. Calgary: Detselig Enterprises, 1981, pp. 213-233.

Dennison, John D. "The Community College in Comparative and Historical Perspective: The Development of the College Concept in British Columbia." *The Canadian Journal of Higher Education* 9, no. 3 (1979): 29-40.

Dennison, John D. "Educational Aspirations of High School Graduates in British Columbia," STOA: *The Canadian Journal of Higher Education* 4, no. 1 (1974): 81-84.

Dennison, John D. and Jones, Gordon. "How B.C. Students Fared in College-University Hurdles." *Canadian University and College.* (April 1970): 40.

Dennison, John D. et al. "Degree Completion at British Columbia's Universities." *The Canadian Journal of Higher Education* 12, no. 2 (1982): 43-57.

Dennison, John D. "Penitentiary Education in Canada—the Role for Community Colleges," *Journal of the Association of Canadian Community Colleges* 3, no. 2 (1979): 12-23.

Dennison, John D. "Post-Secondary Education in British Columbia: 1977—A Coming of Age." *Journal of the Association of Canadian Community Colleges* 1, no. 2 (1977): 13-35.

Dennison, John D. "A Re-examination of the Goals of Higher Education." *College Canada* 4, no. 7 (1979): 3.

Dennison, John D.; Forrester, G.; and Jones, G. "A Study of Students from Academic Programs in British Columbia's Community Colleges." *The Canadian Journal of Higher Education* 12, no. 1 (1982): 29.

Dennison, John D. "University Transfer Program in the Community College." *Canadian Journal of Higher Education* 8, no. 2 (1978): 27-38.

Desbiens, Brian; Peters, Linda; and Wigle, Martha. "A Comprehensive Demographic Study of Community College Students." *Journal of the Association of Canadian Community Colleges* 2, no. 3 (1978): 96-105.

Desroches, Jocelyn. "Authority Conflict in Relation to the Job Satisfaction of Ontario CAATs Instructors." *The Canadian Journal of Higher Education* 8, no. 1 (1978): 33-46.

DeStefano, Dick. "Decentralized Counselling Services at Cambrian College." *Journal of the Association of Canadian Community Colleges* 3, no. 1 (1979): 17-22.

Devlin, Lawrence E. and Gallagher, Paul. "Age-Related Needs of Community College Students." *The Canadian Journal of Higher Education* 12, no. 2 (1982): 33-42.

Dickinson, Gary. "Planning for Team Instruction in the Community College." *Continuous Learning* 10, no. 6 (1971): 230-35.

Dickinson, Gary. "Post-Secondary Education in Quebec." *The Teachers' Magazine.* January 1968.

Dodge, David E. and Wilkinson, Lynn. "Employment Training—A Government Perspective." *The Canadian Journal of Higher Education* 12, no. 3 (1982): 37-46.

Donald, Janet G. "The Phychodynamics of Evaluation." *Journal of the Association of Canadian Community Colleges* 2, no. 1 (1978):37-47.

Donald, Janet G. "Where to Begin! Priorities for Teaching Improvement." *Journal of the Association of Canadian Community Colleges* 2, no. 3 (1978): 39-51.

Donnelly, James J. "Cutting the Cloth: Financial Management in Times of Retrenchment." *Journal of the Association of Canadian Community Colleges* 4, no. 1, 2, (1980): 17-24.

Doughty, Howard A. "Students in the Seventies: A Study of Private Liberalism and Public Conservatism." *Journal of the Association of Canadian Community Colleges* 2, no. 4 (1978): 47-74.

Downey, James and Fritz, Howard. "Direct Funding to Users: A Schematic Analysis." *The Canadian Journal of Higher Education* 12, no. 3 (1982): 65-71.

Downey, Lorne. "How to Tackle the Major Issues First in Planning for a Community College." *School Progress* 35 (July 1966): 27-28.

Downey, Lorne. "Planning Points to Ponder for a Regional College." *School Progress* 35, (August 1966): 31.

Dupre, J. Stefan. "Some Personal Ruminations on Changing Growth Rates." *The Canadian Journal of Higher Education* 7, no. 3 (1977): 51-58.

Dutton, John. "Alternative Approach to Faculty Hiring a Necessity, Teacher Urges," *College Canada* 4, no. 4 (1979): 8.

Dyck, E. "The Saskatchewan Technical Institute." *College Canada* 4, no. 1 (1979).

Edginton, Christopher R. "Expanding Community Services: A Look at Recreation Programming." *Journal of the Association of Canadian Community Colleges* 1, no. 1 (1977): 48-63.

Evans, John R. "Problems of Changing Growth Rates in Higher Education: Internal University Responses." *The Canadian Journal of Higher Education* 7, no. 3, (1977): 41-50.

Faris, Don. "The College in Saskatchewan: Where Community is Campus." *College Canada* 2, no. 4 (1977): 4.

Faris, Ron. "The Challenge of Change." *College Canada* 5, no. 3 (1980): 6-7.

Faris, Ron. "Community College Development in Saskatchewan: A Unique Approach." *Canadian Forum* 51 (1972): 60-61.

Findlay, P. "The OECD Reports on Canada's Educational System." *Canadian Vocational Journal* 12, no. 1 (1976): 34-37.

Fisher, Grant. "Institutional Renewal at Camosun." *Journal of the Association of Canadian Community Colleges* 3, no. 3 (1979): 41-60.

Fleming, Thomas. "Beyond Survival: Policies for Academic Revitalization in an Uncertain Environment." *Canadian Journal of Higher Education* 10, no. 2 (1980):103-115.

Foot, David K. and Pervin, Barry. "The Determinants of Post-Secondary Enrolment Rates in Ontario." *The Canadian Journal of Higher Education* 13, no. 3 (1983): 1-22.

Forbes, W.G. "Solving Illiteracy Problems." *College Canada* 7, no. 1 (1982): 10.

Forsythe, Kathleen. "Long Distance Education a Challenge for Teacher at North Island College." *College Canada* 3, no. 2 (1978): 8.

Forsythe, Kathleen. "North Island College: An Idea Creating Its Reality." *Journal of the Association of Canadian Community Colleges* 3, no. 2 (1979): 60-89.

Franklyn, Gaston J. "Academic Revitalization or Mediocrity." *College Canada* 8, no. 1 (1983): 5.

Franklyn, Gaston J. "Academic, Social & Value Orientations at a Community College in Ontario." *Journal of the Association of Canadian Community Colleges* 1, no. 1 (1977): 15-31.

Fraser, Bruce. "Educational Program Planning in British Columbia: The Context for Institutional Research." *Journal of the Association of Canadian Community Colleges* 3, no. 3 (1979):29-39.

Frey, J.D. "A New Look at Northern Colleges: Haileybury School of Mines." *Canadian Vocational Journal* 6, no. 1 (1970): 31.

Gaber, Mark. "Career Planning and Placement: 'The Onion in the Petunia Patch' New Realities and New Challenges in the 1980's." *Journal of the Association of Canadian Community Colleges* 3, no. 1 (1979): 35-40.

Gallagher, Paul. "Examining Organizational Myths: An Administrator's Approach to Institutional Renewal." *Journal of the Association of Canadian Community Colleges* 3, no. 3 (1979): 83-100.

Gallagher, Paul. "Power and Participation in Educational Reform." *McGill Journal of Education* 7 (Fall 1972): 119-134.

Garrison, R.H. 'What's Different About Community College Teaching." *The Canadian Nurse* 68, no. 1 (1972):30-34.

Gartley, W. "Co-op Education Aids in Student Placement." *College Canada* 4, no. 1 (1979).

Gates, Ruth. "Development of a Self-Evaluation Model for Basic Job Readiness Training Programs." *Journal of the Association of Canadian Community Colleges* 2, no. 3 (1978): 61-66.

Gayfer, M. "Community College: Why This Dynamic Movement Now Faces Problems of Success." *School Progress* 38 (July 1969): 21-23.

Gayfer, Margaret. "La Bataille de la declassification stirs up Quebec College Teachers." *Canadian University and College* (May-June 1973): 26.

Gayfer, M. "Multi-level 'Mix' Core of Ontario's New College Plan." *School Progress* 35 (July 1966): 22-24.

Gayfer, M. "What Role for the Community College?" *School Progress* 35 (July 1966): 22-24.

Gerwig, A. James and Bolting, Gary. "Final Offer Selection as an Appropriate Procedure for Community Colleges." *Journal of the Association of Canadian Community Colleges* 1, no. 3 (1977): 1-10.

Giles, Valerie. "The Case Against College Boards." *College Canada* 6, no. 5 (1981): 22.

Gill, E.B. "Is the Community Served When Numbers of Graduates Exceed Jobs?" *Canadian University and College.* (March 1970): 27.

Giroux, Roy F. and Franklyn, Gaston J. "Accountability: A Conceptual Revue." *Journal of the Association of Canadian Community Colleges* 2, no. 3 (1978): 33-39.

Giroux, Roy F. "The Instructional Revolution: Implications for Educational Leaders." *Journal of the Association of Canadian Community Colleges* 1, no. 1 (1977): 1-14.

Giroux, Roy F. "New Directions for Disadvantaged Adults in the Community College." *Canadian Counsellor* 8, no. 3 (1974): 156-162.

Glendennning, Donald. "Effective Decision-making." *Journal of the Association of Canadian Community Colleges* 4, no. 1, 2 (1980): 117-126.

Goard, Dean H. "The Commission on Vocational Education in B.C." *Canadian Vocational Journal* 13, no. 3 (1977): 53 and 64.

Goodman, Donald. "The James Bay Education Centre." *Community and Junior College Journal* 50, no. 6 (1980): 35-37.

Gordon, Robert A. "Leadership: A Personal Perspective." *Journal of the Association of Canadian Community Colleges* 4, no. 1, 2 (1980):53-66.

Gordon, Robert A. "Organizational Growth and Development and the National Association." *Journal of the Association of Canadian Community Colleges* 3, no. 3 (1979):13-28.

Gradwell, John and Bailey, Miriam "The Organization for Economic Co-operation and Development: Review of Vocational Education in Canada." *Canadian Vocational Journal* 14, no. 3 (1978): 5-6.

Graham, Jean. "Centennial College: A Decade of Growth." *College Canada* 2, no. 9 (1977): 1.

Grant, Lou S. "Canada's Evolving Two-Year Colleges." *Junior College Journal* 37 (February 1967):25-37.

Greenaway, John. "A Block-Matrix Method for Course Development." *Canadian Vocational Journal* 12, no. 4 (1977): 33-38.

Gregor, Alexander, "The Re-alignment of Post-Secondary Education Systems in Canada." *Canadian Journal of Higher Education* 9, no. 2 (1979): 35-49.

Griew, Stephen. "A Model for the Allocation and Utilisation of Academic Staff Resources." *The Canadian Journal of Higher Education.* 10, no. 2 (1980):73-84.

Grossman, H.I. "Solving the Educational Dilemma—The Community College." *Continuous Learning* 4 (May-June 1965):105-109.

Haig-Brown, Roderick. "First Things First." *Community Colleges for British Columbia? Views and Points of View.* Vancouver: British Columbia Teachers' Federation, January, 1963.

Ham, James M. "Technology and the Human Adventure," *The Canadian Journal of Higher Education* 13, no. 3 (1983):97-103.

Isabelle, Laurent. "Transferability: Can Community Colleges and Universities Meet the Challenge? *Journal of the Association of Canadian Community Colleges* 3, no. 2(1979):24-37.

Isbister, Al. "Institutional Evaluation: A Participant's Experience at Camosun College." *Journal of the Association of Canadian Community Colleges* 3, no. 1 (1979):99-108.

Hammons, James O. "Overcoming Barriers to Effective Instructional Change." Proceedings of the 7th Annual International Institute on the Community College. Sarnia: Lambton College, 1976.

Hartle, Douglas G. "The Financing of Higher Education in the '70s: A Viewpoint From Ottawa." *The Canadian Journal of Higher Education.* 3, no. 2 (1973): 113-140.

Hartnett, Richard. "The ABCs of Faculty Collective Bargaining: Projections of American, British and Canadian Directions in the 1980s." *International Journal of Institutional Management in Higher Education.* 4, no. 3 (1980): 221-234.

Heming, D.A. "The Adult Learner: A Challenge to the Educator." *College Canada* 3, no. 9 (1978): 22.

Heming, D.A. "The Forgotten Minority at Community Colleges: The Part-Time Faculty." *Journal of the Association of Canadian Community Colleges* 1, no. 3 (1977): 46-60.

Henchey, N. "Quebec Education: the Unfinished Revolution." *McGill Journal of Education,* (Fall 1972): 95-118.

Jackson, H.W. "Procedures for Planning Colleges of Applied Arts and Technology." *Canadian School Journal* 45 (September-October 1967).

Jala, Tom. "Far East Comes Down East at College of Cape Breton." *College Canada* 2, no. 5 (1977): 3.

Jansen, D. "How Big Is Enough? Vancouver City College Moves on to Its New Campus." *Canadian University and College* 5 (September 1970).

Johnston, E.F. "Community College Environment—Neglected Research in Canada." *Canadian Counsellor* 6, no. 2 (1972): 100-111.

Johnston, Roger J. "Counselling Services at Colleges of Applied Arts and Technology." *The School Guidance Worker* 24, no. 1 (1968).

Jones, Chuck. "Ontario MCU Promotes Apprenticeship Training." *College Canada* 3, no. 1 (1978): 5.

Jones, Gordon. "Community College—A Great Starting Place for University Students." *The B.C. Teacher* 48, no. 6 (1969): 221-223.

Jones, G. and Dennison, John D. "The Community College Opportunity for All." *The B.C. Teacher,* 50, no. 3 (1970): 100-104.

Joyner, Charles W. "The CEGEP Twelve Years Later: Review of a Major System Change." *Canadian Vocational Journal* 16, no. 3 (1980): 5-9.

Judge, David. "Community Colleges: Are They Serving Community Needs Across Canada?" *Canadian University and College* 5, no. 3 (1970): 21-38, 54.

Justesen, Henry E. "Competency Based Care Programs." *Canadian Vocational Journal* 19, no. 2 (1983): 11-15.

Kazi, Sadat. "CEGEPs are Thriving After Ten Years." *College Canada* 3, no. 3 (1978): 2.

Kelly, Gerald O. "Student Participation in College Governance," *Yearbook of the Association of Canadian Community Colleges.* Edmonton, Alberta: The University of Alberta, 1974.

Kelly, Gerry. "College Management Development: The Coombe Lodge Experience." *Journal of the Association of Canadian Community Colleges* 4 no. 1, 2 (1980): 67-76.

Kennedy, Michael P. J. "College Education—Another Dimension." *Canadian Vocational Journal* 18, no. 1 (1982): 22-26.

King, Alan J.C. "Capri: An Institutional Self-Evaluation System." *Journal of the Association of Canadian Community Colleges* 3, no. 3 (1979): 141-158.

Klein, Owen. "Accountability for General Education." *Journal of the Association of Canadian Community Colleges.* 2, no. 3 (1978): 67-76.

Konrad, Abram G. "Clientele and Community: Issues in Canadian Post-Secondary Education." *Journal of the Association of Canadian Community Colleges.* 1, no. 1 (1977): 32-47.

Konrad, Abram G. "College Trustees View Their Selection." *Alberta Journal of Educational Research* 23, no. 2 (1977): 138-50.

Konrad, Abram G. "Community College Boards: A Canadian Perspective." *New Directions for Community Colleges* 3, no. 2 (1975): 1-9.

Konrad, Abram G. "Community College Trustees Examine Their Role." *Canadian Administrator* 16, no. 2 (1976): 1-5.

Konrad, Abram G. "Educational Institutions: A Need to Take a Hard Look at Ourselves." *Journal of the Association of Canadian Community Colleges* 5, no. 1 (1981): 35-53.

Konrad, Abram G. "Evaluation of College Trustees," *Journal of the Association of Canadian Community Colleges* 2, no. 3 (1978): 12-23.

Konrad, Abram G. and Small, J.M. "Institutional Renewal: A Planning Mechanism for the 1980s." *Journal of the Association of Canadian Community Colleges,* 3, no. 3 (1979): 1-12.

Konrad, Abram G. and Long, John C. "Issues and Implications." *Yearbook of the Association of Canadian Community Colleges.* Edmonton, Alberta: The University of Alberta, 1974.

Konrad, Abram G. et al. "Professional Development Needs of Administrators in Higher Education." *Canadian Journal of Higher Education* 6, no. 1 (1976): 1-16.

Konrad, Abram G. "A Profile of Community College Trustees," *Canadian Journal of Education* 2, no. 2 (1977): 65-77.

Konrad, Abram G. "Staff Development in Western Canadian Colleges." *The Canadian Journal of Higher Education,* 3, no. 1 (1973): 47-52.

Krakana, M. "Participatory Educational Evaluation and the Decision Making Process." *Journal of the Association of Canadian Community Colleges* 2, no. 3 (1978): 106-110.

Lacey, Frances. "Ontario College Review of Admissions Policies, Standards and Procedures." *Journal of the Association of Canadian Community Colleges* 3, no. 1 (1979): 59-66.

Ladyman, William. "He is Best Educated, Who is Most Useful." *Canadian Vocational Journal* 10, no. 3 (1974): 9-13.

Landgraf, John and Gilkes, Dave. "Instructor in Front Line." *Journal of the Association of Canadian Community Colleges* 3, no. 2 (1979): 1-11.

Law, H. "Community Colleges: Dead End or Doorway?" *Canadian University and College* 1 (March-April 1966): 32-35.

Law, Harriet. "Community Colleges—Whom Shall They Serve?" *School Administration* 3 (March 1966).

Lawrence, Stephanie. "The Boards and the Future." *Journal of the Association of Canadian Community Colleges* 2, no. 3 (1978): 24-32.

Leach, Barry. "Environmental Education at Douglas College." *College Canada* 2, no. 5 (1977): 4.

Leach, Barry. "Wild Cranes and Tibetan Refugees: Aspects of Community Education at Douglas College." *Journal of the Association of Canadian Community Colleges* 5, no. 2 (1981): 62-64.

LeBlanc, Andre E. "The College Administrator in Quebec." *Journal of the Association of Canadian Community Colleges* 4, no. 1, 2 (1980): 39-54.

LeBlanc, Andre. "Faculty Working Conditions in Canadian Colleges." *College Canada* 1, no. 2 (1976): 3.

Lee, G.H.. "Post-High School Education." *Community Colleges for British Columbia? Views and Points of View* Vancouver: British Columbia Teachers' Federation, 1963.

Lipkin, J.P. "The Academic Tilt in Quebec Post-Secondary Education." *Canadian and International Education III.* 3, no. 1, 1974, pp. 53-60.

Long, Kenneth F. "Learning Skills Programs: The Present and the Future: How Important Are They?" *Journal of the Association of Canadian Community Colleges* 3, no. 1 (1979): 41-48.

McAndrew, J. "At Holland College: Big Plans for a Small Province." *Canadian University and College* 5 (March 1970): 35-36.

McCaffrey, G. "A Labour View of Technical and Vocational Education." *Canadian Vocational Journal* 6 (January 1970): 12-15.

MacDonald, Hesta. "PEI's Holland College Institute Provides Leadership Training." *College Canada* 3, no. 9 (1978): 12.

MacDonald, Steve. "Centre for International Studies Started by College of Cape Breton." *College Canada* 4, no. 2 (1979): 17.

McDonough, Bernice. "Teacher Assistants—College Trained." *The B.C. Teacher* 48, no. 7 (1969): 260-62.

McLean, Ruth. "Part-Time Care for the Part-Time Teacher." *College Canada* 5, no. 5 (1980): 14-15.

McLean, Ruth. "Professional Development and the Part-Time Faculty." *Journal of the Association of Canadian Community Colleges* 2, no. 1 (1978): 105-114.

McMullan, Peter. "Malaspina College Builds on Confidence and Trust." *Community and Junior College Journal* 48, no. 2 (1977): 22-24.

McMullan, Peter. "Malaspina College: Meeting the Needs of Its Community." *College Canada* 2, no. 3 (1977): 1.

McMullan, Peter. "Malaspina College Plays Major Training Role in West Coast Forest Industry." *College Canada* 4, no. 4 (1979): 12.

MacNeil, Kenzie. "College of Cape Breton, An Educational Innovator." *College Canada* 1, no. 2 (1976): 1.

Maltby, Peter. "Financing the Community Colleges." *Continuous Learning* 4 (July-August 1965).

Marguet, A. "Cambrian College Convinced One Picture is Worth a Thousand Words." *Canadian Vocational Journal* 9, no. 1 (1973): 16-17, 31.

Messer, T. "Alberta Study Seeks to Measure Colleges Against Community Needs." *Canadian University and College* 6 (January-February 1971): 8.

Mitchener, R.D. "Junior Colleges in Canada." *Junior College Journal* 20, no. 3 (1960): 400-412.

Mitminger, Sam. "Community College and the Community." *Canadian Vocational Journal* 8, no. 1 (1972): 11-13, 37.

Montagnes, I. "Electronic and Micrographic Publishing, Cost Effectiveness, and Accessibility." *The Canadian Journal of Higher Education* 13, no. 2 (1983): 1-12.

Morgan, Kent. "Keewatin Community College—A Woman at the Helm." *Canadian Vocational Journal* 12, no. 3 (1976): 18-20.

Morisseau, James J. "For Planners, That Shrinking Feeling." *Planning for Higher Education* 2, no. 5 (1973): 13-15.

Morphy, David R. "A Descriptive Study of the Professional Development Activities of Student Affairs Professionals in the Two Year Post-Secondary Educational System of Alberta." *Journal of the Association of Canadian Community Colleges* 3, no. 1 (1979): 91-98.

Morrison, Ian. "Towards Lifelong Learning: The Community College as Oasis." *Journal of the Association of Canadian Community Colleges* 5, no. 2 (1981): 2.

Mowat, Gordon. "Transferability: An Old Problem in a New Setting." *Yearbook of the Association of Canadian Community Colleges* Edmonton, Alberta: The University of Alberta, 1974.

Mukerjee, Roman *et al.* "Humanities and General Education." Montreal: Vanier Press, 1974.

Murphy, T. "Woodstock's Community College." *Atlantic Advocate* September, 1979.

Nelson, Sally Todd. "Literacy and the Aims of Community Colleges." *Journal of the Association of Canadian Community Colleges* 3, no. 3 (1979): 115-40.

Nemiroff, Greta. "The New School of Dawson College: A Humanistic Alternative." *College Canada* 2, no. 5 (1977): 2.

Noble, Howat; Stoll, Robert A; and Calvert, Ian S. "A Participatory Approach to the Development of Centralized Information Systems." *The Canadian Journal of Higher Education* 8, no. 1 (1978): 1-23.

Oliver, David. "Animation: A Creative Learning Experience." *Journal of the Association of Canadian Community Colleges* 2, no. 2 (1978): 13-30.

Olivier, William P. and Lomberg, Evannah J. "Student Skill Deficiencies and Computer Assistance." *Yearbook of the Association of Canadian Community Colleges* Edmonton, Alberta: The University of Alberta, 1974.

O'Neill, G. Patrick. "Post-Secondary Aspirations of High School Seniors from Different Social-Demographic Contexts." *The Canadian Journal of Higher Education* 11, no. 2 (1981): 49-66.

O'Neill, Len. "Community Colleges on the Couch." *Edge* 4, no. 3 (1976): 4.

O'Reilly, Robert R. "Post-Secondary Education for Canadian Police Officers: The Community College." *Canadian Police College* (November 1977.)

Orlowski, S.T. "Procedures for Planning Colleges of Applied Arts and Technology." *Canadian School Journal* 45, no. 5 (1967): 11-12.

Oureshi, M. "Academic Status, Salaries and Fringe Benefits in Community College Libraries of Canada." *Canadian Library Journal* 28 (January-February 1971).

Pantazis, F. "Library Technicians in Ontario Academic Libraries." *Canadian Library Journal* 35 (April 1978).

Park, Michael. "Ontario CAATs: The First Ten Years." *College Canada* 2, no. 9 (1977): 1.

Pascal, Charles E. "The New Reality of Higher Education: The Agony and Ecstasy of Educational Development." *Journal of the Association of Canadian Community Colleges* 2, no. 3 (1978): 77-95.

Paul Ross. "Academic Leadership in Times of Retrenchment: A Clockwork Cumquat." *Journal of the Association of Canadian Community Colleges* 4, no. 1,2 (1980): 25-38.

Picot, Jocelyne. "Toronto Institute of Medical Technology: Meeting the Needs of Medical Technology." *College Canada* 4, no. 5 (1979): 12.

Pike, Robert M. "Sociological Research on Higher Education in English Canada 1970 -1980: A Thematic Review." *The Canadian Journal of Higher Education* 11, no. 2 (1981): 1-25.

Pierre, Gloria. "The CEGEP's and the English Community." *The Montreal Star* (March 4. 1970), 61; (March 5, 1970), 10; (March 6, 1970) 22-23; (March 7, 1970), 71.

Piquette, Andre. "Paraprofessionals in Canadian College Counselling Services." *Journal of the Association of Canadian Community Colleges* 3, no. 1 (1979): 49-54.

Preddie, Calvin. "Education for the Whole Person." *College Canada* 3, no. 3 (1978): 5.

Prokopec, D. "The Community College: Historical Roots and Purposes." *Canadian Vocational Journal* 15, no. 1 (1979): 12-15.

Puffer, Karel. "Students Who Leave College." *Yearbook of the Association of Canadian Community Colleges*, Edmonton, Alberta: The University of Alberta, 1974.

Quick, D. "The CAATS Programme and Planning." *Canadian University and College* (June 1968): 16.

Quick, D. "Community Colleges—The Next Big Step in Education." *School Administration* 3 (July 1966).

Quittenton, R.C. "Brief Calls for Radical Changes in Education." Presentation to the Commission of Post-Secondary Education in Ontario. *Canadian Vocational Journal* 7, no. 3 (1971): 17-19.

Rachlis, Louise. "Intake 60,000: Ontario's Community College System." *Canadian Vocational Journal* 6, no. 1 (1970): 4-7, 48.

Rampaul, Winston; Koodoo, Aaron H.; and Didyk, John. "Self-Reported Differences between Community College Graduates and Non-Graduates." *Canadian Vocational Journal* 19, no. 3 (1983): 32-36.

Ratcliff, James L. "Community Colleges in Western Canada: A Study of the Development of Provincial Colleges and College Systems. Education 570: The Community and Junior College, Winter Semester, 1972." *American Educational Research Association Annual Meeting* New Orleans: February-March 1973.

Rath, Norman S. "Career Education: A Community College Model." *Journal of the Association of Canadian Community Colleges* 1, no. 2 (1977):36-46.

Richards, John. "Planning and Survival." *Journal of the Association of Canadian Community Colleges* 2, no. 3 (1978):1-11.

Riederer, L. "Saskatchewan Community Colleges." *Canadian Vocational Journal* 9, no. 4 (1974):25-26.

Riederer, L. "Saskatchewan Community College Development." *Canadian Vocational Journal* 11, no. 1 (1975):62.

Riendeau, Marcel. "PERFORMA: Helping the Teachers in Francophone Quebec." *Journal of the Association of Canadian Community Colleges* 11, no. 1 (1978):3-17.

Robertson, G.H. "A Study of Training Needs for Community College Administrators in Ontario." *OCLEA* 1 (June 1974):6-8.

Rothery, Allisen. "New Parts Marketing Programme Piloted at Kelsey Institute." *College Canada* 4, no. 2 (1979):10.

Russell, C. Neil. "The College Environment: Assessment Techniques." *Yearbook of the Association of Canadian Community Colleges* Edmonton, Alberta: The University of Alberta, 1974.

Ryan, Doris W. "The Community College: Some Philosophical Issues." *Yearbook of the Association of Canadian Community Colleges* Edmonton, Alberta: The University of Alberta, 1974.

Sainty, Geoff. "The Community College in Newfoundland." *College Canada* 2, no. 4 (1977):6.

Sanguinetti, Sonja, *et al.* "Collective Bargaining in B.C. Community Colleges - First Steps." *CAUT Bulletin* 23 (December 1974):13-14.

Scharf, John S. "A Broken Model for Program Delivery." *Journal of the Association of Canadian Community Colleges* 5, no. 2 (1981):49-55.

Scharf, John S. "Community College Bestiary." *The Canadian Journal of Higher Education* 12, no. 3 (1982):73-76.

Schipper, Sidney S. "Upgrading Ontario Instructors in Fashion Technology." *Journal of the Association of Canadian Community Colleges* 1, no. 3 (1977):29-45.

Schmidt, Lanalee. "Counselling Needs Assessment Project of the Community." *Journal of the Association of Canadian Community Colleges* 3, no. 1 (1979):9-16.

School Progress. "Current and Future Plans for Community Colleges." *School Progress* 35 (July 1966):26.

School Progress. "Ontario: Colleges of Applied Art and Technology." *School Progress* 34 (July 1965):48.

School Progress. Special Edition on the Community College. *School Progress*. Toronto, Maclean Hunter, 1966.

School Progress. "Storefront Campus." *School Progress* 4 (February 1972).

Senechal, Marcel and Lebel, Denis. "Changing an Educational Environment." *Yearbook of the Association of Canadian Community Colleges* Edmonton, Alberta: The University of Alberta, 1974.

Seredick, M.S. *et al.* "Collective Bargaining in Alberta Colleges." *CAUT Bulletin* 23 (December 1974): 17-20.

Sheffield, Edward F. "A Coherent System for Manitoba." *The Canadian Journal of Higher Education* 4, no. 1 (1974): 111-116.

Sheffield, Edward F. "Emerging Provincial Systems of Higher Education." *School Administration* (September/October 1965): 31-34.

Sheffield, Edward; Noah, Harold J.; and Hamm-Brucher, Hildegard. "The OECD Review and Higher Education." *The Canadian Journal of Higher Education* 9, no. 2 (1979): 13-24.

Sheffield, Edward F. "The Post-War Surge in Post-Secondary Education: 1945-1969." in *Canadian Education: A History,* J. Donald Wilson, et al., eds. Scarborough: Prentice-Hall, 1970.

Shore, Bruce M. "Instructional Development in Canadian Higher Education." *The Canadian Journal of Higher Education* 4, no. 2 (1974): 45-53.

Shragge, Phil. "Quality Education Standards in Community Colleges." *Journal of the Association of Canadian Community Colleges* 5, no. 1 (1981): 27.

Siscoe, N. "Two Comments on Ontario's Community College." *Continuous Learning* 5 (September-October 1966): 222-26.

Skolnik, Michael L. "Will High Technology Save Higher Education From Decline?" *The Canadian Journal of Higher Education* 13, no. 2 (1983): 71-77.

Smith, Denis C. "Community Colleges are Really Needed." *Community Colleges for British Columbia? Views and Points of View.* Vancouver: British Columbia Teachers' Federation, January, 1963.

Smith, Denis C. "Preparation of College Teachers: Towards a Rationale for Instruction." *Canadian Educational Research Digest* 8 (September 1968): 230-244.

Smith, Denis C. "Two-Year Colleges Mean New Concepts for Trustees." *The British Columbia School Trustees* (Spring 1963).

Smith, Donald. "For Community Colleges, A Need to be Fertilized by Their Communities." *Canadian University and College* 6, no. 7 (1971): 24-25.

Smith, M. Elena. "Equal Access to College: A Case Study." *Journal of the Association of Canadian Community Colleges* 2, no. 4 (1978): 10-32.

Smith, Stuart L. "Employment and Well-Being: Changing Structures of Work." Notes for and address to the Canadian Mental Health Association, Nov. 1, 1984. Ottawa: Science Council of Canada, 1984.

Soles, Andrew E. "Role of Two Year College in Creating a New Design for Post-Secondary Education in British Columbia." *Journal of Education.* (UBC) 16 (April 1970): 22-31.

Souch, Stanley and Fahy, Patrick. "Self-Study in Alberta: Preliminary Report." *Journal of the Association of Canadian Community Colleges* 2, no. 4 (1978): 33-46.

Sparling, Lorne. "Community College Development in Prince Albert, Saskatchewan." *Saskatchewan Journal of Educational Research and Development* 2, no. 1 (1971): 12-16.

Spencer, John. "The Senate at Work." *Journal of the Association of Canadian Community Colleges* 4, no. 1,2 (1980): 109-116.

Stager, David. "Economics of Higher Education: Research Publications in English in Canada, 1971 to 1981." *The Canadian Journal of Higher Education* 12, no. 1 (1982): 17-28.

Stager, David and Meltz, Noah M. "Manpower Planning in the Professions." *The Canadian Journal of Higher Education* 7, no. 3 (1977): 73-83.

Stamp, Robert M. "Government and Education in Post-War Canada," in *Canadian Education, A History*, J. Donald Wilson et al., eds. Scarborough, Prentice-Hall, 1970.

Stamp, Robert M. "Technical Education, the National Policy and Federal-Provincial Relations in Canadian Education, 1899-1919." *Canadian Historical Review* 52 (1971).

Stevens, Tom J. "Continuing Education: Into the Eighties." *College Canada* 6, no. 6 (1981): 4.

Stevenson, Hugh A. "Crisis and Continuum: Public Education in the Sixties," in *Canadian Education: A History*, J. Donald Wilson et al., eds. Scarborough: Prentice-Hall, 1970.

Stevenson, Hugh A. "Developing Public Education in Post-War Canada to 1960," in *Canadian Education: A History*, J. Donald Wilson et al., eds. Scarborough: Prentice-Hall, 1970.

Stinson, Arthur. "Striving to Meet the Challenges of Community Needs." *Canadian University and College* 6 (May-June 1971): 44-46.

Stone, G.L. "Staff Development: An Integral Part of Any Institution." *Journal of the Association of Canadian Community Colleges* 5, no. 1 (1981): 91-99.

Stubbs, Paul. "Anglophone CEGEP—Mosaic or Maelstrom?" *College Canada* 2, no. 5 (1977): 4.

Terry, John. "Atlantic Canada's Community Colleges." *College Canada* 5, no. 2 (1980): 18.

Terry, John. "Managing, Merging, and Moving." *Journal of the Association of Canadian Community Colleges* 4, no. 1,2 (1980): 127-132.

Thiessen, Umer J. "The Need for Applied Humanities in Postsecondary Technical/Vocational Education." *The Canadian Journal of Higher Education* 15, no. 1 (1985): 69-81.

Thom, Gordon. "Perspectives on Technological Information in the 80s." *Journal of the Association of Canadian Community Colleges* 5, no. 1 (1981): 73-81.

Thompson, Lorne. "B.C. on TRAC: A New Vocational Training Plan." *Canadian Vocational Journal* 19, no. 1 (1983): 54-58.

Thompson, Sheilah D. "Career Mobility: A Community College Nursing Program." *Journal of the Association of Canadian Community Colleges* 1, no. 3 (1977): 11-28.

Thompson, Sheilah D. "Career Mobility." *Edge* 4, no. 3 (1976): 6.

Thompson, Sheilah D. "Student Services in Community Colleges." *Yearbook of the Association of Canadian Community Colleges* Edmonton, Alberta: The University of Alberta, 1974.

Thompson, W.B. "The New Brunswick Community College." *Canadian Vocational Journal* 10, no. 4 (1975): 28-32.

Totten, William and Giroux, Roy. "Student Services: Theory and Practices." *Journal of the Association of Canadian Community Colleges* 3, no. 1 (1979): 1-8.

Van Nest, Paul and Warren, Wendy K. "The Implementation of CAPRI at St. Lawrence College." *Journal of the Association of Canadian Community Colleges* 3, no. 3 (1979): 159-175.

Wales, B.E. "Post-Secondary Education in British Columbia." *1970 Yearbook* Canadian Association of School Administrators, 1970.

Watson, Ron. "The C.E.G.E.P." *Canadian Vocational Journal* 6, no. 2 (1970): 4-9.

Weihs, J. "Survey of Library Technician Programs in Canada." *Canadian Library Journal* 36 (December 1979).

Well, C.V. "Alberta Colleges: A Product of Their Times." *College Canada* 2, no. 7 (1977).

Wensley, Roland J. "Quebec's Anglophone CEGEPs. Success or Failure?" *College Canada* 2, no. 2 (1977): 3-12.

Whale, W. Brock and Riederer, Lewis A. "Colleges That Encourage Life-Long Learning." *Yearbook of the Association of Canadian Community Colleges* Edmonton, Alberta: The University of Alberta, 1974.

Whitelaw, J.A. "The CEGEP Revolt and After." *Canadian University and College* (November 1968): 30.

Whitelaw, J.A. "From CEGEP to University: Problems of Articulation in Quebec." *Canadian University and College* (March 1971): 52-55.

Wieler, Dennis. "Regional Commitment and the Community College at Grande Prairie Regional College." *College Canada* 4, no. 3 (1979): 10-11.

Williamson, David. "Co-operative Education: Separating the Facts From the Fad." *Journal of the Association of Canadian Community Colleges* 2, no. 2 (1978): 1-12.

Wilson, H.V. and Marbell, F.E. "Community College in Canada." *CAHPER Journal* 33 (October-November 1966): 21-23.

Wilson, J.D. "Vocationalism in Education: Some Comments from Ontario" in *Journal of Educational Thought* (August 1968): 91-96.

Wolansky, William D. "Evaluation of Employer Sponsored Skill Training and Development Programs." *Canadian Vocational Journal.* 20, no. 4 and 21, no. 1 Feb.-May 1985.

Wootton, George C. "How to Build a College—Some Guidelines for Physical Planners." *Canadian University and College* (November/December 1981): 40-44.

Wormsbecker, John H. "City College: New Concept in Adult Education." *School Administration* 2 (May 1965): 43-46.

Worth, Walter H. "Perspectives on Policy Formation." *The Canadian Journal of Higher Education* 8, no. 2 (1978): 1-7.

Wragg, Gordon, "Division of Post-Secondary Provincial Funding Between Colleges/ Universities: A Letter to the Editor." *College Canada* 4, no. 6 (1979): 3.

Wright, Phillip C. "Association-Sponsored Education: Is It An Alternative to the Community College?" *Canadian Vocational Journal* 18, no. 4 (1983): 24-25.

Wyman, William. "Who Controls Programme Quality?" *College Canada* 5, no. 7 (1980): 4-5.

Young, William A. "The Ministry of Education as Policy-Maker. Toward Centralization of the Cegeps of Quebec." *College Canada* 18, no. 5 (1984):7; 9, no. 1 (April 1984): 7-8.

THESES IN ENGLISH

Ali, Ameer H. "Federal Aid to Education in New Brunswick; the Effects of Federal Aid on the Development of Technical and Vocational Education in New Brunswick." M. Ed. thesis, University of New Brunswick, Fredericton 1966.

Anderson, Darrel Vail. "The Adoption of Recommended Administrative Practices by Directors of Public School Adult Education in the Province of British Columbia. Ed. D. thesis, University of British Columbia, Vancouver 1975.

Aumont, Marcel. "The Relationship between Early Withdrawals and Selected Institutional Factors in Colleges of the Montreal Metropolitan Area." Ph.D. thesis, The Catholic University of America, Washington 1974.

Bacon, John A. "Communications and Role Satisfaction in Post-Secondary Institutions." Ph.D. dissertation, University of Alberta, Edmonton 1973.

Barrington, Gail Vallance. "The Impact of Environmental Forces on Alberta Community Colleges 1980-1990." Ph.D. dissertation, University of Alberta, Edmonton 1981.

Barron, Marion. "Possible Consequences for Diploma Nursing Education in Ontario as a Subsystem of the System of Colleges of Applied Arts and Technology." Ph.D. thesis, Catholic University of America, Washington, D.C. 1972.

Bartram, Peter Edward Raven, "The Ontario Colleges of Applied Arts and Technology—a Review and Analysis of Selected Literature 1965-1976." Ed.D. thesis, University of Toronto, Toronto 1980.

Beckman, Harold R.D. "A Survey of Agencies Responsible for Co-ordination of Post-secondary Education in Canada." M.Ed. thesis, University of Alberta, Edmonton 1973.

Berghoffer, D.E. "The Future's Perspective in Educational Policy Development." Ph.D. dissertation, University of Alberta, Edmonton 1972.

Berghoffer, D.E. "General Education in Post-Secondary Non-University Educational Institutions in Alberta." M.Ed. thesis, University of Alberta, Edmonton 1970.

Bernard, Jean-Louis. "Perceived Constraints Operating on Adult Students, Teachers, and Directors in CEGEPS Regarding the Adoption of New Practices in Adult Education in Quebec." Ph.D. thesis, Boston University, Boston 1972.

Bigsby, Kathleen Mary. "Continuing Education at Capilano, Douglas and Vancouver Community Colleges," M.Ed. paper, University of British Columbia, Vancouver 1977.

Biles, Penny. "Sex Differences and Work Patterns: A Case Study of a Community College." M.A. thesis, McMaster University, Hamilton 1978.

Bryce, R.C. "The Technical and Vocational Training Assistance Act of 1961-67: An Historical Survey and Documentary Analysis." Ph.D. thesis, University of Alberta, Edmonton 1970.

Burgess, Donald A. "Education and Social Change: A Quebec Case Study." Boston: D.Ed. thesis, Harvard University, Cambridge 1978.

Cameron, Donald Alan. "An Examination of Social Service Programs in Ontario Community Colleges, with Special Reference to Field Instruction." D.S.W. dissertation, University of Toronto, Toronto 1975.

Campbell, Gordon. "History of the Alberta Community College System 1957-1969." Ph.D. dissertation, University of Alberta, Edmonton 1972.

Chowdhury, Gajinder S. "Administration and Growth of Vocational Education in Nova Scotia." M.A. thesis, Dalhousie University, Halifax 1973.

Churchill, Edgar. "Developing an Individualized Reading Programme at the College of Fisheries, Navigation, Marine Engineering and Electronics." M.Ed. thesis, Memorial University of Newfoundland, St. John's 1974.

Collin, Wilbur J. "A Follow-up Study of the 1966-70 Graduates of the Alberta Agricultural and Vocational Colleges." M.Ed. thesis, University of Alberta, Edmonton 1971.

Cooper, Norma Colleen. "Instructor Evaluation in Community Colleges." Master's thesis, University of Alberta, Edmonton 1972.

Corbet, R. "The Classical College of Quebec." Master's thesis, McGill University, Montreal 1966.

Cornish, D.J. "A Comparison of Student and Faculty Perceptions of Their College Environment," M.Ed. thesis, University of Alberta, Edmonton 1971.

Cornish, D.J. "The Impact of Participation and Information in Perception of College Goals," Ph.D. thesis, University of Alberta, Edmonton 1977.

Costello, E.P. "A Report on the Saint John Mechanics Institute, 1838-1890." M.A. thesis, University of New Brunswick, Fredericton 1974.

Crookshanks, James Douglas. "Some Predictors of Academic Success and Student Status of First Term Freshman Students at Mount Royal College." M.Sc. thesis, University of Calgary, Calgary 1974.

Datey, Blaise S. "The Sociopolitical Process of Innovation and Planning as Demonstrated by the Introduction of CEGEP's in Quebec's Education System." Toronto: Ph.D. thesis, University of Toronto, Toronto 1973.

Day, T.C. "Administration-Faculty Conflict over the Distribution of Control in Policy Formulation in Alberta Colleges." Ph.D. dissertation, University of Alberta, Edmonton 1971.

Desroches, J.J. "The Concepts of and Determinants of Job Satisfaction: an Exploratory Study in the Colleges of Applied Arts and Technology in Ontario." Ph.D. thesis, University of Toronto, Toronto 1976.

Dickinson, James Gary. "An Analytical Survey of the Pemberton Valley in British Columbia with Special Reference to Adult Education." Ed.D. thesis, University of British Columbia, Vancouver 1968.

Dunn, Timothy Allan. "Work, Class and Education: Vocationalism in British Columbia's Public Schools, 1900-1929." Ed.D. thesis, University of British Columbia, Vancouver 1977.

Epstein, Maurry Hart. "Relationships between Interpersonal Relations Orientations and Leader Behaviour of Canadian Community College Administrative Leaders." Ph.D. dissertation, George Peabody College for Teachers, Nashville 1976.

Evancio, Edward W. "The Identification of Program Needs for a Community College in Regina as Perceived by Business and Industry and Grade Twelve Students." M.Ed. thesis, University of Regina, Regina 1974.

Falkenberg, Eugene Edward. "A Study of the Success of Junior College Transfer Students to the University of Alberta, Edmonton, and the University of Calgary from Public Junior Colleges in the Province of Alberta, Canada," Ed.D. thesis, University of Montana, Missoula 1969.

Farquhar, Hugh Ernest. "The Role of the College in the System of Higher Education in Alberta." Ph.D. dissertation, University of Alberta, Edmonton 1968.

Flynn, John David. "Structural Congruence of Community Colleges and Economic Development Areas in Ontario." Ph.D. dissertation, Cornell University, Ithaca 1975.

Ford, Barbara C. "Factors Involved in the Reading Ability of Students in Ontario Colleges of Applied Arts and Technology." Ph.D. thesis, University of Toronto, Toronto 1972.

Ford, Donald W. "A Taxonomic Study of Post-Secondary Programs in Alberta," Master's thesis, The University of Calgary, Calgary 1969.

Foster, John Keith. "Education and Work in a Changing Society: British Columbia, 1870-1930." M.A. thesis in Education, University of British Columbia, Vancouver 1970.

Frederick, Nicholas O. "The Autonomy of Universities and Colleges: a Tentative Theory of Power Distribution Based on a Comparative Case Study of Government Relations with Universities and Colleges in Ontario," Ph.D. thesis, University of Toronto, Toronto 1978.

Garland, John James. "A Study of the Intramural Sport Programs in Selected Colleges of Applied Arts and Technology in the Province of Ontario, 1975-1976. M.A. thesis, University of Western Ontario, London 1976.

Gelowitz, Arnold Charles. "A Proposal for Professional Preparation in College Student Personnel Work for Western Canada." Ed.D. thesis, Oregon State University, Corvallis 1979.

Gentles, Helen Rosemaree. "Drug Abuses: Perceptions of Regional College Science Students." M.A. thesis, University of British Columbia, Vancouver 1976.

Girard, Hermann C. "A Conceptual Model for Implementing a New Decision-Making Process at the Saguenay and Lake St-John Community College in Quebec." Ph.D. dissertation, University of Toledo, Toledo 1972.

Gordon, P.A. "Student Services in Alberta Colleges," M.Ed. thesis, University of Calgary, Calgary 1970.

Goss, Anthony John. "The Effectiveness of the Colleges of Applied Arts and Technology of Ontario." Ph.D. thesis, State University of New York at Buffalo, Buffalo 1972.

Gray, Robert William. "The Governance of Three Post-Secondary Two-Year Colleges in British Columbia, Canada." Ed.D. thesis, University of British Columbia, Vancouver 1975.

Gunn, Charles R. "The Role of the Atlantic Provincial Governments in Adult Education." Ph.d. dissertation, The University of Toronto, Toronto 1967.

Hamblin, Frederick. "An Analysis of the Policy Formation Process Leading to the Establishment of The Colleges of Applied Arts and Technology of Ontario." Ed. D. thesis, University of Toronto, 1984.

Harper, Jane Kathryn. "The Relation of High School Academic Achievement and Curricula and Other Factors to Academic Achievement at a Community College." M.A. thesis, University of British Columbia, Vancouver 1978.

Harrison, William George. "A Survey of Indian Education in Five Selected Alberta Community Colleges: Some Models and Recommendations," Ed. D. dissertation, Washington State University, Pullman 1977.

Hassen, Matthew Robert. "Intraorganizational Relationship between Work Technology, Structure and Organizational Effectiveness in a Community College." Ph.D. dissertation, University of Alberta, Edmonton 1976.

Haughey, Denis Joseph. "Sources of Information Used by Community College Students." M.Ed. thesis, University of Alberta, Edmonton 1972.

Havard, Ronald James. "The Philanthropic Support of Community Colleges in Canada." Ed.D. thesis, Indiana University, Bloomington 1975.

Hendry, Andrew. "Student Services in the Community Colleges of British Columbia," Ph.D. thesis, University of Alberta, Edmonton 1974.

Heron, Robert Peter. "Growth Stages in the Development of College Structures," Ph.D. thesis, University of Alberta, Edmonton 1972.

Hoek, Margaretha Sophia Maria. "A Descriptive Study of Women Enrolled in the Office Careers Programmes at Selected Community Colleges." M.A. thesis in Education, University of Victoria, Victoria 1979.

Hollick-Kenyon, Timothy Hugh. "An Analysis of the Co-ordination of Community Colleges in British Columbia," Ph.D. dissertation, University of Oregon, Eugene 1979.

Hollington, Kenneth Charles. "Fault-Free Approach to Management Development Programs: Alberta Community Colleges." Ed.D. dissertation, Brigham Young University, Provo 1979.

Innes, Robert John. "Issues in the Design of a Program of Professional Preparation for Community College Instructors in Manitoba." Ph.D. dissertation, The University of Manitoba, Winnipeg 1980.

Jeffares, D. "Student Involvement in Governance of Alberta Colleges." M.Ed. thesis, University of Alberta, Edmonton 1971.

Johnson, Richard Dale. "Mount Royal College: A Case Study." M.Ed. thesis, University of Alberta, Edmonton 1977.

Justus, Marian. "A Descriptive Study of the Female Nonpersisters Enrolled in the Office Careers Programs at Douglas College between 1976-1979." M.A. thesis, Simon Fraser University, Burnaby 1981.

Kalyn, P. "Saskatchewan Community Colleges—a Shattered Dream, 1971-1981." Thesis, University of Regina, Regina 1983.

Kelly, Gerald Oliver. "A Study of Participation in College Governance." Ph.D. dissertation, University of Alberta, Edmonton 1973.

Knoll, Alexander. "Guidance Personnel Worker Accuracy of Predicting College Freshmen Attitude toward Drugs in Montreal CEGEPs." Ph.D. thesis, Syracuse University, Syracuse 1975.

Kolt, Stanley. "The Establishment and Financing of Junior Colleges in Rural Manitoba." Ph.D. thesis, University of North Dakota, Grand Forks 1969.

Koodos, Aaron H. "Differences between Community College Graduates and Non-Graduates on Three Dimensions: Demographic Variables, Personal Characteristics and Student Perceptions." M.Ed. thesis, University of Manitoba, Winnipeg 1982.

Korella, Lynell. "Administrator Frustration in a Community College." Ph.D. thesis, University of Alberta, Edmonton 1983.

Lazar, Morty M. "A Comparative Analysis of Canadian and American Community College Students." Ph.D. dissertation, York University, Toronto 1975.

Leduc, Ronald J. "Perceptions and Expectations of Behavior of Community College Academic Deans: A study of Canadian Community College Deans of Themselves, Their Superordinates and Subordinates." Ed. D. dissertation, Brigham Young University, Provo 1982.

Lemessurier, Robert Thomas. "Prediction of Achievement at a College of Fisheries and Marine Technology in St. John's, Newfoundland," M.Ed. thesis, University of Western Ontario, London 1976.

Letts, Alex. "The Characteristics of Students in Alberta Public Junior Colleges," M.Ed. thesis, University of Alberta, Edmonton 1968.

Loken, G. "Analysis of the Junior College in Alberta," M.Ed. thesis, University of Alberta, Edmonton 1965.

London, James Bruce. "The Editorial Significance Given to Education by Victoria's Leading Newspapers during three Periods of Educational Study by the British Columbia Government: 1932-36, 1942-46, 1957-61." M.A. thesis in Education, University of Victoria, Victoria 1976.

Long, John Clifford A. "An Historical Study of the Establishment of College Systems in Ontario and Alberta in the 1960s." M.Ed. thesis, University of Alberta, Edmonton 1972.

Long, John Clifford A. "The Transferability Issue in Alberta. A Case Study in the Politics of Higher Education." Ph. D. dissertation, University of Alberta, 1979.

Macrae, Douglas Howard. "The Prediction of Freshman Academic Achievement at a Vocational College." M.Ed. thesis, University of Regina, Regina 1974.

Maddocks, G.R. "A Comparative Analysis of Approaches to Planning Development in Post-Secondary Education." Ph.D. dissertation, University of Alberta, Edmonton 1972.

Mann, Jean Simpson. "Progressive Education and the Depression in British Columbia." M.A. thesis in Education, University of British Columbia, Vancouver 1978.

Markle, A.G. "Genesis of the Lethbridge Public Junior College." M.Ed. thesis, University of Alberta, Edmonton 1965.

Martin, R. "Future Issues in Co-ordinating Alberta Post-Secondary Education." M.Ed. thesis, University of Alberta, Edmonton 1970.

Meen, Donald John. "An Assessment of the Youth Development Program of Grant MacEwan Community College." M.Ed. thesis, University of Alberta, Edmonton 1979.

Michaels, Jayne Dale. "A Study of the Reasons Women Give for Participation in Adult Career Education Courses and a Comparative Analysis of Some Demographic Characteristics." M.A. thesis in Education, University of British Columbia, Vancouver 1979.

Miles, Frederick Alex. "The Nature and Extent of Community College Counselling Services in Western Canada." M.Sc. thesis, University of Alberta, Edmonton 1973.

Moore, Barry David. "Two Approaches to Educational Planning: Freire and Worth." Ph.D. dissertation, University of Alberta, Edmonton 1973.

Murphy, Peter James. "An Analysis of Selected Characteristics Related to Adults Attending and Dropouts from the Evening Division of the Red River Community College." M.Ed. thesis, University of Manitoba, Winnipeg 1972.

Naismith, Earl George. "Profile and Problems of Part-Time Faculty in Selected British Columbia Community Colleges." M.A. thesis in Education, University of British Columbia, Vancouver 1978.

Narine, H.C. "Perceived Parental Influence and Student Preference of Post-Secondary Options." M.Ed. thesis, University of Alberta, Edmonton 1971.

Nekolaichuck, D.M. "Student Vocational Plans: A Three Year Follow-up Study." M.Ed. thesis, University of Alberta, Edmonton 1970.

Newberry, J.F. "A Comparative Analysis of the Organizational Structures of Selected Post-Secondary Educational Institutions." Ph.D. dissertation, University of Alberta, Edmonton 1971.

Okihiro, Norman R. "Community Colleges and Early Job Outcomes: the Role of Colleges of Applied Arts and Technology in the Distribution of Job Tasks, Rewards, and Fulfillment among Young Men in Ontario." Ph.D. dissertation, York University, Toronto 1982.

Olson, Corliss Patricia, "A Follow-up Study of 1978 Northern Lights College Students." M.A. thesis, University of British Columbia, Vancouver 1981.

O'Quinn, Augustine Gerard. "An Examination of the Community College System in Quebec with Emphasis on the Collèges d'enseignment general et professionel." M.Ed. thesis, Memorial University, 1981.

Papale, Antimo. "A Model of Collective Bargaining and its Application to the Evolution of Collective Bargaining in the Public College (CEGEP) Sector of Quebec (1967-1980)." Ph.D. thesis, McGill University, Montreal 1983.

Patrick, Glenda M. "The Establishment and Development of Colleges of Applied Arts and Technology a Study of Vocational and Technical Education Policy in the Province of Ontario." Ph.D. thesis, University of Toronto, Toronto 1982.

Pearce, Sandra Dale. "Citizen Participation in the Community College." M.A. thesis, University of Alberta, Edmonton 1972.

Pepper, Elizabeth Frances. "A Case Study of Citizen Participation in the Involvement of Adult Educators with Provincial Governments in Developing a Community College System for Saskatchewan." M.C.Ed. thesis, University of Saskatchewan, Saskatoon 1973.

Peszat, L. "The Development of Health Science Education Programs in Metropolitan Toronto Region Colleges of Applied Arts and Technology, 1967-1977: a Study of Selected Factors Influencing their Development." Ph.D. thesis, University of Toronto, Toronto 1980.

Pickard, Brent William. "The Role of Community College Community Services as Perceived by Community Organizations." Ph.D. Dissertation, University of Alberta, Edmonton 1975.

Pollard, Harry Vickery. "A National Community College Information System." M.A. thesis, University of Alberta, Edmonton 1973.

Proulx, Monique Cecile. "Personal, Family and Institutional Factors Associated with Attitudes toward Women's Roles among French-Canadian College Students." Ph.D. dissertation, Michigan State University, East Lansing 1976.

Robertson, George Hawthorne. "A Proposed In-Service Training Program for Academic Administrators in Ontario Community Colleges." Ph.D. dissertation, The Florida State University, Tallahassee 1976.

Robillard, Elaine. "Women Administrators in Alberta Community Colleges." M.Ed. thesis, University of Alberta, Edmonton 1979.

Rozenhart, Robert N.L. "The Process and Effects of a Governance Change at Four Alberta Colleges." M.Ed. thesis, University of Alberta, Edmonton 1981.

Rosenzveig, Frederic Michael. "Student Self-Actualization in Different College Courses." M.A. thesis, McGill University, Montreal 1973.

Russell, Charles Neil. "Environmental Processes within an Academic Community of an Evolving Canadian Community College." Ed.D. dissertation, University of Southern California, Los Angeles 1974.

Schindelka, D.J.J. "Characteristics of Students in the Alberta Institutes of Technology." M.Ed. thesis, University of Alberta, Edmonton 1979.

Selman, Gordon Rex. "A History of the Extension and Adult Education Services of the University of British Columbia, 1915 to 1955." M.A. thesis in History, University of British Columbia, Vancouver 1963.

Small, James Matthew. "College Co-ordination in Alberta: System Development and Appraisal." Ph.D. dissertation, Michigan State University, East Lansing 1972.

Smyth, Delmar MacCormick. "Some Aspects of the Development of Ontario Colleges of Applied Arts and Technology." M. Phil. thesis, University of Toronto, Toronto 1970.

Smyth, Kathaleen Celia. 'Psychological, Demographic and Educational Correlates of Persistence in College," M.Ed. thesis, University of Alberta, Edmonton 1979.

Soles, Andrew Edwin. "The Development of the Two-Year College in British Columbia," M.Ed. thesis, University of British Columbia, Vancouver 1968.

Swayze, R.M. "Characteristics of Manitoba Vocational Staff." M.Ed. thesis, University of Alberta, Edmonton 1969.

Tingley, C. "Technical Programs in the Alberta College System." M.Ed. thesis, University of Alberta, Edmonton 1970.

Tod, A.J. "A Survey of Staff Characteristics in Post-Secondary Institutions in Alberta." M.Ed. thesis, University of Alberta, Edmonton 1969.

Townsend, Joan Helen. "Protestant Christian Morality and the Nineteenth Century Secular and Non-Sectarian British Columbia Public School System." M.A. thesis in Education, University of British Columbia, Vancouver 1974.

Tower, Gael Wells. "The International Transfer of Students from Community Colleges to Senior Institutions in Canada and the United States." Ph.D. dissertation, University of Arizona, Tucson 1979.

Treslan, Dennis L. "A Survey of Student Involvement in Decision-Making in the Mathematics Program at an Alberta Community College." M.Ed. thesis, University of Calgary, Calgary 1972.

Urvet, Matti. "Academic Achievement of Medicine Hat College Students at Alberta Universities." M.Ed. thesis, University of Alberta, Edmonton 1972.

Webb, David Charles N. "The Introduction of the Two-Year College in Quebec: A Case Study in Educational and Social Reform." Ph.D. dissertation, University of Pittsburgh, Pittsburgh 1971.

Weeks, Donald Ralph. "The Preparation and Selection of Community College Presidents in Ontario." Ph.D. dissertation, Michigan State University, 1979.

Weleschuk, Marian. "A Study of the Need for Instructor Development Perceived by Instructors and Administrators in Alberta Colleges." Ph.D. thesis, University of Alberta, Vancouver 1977.

West, P.M. "The Formation of the Department of Advanced Education: a Case Study in Post-Secondary Education, 1966-1973." Ph.D. dissertation, University of Alberta, Edmonton 1982.

Westley, Margaret W. "Environment, Goals and Structure and Academic Disciplines: A Study of Two Departments in Two Colleges in Quebec." M.A. thesis, Concordia University, Montreal 1974.

Williams, David Rees. "Structure and Perceived Adequacy of Performance in British Columbia Community Colleges." Ed.D. thesis, University of British Columbia, Vancouver 1980.

Williams, John G. "Goals in Technical Education." M.Ed. thesis, University of Alberta, Edmonton 1967.

Woodrow, James. "Authority and Power in the Governance of Public Education: A Study of the Administrative Structures of the British Columbia Education System." Ed.D. thesis, University of British Columbia, Vancouver 1974.

Workman, W.L. "Cost Analysis: Alberta Junior Colleges." M.Ed. thesis, University of Alberta, Edmonton 1969.

Workman, William Laurence. "Factors Associated with the Emergence of Selected Two-year Colleges in British Columbia." Ph.D. thesis, University of Alberta, Edmonton 1975.

Wroot, R.E. "Training Needs for Technical Instructors," M.Ed. thesis, University of Alberta, Edmonton 1970.

BASIC BIBLIOGRAPHY IN FRENCH

Arguin, Gérard. *Une théorie de l'organisation scolaire. Les nouveaux collèges québécois.* Paris: R. Pichon & R. Durand-Auzias, 1972.

Asselin, Pierre-Paul. "Les cégeps ont-ils leur autonomie," *College Canada,* II, no. 3 (mars 1977), 2-3.

Association québécoise de pédagogie collégiale. *L'étudiant de cégep: le connaître pour quoi . . . faire?* Actes du troisième colloque annuel de l'Association québécoise de pédagogie collégiale tenu à Québec les 8, 9, 10 juin 1983. Montréal: 1984.

Aubin, Gabriel et Madeleine Leroux. *Les Objectifs généraux de la formation professionnelle.* Montréal: C.A.D.R.E., 1976. 2 volumes.

Aubin, Gabriel et Mathieu Girard. *Recherche prévisionnelle sur l'enseignement collégial au Québec.* Montréal: C.A.D.R.E., 1975. 2 volumes.

Béland, Paul. *Les attentes des étudiants de niveau collégial, traduction scolaire d'un milieu socio-économique.* Québec: Gouvernement de Québec, Conseil supérieur de l'éducation, 1974.

Bernard, Jean-Louis et Danièle Geoffrion-Guay. *Etude de l'évolution de la clientéle et des programmes d'études dans les services d'éducation permanente de cégep, de 1967 à 1972; rapport d'étape.* Montréal: Université de Montréal, Faculté des sciences de l'éducation, Départment d'andragogie, 1974. 2 volumes.

Bernier, Léon. *Attitudes des études du collégial face à leur activité et à leur contexte scolaires.* Québec: Gouvernement de Québec, Conseil Supérieur de l'éducation, 1975.

Boisvenu, Paul et al. *Description des structures et inventaire des activités de formation à l'éducation des adultes dans les collèges publics du Québec.* Chambly: Cégep Edouard-Montpetit, Association des coordonnateurs de l'éducation des adultes des cégeps du Québec, 1983.

Bonin, Jacques et Jacques DesGroseilliers. *L'éducation populaire au cégep; rapport final de l'opération REPO* Montréal: Féderation des cégeps, 1980.

Bordeleau, H.-Paul. *Les services de psychologie, d'orientation, d'aide pédagogique individuelle et d'information scolaire et professionnelle dans les collèges.* Saint-Jérôme: Cégep de Saint-Jerôme, 1973.

Bouchard, Benoît et al. *L'enseignement professionnel au cégep: les programmes; document de travail.* Montréal, Féderation des cégeps, 1981.

Breton, Lise et Jean-Luc Roy. *Le collége québécois. Introduction bibliographique.* Montréal: C.A.D.R.E., 1976.

Campeau, Daniel et Jeanne Leroux. *La formation sur mesure; rapport final.* Montréal, Féderation des cégeps, 1978. 2 volumes.

Cantarella, Claudette. *Valeurs de travail des étudiants de niveau collégial.* Montréal: thése de Ph.D., Université de Montréal, Faculté des arts et des sciences, Départment de psychologie, 1981.

Caron, Louise et Nicole J. Leblanc. *Vie étudiants et services aux étudiants; bibliographie commentée sur les services offerts aux étudiants au niveau collégial, le personnel de ces services, la clientèle étudiante concernée.* Québec: Ministère de l'éducation, Direction générale de la planification, 1975.

Cegep-Realité. *Si CEGEP m'était conté . . .* Sherbrooke: Les Presses Coopératives, 1972.

Centre de recherches sur l'opinion publique. *Préoccupation des étudiants des CEGEP de Montréal.* Montréal: 1969.

Cleaver, Roseline et al. *Ecole et société: Continuité ou rupture? Les attentes de la société à l'égard de l'enseignement collégial.* Québec: Gouvernement du Québec, Conseil supérieur de l'éducation, 1974.

Cloutier, Marcel et al. *Le Perfectionnement des maîtres de l'enseignement professionnel au collégial: problématique.* Sherbrooke: Université de Sherbrooke, Performa, 1976.

Comeau, Hubert. *Analyse de regroupement des collèges publics francophone de l'Ile de Montréal* Montréal: Thèse de maîtrise en administration, l'Université Sir George Williams, 1974.

Commission d'étude de la tâche des enseignants du collégial. *La tâche des enseignants du collégial; rapport final.* Québec: Service général des personnels des organismes d'enseignement, 1975. 3 volumes.

Côté, Julien. *L'enseignement professionnel au cégep: les programmes: historique et conjoncture actuelle; document de référence.* Montréal: Fédération des cégeps, 1981.

David, Guy et al. *La situation de l'enseignment privé au Québec.* Québec: Centrale de l'enseignement du Québec, 1975.

Demers, Marius et Jacques Lavigne. *Une analyse des dépenses des cégeps de 1972-1973 à 1978-1979.* Québec: Ministère de l'Education, Secteur de la planification, Direction des études économiques et démographiques, 1980.

Desbiens, Jean-Paul. "L'éducation au Québec, dix ans après la reforme scolaire," dans *Dossier Untel.* Montréal: Editions du Jour, 1973.

Desbiens, Jean-Paul. "Les Cégep Après 9 ans," *College Canada,* II, no. 2 (Fèvrier 1977), 9.

DesGroseilliers, Pierre. "A la recherche d'une philosophie de léducation pour le niveau collégial: eduquer ou instruire les cégepiens?" *Journal of the Association of Canadian Community Colleges/Journal de l'Association des collèges Communautaires du Canada,* I, no. 1 (printemps 1977), 77-93.

Dessureault, Guy. *Recherche documentaire sur les professeurs du collégial. Volume 1: Formation et perfectionnement.* Québec: Ministère de l'éducation, Secteur de la planification, Direciton de la recherche, 1981.

Dessureault, Guy. *Recherche documentaire sur les professeurs du collégial. Volume II: Caractéristiques professionnelles et socio-culturelles.* Québec: Ministère de l'éducation, Direction de la recherche, 1983.

Des Trois Maison, Louise. *Dix années d'innovation pédagogique dans les cégeps du Québec.* Québec: Ministère de l'éducation, Direction des Programmes, 1981.

"Dossier sur le Rapport Roquet," *Prospectives,* VII, no. 2 (avril 1971), 83-106.

Dubuisson, Régis. *L'enseignement professionnel au cégep: accessibilité et démocratisation: les obstacles; document de travail.* Montréal: Fédération des cégeps, 1981.

Dumont, Fernand et Guy Rocher. "L'expérience des cegeps: urgence d'un bilan," *Maintenant,* no. 122 (janvier 1973), 17-23.

Escande, Claude. *Les classes sociales aux cégep; sociologie de l'orientation des étudiants.* Montréal: Editions Parti pris, 1973.

Fédération des cégeps. *Bilan de dix années de réalisation, opération Cégepdix.* Montréal: 1978.

Fédération des cégeps. *La vie associative des étudiants: lieux et formes de regroupements et de participation des étudiants dans les cégeps (décembre 1982).* Montréal: 1983.

Fédération des cégeps. *Réalisations des Cégeps depuis dix ans, 1967-1977.* Montréal: 1977.

Fédération des cégeps. *Six facettes du développement des cégeps.* Montréal: 1974.

Fédération des cégeps. *Vers des politiques institutionnelles d'évaluation.* Montréal: 1982. 4 volumes.

Fédération des cégeps. Comité sur l'éducation des adultes. *La formation des adultes, une contribution de cégep au développement de son milieu.* Montréal: 1984.

Fédération des enseignants de CEGEP. *Enquête sur le rôle social du CEGEP; rapport préliminaire.* Montréal: 1978.

Fédération des collèges classiques. *La Fédération des collèges classiques et son évolution à l'heure des CEGEP.* Montréal: 1967.

Fédération des collèges classiques. *Notre réforme scolaire.* Montréal: Centre de Psychologie et de Pédagogie, 1962-1963. 2 tomes.

Fortier, Claude. *Les Structures et l'administration pédagogique des CEGEP.* Montréal: Féderation des cégeps, 1970.

Galarneau, Claude. *Les collèges classiques au Canada français (1620-1970).* Montréal: Fides, 1978.

Gaudet-Chandler, Hélène. "Les relations de travail dans les cégeps: Centralisation et politisation," *College Canada,* VI, no. 7 (novembre-décembre 1981), 16-17.

Gingras, Paul-Emile. "C.A.D.R.E.—L'institutionnelle," *Journal of the Association of Canadian Community Colleges/Journal de l'Association des Collèges Communautaires du Canada,* III, no. 3 (automne 1979), 61-81.

Gingras, Paul-Emile. *La vie pédagogique des collèges, 1960-1970.* Montréal: Centre d'animation, de développement et de recherche en education, 1969.

Isabelle, Robert. *Les CEGEP, collèges, d'état ou établissements autonomes? L'évolution de l'autonomie des cégeps de 1967 à 1982.* Québec: Conseil des collèges, 1982.

Lamontagne, Jacques. *Les professeurs de collège pendant la réforme scolaire des années soixante au Québec: analyse psycho-sociologique d'un changement social.* Montréal: thèse de Ph.D., Université de Montréal, Département de sociologie, 1973.

Lamontagne, Jacques et Rita Therrien. *Les valeurs des professeurs de cégep.* Montréal: Université de Montréal, 1977.

Langlais, Jacques. "Les collèges du Québec et l'étude de la religion," *Journal of the Association of Canadian Community Colleges/Journal de l'Assoication des Collèges Communautaires du Canada.* IV, no. 3/4 (été-automne 1980), 72-83.

Lanoix, Jean. *Comment réussir et vivre heureux au cégep.* Montréal. Editions internationales, Alain Stanke, 1978.

Lapierre, René. *La relation cégep-milieu: entre le discours et la réalité.* Québec: Conseil des collèges, 1983.

"La régionalisation de l'enseignement collégial," *Prospectives,* VIII, no. 5 (décembre 1972), 319-403.

Larouche, René et Paul Godbout. *La pratique de l'activité physique de type para-scolaire au niveau collégial.* Québec: Haut Commissariat à la jeunesse, aux loisirs et aux sports, 1978.

Lebel, Maurice. "Succès ou faillite des cégeps," dans *Le rapport Parent, dix ans après,* Académie des lettres et des sciences humaines de la Société royale du Canada. Montréal: Bellarmin, 1975.

Le CEGEP 5 ans après. Succes ou échec. St. Laurent: Cegep de Saint-Laurent, 1973.

Legault, Ginette et Normande Levesque. *Le cégep de demain: pouvoirs et responsabilités; synthèse de la consultation.* Québec: Conseil des collèges, 1984.

"Le livre blanc sur les collèges," *Prospectives,* XV, no. 1 (février 1979), 5-46.

"L'Enseignement Collégial," *Critère,* no. 8 (janvier 1973), 1-281.

"Le Rapport Nadeau", *Prospectives,* XI, no. 4 (octobre 1975), 157-258.

"Les Cégeps 17 ans après," *Le Devoir (Montréal),* (27 janvier 1984), 15-28.

Lucier, Pierre. "Bilan et prospective de l'enseignement collégial: éléments pour une comparaison," *Prospectives,* XIII, no. 3 (octobre 1977), 145-168.

Lucier, Pierre. "Les dix ans des Cégeps: tendances et orientations du symposium Cégepdix," *Prospectives,* XIII, no. 4 (décembre 1977), 230-239.

Nocaudie, Dominique. *Etude administrative des CEGEP.* Québec: Direction générale de l'enseignement collégial, 1969.

Nocaudie, Dominique. *Les collèges d'enseignement général et professionnel au Québec.* Paris: thèse de doctorat, Université de droit, d'économie et de sciences sociales de Paris, 1972.

Pineau, Gaston. *Le Perfectionnement des enseignants du collégial et Performa.* Sherbrooke: Université de Sherbrooke, 1976.

Pronovost, Jean. *La Qualité de l'enseignement dans les cégeps: quelques éléments d'une problématique.* Québec: Direction générale de l'enseignement collégial, 1977.

Québec. Commission d'étude sur la formation des adultes. *Apprendre: une action volontaire et responsable; énoncé d'une politique globale de l'éducation des adultes dans une perspective d'éducation permanente.* Montréal: Ministère des communications, Direction de l'éducation, 1982.

Québec. Conseil des collèges. *Le Cégep de demain. Pouvoirs et responsabilités.* Québec: 1984.

Québec: Conseil des collèges. *Le partage du pouvoir dans les CEGEP: le rôle du conseil d'administration.* Québec: 1983.

Québec. Conseil des collèges. *Rapport annuel.* Québec: 1979-

Québec. Conseil supérieur de l'Education. *Le Collège. Synthèse de la consultation sur l'état et les besoins de l'enseignement collégial.* Québec: Service général des communications du Ministère de l'Education, 1975.

Québec. Conseil supérieur de l'éducation. *L'Education au niveau post-secondaire en 1975-1976. Analyses réflexives.* Québec: Service général des communications du Ministère de l'Education, 1976.

Québec. Conseil supérieur de l'éducation. *Rapports annuels.* Québec: 1967-

Québec. Conseil supérieur de l'éducation. Commission de l'enseignement technique et professionnel. *La première année du développement des collèges d'enseignement général et professionel.* Québec: 1968.

Québec. Direction générale de l'enseignement collégial, Service de la recherche et du développement. *Bulletin statistique.* Québec: 1976-

Québec. Direction générale de l'enseignement collégial, Service de la recherche et du développement. *Le Rôle d'un service audio-visuel du collège.* Québec: 1973.

Québec. Minstère de l'Education. Direction Générale de la Planification. *L'Edudiant Québécois. Défi et dilèmmes.* Québec: Editeur officiel, 1972.

Roquet, Ghislaine *et al. Rapport du comité d'étude des cours communs à tous les étudiants de C.E.G.E.P.* s.p., s.ed., 1970.

Taschereau, Yves. "Les cegep de Babel. Un bilan inquétant des dix premières années de nos nouveaux collèges", *L'Actualité,* (septembre 1977), 19-23, 50; (octobre 1977), 43-46.

Tremblay, Arthur. "La démocratisation de l'enseignement" dans *Le rapport Parent, Dix Ans Après,* Académie des lettres et des sciences humaines de la Société royale du Canada. Montréal: Bellarmin, 1975.

Van Der Donckt, Pierre. "Le CEGEP: vers une intégration des divers types d'enseignement", *Prospectives,* IV, no. 2 (avril 1968), 125-128.

Watson, Cicely. *Les Nouveaux systèmes collégieaux au Canada.* Paris: Organization de coopération et de développement économiques, 1973.

Index

Committee of University Presidents, 32-34
Council of Regents, 98-99, 183, 193, 217, 245, 259
general education, 31-34
General Industrial Training, 96
Grade 13 Study Committee, 166
Institute for Studies in Education, 34
Ministry of Colleges and Universities, 98
Public Service Employees Union (OPSEU), 217
Post-Secondary Education in Ontario, 1962-1970, 32
stability of college system, 95-96
technical education, 35-36

Parent, Alphonse-Marie, 39-43
Peterson, Gilbert C., 18
Policy
formulation, 78-79, 157-61, 195-204
responsibility for, 94-95, 105, 120-21, 205-12
Porter, J.M., 219
Post-secondary education
alternative models, 12-15, 141-77
tradition, 11-12, 142
Prince Edward Island
Board of Governors, 107
college programs, 106
Department of Education, 107
Designing a Curriculum Chart (DACUM), 108
history of post-secondary education, 45-48
Holland College, 47-48, 106, 148-49, 233, 276
labour relations, 107
provincial vocational centres, 46, 106
Self-Teaching and Evaluation Plan (STEP), 108, 259-61
University Grants Commission Bill, 47
University of PEI, 47
Professional development, 219-25, 230-32
Programmes
allocation of, 232-37
diversity, 237-51, 273-83
evaluation, 230-32, 252-62
Provincial role in community colleges, 86-87, 178-79, 181-83

Quebec
Collèges d'Enseignement Général et Professionnel (CEGEP), 43-45, 100-3, 159, 217, 247-48
Conseil des Collèges, 104-5, 183, 193, 259
Council of Public Instruction, 38
diversification of college programs, 39-43
enrolment in colleges, 105
history of education, 38-41
goals for colleges, 100-2
Institut de Technologie de Montréal, 41
labour relations in colleges, 105, 217
Ministry of Education, 43, 105
Ministry for Higher Education, Science, and Technology, 105
"Quiet Revolution," 38, 100
Royal Commission of Inquiry on Education (1961), 39
White Paper on Colleges (1978), 103-4

Research
agenda, 268-69
institutional, 265
kinds, 269-71
need for, 263-64
priorities and purpose, 269
responsibility for, 265-67
role of colleges, 262-63
Riederer, L.A., 54
Robbins, L.C., 182
Ross, Murray, 34-36
Rowe, F., 65-66
Royal Commissions
on Agriculture and Rural Life (Sask.), 52
on Education in Alberta, 20
on Education in B.C., 25
on Education in Ontario, 31
on Education, Public Services, and Provincial-Municipal Relations (NS), 61-62
on Education and Youth (Nfld.), 66, 123
on Higher Education in New Brunswick, 58
on Higher Education in Prince Edward Island, 46
on Industrial Training and Technical Education, 15
of Inquiry on Education (Que.), 39, 143
on National Development in the Arts, Letters, and Sciences, 15, 46
on Post-Secondary Education (NS), 121

Saskatchewan
Adult Basic Education (ABE), 113-15
college concept, 111-12
Community College Trustees Association, 115
community life, 113, 115
Continuing Education Department, 53, 113
Mandate Review, 114
Ministry of Advanced Education and Manpower, 113
post-secondary education, 52-57, 115
rural colleges, 52-57
technical institutes, 53, 111
University of Saskatchewan, 52
Wascana Institute of Applied Arts and Sciences, 111